SHAKTI

✳ AN EXPLORATION OF THE DIVINE FEMININE ✳

SHAKTI

❋ AN EXPLORATION OF THE DIVINE FEMININE ❋

NILIMA CHITGOPEKAR
FOREWORD BY SHASHI THAROOR

contents

Editor Vatsal Verma
Editorial support Ayushi Thapliyal
Project Art Editor Devika Awasthi
Art Editor Priyal Mote
Design support Bhavika Mathur
Jacket Designer Priyanka Thakur
Project Picture Researcher Deepak Negi
DTP Designers Narender Kumar, Mohammad Rizwan
Senior DTP Designer Tarun Sharma
Pre-Production Manager Balwant Singh
Production Manager Pankaj Sharma
Picture Research Manager Taiyaba Khatoon
Managing Editor Chitra Subramanyam
Managing Art Editor Neha Ahuja Chowdhry
Senior Managing Art Editor Priyanka Thakur
Managing Director, India Aparna Sharma

Author Nilima Chitgopekar
Translations by Tarinee Awasthi

First published in Great Britain in 2022 by
Dorling Kindersley Limited
DK, One Embassy Gardens, 8 Viaduct Gardens,
London, SW11 7BW

The authorised representative in the EEA is
Dorling Kindersley Verlag GmbH. Arnulfstr. 124,
80636 Munich, Germany

Copyright © 2022 Dorling Kindersley Limited
Translated text copyright © Tarinee Awasthi 2022
A Penguin Random House Company
10 9 8 7 6 5 4 3 2 1
001–326294–Jan/2022

A CIP catalogue record for this book
is available from the British Library.
ISBN: 978-0-2415-3134-1

Printed and bound in India

For the curious
www.dk.com

This book was made with Forest Stewardship
Council ™ certified paper – one small step in DK's
commitment to a sustainable future.
For more information go to
www.dk.com/our-green-pledge

Publisher's note

Shakti *attempts to examine and relate multiple strands of the Goddess tradition. It brings together the interpretations of various scholars spanning many years. Some of the primary sources that have been referred to in this book seem to be products of a patriarchal ethos. The publisher and the author are cognizant that some of the goddesses, therefore, appear to have characteristics constructed from a male perspective. The book endeavours to build an objective narrative without prejudice as far as possible. At the same time, although there is some degree of course correction, the breadth of the subject and the structure of the book may have, at times, posed certain limitations.*

1 ❋ INTRODUCTION
TO THE GODDESS

2 ❋ RISE OF
THE GODDESS

3 ✷ EVOLUTION OF GODDESS WORSHIP

4 · BUDDHIST AND JAIN GODDESSES

5 · TANTRA AND THE GODDESS

6 · DIVINE LANDSCAPES

Foreword

By Shashi Tharoor

※

In this beautifully illustrated book, Nilima Chitgopekar delves into the ancient, profound, and deeply moving story of the Goddess and Her portrayal throughout India's long history. Examining Her many manifestations, through sculpture, literature, writing, and art, it becomes clear that the way She is depicted reveals fascinating clues to the way Indians throughout history saw themselves and what they valued. Chitgopekar explores the various angles that made the Goddess what She is today – the syncretic blend of multiple faiths, the oral traditions that shaped Her image, the various manifestations of Her divine being. The history of Her worship is traced, from the 5,000-year-old clay figures of Mohenjo-Daro to the elaborate religious processions of the modern day. After going through this book, one thing is very clear that whether She be imagined as Parvati, Durga, Sita, or any other of Her countless forms, the Goddess has been a constant companion for so many Indians, manifestations of their hopes, fears, and values.

Chitgopekar has created a work that is true to history while remaining original and insightful. The book traverses the length and breadth of India's geographical and historical landscapes, seeking out the various ways in which the Goddess is revered. Through her exploration of this one important facet of spiritual life, she has given us key insight into the way Indian society has evolved and changed across time and place. This is a book to be read by all – believers and atheists, those interested in the spiritual, those more fascinated by the material, and above all, anyone who believes India is a place worth understanding, and that the essence of a people's lives are so often expressed by the stories they tell. *Shakti* is inspiring – an evocative and insightful book that is a fine guide to this beautiful part of the story of Hinduism and of India.

Dr Shashi Tharoor, a third-term Member of Parliament for Thiruvananthapuram, is the bestselling author of 22 books, both fiction and non-fiction, besides being a former Under Secretary-General of the United Nations and a former Minister of State for Human Resource Development and for External Affairs in the Government of India. He has won numerous awards, including the Pravasi Bharatiya Samman, a Commonwealth Writers' Prize, and the Crossword Lifetime Achievement Award. In 2019, Dr Tharoor was also awarded the Sahitya Akademi Award in the category of "English Non-Fiction" for his book *An Era of Darkness*. He chairs Parliament's Standing Committee on Information Technology.

Reverence to Her
This painting of the Goddess, created in c. 1850 in Kota, Rajasthan, depicts Her sitting on Her throne and being worshipped by devotees. The crescent moon and the third eye emphasize Her association with Shiva.

INTRODUCTION TO THE GODDESS ❊ 1

The story of Goddess worship in the Indian subcontinent is diverse and intricate. It is firmly entrenched within an equally complex matrix, constituting many texts, traditions, and belief systems. Before one begins to understand the Goddess in Her entirety, it is significant to appreciate and unfold the larger religious and literary model that informs Her story.

△ **The three principal deities in Hinduism**, Shiva, the destroyer, Vishnu, the preserver, and Brahma, the creator (from left), bow before the Great Goddess in this painting from c. 1710.

The Goddess tradition

Existing in myriad ways, the Goddess epitomizes a plethora of riches, such as feelings, concepts, and materials. She is the female shining one, ubiquitous across the land, and in the minds and everyday life of the people.

It is widely believed that the Goddess made Her first appearance in the hundreds of terracotta figurines (See pp 36–39) of the Indus Valley Civilization, and in this form, She is regularly referred to as Mother Goddess. The precise nature and context of these female sculptures are increasingly becoming a matter of debate. However, the fact that modern research has time and again looked at them as a form of the divine feminine itself points to the widespread preoccupation with the Goddess tradition. The earliest texts, the Vedas, perceived as the roots of Hinduism, are the first site where

one encounters the Goddess, or the Devi (See pp 42–43). Here, She is identified with a range of natural spectacles and appears as different entities personifying aspects of nature and physical phenomenon. During the Vedic times, however, Her presence seems to be only on the fringes, having been relegated to the sidelines by boisterous male divinities.

Coming into Her own
It is the Puranic corpus that brings forth a torrent of vigour and introduces a comprehensive Goddess tradition. In this,

Her greatness rivals that of the male gods. The period is replete with visual art and mythology related to Her, pointing to Her gigantic presence in the Indic culture that emerged by this time.

She had always existed, but it is in the Puranic period that She made an "official" appearance in the Sanskrit domain, and slid into the focus of the influential, hegemonic sections of society.

Her many manifestations

The Puranic corpus amalgamated non-Brahmanical religious systems. The Goddess proved to be the suitable modus operandi for the Brahmanical attempt to assimilate local cults. So She was engorged and infused with many of "herselves". She came to assimilate many local divinities with varied characteristics and some similarities. With many forms, She also came to represent an assortment of things, such as fertility, nature, abundance, and, Her most popular role became that of a mother. It is ironical that none of the goddesses actually give birth in physical ways. The label of motherhood is abstract and refers to someone who nurtures and gives birth to ideas. In this manner, She is a creator, the source of all life, and a protector, a saviour, and a warrior.

Two waves

The process of absorbing local goddesses into the Puranic pantheon also imbued the Puranic Goddess with a unique and seemingly

GODDESS AS A MOTHER

Both the Brahmanical and the non-Brahmanical traditions encompass a strong theological notion that the Goddess is a mother. She is addressed variously as Amba, Mata, Ma, Maiyya, Amman, and Matrika, all of which mean mother in different languages and dialects. Interestingly, the male gods rarely have the noun "father" affixed to their epithets. This characteristic is reserved only for female divinities, whether virginal, ferocious, protective, or benign.

> "... for God is also our **Mother**... To understand **Hindu wisdom** more completely, we must therefore also think about **goddesses**."

FRANCIS X CLOONEY, S J, *HINDU WISDOM FOR ALL GOD'S CHILDREN* (1998)

intangible concept of Shakti. Many philosophical traditions put forth the idea that both female and male principles are necessary for creation and orderly functioning of the universe. At the same time, it is Shakti as energy that activates the power of male gods. In this context, Shakti could be the energy that manifests and also the manifestation itself. So, all divine, cosmic, and earthly power emanates from the supreme Great Goddess. All deities – male, female, Vaishnava or Shaiva – are the manifestation of this divine power. Shakti, therefore, is a characteristic peculiar to Her alone.

The idea of Shakti has also given rise to a tendency to identify the Goddess as a singular entity, but the reality is far more nuanced. Attempts at taxonomy and encapsulation have revealed that almost all the goddesses have their predominant personal and regional flavour. So, all classifications should be seen as permeable and essentializing should never be a maxim for those engaged in the study of goddesses. Some definitions of them are pan Indian and some local. At best, they are like two intermingling waves that come together and separate, only to merge again.

There is no doubt that there is a long tradition of honouring the Goddess, and She is celebrated and lauded for Her antiquity and eternal nature. She is also dynamic and enjoys a living and thriving tradition in the entire subcontinent.

The religious fabric

The countless faiths of the Indian subcontinent, living cheek by jowl, are in constant dialogue with each other, giving rise to the process of syncretism. All these faiths, with their contradictions and similarities, present a beautiful, composite sacred fabric of the subcontinent.

The religious domain of the subcontinent is akin to a mosaic of different, but also interrelated, religions. Every religion encompasses a plethora of effects in its every sphere and aspect, whether it is the number of divinities and their forms, or scriptural texts and bhakti trends, or theological and metaphysical ideas.

Pluralism in Hinduism

One of the prime religions of the subcontinent is Hinduism, which does not lend itself to easy characterization due to its vastness and intricate history. There is hardly a single important teaching, unified field of doctrine, or solo text valid for all Hindus. Its cauldron is large and deep enough for all concoctions – everyone is free to dip their chalice and get what they desire. It encompasses all phases and levels of religious consciousness and brings into its fold diverse practices, such as the worship of ancestors, spirits, child, female, local heroes, animals, and trees, onerous fasting, fire walking, consumption of liquor, and animal sacrifices.

▽ **The ritual of an aarti,** wherein lit oil lamps are offered as homage to the divine, is common in most Hindu denominations who believe that fire sanctifies the atmosphere.

Major sects

The contours of Hinduism may seem heavily influenced by the Sanskritic tradition of Brahmanical orthodoxy. However, ethnographic field studies in the countryside indicate that its fabric is also composed of the heterogeneity of local traditions, providing a bewildering array of diverse paths to Hindu ideals.

Though there is no major cleavage between Sanskritic and local traditions, one cannot deny the existence of multiple denominations within Hinduism. These are belief systems centred on some shared features, such as ritual patterns, pilgrimages, or reincarnation.

The beauty of Hinduism is not merely in the existence of many systems, but their elasticity as well. Each accommodates a mind-boggling plurality within its pantheon. This gives the appearance that there has been no discarding of sacred elements and instead an assimilation process is constantly in motion. Therefore, in Hinduism, polytheism is not antithetical to monotheism, as the main deity has the ability to transform in different manifestations.

Some of the most popular theistic sects are based on devotion to a particular divinity. Among these are three major belief systems – Vaishnavism, Shaivism, and Shaktism. While Shakta worshippers believe in the supremacy of the feminine principle, that is Shakti, Vaishnavism gives prime importance to Vishnu, the preserver, and his avatars, and Shaivism to Shiva, the destroyer, and his retinue. However, there does exist some degree of permeability between the three.

Vaishnavism

Goddesses are worshipped within Vaishnavism and Shaivism as well, but their forms are dependent on the prime male gods. For instance, Vaishnavites worship Lakshmi (See pp 168–171, a prominent goddess in the Vishnu arena. She dwells with Vishnu and shares a close relationship with him. Other examples include Sita, Rama's wife, and Radha, Krishna's lover – both Rama and Krishna being manifestations of Vishnu. Even in the avatar system, Sita and Radha are considered forms of Lakshmi.

There might also be regional variations within each belief system. For instance, in South India, Vaishnavites worship Lakshmi, who is Vishnu's consort, as a messenger to her rather aloof husband. In North India, she is worshipped autonomously and Vishnu is rarely invoked. She is given importance as one who bestows good fortune on individuals, their families, and their businesses.

Shaivism

Similarly, although Shaivism primarily puts forth the worship of its chief deity Shiva, different ≫

◁ **Feet of the Shaiva goddess** Chamunda in Chamundi Hills, Karnataka

"We may be yet far from knowing with certainty **what led to the birth of so many divergent views** at such an early period of our history."

DEBIPRASAD CHATTOPADHYAYA, *INDIAN PHILOSOPHY: A POPULAR INTRODUCTION* (1964)

△ **Jain Prateek Chihna**, a symbol associated with Jainism

deities get associated with him depending on the region. For instance, the elephant-headed god Ganesha, his son, is a much-loved divine presence in many regions. Shiva's spouse, the powerful goddess Parvati, encapsulates and epitomizes the concept of Shakti. Her various forms, such as Durga and Kali, as well as manifestations in local cultures, are also viewed as Shiva's spouse.

Shiva, however, is dissimilar to Vishnu or his avatars, as are his female counterparts. So from Sati and Parvati to Durga and Kali, one encounters a bevy of female consorts, who impart knowledge and truth in sometimes very contrarian and seemingly inexplicable ways. It is through them that one encounters Shaktism in which the supreme universal entity is the Goddess who rules all. Shiva himself, in this religion, is subservient to Her and Her might. She destroys Asuras and imparts courage to everyone to deal with adversaries. As the prime divinity, the Goddess in Shaktism has a power unsurpassed in any other theistic cult.

Buddhism

An ancient religion that appeared in northern India in the 6–4th century BCE, Buddhism is another important religion in the subcontinent. It is based on teachings attributed to Gautama Buddha, its founder. Over centuries, the religion, similar to Hinduism, has managed to encompass a variety of traditions, beliefs, and spiritual practices. Its several sects worship the Buddha, the Bodhisattvas, and the goddesses.

As expressed in the Buddha's Four Noble Truths, the goal is to achieve nirvana by overcoming suffering, or dukkha, caused not by some planetary disturbances but by ignorance of reality's true nature, which constitutes impermanence, or anicca, and the non-existent self, or anata. Buddhism emphasizes transcending the individual self through the attainment of nirvana, or ending the cycle of death and rebirth, by following the path of Buddhahood.

Buddhist schools vary in their interpretation of the path to liberation, the relative importance and canonicity assigned to the various Buddhist texts, and their specific teachings and practices. They do recognize similar practices such as meditation, observance of moral precepts, monasticism, taking refuge in the Buddha, the Dharma and the Sangha, and the cultivation of the Paramitas, or perfection. Goddesses were introduced into the religion to bring a larger population under its sphere of influence.

Jainism

Among the world's oldest religions, Jainism denies the authority of the Vedas and opposes animal sacrifice. It traces its spiritual ideas and history through a succession of 24 spiritual teachers, or Tirthankaras, guiding every time cycle of the cosmology.

It conceives the universe as functioning according to the eternal law. It is known for its rigorous practice of asceticism, meaning abstinence from sensual pleasures. Immense importance is given to subjecting the body to fasting.

The sole purpose is the purification of the soul and Jains widely believe that it is asceticism and not knowledge that would free the soul from sorrows. Other essential ingredients of Jain philosophy are ahimsa, or non-violence, *anekantavada*, or non-absolutism, and *syadvada*, or the theory that all knowledge is relative, and *aparigraha*, or

---

HINDU DOCTRINES

Hindus believe in a set of doctrines that include samsara, atman, dharma, karma, and moksha. While samsara is a continuous cycle of life, death, and reincarnation, atman is the soul, which is immortal and a part of the divine soul. Hindu philosophy also believes that everyone should try to act according to dharma, that is the ethical code as per one's station in life, and one's life unfolds as per their karma, that is the universal law of cause and effect. The ultimate goal of life or one's being is moksha, or freedom from life cycle, which unites the soul with the divine.

non-attachment. These principles have affected Jain culture in many ways. There are two major ancient sub-traditions, the Digambaras and the Shvetambaras. Each has different views on ascetic practices, gender, and which texts can be considered canonical. Both have mendicants supported by laypersons.

Like Hinduism and Buddhism, Jainism also could not ignore the Goddess tradition. The divine feminine found her way into it through the veneration of Yakshi, or female spirits, who formed an integral aspect and part of the entourage of the Tirthankaras. The Yakshis grew in stature and power with the permeation of Tantrism within Jainism.

Considered as Avarana Devatas, or surrounding divinities, and Shasana Devis, or protective attendant goddesses, the figures

> "To **survive and flourish** over so long a period is a striking testimony to **Hinduism's ability** to adapt itself to **changing circumstances**…"

JL BROCKINGTON, *THE SACRED THREAD* (1996)

of Yakshis are found depicted in association with their Tirthankaras. Through accepting these goddesses, it became easier for Jainism to spread in such areas where belief in these goddesses was more popular.

▽ **Buddhist women turn prayer wheels** during the festival of Yuru Kabgyat in Lamayuru Monastery in Ladakh.

Hindu literary tradition

The core of Hindu thought and practices is an assortment of texts that have informed it over the centuries. These codify philosophical concepts and provide a complex matrix to study the religion in all its glory and diversity.

In the Hindu tradition, the oldest, and, for some, the most sacred body of texts are the Vedas – the *Rigveda*, the *Yajurveda*, the *Samaveda*, and the *Atharvaveda*. Composed in Sanskrit and constituting mantras and prayers, which are chanted during *yagnas*, or sacrifical offerings, the Vedas are *nitya*, or eternal, and *shruti*, or that which is heard. As Shruti texts, the Vedas are *apaurusheya*, or not written by humans. Instead, it believed that the gods revealed these to ancient Rishis in a state of deep contemplation. Over centuries, this large body of work was orally transmitted from one generation to another, until they were composed probably around c. 1500–1000 BCE.

Each Veda has four parts. The first two include the Samhitas that are collections of hymns by a number of priestly families and the Brahmanas, which are attached to the Samhitas and describe the rituals. Then, there are the Aranyakas and the Upanishads, both philosophical treatises and presented as appendages to the Brahmanas. The Upanishads are also considered a part of Vedanta, literally the *anta*, or end, of the Vedas. This is because they form the end of the last portion of Vedic literature and perceived to be the essence and culmination of all the knowledge within the Vedas.

The epics

It is widely accepted that, in terms of chronology, the next set of texts to appear are the two epics – the *Ramayana* (See pp 64–65) and the *Mahabharata* (See box). Bardic in origin, these are understood as Smriti texts, or those that were remembered by the sages. Eventually, they gained as much religious importance as the Vedas.

Scholars have dated the composition of *Mahabharata* to around the 4th century BCE, but additions were made right up till the 4th century CE. With 100,000 verses, the epic poem has 18 *parvas*, or sections. Apart from the central story, the text also contains ancient myths and advice on living an ethical life.

The second epic, the *Ramayana*, centred around the story of prince Rama, is also a great source of information for societal norms and cultural preferences of the time. The precise date of its composition is debatable, but many scholars agree on the period between the 2nd and 4th centuries BCE. There are various versions of the story, but sage Valmiki's version, with 24,000 *shlokas*, or verses, and seven *kandas*, or sections, is considered the earliest.

"…the **purpose** of the epics, the *Puranas* and the *Vedas*, was **different**. Since the last were the earliest in time, Indian history was said to **begin** with the information that they contained."

ROMILA THAPAR, *THE PENGUIN HISTORY OF EARLY INDIA: FROM THE ORIGINS TO AD 1300* (2002)

The Puranic corpus

The Puranas, also a part of the Smriti literature appeared around the early centuries. Each Purana is like a manual or a guide for worshippers of a specific deity. To a large extent, the Puranas could be looked at as explanatory texts rather than those preoccupied with rituals.

They are valuable because they point to a dynamic process whereby the Brahman mythographers remodelled and incorporated several folk deities and local traditions into the Hindu fold. This approach was likely adopted in order to popularize and expand the reach of Hinduism. Therefore, the Puranas essentially project Brahmanical ideas imparting social codes and mores, and as they go about absorbing local traditions, they regularly attempt to give an integrated world view. The process of intermeshing and synthesis of Sanskritic and local traditions is best presented in these texts. The Puranic corpus also brought into its fold other types of texts, such as the Mahatmyas, which are legends that portray the greatness of a particular place or a deity. Sometimes, these texts are interpolated into a well-known Purana or any other important scriptural text, in order to achieve legitimacy and acceptance. There is a symbiotic relationship at play wherein the larger text as well as the Mahatmya benefit by way of association. The most common example is the *Devi Mahatmya*, which is a part of the *Markandeya Purana*.

△ **The elephant-headed god** Ganesha wrote the *Mahabharata* as the great Rishi Ved Vyasa narrated the story to him. This painting from Mehrangarh Fort, Jodhpur, Rajasthan, depicts the god transcribing the epic.

THE STORY OF THE MAHABHARATA

Aeons ago, the Kuru clan consisted of two sets of paternal first cousins, the five Pandavas and the 100 Kauravas, who were vicious rivals as both groups vied for the throne of Hastinapur, the capital of the Kuru Kingdom. In a game of dice, the Kauravas defeated the Pandavas by cheating and banished them into the wilderness for 12 years. After their exile, the Pandavas laid claim to their kingdom, but the Kauravas refused to return it. This led to an 18-day battle, which was fought in Kurukshetra. In the end, the Pandavas were victorious and Yudhishthira, the eldest brother, became the king.

To gain her favour

Every year, women throng the streets and lanes of Thiruvananthapuram, Kerala, in southern India to celebrate Attukal Pongala. They build makeshift hearths with bricks and prepare pongala, a sweet pudding of rice, jaggery, coconut, and plantains, as an offering to the goddess Bhagavati also known as Bhadrakali or Kannaki. The popular festival sees what is possibly the largest gathering of women devotees in the Indian subcontinent.

Decoding Tantrism

Through the use of complex techniques, Tantrism is a practical way to render the individual free from worldly fetters while remaining in this world. It involves the interaction of the macro and the micro – the Shakti and the worshipper.

Tantrism has a lineage in historiography of being such an esoteric, mystical religion that any exposition on the subject inevitably commences with the thorny issue of its definition. Tantra, or Tantrism, is often used as a comprehensive name to designate a denomination that has differed from the mainstream, especially providing an alternative view to the Vedic thoughts since about the 6th century. One of the most powerful factors in the development of Indian culture, it is a particular kind of gnosis and a network of intellectual and ritual systems. Over time, it has witnessed the evolution of different sects, but their emphasis is always on Shakti – the female creative power, who in embodied form, is the consort of Shiva, the destroyer.

Emphasis on the body

Shakti is both cosmic as well as human. It resides in the body in the form of a serpent power called *kundalini*, which means coiled and is likened to a snake. It is untapped energy that lies dormant. Tantra practitioners must awaken and stimulate it. They seek to harness its power to extend their own bodily experience and consciousness to a state of *satchitananda*, or the ultimate spiritual bliss.

Thence the human body is central to Tantrism. It is understood that the clue to the mysteries of the universe is to be sought in

the body, so much so that it is glibly declared that what is not in the body, is not in the universe. Assuming that the universe is the macrocosm and the human being is the microcosm, it could be said that a homology is seen between the two leading to "cosmicization" of the human.

Key features

Followers of Tantrism believe that one obtains emancipation by means of special rituals and procedures, such as yogic exercises, yantras, and mantras. While mantra is the uttered word, yantra is the symbolic representation of the divine in mystic diagrams. Many scholars have noted that Tantric practitioners conceive the divine ontologically and epistemologically through imagery or the physical anthropomorphic, mantric or verbal, and yantras, which is diagrammatic.

The Tantric belief that salvation could be sought through the mastery of visualization also fostered a rich legacy of art in the form of temple building and sculpture. Tantric art frequently depicted the perennial theme of *kama*, or love, and the idea that all aspects of this world can be utilized to gain both worldly and supernatural enjoyments – *bhukti*, or pleasure of the world, *siddhi*, or supernatural powers, and

△ **A 19th-century copper yantra** meditation plaque

◁ **A Tantric painting** depicting the chakras and *kundalini* of a yogi sitting in a meditative posture

> " … Tantric vision is the cosmos as permeated by power… wherein energy (*shakti*) is **both cosmic and human** and where the **microcosm and macrocosm** correspond and interact."

ANDRE PADOUX, "WHAT DO WE MEAN BY TANTRISM?" (2002)

expanse, especially the outer tribal circles. Tantrism exploded in the early medieval period, and penetrated the areas of Kashmir, Nepal, Bengal, Assam, and even the far southern regions. The spread of Tantrism during this time coincided with feudal developments, and it meant many areas were getting "Brahmanized" as land grants were being donated to Brahmans.

The fusion and interaction of the indigenous cultures gave a fillip to Tantrism. One essential feature that emerged was the abundance of female deities, such as Kali (See pp 126–29) and Tara (See pp 272–73), and the emphasis on the *Shakti pithas* (See pp 104–07).

Tantric rituals are regarded by some as the resurgence of indigenous beliefs associated with subordinate social groups which eventually became popular at every level of society, including the royal courts. This idea is most clear in the aboriginal background of the Tantric mother goddesses, such as Matangi (See pp 308–09) and Chandali.

ultimately *jivan mukti*, or freedom from life. Tantra also deliberately reverses Brahmanic values. It is evident in the ritual use of the *panchamakaras*, the five transgressive substances – alcohol, meat, fish, gesture, and sexual intercourse. There is emphasis on personal autonomy, generated by the mystical experience, whereby the practitioner feels above societal morality.

Historical development

The early history of Tantrism is obscure, but it eventually becomes a pan Indian phenomenon, in Buddhism and Hinduism, with varying forms, by the 9th century. Precise geographical location of its source is not known, but it seems to have originated in the peripheral

CHANGING PERCEPTION

For a long time, Tantrism was dismissed and looked upon as inconsequential to the mainstream. It was rarely a subject of scholarly attention. A reason for this cavalier attitude is because this tradition was considered morally suspect and religiously antinomian. However, in the last few years, there has been a course correction wherein both academic and popular discourses have recognized it as an important variation in the religious sphere.

Incarnation and manifestation

Most Hindu traditions favour the idea of an overarching oneness existing beyond time and space, but also portray a multiplicity of gods and goddesses. What one encounters in this theology is one of Hinduism's crucial markers – the relationship between the transcendent one and its many manifestations.

▽ **Kalamkari**, a traditional textile art form from Andhra Pradesh, usually portrays scenes from Hindu mythology, such as the Dasavatar, as seen here. The two panels depict the 10 forms that Vishnu, the preserver, took to restore cosmic balance.

The Sanskrit word avatar means to descend and, by extension, it denotes the process whereby an incarnation of the divine consciousness – male or female – descends on the Earth to show humankind how to live a virtuous life based on dharma or to save the world from disaster. As opposed to ordinary human beings, an avatar is born not as a result of karma, but from an act of free will. Avatars are also conscious of their divine mission throughout their life and find new paths for spiritual awareness corresponding to different time periods in which they are born.

Inception

The concept came up in the epic period when Vishnu, the preserver, took the incarnation of Rama in the *Ramayana* and Krishna in the *Mahabharata*. It became a full-fledged doctrine by c. 4th century, when several local figures and regional divinities were assimilated via the avatar system. This is most clearly enunciated in the mythology of the sectarian Puranas.

Devi as a saviour

The Devi is also firmly entrenched in the avatar system. Her multiple appearances are dramatic and full of rigour and vigour, as seen in the Shakta texts. In the Shakta mythology, devotees beseech Her for help and She manifests before them and offers Her assistance. In the *Devi Mahatmya*, for instance, Her incarnation's sole aim is to kill the Asura Mahisha who had been granted immunity from everyone, except a

DASAVATAR

The most popular avatars are those of Vishnu, widely believed to be 10 in number. These include: Matsya, or the fish; Kurma, the tortoise; Varaha, the great boar; Narasimha, the man-lion; Vamana, the dwarf; Parashurama, or Rama with an axe; Rama, the king of Ayodhya and the protagonist in the epic *Ramayana*; Krishna, the son of Vasudeva and Devaki; and Kalki, who is yet to come. While Hindus also include Buddha in this list, Buddhists view him as an independent figure with no connection to Hinduism.

> " …she incarnates in **manifold ways**… When she **manifests herself**… she is said to be **born in the world**, though she is eternal."

VERSES 64–66, CHAPTER 1, *DEVI MAHATMYA*

woman (See pp 86–87). In the *Adbhuta Ramayana*, She helps Rama win against Rakshasa Ravana by giving him the strength to build a bridge. Towards the end of the *Devi Mahatmya*, the Devi foretells Her future appearances in times of crisis. She promises Her return when fearsome Asuras rise, or when there is a drought, or there is a need for food on the Earth.

It can be said that She is then similar to Vishnu who oversees the world and, when danger is imminent, descends in different avatars to combat the evildoers (See box). The Devi's avatars, however, emerge in a system different to that of Vishnu. Her forms are mature from the beginning, unlike most of Vishnu's avatars, who take birth as an infant and then experience the different stages of life. For example, in Her quelling of Asuras of different dimensions, Her fully formed avatars appear immediately from Her anger.

Multiplicity in the Hindu pantheon

There are many divinities in the Hindu pantheon, but the way they appear and the way they are explicated is key. Through an elaborate process of accretion, Vishnu has avatars, Shiva, the destroyer, has an extended family, and the Devi has innumerable forms. The multiplicity is due to the assimilation of local divinities who acquire a place in an organized, developed and hierarchal religion. The understanding and usage of terms such as polytheistic and monotheistic would betray a partial and superficial understanding of such a complex and nuanced a system.

Adbhuta Ramayana

Unlike other versions, the Shakta orientation of the *Ramayana*, the *Adbhuta Ramayana* focuses on Sita and presents her as the ultimate reality. It is sometimes referred to as *Sitayana* and highlights the significance of omnipotent femininity.

Sage Valmiki, credited with composing the *Ramayana*, is also believed to be behind the writing of the *Adhbuta Ramayana*, a Sanskrit text dated to the 14th or 15th century. Unfolding in 27 cantos, the work presents itself as an appendix to the *Ramayana*. It is an unconventional depiction of Rama's story, with Sita getting more prominence in the text.

A part of the narrative is similar to the *Ramayana*. Here too, Ravana abducts Sita and Rama in turn, kills him and rescues his wife. However, Sita later tells everyone of a far more formidable enemy – the 1000-headed Ravana of Pushkar, who is the twin brother of the 10-headed Ravana of Lanka.

A vicious battle between Rama and the new Ravana ensues, and in the end, Rama faces defeat. The gods panic. It is then that Sita assumes the frightening form of Mahakali (See pp 126–29), carrying all the marks of Shiva – the third eye, the crescent moon, and the trident. She kills the brutal Rakshasa along with his sons and army.

Sita then gives Rama the divine vision so that he can see her true form. He praises her as both the Supreme Goddess and Supreme Brahman. Finally, she grants him a wish that she would keep her superlative form in his heart, but returns with him to his kingdom in Ayodhya in human guise.

The Incredible Ramayana

The following selection of verses is from cantos 26 of the *Adbhuta Ramayana*. At the end of the battle, Sita is still in her terrifying form. Rama propitiates her with a recitation of 1000 names and then asks her to take on a less terrible form. Once she is in her beneficent form, Rama praises her as the Supreme Goddess, before taking his place by her side. Sita then explains how she resides in different places in different forms.

एवं नामसहस्रेण स्तुत्वासौ रघुनन्दनः | भूय प्रणम्य प्रीतात्मा प्रोवाचेदं कृताञ्जलिः ||

That delight of the Raghus, having so praised her with a thousand names, and having prostrated himself again, was pleased in his heart and spoke thus with his hands together:

यदेतदैश्वरं रूपं घोरं ते परमेश्वरि | भीतोऽस्मि साम्प्रतं दृष्ट्वा रूपमन्यत्प्रदर्शय ||

"I am presently afraid of looking upon this majestic, terrible form of yours, Supreme Goddess! Show me a different form."

एवमुक्ताथ सा देवी तेन रामेण मैथिली | संहृत्य दर्शयामास स्वं रूपं परमं पुनः ||

That goddess Maithili, so addressed by that Rama,
withdrawing (that form), then showed her supreme form,

काञ्चनाम्बुरुहप्रख्यं पद्मोत्पलसुगन्धिकं | सुनेत्रं द्विभुजं सौम्यं नीलालकविभूषितम् ||

which resembled a golden lotus, and was fragrant as lotus flowers.
It was gentle, two-armed, and with beautiful eyes, adorned with dark tresses.

तदीदृशं समालोक्य रूपं रघुकुलोत्तमः | भीतिं संत्यज्य हृष्टात्मा बभाषे परमेश्वरीं ||

When he saw that form, the best of the Raghu lineage abandoned fear
and addressed the Supreme Goddess, delighted,

अद्य मे सफलं जन्म अद्य मे सफलं तपः | यन्मे साक्षात्त्वम् अव्यक्ता प्रसन्ना दृष्टिगोचरा ||

"Today, my life is successful, today, my austerities have borne fruit,
for you, the unmanifest one, are pleased and in the scope of my vision."

त्वया सृष्टं जगत् सर्वं प्रधानाद्यां त्वयि स्थितं | त्वय्येव लीयते देवि त्वमेव च परागतिः ||

"Goddess! This entire world, beginning with primordial matter, is created by you, exists in you, and dissolves in you. You are the ultimate refuge."

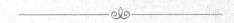

त्वमेव परमं व्योम महाज्योतिर्निरञ्जनं | शिवं सर्वगतं सूक्ष्मं परं ब्रह्म सनातनं ||

"You alone are the transcendental space, the great immaculate light, the eternal Supreme Brahman, which is auspicious, omnipresent, and subtle."

एतावदुक्त्वा वचनं रघुराजकुलोद्रहः | सम्प्रेक्षमाणो वैदेहीं प्राञ्जलिः पार्श्वतोऽभवत् ||

Having uttered this speech, the best of the royal lineage of Raghus, looking at Vaidehi with folded hands, stood by her side.

अथ सा तस्य वचनं निशम्य जगतीपतेः | सस्मितं प्राह भर्तारं शृणुष्वैकं वचो मम ||

And she, having heard the words of that lord of the Earth,
spoke smilingly to her husband, "Listen to one thing I say."

———————————⁂———————————

गृहीतं यन्मया रूपं रावणस्य वधाय हि | तेन रूपेण राजेन्द्र वसामि मानसोत्तरे ||

"Best of kings! I live to the north of the Lake Manasa in the form
that I took for the killing of (the 1000-headed) Ravana."

———————————⁂———————————

प्रकृत्या नीलरूपस्त्वं लोहितो रावणार्दितः | नीललोहितरूपेण त्वया सह वसाम्यहम् ||

"You are naturally blue, and struck by (the 1000-headed) Ravana,
you are rendered red. (Thus) I live with you in the blue-red form."

Forms of the divine

One of the most common methods of worship in Hinduism is the devotion and care bestowed upon images. The appearance of the divine in a tangible form makes Him or Her believable and far more accessible.

The Sanskrit language has a treasure trove of lexicon when referring to icons – as *archa*, or the entity of adulation, murti, or the one that has a fixed shape, *bimba*, or a sample of the original, *pratima*, or resemblance, and *rupa*, or form. All these indicate the significance and popularity of the worship of form in Hinduism.

Belief in the manifest

Yet, there is the concept of Nirakara, or without a form, such as the Brahman, or the ultimate reality, which is devoid of attributes. The understanding is that the deity is *nishkala*, or transcendent. But, on donning the mantle of appearance, He or She becomes *sakala*, or the material, like the entire phenomenal universe, subject to the categories of space and time.

To people who have realized the Brahman within themselves, there is no need for a divine image for worship. Icons are prescribed to those who have not attained this realization. This explains why sometimes, there is a subtle disdain towards those who need an icon to experience the divine. The visuals have their own advantages. For the devotee, the murti is alive and presents the most instant medium to experience the divine. With its graphic and anthropomorphic form, the murti articulates the mythology behind the Goddess and makes her more believable and relatable.

Myriad depictions

Over the centuries, an astonishing amount of diversity in the forms of the Goddess has emerged. She may have a youthful appearance with a strong, stout body and full breasts. She may be embellished in ornaments, from those made of gold to ones carved out of bones, such as a *mundamala*, or garland of skulls. She may be two-armed or many-armed, wielding various *ayudhas*, or destructive weapons, musical instruments, and lotuses. At times, the hands don't hold any object but are presented in different mudras, or gestures, such as the *abhaya mudra* for fearlessness or the *varada mudra* for bestowing gesture.

The images that one encounters of the Goddess are an amalgamation of at least two, if not more, streams of expressions – the classical and the vernacular. The classical tradition was the "great" tradition which covered the science of *shilpa*, or arts and crafts, delineated in the established body of manuals or canons describing design rules and proportions. This form of expression was patronized by diverse groups of individuals and changed from one region to another, and many exceptional schools of inherited craftspeople thrived under the beneficence of royalty.

> "O Devi, how can we **describe your inconceivable form**... displayed in battles among all the hosts of gods, asuras and others?"

VERSE 6, CHAPTER 4, *DEVI MAHATMYA*

PRANA PRATISHTHA

The ritual of the consecration of an idol or an image is called *prana pratishtha*. A number of steps must be taken before the idol can be considered divine. First, it is purified by materials, such as grass, honey, or ghee, followed by a practice of *nyasa*, or touching, where each part of the idol is touched while chanting mantras. In the end, *prana*, or breath, is infused into the idol by reciting more mantras. Then, the deity, it is believed, enters into the idol, ready to be worshipped by the devotees.

◁ **Placed outside** the Sri Gangamma Devi Temple in Bengaluru, Karnataka, this trident incorporates the face of the Goddess.

Therefore, the images that emerged out of this tradition were mostly made of long-lasting and expensive materials, such as stones and metals. They also followed prescriptive requirements as per the canonical literature.

On the other hand, the images that appeared in the rural areas were part of a vernacular or "little" tradition, which operated through individual artisans, guilds, and even worshippers. Here, the goddess iconography was built upon the repertory of local cults seen in fairs, festivals, pilgrimages, and in countless tribal shrines. Therefore, the images, made of everyday materials, such as terracotta and wood, appear with less technical finesse.

Social commentary

The Goddess's many forms also represent the many phases in the life cycle of a woman – youthful, married, maternal, widowed, and old. For instance, Lakshmi and Sita could symbolize the devoted wife, in Radha one could see a selfless lover, and Parvati could embody the devoted mother or equal partner. Ultimately, the crone and hag Chamunda, grimacing and emaciated, with prominent ribs and drooping breasts shows the inevitability of aging.

It also puts forth a take on the conceptualization of beauty. Through the many forms of the Goddess, the idea of beauty appears to be fluid. The sanitized version of the Goddess – fair, voluptuous, and bedecked – is not Her only comely form, for the fearsome goddesses are considered alluring by their followers. At the same time, the conventionally beautiful may appear fearsome for others.

RISE OF THE GODDESS $\cdot$ 2

The first possible signs of feminine worship in the Indian subcontinent emerge from the ruins of the Indus Valley Civilization. These fragmentary and speculative indications take a definite shape in the Vedic period when, in the labyrinth of male gods, the Vedic feminine makes its presence felt through occurrences of everyday life, such as the dawn, the night, the forest, and the rivers.

Early goddesses

The earliest signs of feminine worship in the Indian subcontinent are seen in the Indus Valley Civilization, after archeological excavations yielded hundreds of enigmatic female figurines. While these have been widely interpreted as having religious relevance, their significance is still a matter of much debate.

An abiding civilizational characteristic of India is the worship of the feminine. The fertility of the land and the livestock was of paramount importance to ancient societies. The belief seems to be that since the female body also procreates, it is considered sacred and a symbol of overall fertility.

Even though there are some caveats, the earliest signs of such worship are seen in the hundreds of terracotta female figurines unearthed at different sites of the Indus Valley Civilization (c. 3300–1750 BCE), such as Mohenjo-Daro, and Harappa. From their first discovery, they have been referred to as mother goddesses.

The Mother Goddess is often understood to be the central figure of the Harappan religion. This is because archaeologists, who discovered these figurines, were aware of Goddess worship in later historical periods and its prevalence in modern times. Hand-modelled terracotta figurines are still used in traditional Hindu society for domestic rituals where a woman seeks specific benefits, such as a child, good health, or long life for husband and family.

INDUS VALLEY CIVILIZATION

One of the earliest urban cultures, the Indus Valley Civilization emerged on the plains of the River Indus, across present-day northwestern India, Pakistan, and Afghanistan, in the 3rd millennium BCE. Archaeologists discovered several urban cities, which had baked-brick houses and extensive drainage systems. These include Harappa and Mohenjo-Daro in Pakistan, and Dholavira, Rakhigarhi, and Lothal in India.

Iconography

The figurines found at Indus Valley sites are somewhat crudely made and fashioned out of clay. The figurines have elaborate headdresses, prominent eyes, and thick lips. The breasts are separately moulded and attached to the body, and the navel is deep. The head region of the figurines usually shows a complex arrangement of hair and flowers. There seems to be cultural interest in hairstyle, likely related to a particular

△ **Motherly figurines**, such as this one from Mohenjo-Daro dating between 2600–2500 BCE, portray what appears to be a mother carrying a small infant – a theme associated with fertility and procreation.

"In one figurine, a plant is shown growing out of the **embryo of a woman**… represents the **goddess of earth**… connected with the **origin and growth** of plants."

RS SHARMA, *INDIA'S ANCIENT PAST* (2005)

ethnic community or family within the Civilization. Rarely nude, clothing includes short skirts. Additional ornaments comprise belts, necklaces, and bangles. In reality, this jewellery would have been in metal, agate, ivory, and semi-precious stones, but in the figurines, they are simply outlined and sculpted onto the surface. Some figurines carry a child and some are matron-like with a potbelly, which could represent a pregnant or prosperous woman.

Cult figures

There are many theories that discuss the relevance of these figurines. American archaeologist Jonathan Mark Kenoyer suggests that the different styles may represent different cults. The earliest archaeologists saw these sculptures as an indication of the existence of a fertility cult, which was vital in a civilization where agriculture played an important role. Residues that may indicate burning of oils or other substances in the panniers have also prompted a cultic interpretation. However, there is no contextual evidence to support such an interpretation.

Votive offerings

Most of the figurines were found broken and none were found in contexts that would suggest a temple, such as structures or paraphernalia attached to worship. British archaeologist Sir John Marshall was the first to suggest that these were votive offerings and could have been part of a ritual cycle and meant for short-term use for specific rituals.

Indian art historian Vidya Dehejia seems to give weightage to this as many terracotta figurines were found in an ancient tank, dating to the 1st and 2nd millennium CE, at Shringaverapura, near Allahabad, Uttar Pradesh. Judging from later practices, it seems that these were deposited in water after the fulfilment of the vow that led to their creation. Some broken figurines were even part of the garbage in street jars used for urban

disposal of waste or post-cremation urns. However, Indian archaeologist Shereen Ratnagar argues that since they are not found near street junctions or trees or wells, they may have been goddesses who presided over birth and death.

Different perspectives

Indian historian DD Kosambi views them as toys, decorative items, or figurines that show women wearing a heavy bird mask. They may represent actual women as brides. Indian historian Upinder Singh, however, points out that not every depiction of a woman needs to have religious significance and not all goddesses had maternal associations.

△ **This figurine from Mohenjo-Daro** is 7.9 cm (3.1 in) in height and was possibly produced between 2500–2000 BCE.

◁ **Bust of a mother goddess**, with a pannier on one side, discovered at Mohenjo-Daro

Fan-shaped elaborate
headdress

Smoke stained
panniers suspended
on either side

Pinched nose

Two round pellets
of clay for the eyes

Separately
moulded breasts

**Complete view
of the figurine**

In her image

A mother goddess figurine from Mohenjo-Daro, 2700–2100 BCE

The slim female figurine, such as the one on the left, is among the most prominent type of terracotta figurines from the Indus Valley Civilization found during excavations. Displayed in the National Museum, New Delhi, this figurine is about 230 cm (90.6 in) in height and 85 cm (33.5 in) in width.

It is seen with a short kilt around the waist, which is heavily ornamented with a belt that has three strands and a circular clasp. With a deep navel, the figurine doesn't appear to have any clothes above the waist but the upper segment is adorned with several rows of necklaces, including a choker with many pendants. One particular necklace is longer than the others and it sits between her breasts, which are separately moulded and attached to the body. It is possible that the conical object on the forehead could be another type of ornament. This figurine has a forward-projecting face with prominent eyes and thick lips. The handiwork is so rudimentary with the technique of pellets of clay applied to create eyes, breasts, and ornaments.

Although badly broken, the headdress is elaborate. While some figurines may have flowers on either side, others, such as this one, have cup-like attachments. The cups of the fan-shaped pannier headdress in this figurine were found to contain black residue. The black residue suggests that these sculptures were of religious significance since the cups may have been used to burn oil or some sort of incense.

On the fringes

The Indus Valley Civilization had some archaeological evidence of female worship unlike the textual sources from the following Vedic period. Here, goddesses made a fleeting appearance in the hymns, yet they were noteworthy in their message and elaborate description.

Starting around 1500 BCE, a group of nomadic peoples who called themselves Arya, or the noble ones, became dominant in northern India. Their sacred literature was composed in Sanskrit and known as the Vedas. Of these, the *Rigveda*, the earliest of all the Vedas, reflects a religion of naturalistic polytheism. It speaks of gods representing natural phenomena and provides anthropomorphic descriptions of the deities. There are three categories – the celestial and heavenly called *dyusthana*, the aerial, intermediate, and atmospheric called *anatarikshasthana*, and the terrestrial called *prithivisthana*. It projected an overwhelmingly masculine world view, particularly in the religious sphere. This is perhaps why the Vedic divinities were predominantly male (See box), as was natural in a patriarchal society.

Unsteady appearance

The Vedic texts do not place much power on their goddesses, who remain somewhat in the background. Some historians attribute it to the fact that this was a period of constant warfare between different tribes. So, the male gods became paradigmatic models of warriors. Another reason could be that this was mostly a pastoral society, not an agrarian one.

The goddess usually plays a prominent role in agricultural economies and societies because of her connection with fertility as a mother. There is also a homology with land and livestock. It is, of course, surprising that there are no encounters with the fierce and strong goddesses of later periods. Also, while there is a mention of some goddesses, they do not form the core of the Vedic religion.

"I am the **Queen**, the gatherer-up of treasures, most thoughtful, **first** of those who **merit worship**. Thus Gods have stablished me in **many places** with **many homes** to enter and abide in."

VERSE 3, HYMN 125, CHAPTER 10, *RIGVEDA*

The goddess of dawn

Among these is Ushas, who appears to be an important divinity in the *Rigveda* as she is mentioned 300 times with 20 hymns that address her. The daughter of Heaven and sister of the Adityas, she is portrayed as a physical phenomenon. The Sun is her lover, but as she precedes him, she is also said to be his mother. Reddish horses, probably representing the red clouds of dawn, draw her chariot. Like a dancer with a garment of light, she rises in the east and awakens all life, chasing away evil dreams. She exhibits her graces before the world, shines bright, and is strong and ever-youthful, being born repeatedly. She is always the same, as age cannot touch her. She does not despise the small or the great, as she goes to every house. Representing victory of light over darkness, she is generous, which is why those desiring wealth often invoke her. German scholar of religion Max Müller notes that her description is so allegorical that, sometimes, one wonders whether the poet is speaking of a bright apparition or of a bright goddess.

The guardian mother

Aditi is one of those distinct goddesses whose traits can be reconstructed from the hymns. The word *aditi* is primarily a noun, the personification of an abstract idea, and means non-binding. So, her name means freedom, and she is the mother of the Adityas.

Indian historian Roshen Dalal points out that there is no separate hymn to her, but has almost 80 references in the *Rigveda*. She nourishes and sustains the universe and all existence. She is bright and luminous, invoked in the morning, at noon, and at sunset. She is the sky and space or air.

THE MALE PANTHEON

In the Vedic pantheon, Indra seems to be the most prominent of the male gods. He was the god of thunder whose lightning, thunderbolt, and the *vajra* caused havoc among demons, dragons, and enemies. Agni was the other important male deity, said to have descended from the Sun. He was believed to be the mouth of the deities as he received the offerings from devotees not only for himself but also for transmission to the other gods. Both Indra and Agni were associated with virility, sexual potency, aggression, and strength. Varuna, who personified water, was the guardian of the cosmic order, and Soma, the god of plants, whose mystery was embodied in the immortal nectar, drunk on ceremonial occasions. Apart from these, there were the Vishvedevas, a class of semidivine beings, who were preservers of human beings, bestowers of rewards, and the Ashvins, who were the supreme healers.

▷ **A 16th-century Nepalese metal sculpture** of Indra, decorated with gemstones

>> Some hymns speak of her as a mother, and worshippers invoke her to bestow freedom from sickness, harm, evil, and release from the bondage of suffering.

Ratri and Nirriti

Goddess Ratri's association is with night but not the dark night. She has only one hymn to her in the *Rigveda*. She is the daughter of Heaven and the goddess of the starlit night. She fills the valleys and the heights, driving away the darkness with her light.

Nirriti has 12 mentions and in association with Yama, the god of death. Indian historian Kumkum Roy indicates that she is a female deity of destruction in later texts, who is often asked to consume decay associated with *jara*, or aging. Interestingly, Nirrti is also a male deity in the *Rigveda*.

Sarasvati and her associations

Sarasvati is a goddess first mentioned in the *Rigveda*. She is personified as a great, sacred river flowing into the sea. She is the best

> "... O Blessed One, bestowing food of thousand sorts.
> O **broad-tressed Sinivali**, thou who art the Sister of the Gods,
> Accept the offered sacrifice, and, **Goddess, grant us progeny**.
> With lovely fingers, lovely arms, prolific **Mother of many sons** —
> Present the sacred gifts to her, to **Sinivali Queen of men**."

VERSES 5–7, HYMN 32, CHAPTER 2, *RIGVEDA*

of mothers, the best of rivers, and the best of goddesses. As Amba, that is mother, she gives renown to those who are unknown. She defeats enemies and protects her worshippers. She is also connected with deities, such as Pushan, Indra, the god of heavens, the Maruts, and the Ashvins. She is also associated with the goddesses Ila and Bharati and sometimes with Hotra. Ila is also mentioned in the *Rigveda*. Her name means nourishment and she is the personification of the offering of milk and butter, representing the nourishment provided by the cow. She is alternatively called the "butter footed" and "butter handed" and Agni, the god of fire, is once said to be her son. Roy points out that she is not so clearly defined and, much like Bharati, her association is with sacrality, nourishment, and prosperity. Another goddess, Dhishana, unrelated to Sarasvati, is also connected with nourishment, particularly the kind received from the cow in the form of milk and butter. A goddess named Vac is later

FEMALE SEERS

The Brahmavadinis or Rishikas were women seers who strove for the highest philosophical knowledge of Brahman. They authored hymns and featured in dialogues in the Vedic texts. Prominent among them are Vac Ambhrini, Ghosha, Gargi, Maitreyi, and Lopamudra. Although their verses are only one per cent of 1028 hymns of the *Rigveda*, theirs is the only female voice in the Vedic literature. They should be celebrated, no doubt, as some of the verses are striking and beautiful. They are cited as symbols of enlightened, liberated women and also provide evidence of an egalitarian society, where women were also educated. Vac Ambhrini's hymn in the *Rigveda*, for instance, is one of the rare early hymns where the poetess is speaking experientially of herself as a goddess in the first person.

▷ **A contemporary depiction** of Lopamudra

identified with Sarasvati (See pp 186–89). She appears to be the personification of speech by whom human beings receive the communication of divine knowledge. The gods created her, and while there is but one hymn to her, she finds mention in many others. She is often referred to as the queen of the gods and is said to accompany deities.

With male gods

There are many goddesses in the Vedic literature who are inextricably linked to male gods, and they make an appearance only in the context of their relationships with these gods. So Varunani is the wife of Varuna, Agnayi is the wife of Agni, and Indrani, also known as Shachi and Paulomi, is the wife of Indra. At the same time, Suryaa is the daughter of the Sun god Surya. There is a reference to her marriage in a wedding hymn. In different verses, she marries Soma, the Ashvins, or Pushan. According to Dalal, she may be the same as Ashvini, the wife of the Ashvins. Another goddess Rodasi is associated with the Maruts, probably as their wife. She sings the praises of Agni and receives wealth from him thus becoming a *supatni*, or good wife.

Other minor goddesses

There are other minor goddesses that make an infrequent appearance in the Vedic literature. Some are associated with abundance, wealth, strength, and longevity. Others are linked with progeny. For instance, Sinivali, a sister of the gods, bestows children. In the *Atharvaveda*, she is the preserver god Vishnu's wife. In the Brahmanas, she is a deity associated with the Moon.

There are three other Moon goddesses – Kuhu, Anumati, and the benevolent and bountiful Raka. Dalal describes them as being connected with different phases of the Moon. Dowson also points out that the Moon on its 15th day, when just short of its fullness, is personified and worshipped as goddess Anumati. These goddesses are also related to childbirth fertility and cattle. So, the *Atharvaveda* portrays Anumati as a goddess of love, prayed to for children.

There are also goddesses, such as Sarama, Saranyu, and Brihaddiva, whose description, nature, and traits remain obscure along with other rivers in one hymn.

It is clear that, in the Vedic period, none of the goddesses equalled the power and stature of the male gods. Subsequent periods saw some of them disappear while others merged or transformed into different goddesses.

▽ **This is an 11th-century stone sculpture** from Sun Temple, Konark, Odisha, depicting Goddess Varunani riding a *makara*, or crocodile.

Devi Sukta

The "Devi Sukta" is the 125th hymn of the 10th *mandala,*
or book, of the *Rigveda.* Composed in the first person, it is
wonderfully direct and seems like the Devi's proclamation
of her own power and the pervasiveness of her glory.

The "Devi Sukta", also called the "Vac Sukta" or "Ambhrini Sukta", consists of eight *riks*, or verses. The 10th *mandala* is one of the later portions to the *Rigveda*, so it may have been composed probably around 1100 BCE. The hymns of the *Rigveda* were not written, but envisioned by its composers or revealed to them by the gods themselves. Its composers are called *mantra drashta*. Brahmavidushi Rishika Vac is the *mantra drashta* of the "Devi Sukta".

In the hymn, the word *vac,* meaning "speech" and the goddess Vac are used interchangeably. This has led some scholars to argue that the hymn is about the power of speech and is not related to a goddess. However, in the hymn, the goddess exults in her own supremacy and declares herself as maya and the one who brought the progenitors to the Earth. She experiences herself as the source and power of all that exists. She expresses that she is the yoni, the source of all, and asserts her identity as the absolute one.

It is often believed that this is the very first hymn that expresses Shakti and so is considered the first reference point in understanding the philosophy of the Great Goddess (See pp 60–61). Traditionally, it is chanted in the worship of the Goddess, along with the *Devi Mahatmya* (See pp 70–75).

Hymn to the goddess

In this selection of verses from the "Devi Sukta", the speaker Vac identifies herself with the deity praised in this passage, the all-pervasive supreme self. Experiencing identity with that, she praises herself saying, "I alone am everything, having the form of all the world and as the foundation of everything."

ॐ अहं रुद्रेभिर्वसुभिश्चराम्यहमादित्यैरुत विश्वदेवैः ।

अहं मित्रावरुंणोभा बिभर्म्यहमिन्द्राग्नी अहमश्विनोभा ॥

Om. I move as the Rudras, Vasus, Adityas and as the world-gods. I bear the pair, Mitra and Varuna, I bear Indra and Agni, and I bear the pair of Ashvins.

अहं सोममाहनसं बिभर्म्यहं त्वष्टारमुत पूषणं भगम् ।

अहं दधामि द्रविणं हविष्मते सुप्राव्ये३ यजमानाय सुन्वते ॥

I bear the Soma, which is to be pressed (or the deity Soma who destroys enemies), Tvashtri, Pushan, and Bhaga. I bestow riches upon the sacrificer who sacrifices with offerings, causes offerings to reach gods, and presses Soma.

अहं राष्ट्री संगमनी वसूनां चिकितुषी प्रथमा यज्ञियानाम् ।
तां मा देवा व्यदधुः पुरुत्रा भूरिस्थात्रां भूर्या वेशयन्तीम् ॥

I am the sovereign who cause attainment of riches. I cognize. I am the first of those unto whom offerings are made. It is I, who pervade many things, who am placed severally by gods in various places. It is unto me who am present in various places and pervade many things that the gods act variously.

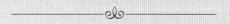

मया सो अन्नमत्ति यो विपश्यति यः प्राणिति य ईं शृणोत्युक्तम् ।
अमन्तवोमान्त उप क्षियन्ति श्रुधि श्रुत श्रद्धिवं ते वदामि ॥

It is through me that he eats food who eats, through me that he sees who sees, through me that he breathes who breathes, and through me that he hears what is said. Those who do not know me waste away. Well-known one, listen to what I say to you, which is to be believed.

अहमेव स्वयमिदं वदामि जुष्टं देवेभिरुत मानुषेभिः ।
यं कामये तंतमुग्रं कृणोमि तं ब्रह्माणं तमृषिं तं सुमेधाम् ॥

I myself state this, which is welcomed by the gods and humans. Whomever I desire, I make him the very best — the creator, the seer, the one with an excellent intellect.

Prithivi and Varaha
This sandstone sculpture from Central India, belonging to the 8th–9th century, depicts a popular legend where Vishnu, in his boar avatar, rescued the goddess from the depths of the cosmic ocean.

Prithivi

Goddess of the Earth and the embodiment of life

"**Thou, of a truth**, O Prithivi, bearest
the tool that rends the hills:
Thou **rich in torrents**, who with might
quickenest earth, O Mighty One."

VERSE 1, HYMN 84, CHAPTER 5, *RIGVEDA*

Firm and steady, Prithivi, the goddess of the Earth, is *mahi*, or great, all-encompassing, and shining. She is stationary and yet accommodates everything and every being, whether biped or quadrupeds, from the hyena and tiger to the horse and the birds. She supports the snow-clad mountains, the plains, the cornfields, the forests, the oceans, and the rivers. She also scatters the rain. This is how the "Prithivi Sukta", a celebrated hymn of 63 verses from the *Atharvaveda*, refers to this mighty goddess.

Linked to Dyaus

The first reference to Prithivi, however, is found in the *Rigveda*, though she is never addressed alone. Literally, her name means "one who is broad and wide", and reflects the expansive nature of the Earth. She is always associated with Dyaus – the male deity of the heavens and the sky. Together, they are referred to as the "Dyavaprithivi". There are six hymns solely dedicated to this duo, but they are mentioned together in many other hymns as well. Both these deities are interdependent. The heaven produces rain, which fertilizes the Earth, giving birth to all life forms. They are considered the parents who have created the world and sustain the creatures therein.

Prithivi Sukta

The *Atharvaveda* is the first text where Prithivi is addressed as a separate deity. It mentions her as the god of the heaven Indra's wife. It also speaks of Agni, the god of fire, who pervades her, preserver Vishnu who strides over her, and Parjanya, Prajapati, and Vishvakarma, who protect and provide her requirements. However, despite these associations, she is a powerful deity in her own right.

Protection

Goddess Prithivi, along with Dyaus, is worshipped for wealth and power. People also worship them together for protection from danger and to compensate sin, thereby bringing happiness. Additionally, she is believed to bestow psychological strengths that the supplicant wishes for, such as truth and dharma.

Supportive nature

Prithivi is primarily associated with fertility as she is the source of all plants and is responsible for the nourishment of all living creatures. The significance of Prithivi goes beyond creation and sustenance of life. So, the dead are asked to retreat to her lap so that she may cover them tenderly. No doubt, her relevance has continued well beyond the Vedic times.

IN TODAY'S TIMES

BHUMI PUJAN

In Hindu culture, there's a practice of invoking the goddess Earth before commencing any construction project. People seek her approval as well as forgiveness for any unintended harm to the living creatures she sustains. Called Bhumi Pujan, the worship takes place at the site of construction, though specific rituals may vary across regions and communities. Often, the foundation stone is also laid during this ceremony.

The holy woodlands
Forests and groves across India often have tiny shrines or temples dedicated to local forest gods or goddesses, much like Aranyani. This 1782 illustration by British artist James Forbes shows a similar sacred grove near Chandod, Gujarat, with what appears to be a temple hidden among the trees.

Aranyani

The fearless goddess of the woods

"Goddess of wild and forest who **seemest to vanish** from the sight.
How is it that thou seekest not the village?
Art thou not afraid?"

VERSE 1, HYMN 146, CHAPTER 10, *RIGVEDA*

Sweet-smelling, redolent of the balm of trees, Aranyani is the mother of all forest things. There is one hymn in the *Rigveda* dedicated to her and that is her only mention. She is not cited along with any other deity in any other hymn.

The poignant beauty of this short song is extraordinary for it is almost sonic in its descriptions. The vivid observations are shared by a dweller in the wood.

Calls of the goddesss

Aranyani is described as an elusive goddess who revels in the sounds. Sometimes, one may hear the tinkling bells of her anklets. Those who spend the night in the woodland occasionally think they hear her call. Also, the sounds are heard of a cowman calling his cattle or of a tree falling as a woodman does his work.

In the hymn, there is a reference to certain creatures, such the *chichala*, which may be a grasshopper or some other little creature that cries *chichi*. There is also the mention of a *vrishrava*, which

may be a sort of cricket. Some take them to be birds of a certain kind. One can imagine the myriad evocative sounds and sights which seem to mystify and enthrall the listener on an evening in the darkening forest.

The forest queen

There is also a description of deer feeding in the glade and a statement that the goddess Aranyani never slays unless provoked by some murderous enemy. This could be a reference to a tiger or even a robber.

In the hymn, the supplicant entreats the goddess to explain how she wanders so far from the fringe of civilization, that is the villages, without becoming afraid or lonely.

Aranyani is also described as a dancer and a forest queen. Her ability to feed savoury fruit and other food, though she "tills no lands", is what the supplicant finds most marvellous. She is indeed the sylvan mother for animals and humans alike.

◁ **This red sandstone sculpture** from Mathura, Uttar Pradesh, dated c. 200, is sometimes interpreted as a nature goddess.

IN TODAY'S TIMES

ARANYA DEVI TEMPLE, BIHAR

The Aranya Devi Temple in Arrah, Bihar, is one of the most prominent shrines dedicated to the deity of the forest. Its sanctum sanctorum houses two idols, made of black touchstone, in standing pose, and the two goddesses are believed to be sisters. According to some legends, the temple dates back to the *Mahabharata* period, when it was built by King Mordhwaj of Arrah. However, the temple as it exists today, was constructed in 1953.

A sacred grove
Nestled amidst a dense forest and accessible only through long and winding tracks, Iringole Kavu in Ernakulam, Kerala, is the forest home of the goddess Durga. Here, the gods, in the form of trees and plants, pay obeisance to her. The folklore is replete with interesting stories about its origins. One popular legend connects this temple to Krishna's sister (See pp 206–07) who escaped the evil Kamsa with a bright show of light. That beam of light fell here giving birth to this place.

Symbol of fertility

A 6th-century miniature sandstone sculpture of
Lajja Gauri from Madhya Pradesh

Perceiving the female body as a site for manifesting life-affirming forces is the strongest notion in Indian iconography, especially during the 1st millennium in Central India and the Deccan. So, among the myriad ways in which one encounters a Hindu goddess, the image of Lajja Gauri is profoundly striking.

The word *lajja* means shame and *Gauri* is an epithet of Parvati. So Lajja Gauri may translate as "goddess having shame". However, more than 25 names are prevalent to describe this goddess and they vary across regions. Among them, Aditi Uttanapada, meaning outstretched supine, and Nagna Kabandha, meaning nude headless body, are particularly descriptive. Since there are no texts to explain her form, it is possible that she was assimilated into Hindu tradition from tribal worship. She is often invoked for abundant crops and good progeny.

Her sculptures are most visible from the 1st century onwards in many different regions of the country, including Gujarat, Chhattisgarh, all the states in South India, and even the northeastern region. The images are regarded as auspicious and beautiful. They are also meant to protect against evil forces. Their size may vary from a few centimetres to life-sized, but Lajja Gauri is usually represented as a small sculpture in terracotta or stone.

The image is a female torso in a squatting or lying-down position, with a lotus flower in place of the head. This is in continuation with the depiction of most fertility goddesses of the ancient world, who are similarly shown headless, while giving prominent focus to the genitals. The spread-out legs are drawn up laterally and bent at the knees in a pose akin to parturition, though there is no outward sign of pregnancy. The torso is extended to include the breasts. The soles of the feet are turned upwards, with it appearing as though there is a contraction of the toes. The image could, alternatively, suggest sexual fecundity and receptivity. The arms of the goddess are bent upwards, each, sometimes, holding a lotus stem, at the level of the head.

Lajja Gauri appears to be an explicit icon of fertility, which is emphasized by the representation of the exposed yoni. The artists who created these images definitely drew on various ancient symbols of fortune, fertility, and life-force. It is perhaps a part of a long, highly evolved tradition of expressing fertility in Indian art. This would include the very lofty cosmic feminine procreative energy, nature's fertility, and cyclic existence through human birth.

Lotus flower in place of the head implies blooming youth

Heavy bosom indicates an association with fertility

Malasana, or squatting position

Deep navel

Payals, or anklets

Contracted toes

Continued legacy

The shift from Vedic to the Puranic period is complex and outlines themes of continuity, transformation, and assimilation. This is also the time when the characteristics of many goddesses transmute in interesting ways as they acquire a definite identity.

Goddesses may have been on the margins of Vedic religion, but they certainly laid the foundation for the worship of the divine feminine in subsequent periods, when it exploded in a massive way. The thought process they produced percolated on to later goddesses, giving birth to an attenuated, yet viable, continuity.

Evolved advancement

The Puranas are the first juncture in Hinduism when goddess worship become paramount. One such example is that of Prithivi (See pp 48–49). Unlike the Vedas, where her description is skeletal, the Puranic stories develop her identity in more definite ways. This is when she becomes associated with Vishnu. It is during his third incarnation, as the gigantic boar, that he rescues her from drowning in the cosmic ocean. In another story, Prithivi allows king Prithu to milk her and vegetation comes into being.

Indian art historian Vidya Dehejia draws attention to how Prithivi's identity becomes more complex with regional variations. She notes that in South India, Bhu Devi, another name for Prithivi, comes to denote Vishnu's additional love and she becomes his second consort.

Amalgamation

While some goddesses made an effortless transition to the post-Vedic times, others transformed, via assimilation, into different goddesses with similar characteristics. For instance, the elemental Vedic figure of Aditi has a successor in the image of Aditi Uttanapada, also called Lajja Gauri (See pp 54–55). In the *Rigveda*, she is not a spouse. Her salient characteristic is her motherhood and she is not tied to a husband, family, or lineage. This feature continues as she is portrayed faceless with most focus on her fecundity.

Similarly, Shri blends with Lakshmi (See box), who has since become a favourite deity of the trading community. Sarasvati (See pp 186–89) is another goddess who continues into later traditions, and becomes popular as the goddess of learning and wisdom. In later Vedic literature and the *Mahabharata*, her nature as a river is de-emphasized and she is consistently equated with the goddess Vac.

Another example is Aranyani, the goddess of forests (See pp 50–51), whose worship declines in the post-Vedic times. However, she seems to continue in other forest deities, such as Bonbibi in West Bengal, Vanadevata in Goa and Konkan region, and Vanadurga in parts of South India. American scholar of religious studies David Kinsley points out that Yakshis,

△ **Red sandstone gateway bracket** from 1st–2nd century and belonging to Mathura, Uttar Pradesh, shows a Yakshi, or a nature spirit, holding a branch

---

SHRI SUKTA

The "Shri Sukta", a part of an appendix to the *Rigveda*, is a hymn in praise of Shri. "*Shri*" literally means auspicious or prosperous and is another name for the goddess Lakshmi. Shri and Lakshmi are identified as a single goddess in this *sukta*. This hymn was added somewhere between the 7th and 6th century BCE, but Vidya Dehejia dates it to around 5th century BCE. Nevertheless, it is the earliest hymn to Shri and Lakshmi's identity is also first clearly expressed in this. It is here that she is described as radiant as gold and as resplendent as the Sun. She sits on a lotus and is also bedecked with it to indicate that she as lovely as a lotus.

who are nature spirits in later Hindu traditions, are somewhat similar to Aranyani. Both inhabit forests and have benevolent traits.

Philosophical underpinnings

While Vac disappears, the sublime conception of "*vac*", or speech, outlined in the "Devi Sukta" (See pp 44–45), can be seen as one of the greatest and, at the same time, the simplest expositions of the concept of divine energy or Shakti. It forms an integral and the most arresting principle of goddess worship in later times. The overriding belief is that Shakti is present in gods, humans, and all creation. The thriving and fully developed Shakti worship of the epic and Puranic times was surely beholden to these early goddess concepts. The very idea underlying Shakti is based on the central theme of the "Devi Sukta".

Later goddesses

Names of goddesses, such as Durga, Kali, Uma, and Ambika, which came to designate, singly or collectively, the central figure of the Shakta culture, do not occur in the *Rigveda*, though they are found in the later Vedic texts. What is significant is that Durga, who is connected with battle, has no such association in the *Rigveda*. Yet, this has become such a crucial trope for many goddesses, such as Chandika, Durga (See pp 80–83), and Kali (See pp 126–29). It is clear that this concept was assimilated from the non-Vedic fold into the Brahmanical via the *Devi Mahatmya* (See pp 70–75). It is a seemingly continuous process of acculturation and adaptation.

A symbiotic relationship existed between Brahmanical, classical Sanskritic, and non-Brahmanical, and sophisticated theologies and oral traditions. There was a propelling power of the goddesses that mingled constantly with different autochthonous goddesses of villages, localities, and tribes. Eventually, even if they had different names, they were likened to each other through their characteristics and gained common identity. The water spirits, Earth spirits, serpent goddesses, Bhutnis, Dakinis, Yoginis, Kula Devi, and the village tutelary goddesses were all forms of the feminine sacred that kept transforming and forming linkages, until they were absorbed.

> " ... they have been portrayed as sovereign **all-powerful** figures... or as **terrifying violent**... or as **loving mothers**."

SJ FRANCIS X CLOONEY, *DIVINE MOTHER, BLESSED MOTHER: HINDU GODDESSES AND THE VIRGIN MARY* (2005)

▽ **This makeshift shrine** just outside the Sundarbans National Park, West Bengal, is of Bonbibi, a prominent forest goddess. Inhabitants of the Sundarbans often turn to her, seeking her protection before venturing into the forest.

EVOLUTION OF GODDESS WORSHIP 3

The Sanskrit texts, called the Puranas, assimilated all the regional female divinities into a single entity, remodelling and rehabilitating the Goddess tradition. It served as a vehicle for the profusion of the Goddess within the Brahmanical fold. It is in the Puranic period that the story of the Goddess unfolds in all its glory, full of colourful mythology and elaborate renditions.

The Great Goddess

The feminine divine acquires a more definite form in the Puranic period. This is when She is envisioned as the all-powerful Great Goddess with elaborate mythology and philosophical ideas. Her assimilation into the mainstream Hindu pantheon gives rise to the separate tradition of Shaktism.

△ **Gods (left) and Asuras (right)** entreat the Great Goddess in this painting from Rajasthan. Created in the late 18th or early 19th century, the work depicts the Devi seated on a tree-like throne, symbolic of her ultimate authority.

In Hinduism, all goddesses are believed to emanate from a singular feminine entity imagined as the Great Goddess. Conceptualized through complex sociological and psychological processes, She came to represent a variety of elements at diverse historical stages.

One witnesses Her imagery for the first time in *Rigveda*'s "Devi Sukta" (See pp 44–45). That She was multifaceted is also evident from the different goddesses seen in the Vedic texts. The Vedic connection is important because its antiquity supplied the required legitimacy and helped make Shaktism acceptable. However, the Great Goddess acquires a more concrete identity in the Puranas, where She is injected with colourful and detailed mythology, and connected with philosophical ideas. Both these apparatuses stimulate Her absorption in the mainstream Hindu religion, and places Her at its forefront.

Devi in the Puranas

In the Puranic corpus, the *Devi Mahatmya* (See pp 70–75) is one of the most significant texts for understanding the divine feminine. It delineates two crucial processes for the continuous ascent of the Goddess. Firstly, the Vedantic concept of maya forms a characteristic trait of the Goddess as Mahamaya. Then, there is the identification of the Goddess with abstract philosophical attributes as *prakriti*, or materiality, and *purusha*, or consciousness (See pp 76–77). The Devi gradually came to symbolize all these intangible ideologies. She also gets identified with creation myths and transcendental cosmogonic principles.

Another facet lending weight to the Devi can be seen in diverse epithets, such as Ambika, Chamunda, Chandika, and Bhagavati, used in the *Devi Mahatmya*. This proves that She amalgamated various lesser-known goddesses, including Kali and Durga. All of them appear in the text as powerful and paradoxical female symbols. This made way for different types of goddesses gaining acceptability in a Sanskrit text.

By the end of the 12th century, the composition of the *Devi Bhagavata Purana* (See pp 156–57) attempted to elevate the Devi's spiritual position to the level that Vishnu, the preserver, had in the *Bhagavata Purana*. It showed how the authors of the Puranas reinterpreted older theological models to assert the supremacy of the Goddess over male deities and transformed Her into a figure of broad devotional appeal. In it, She is triumphant against the demonic forces threatening cosmic or social order.

Growth and evolution

In many ways, the *Devi Bhagavata Purana* can be seen as a continuation of the *Devi Mahatmya*. The composers examined and reinterpreted the traditions assembled in the *Devi Mahatmya* and transformed the Goddess from partially martial and erotic goddesses to the "World Mother" (See pp 160–61) of infinite compassion.

Scholar of religious studies C Mackenzie Brown has pointed out that many ancient themes and motifs were taken from masculine texts and were thoroughly incorporated into a feminized theological framework. The Goddess also became the central figure in some Upapuranas, or secondary Puranas, such as the *Kalika Purana*, probably because of the regional context where these Puranas were written. Indian historian Kunal Chakrabarti has noted that the later accounts are either repetitious or confirming

> ## "O Devi, you are the **Intellect**, by which the **essence** of all scriptures is comprehended."
>
> VERSE 11, CHAPTER 4, *DEVI MAHATMYA*

elaborations of the model set by the *Devi Mahatmya*. The Goddess is neither wholly non-Vedic nor entirely Brahmanic, She is a product of interacting traditions.

Drawing legitimacy

The Puranas exemplify the process by which the assimilation of the non-Vedic religious trends and divinities was accomplished. Many of the goddesses may have shared characteristics and separate identities, but were now amalgamated and crystallized into the Great Goddess.

The mythographers reinforced Her legends, myths, and emanations. Consolidating Her influence, they provided Her the textual stamp of validation and transformed local traditions into an elite one by writing it in Sanskrit. Scholar of religious studies Thomas Coburn stresses that the use of Sanskrit language connects a tradition to a sacred past. Hence, the Puranic process brought the great Devi into the mainstream of Hinduism.

GODDESSES IN THE EPICS

The two Sanskrit epics, the *Ramayana* and the *Mahabharata*, composed between c. 300 BCE and c. 300 CE, denote a period of transition from the Vedic to the Puranic. Both the epics have references to some goddesses. In the *Mahabharata*, one encounters elaborate mythology for the origin of certain goddesses, such as Shri Lakshmi in the Samudra Manthan myth (See pp 174–75). The Goddess also makes an appearance through Arjuna's prayers to Durga for Shakti. At this time, social prescriptions begin to idealize women and the epic goddesses Sita and Draupadi are therefore known for their wifely devotion and marital fidelity. Both the epics also discuss the goddess Ganga.

AN EXTRACT FROM A PALM LEAF MANUSCRIPT OF THE *MAHABHARATA*

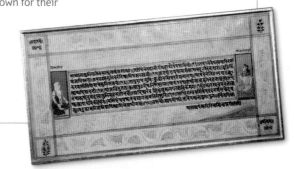

In captivity
A forlorn Sita sits in Ravana's grove in Lanka, surrounded by Rakshashis in this 18th-century folio from the "Shangri" *Ramayana*.

Sita

The steadfast and devoted wife

△ **Sita presents Rama** with a garland in this folio from Tulsidas's *Ramcharitmanas*.

> "**Auspicious Sita**, come thou near:
> we **venerate and worship thee**
> That thou mayst **bless and prosper us**
> and bring us fruits abundantly."

VERSE 6, HYMN 57, CHAPTER 4, *RIGVEDA*

Revered as the model wife in popular Hinduism today, Sita existed much before Valmiki's *Ramayana* (See pp 64–65), a Sanskrit text composed between the 5th–4th century BCE and 3rd century CE. While Sita finds only a fleeting mention in the *Rigveda*, it is enough for one to realize her ancient connections to fertility and earth. Over centuries, other goddesses representing fertility have overshadowed her, relegating her to the role of Rama's wife.

Eclipsed by Rama
Among all the versions of *Ramayana*, including the seminal Valmiki's *Ramayana*, Sita plays a subsidiary role vis-à-vis Rama, the supreme deity. She is the ideal devotee, subsumed in Rama's omnipresent aura and never achieves the position of a great goddess. Though a deity, she is rarely revered in her own right, and worshipped as a part of the Rama–Sita couple. Most temples today show her standing with Rama and his brother Lakshmana, with Hanuman kneeling before them.

Through the feminist lens
Feminists view Sita's personality from a slightly different perspective where they challenge her role as an individual and a woman. They consider her character an example of the oppression of women in Hindu culture. They proclaim that Sita as "a role model" endorses male supremacy. For instance, it is clear in most versions of the story that she has to face dire consequences, such as abduction, when she does not follow the injunctions of the men in her life.

Paradigm of womanhood
Many believers, however, feel that she is not helpless and can never be taken for granted. Her sense of pride and dignity are admired and, for all the sweetness and amiability of her character, she speaks her mind when necessary. She stands by Rama. Her life is a strange mixture of the real and the ideal. The dangers and the discomforts of the forests do not daunt her. She threatens to end her life when, initially, Rama refused to take her with him.

Some devotees feel that she had a mind of her own and raised her twin sons according to dharma. There is wide admiration for Sita's courage. It indicates a respect for her loyalty, dignity, and keen moral sense. It is Sita who is proclaimed a model Hindu wife, for she and Rama are considered the divine couple and avatars of Vishnu and Lakshmi.

IN TODAY'S TIMES

TEMPLES FOR SITA

Most temples worship Rama and Sita as a couple. The handful dedicated only to her are of great significance within the larger *Ramayana* universe. For instance, there is the Sita Mai Temple in Haryana, believed to be the place where she disappears with Mother Earth. Sita Kund in Bihar is where she passed the test of fire, while Seetha Devi Temple in Kerala is where she spent her time in exile with her sons Lava and Kusha. There is also the Janaki Mandir in Nepal, and Seetha Amman Temple in Sri Lanka.

Sita and Rama

The dramatic story of Sita and Rama was first told in Sanskrit poet Valmiki's *Ramayana*. While Rama may be the central figure in this epic, the story hinges as much on his wife, Sita.

The Rakshasa Ravana had ravaged the Earth and heavens alike. In despair, the gods turned to Vishnu, the preserver, seeking his favour. The great god agreed to be born as the son of Ayodhya's king Dasharatha and his wife Kaushalya.

Meanwhile, in Mithila, king Janaka found a baby girl as he was ploughing a field. He named her Sita, and raised her as his own daughter. As she came of age, he set a condition for her marriage — only he who could string the destroyer Shiva's mighty bow could marry Sita.

Rama, now a righteous, young prince, arrived in Mithila, after a successful battle with two Rakshasas. He was successful in breaking Shiva's bow, which led to the joyous union of Rama and Sita.

The two lived happily in Ayodhya, but palace intrigue and divine design soon came into play. On the eve of Rama's consecration as crown prince, he was exiled for 14 years. Sita and Rama's younger brother, Lakshmana, accompanied him. The three spent most of their exile in the forests and defeated many powerful Rakshasas and Rakshasis.

Among them was Ravana's sister Shurapanakha. Enraged at his sister's defeat, Ravana concocted an elaborate plan. He tricked Rama and Lakshmana into stepping away from their hermitage and abducted Sita.

Distraught, Rama was determined to rescue his beloved wife and in the process made unlikely allies. They helped him defeat Ravana's powerful armies and kill him.

At the end of the great battle, when Sita went into Rama's presence, he expressed his doubt at her conduct during their separation. The god of fire testified to Sita's integrity and the couple was reunited. Rama proclaimed that his initial rejection was by design, for it was not he, but the rest of the world that needed proof of Sita's love for him.

They returned to Ayodhya and ruled over the kingdom. Sita became pregnant. Around that time some of Ayodhya's people cast aspersions on her character as Ravana had abducted her. Rama knew these were false accusations, yet renounced Sita. Lakshmana left her at the sage Valmiki's hermitage, where she gave birth to the twins, Lava and Kusha.

Some years later, Rama saw his sons and learnt about their mother Sita. He called for her and asked her to prove her integrity one more time. It is at this moment that Sita silently returned to the earth, in Mother Earth's arms.

Portrait of a divine couple
This kalamkari painting depicts Rama (in blue) and Sita (in yellow) sitting on a throne, with Rama holding the goddess by her waist.

In all her glory
The idol of Subhadra is always decorated beautifully during the Ratha Yatra festival in West Bengal. Here, she is seen in a bejewelled crown and silk clothes with heavy golden embroidery.

Subhadra

The fearless sister goddess

"... salutations to that **"Subhadra Devi"**, who procures all **auspiciousness** to Her devotees... "

VERSE 61, CHAPTER 26, BOOK 3, *DEVI BHAGAVATA PURANA*

△ A *Mahabharata* **folio in opaque watercolour** from c. 1850 and from Paithan, Maharashtra, depicting Subhadra with her son Abhimanyu (left)

A somewhat lesser-known goddess, Subhadra is encountered in the epic *Mahabharata* and the *Bhagavata Purana*, which is centred around Vishnu, the preserver, and his avatars, including Krishna. Her name is made up of two words *su* and *bhadra*, and translates to glorious, fortunate, or auspicious.

In Hindu mythology, Subhadra was the daughter of Vasudeva, the king of the ancient Vrishni clan, and his first wife Rohini. She was also the younger sister of the deities, Krishna and Balarama, and wife of Arjuna, one of the Pandava brothers in the *Mahabharata*.

Flanked by her brothers

Her popularity specifically comes from the Jagannatha Temple at Puri, Odisha, dedicated to Jagannatha, a regional representation of Krishna. Here, Subhadra is depicted between her two brothers. Unlike most temples which throw light on spousal relationships, the Jagannatha Temple, epitomizes the relationship between siblings. According to the Vaishnavites, as Jagannatha's associate deities, Balarama is his mystical guiding force, while Subhadra is the embodiment of his delusion.

British scholar of Hinduism John Dowson notes that, according to one tradition, Jagannatha and Subhadra had an incestuous intimacy. When Jagannatha's *ratha*, or chariot, is brought out, the image of Subhadra and Balarama accompanies the idol. It reminds the followers of the incestuous relationship, and evokes jeers and taunts from the crowd.

Subhadra's marriage to Arjuna

There are many versions of the story of Subhadra's marriage to Arjuna. The epic *Mahabharata* delineates that during Arjuna's stay in the ancient city of Dwarka, he fell in love with Subhadra. However, Balarama wished to give her away to Duryodhana, the eldest Kaurava brother. On Krishna's advice, Arjuna abducted her, and Balarama subsequently acquiesced to their union.

At the same time, the *Bhagavata Purana* narrates how Balarama chose Duryodhana as Subhadra's groom regardless of her feelings towards Arjuna and without her consent. Knowing that after getting the news of Subhadra's elopement Balarama would wage a war against Arjuna, Krishna decided he would be their charioteer. Convinced, Arjuna proceeded to take Subhadra and, with Krishna in tow, they left.

According to the Pradhans, a group of people belonging to the Gond community, when Arjuna saw his friend Krishna's success with women, he grew jealous. He retired to the forest and prayed to him. Touched by his prayer, Krishna granted his friend's wish and brought Subhadra and Arjuna together.

IN TODAY'S TIMES

PURI RATHA YATRA

Every year, in June–July, the Ratha Yatra festival is held at the Jagannatha Temple in Odisha. The main ritual involves bringing out the idols of Jagannatha, Subhadra, and Balarama on grand chariots, pulled by many volunteers. According to a popular legend, the deities suffer from high fever after their annual ceremonial bath, and need a change of place to recover faster. So, they travel from their home temple to a nearby temple called Gundicha, believed to be their aunt's home. The deities stay there for a few days before returning.

Songs for the gods
Every year, the sky reverberates with the sounds of drums, cymbals, and fervent chants as the deities Jagannatha, Subhadra, and Balaram emerge from the Shree Jagannath Temple, on their chariots. This annual festival, the Rath Yatra, takes place in Bhubaneswar, Odisha.

Devi Mahatmya

The *Devi Mahatmya* marks the beginning of an integrative approach to the Great Goddess. At the same time, it is like a textbook for the Devi worshipper. It marks Her arrival into the Brahmanical world, providing legitimacy as well as explanations in the most alluring way.

The tripartite vision
This late 18th-century miniature gouache painting from Jaipur depicts the three incarnations of the Great Goddess. Of these, Mahakali (extreme right) can be seen with the severed head of an Asura in her hand.

The *Devi Mahatmya*, also called the *Chandipatha* and the *Durga Shaptashati*, is a Sanskrit poem of 700 verses and comprises chapters 81 to 93 of the *Markandeya Purana*. The general opinion is that the *Devi Mahatmya* was probably composed in the first part of the 6th century and interpolated into the Purana. However, over the years, the *Devi Mahatmya* has achieved great autonomous popularity.

The text is believed to have been composed in the ancient kingdom of Mahishmati, identified with present-day Omkar Mandhata, Madhya Pradesh, on the basis of popular regional folklores, especially Asura legends.

The text is a group of mythological stories and the framing storyline features a sad king, a betrayed merchant, and the celebrated sage Markandeya. The sage narrates the tale of three great battles between the Devi in her different manifestations with a variety of Asuras. The chapters are divided on the basis of these battles. The goddess Mahakali features in chapter 1, Mahalakshmi in chapters 2–4, and Mahasarasvati in chapters 5–13. Indian art historian Vidya Dehejia says, "As a narrative, the *Devi Mahatmya* appears to speak for itself, the oldest full account in words of the Great Goddess and her activity, an important complement to the artistic testimony to Devi."

Glory of the Goddess

In these excerpts from the *Devi Mahatmya*, the gods propitiate the Great Goddess as they are tormented by Asuras. They address their praise to an unmanifest deity and this makes Parvati curious. The Great Goddess manifests, this time from Parvati's own body (See pp 124–25). These verses are significant in understanding the relationship between the Great Goddess and Her various manifestations.

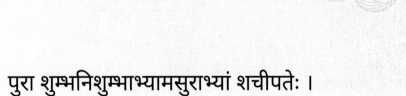

पुरा शुम्भनिशुम्भाभ्यामसुराभ्यां शचीपतेः ।

त्रैलोक्यं यज्ञभागाश्च हृता मदबलाश्रयात् ॥

Once, Shumbha and Nishumbha, relying on their pride and strength, took from Indra the three realms and shares in sacrifices.

हृताधिकारास्त्रिदशास्ताभ्यां सर्वे निराकृताः ।

महासुराभ्यां तां देवीं संस्मरन्त्यपराजिताम् ॥

All the gods, robbed of their authority and driven away by those two great Asuras, remembered that invincible Goddess.

तयास्माकंवरो दत्तो यथापत्सु स्मृताखिलाः ।

भवतां नाशयिष्यामि तत्क्षणात्परमापदः ॥

We were given a boon by her, "Remembered in calamities,
I shall destroy all your greatest calamities that very moment."

इति कृत्वा मतिं देवा हिमवन्तं नगेश्वरम् ।

जग्मुस्तत्र ततो देवीं विष्णुमायां प्रतुष्टुवुः ॥

Having thought in this way, they went to the lord of mountains, the
Himalaya, and propitiated the Goddess, Vishnu's Maya.

अतिसौम्यातिरौद्रायै नतास्तस्यै नमो नमः ।

नमो जगत्प्रतिष्ठायै देव्यै कृत्यै नमो नमः ॥

We are obeisant before Her who is exceedingly gentle and exceedingly
fierce – obeisance, obeisance! Obeisance unto the foundation of the
world! Obeisance unto the effulgent one! Obeisance unto the one who
consists of the acts (of creation, maintenance, destruction)!

चितिरूपेण या कृत्स्नमेतद्व्याप्य स्थिता जगत् ।
नमस्तस्यै, नमस्तस्यै, नमस्तस्यै नमो नमः ॥

Unto the one who stands having pervaded this entire world as consciousness, obeisance! Obeisance unto Her, obeisance unto Her, obeisance, obeisance!

———— ✤ ————

एवं स्तवाभियुक्तानां देवानां तत्र पार्वती ।
स्नातुमभ्याययौ तोये जाह्नव्या नृपनन्दन ॥

Prince! As the gods were thus engaged in praise, Parvati arrived to bathe in the waters of the River Ganga.

———— ✤ ————

साब्रवीत्तान् सुरान् सुभ्रूर्भवद्भिः स्तूयतेऽत्र का।
शरीरकोशतश्चास्याः समुद्भूताब्रवीच्छिवा ॥

The one with beautiful eyebrows said to the gods, "Who is being praised by all of you here?" And the auspicious one, who emerged from the sheath of her body, said:

स्तोत्रं ममैतत्क्रियते शुम्भदैत्यनिराकृतैः ।
देवैः समेतैः समरे निशुम्भेन पराजितैः ॥

It is my praise that is sung by the gods who are gathered together, driven away by the Asura Shumbha and defeated by Nishumbha.

शरीरकोशाद्यत्तस्याः पार्वत्या निःसृताम्बिका ।
कौशिकीति समस्तेषु ततो लोकेषु गीयते ॥

Because the Mother emerged from the sheath of Parvati's body, She is called Kaushiki in all realms.

तस्यां विनिर्गतायां तु कृष्णाभूत्सापि पार्वती ।
कालिकेति समाख्याता हिमाचलकृताश्रया ॥

And Parvati, who became dark when She came out, was called Kalika. She lived in the Himalaya.

The Goddess and cosmogony

The Goddess is often extolled by associating Her with cosmogony and its principles. In many philosophical explorations, She is often identified as Shakti, *prakriti*, and maya. This means the world is Hers and She is the world.

In the Puranas, association with cosmogony, that is the creation, preservation, and destruction of the universe, is one of the ways in which a deity is afforded a place in the mainstream Hindu pantheon. It is why the three deities Brahma, Vishnu, and Shiva come to occupy the foremost positions as creator, preserver, and destroyer, respectively.

One could argue that one of the ways in which the position of the Goddess was escalated was through Her increasingly prominent role in the cosmogony. Therefore, from around the 3rd to the 16th centuries,

there are several accounts in the Puranas where the Goddess occupies a primary role in creation.

Cosmic principles

The notion of a single Great Goddess hinges at least in part on the identification of a female divinity with unique cosmic principles. In the Puranas, the Goddess is equated with the cosmogonic principles of *prakriti* and Shakti. While *prakriti* refers to the concept of materiality and manifestation, Shakti is often understood to be the energizing

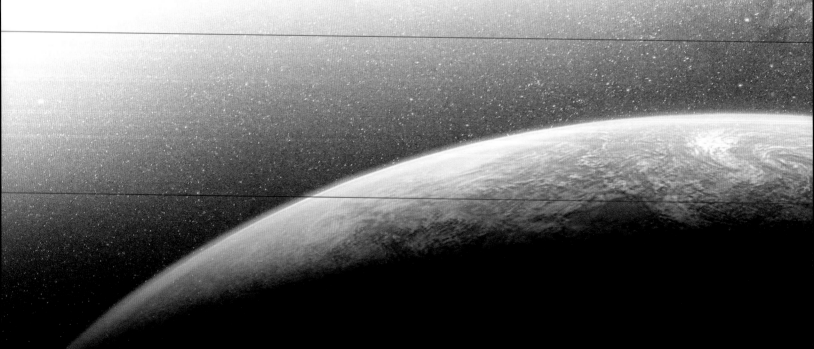

"Who is there **except you** in the sciences, in the scriptures, and in the Vedic sayings that **light the lamp** of discrimination?"

VERSE 31, CHAPTER 11, *DEVI MAHATMYA*

dimension of Brahman, or the ultimate reality. The third principle maya, or illusive power, links these two factors.

As creator in Devi Mahatmya

In the *Devi Mahatmya*, amongst the most striking epithets used are those that relate Her to cosmogony. As scholar of religious studies Tracy Pintchman argues, the *Devi Mahatmya* introduces philosophical terms about creation and relate the Goddess to these. Pintchman points out two particular episodes of Her manifestation. First, when She manifests herself from Vishnu and second, when She appears as a combination of *tejas*, or heat energy that emerges from the gods. Pintchman suggests that *tejas* in the Upanishads is understood to be the source of primordial waters. So, the *Devi Mahatmya* understands the Goddess as the source of all creation as well as creation itself. Although the text does not go into the details of cosmogony, it portrays the Goddess as intrinsic to creation. She is the cause, source, and the creation itself.

Goddess as maya and prakriti

The Goddess is also identified as maya, and is allied with Shakti and *prakriti*. The Devi plays a cosmogonic and a cosmological role. Pintchman notes, "She is also the power of delusion that prevents one from realizing Brahman." One invokes Her in this capacity to seek liberation. She writes that the Goddess also maintains creation, that is *prakriti*, and it is through this manifestation that one encounters Her.

SANKHYA PHILOSOPHY

Sankhya is one of the oldest six major systems of Hindu philosophy expounded in the 1st century. According to it, *prakriti* is an unstable composition of three kinds of substances, called the *gunas*. These are *sattva*, *rajas*, and *tamas* and are present in the composition of the different objects of the world. In the *avyakta*, or non-manifest, stage of *prakriti*, these form a stable equilibrium. A loss of this equilibrium is conceived as the starting point of the evolution of the world.

Death of Madhu and Kaitabha
From Chhatarpur, Madhya Pradesh, this folio from the *Devi Mahatmya* is dated 1775. It shows the end of Vishnu's battle with the Asuras, as the goddess Mahamaya looks on. The marine elements in the composition indicate that this was an underwater battle.

A plea to Mahamaya

The first episode in the *Devi Mahatmya* recounts the story of a goddess so mighty that she even controlled Vishnu, the preserver. She manifests herself in the form of his transcendental sleep.

Once upon a time, an unhappy, bereft king and an equally disgruntled merchant chanced upon each other. Discarded by their greedy families, they wondered at their sadness. As they wandered through a dense forest, they met a sage. They asked him why they continued to feel so sad when they knew the cause of their delusion.

The sage told them that the power of Mahamaya hurled human beings into a whirlpool of attachment. The wise sage then proceeded to tell them that Mahamaya was Vishnu's *yoga nidra*, or yogic slumber. She had the ability to forcibly draw the minds of even the wisest and throw them into a state of delusion. When propitious, she could liberate through Supreme Knowledge.

The sage then told them of a time at the end of a *kalpa*, or eons, when the universe was a large ocean and Vishnu lay on Shesha, his serpent bed, and took to mystic slumber. Two terrible Asuras, Madhu and Kaitabha, sprung into being from the dirt of Vishnu's ears. They decided to slay the creator, Brahma, who sat on the lotus that grew from Vishnu's navel.

In dire straits, Brahma propitiated Mahamaya: "You are the goddess of good fortune, the queen of the cosmos, and the supporter of the world. You are the sacrifice, the heaven attained through the performance of the sacrifice, and the cause of sustentation and dissolution alike. You are armed with sword, spear, club, discus, conch, slings, and iron mace. You are both terrible and yet pleasing. You can put the very creator to sleep. You have such power. Let Vishnu be awakened from sleep and rouse up his nature to slay these two Asuras."

On hearing this invocation, Mahamaya withdrew from Vishnu's eyes, mouth, nostrils, arms, heart, and breast. Vishnu arose and fought the Asuras for 5,000 years, using his arms as weapons. Frenzied by their exceeding power and deluded by Mahamaya, they told Vishnu that he could ask them for a boon.

Vishnu replied that he would slay them and that there was no need for a boon from them. They said, "Slay us at the spot where the Earth is not flooded by water."

Vishnu then took them to his loins and severed their heads with his discus. Thus, praised by Brahma, all witnessed the power of the great goddess Mahamaya.

Durga

The warrior goddess

> "**O Queen of all**, you who exist in the **form of all**, and possess **every might**, save us from error, O Devi. Salutations to you, **Devi Durga**!"

VERSE 24, CHAPTER 11, *DEVI MAHATMYA*

Durga luxuriates in war. She knows her weapons and uses them efficiently, from arrows, sword, dagger, and *chakra*, or disc, to the shield, trident, and noose. She knows her strategies and uses them effectively. She pounces, kicks, impales, yells, quaffs wine, laughs, and stuns with every movement. Finally, she knows her enemies and is merciless, as they hurl pikes at her. She destroys chariots, elephants, foot soldiers, and Asuras of gargantuan dimensions, for she is the warrior goddess par excellence.

She is worshipped in almost all corners of the Indian subcontinent under different epithets and overlapping conceptual identities. In eastern states, such as Bengal and Odisha, where she is the reigning deity, she is known as Durga. In North India, around Punjab and Himachal Pradesh, she is called Sheranvali (See pp 94–95). The *Devi Mahatmya* uses names such as Ambika and Chandika interchangeably with Durga. This multi-named female divinity fits in well with the belief in Hinduism that the abundance of names is but a manifestation of divine power, as stated in *Brihaddevata*, a text of the 5th century.

Exploring the origins

There is no Vedic mention of such a goddess, literally, or even conceptually. It is widely understood that she was a non-Vedic goddess of the autochthonous, and originally associated with fertility and war. Eventually, she was elevated to the top ranks of the Hindu pantheon. In terms of the antiquity of the name Durga, the *Taittiriya Aranyaka*, a text of the 3rd century BCE, makes the earliest reference, though there is little trace of her role as a vanquisher of Asuras.

This reference is followed by the hymns in the epic *Mahabharata*, where the princes Yudhishthira and Arjuna invoke her at different moments. French scholar of architecture Odile Divakaran notes that at the beginning of "Durga Stotra", Yudhishthira praises the goddess Durga in his mind

HYMN FOR DURGA

"Mahishasuramardini Stotram" is a hymn in praise of Durga in her avatar as Mahishasuramardini. Its authorship is unclear, but scholars often attribute it to Indian philosopher Adi Shankaracharya or poet Tenali Ramakrishna. Traditionally, it is chanted in South India, especially during Navaratri. The hymn is so mesmerizing and powerful that there are several musical interpretations and renditions by contemporary artists.

◁ **Ambika Mata temple** in Jagat, Rajasthan

Later, at the start of the great battle, Krishna tells Arjuna to recite the "Durga Stotra" for the sake of conquering his enemies. The Mahabharata also states that tribes, such as Shabaras, Barabaras, and Pulindas, worshipped Durga. There is no doubt that, over time, she became assimilated into mainstream Hinduism.

Appearance in texts

The first detailed Brahmanic appearance and textual source for the myth of the goddess vanquishing the Asura is found in the *Devi Mahatmya*. The text glorifies the victorious power of the goddess over Asuras in a manner that was not attempted before. This is the most well-known account of Durga's origin.

Her creation occurs when there is a cosmic crisis as no one but a female can destroy the Asura Mahisha. The gods release fiery emissions which, lo and behold, manifest as Durga. She is beautiful and suffused with power, created through the combined *tejas*, or valour, of the gods. Although a derivative of them, she is also their power and personifies

> "Where can one find this **beauty**… **striking fear** in enemies? **Compassion in heart** and **relentlessness in battle** are seen…"

VERSE 22, CHAPTER 4, *DEVI MAHATMYA*

▽ **An early 19th-century** painting from Guler, Himachal Pradesh, depicts the creation of Durga. She is shown seated on a lotus and surrounded by gods, who created her to defeat an Asura, whom they themselves could not defeat.

energy. She is an autonomous feminine divinity, epitomizing an independent goddess. Later Puranas, such as the *Devi Bhagavata*, the *Brahmavaivarta*, and the *Vamana*, speak of Durga as well, with many twists and turns to the myths that they recount.

Etymology

The word Durga has many meanings. Etymologically, *dur* means she who is difficult and *ga* means to go against. So, it refers to the unfathomable one or the one who is difficult to penetrate. Durga is a name that can also be a play on words – she is the great protectress from worldly adversity and is at the same time herself unassailable and hard to approach.

Divakaran notes that the ambiguity inherent in the identification of the goddess with the very same threats and difficulties, which she has the power to help overcome, is an essential element of her nature.

Worship in Bengal

Durga's worship is most prominent for 10 days in the Hindu month of Ashvin (September to October), every year during the Dussehra festival. Also called Navaratri, this festival eulogizes Durga's battle with the Asura Mahisha. Particularly celebrated in Bengal, Assam, and other eastern states, the first day, or Mahalaya, heralds the advent of the celebrations. She is worshipped in various forms, including Sarasvati and Lakshmi. For nine days, devotees chant the complete text of the *Devi Mahatmya*, and at the end, present the goddess with red flowers and red cloth.

Her worship, it seems, took on a standardized format from the middle of the 18th century. This was because, in the 17th and 18th centuries, Bengali zamindars became wealthy through trade with Europe and sponsored lavish Durga pujas in their family *rajbaris*, or palaces. Today, this has become a community celebration – ranging from simple to lavish – organized by neighbourhood

cooperatives. Buffalo and goat sacrifices have been replaced by a pumpkin, cut as ceremonial offering. Devotees sing, dance and feast, watched by the goddess and her family.

It is interesting to note that the Bengali Durga, with her make-up and jewellery, appears as an ideal Bengali housewife. She is not just a mother, but a daughter as well and her parents Himavat and Mena worry about her. Popular legends believe that during the Durga Puja festival, she is on a brief visit from her abode in the Himalayas, where she lives with Shiva, the destroyer. On the last day, devotees immerse her idol in the nearest river, symbolic of her return to her marital home. There is no doubt that despite so much violence within the Durga legend, as American theologian Francis Xavier Clooney notes, the goddess is also a great mother, and the source and protector of every being. All of life comes from her and she is every experience.

△ **A contemporary tableau** of Durga from 2003 in Kolkata, West Bengal, where she is flanked by armed terrorists. Such thematic depictions are quite common during Durga Puja. They change every year and can sometimes be a commentary on contemporary social and political issues.

◁ **The carvings on this Nepalese hilt** from the 13–14th century depict Durga's battle with the Asura Mahisha. Severed heads can also be seen on the handle.

Killing of a demon

Stories from the *Devi Mahatmya* are often a popular source of inspiration for traditional dancers from across India. Here, performers of the Chhau, a semi-classical folk dance from eastern India, re-enact the moment Durga (left) and her lion mount killed a demon (right). The Chhau uses elaborate and vibrant masks and is a mix of martial arts, tribal, and folk traditions.

Mahisha slayed

The second episode in the *Devi Mahatmya* tells a tale replete with valour, power, and bloodshed, as the goddess Durga battled the mighty buffalo-Asura Mahisha. It is indeed a paradigmatic battle played out over and over again, in different eras and regions.

In a bygone era, the Devas, or the gods, were always at war with the Asuras, and regularly had the upper hand. Until, one day, the Asura Mahisha became the king of Asuras. After years of arduous penance, he cunningly tried to compel the creator, Brahma into granting him a boon of immortality. The great god replied sagely that this was an impossible boon, as all beings once born must die. "So be it, let me die then, but by a woman's hands," Mahisha replied. Armed with what appeared to him to be an everlasting promise of immortality, he felt invincible. For how could a fragile woman smite *him*?

The swashbuckling Asura strutted around with unbecoming confidence. In a war that lasted 100 years, he defeated Indra, the god of the heavens, and dethroned him from his abode. Mortified, fearful, and helpless, the vanquished Devas sought help from Shiva, the destroyer, and Vishnu, the preserver. Together, they plotted their next move. Finally, they combined their strengths to create a woman.

She emerged a wonderful goddess, carrying various weapons in her many hands. She was Durga, the unsurpassable and fortress-like. She was the one who could annihilate a foe of any dimension. Raring to go, Durga set out on her mission. "Victory to you," the gods chanted as they gazed at the resplendence of their creation. Mahisha saw the woman approach and sneered. His derision soon disappeared when he saw how she attacked his army and Asura generals. She killed them with loud cries of glee. Yet, her face held a strange look of complete equanimity. What was this force?

Mahisha was mesmerized, yet flummoxed. Soon, he stood before her in battle, his army destroyed. He tried everything, drawing from his repertoire of combative skills and, what he thought was substantial power.

When everything failed, he resorted to form-shifting. He became a lion, then an elephant, and finally a buffalo. At that moment, Durga jumped on him. As she landed on his back, she pinned his neck with her foot and struck him with her spear. Mahisha, caught as he was shifting his shape, half human half animal, lay there helpless. Then, she beheaded him with her sword. Her valour beyond compare, this is how Durga rendered the world safe from an unscrupulous Asura of gargantuan proportions.

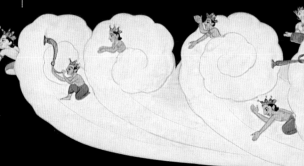

The Mahisha myth

▽ **This 12th-century miniature sculpture** from the Pala empire depicts Durga in her 16-arm form slaying Mahisha.

Mahisha's death is central to Durga's identity. Without him, she could not have achieved the sobriquet of "Mahishasuramardini", or the one who kills the buffalo Asura, Mahisha. Over the years, this story and its significance has acquired many meanings.

Of all the beings mentioned across the *Devi Mahatmya* that broadly fall into the "evil" category, Mahisha or Mahishasura (the Asura called Mahisha) is perhaps the most dreaded. Like the other beings – Asuras, Daityas, Rakshasas, and Danavas – Mahisha too has superhuman qualities, not unlike the gods. He practices austerities so that he receives boons. Craving immortality, he can be killed only under exceptional circumstances.

Significance of the myth for the devotees
At the most straightforward and rather hackneyed level, the Durga–Mahisha myth is seen as a battle between good and evil. At a historical level, this may be interpreted as a conflict between two tribes or sects. Mahisha may perhaps represent a tribe from around Mahishmati in Madhya Pradesh or a sect whose totem or most favoured animal is a buffalo. For the oppressed, Durga is seen as a saviour and protectress, who will combat all malevolent occurrences and characters on their behalf.

This myth, additionally, satisfies a psychological need in worshippers and believers. It helps the individual to come to terms with hindrances and shows how to battle and rid oneself of demonic tendencies, such as lust and pride. It demonstrates the way one can awaken divine latent power within us. During the battle, Mahisha reveals all his alter egos as he shape-shifts from one beast to the other, in an attempt to confuse Durga. The goddess is part of the celestial world, but she instructs on how to deal with the present in the most dramatic way. So, she fights Mahisha, who represents the chthonic forces par excellence, and concomitantly those forces which keep humankind ensnared in the material world. The buffalo is also a vahana, or mount of Yama, the god of death. Durga shows her mastery over death and danger. Her subjugation of this Asura suggests that for the coming year she has conquered death for her devotees.

Durga, an independent figure

That Durga is the embodiment of such awesome power is significant for women. She takes the inner fiery energies from the male gods in order to perform her own heroic exploits. However, that does not dent or diminish her own strength and potency. In the *Devi Mahatmya*, she is independent and fights the demons with tremendous might along with panache and delight. Her awesomeness lies in the manner in which she kills. It is interesting too that, even in the celestial realm, it is the female who brings the males together for a common cause. These male deities, who in other cosmic cycles, are bitter rivals, combine in a true show of strength, only for the goddess.

> "Having **killed them**... you have led even those **hosts of enemies to heaven**, and you have **dispelled our fear** from the frenzied **enemies** of the devas."

VERSE 23, CHAPTER 4, *DEVI MAHATMYA*

MAHISHA'S SHENANIGANS

Once the boon of immortality was granted, Mahisha's vanity knew no bounds. He dragged the goddesses and told them to do housework, and made the gods his servants. He sent many of the deities to dwell in the forests on the Earth and abolished all religious ceremonies. He compelled the wives of the Rishis to sing songs in his praise. Brahmans gave up reading the Vedas, rivers changed their course, and fire lost its energy. The terrified stars retreated from sight. Mahisha assumed the shape of clouds and brought rain whenever he pleased. He had no rival, there was no cause for him to fear for he became the lord of the three worlds.

Mythology of buffalo

The buffalo has a significant specific meaning within the myth. It is considered the only animal of the Asuras, and not of divine creation. Incapable and lacking in all aesthetic sense, they create a short creature with, as German scholar of religion Heinrich von Stietencron puts it "an immense misshapen belly, hairless, black, leathery skin, short and stiff legs, a disproportionately long neck, and a massive head with dull and lazy eyes. It was ugliness incarnate. The gods broke out into raucous laughter..." Yet remarkably, the buffalo is an important animal in the domestic sphere. Its uses are most evident in the rural agricultural sphere where it is used for ploughing and hauling loads. It produces more milk than any other type of cattle. However, its milk is considered impure and therefore not fit for use in rituals.

Drama in the myth

During the recitation of the myth among devotees as well, there is a sheer awakening of the senses, or rasas. The accompanying sounds of the drums and the bells add to a cathartic dramatic experience. Mahisha is decapitated – a method that has the advantage of ghoulish drama. When the head is severed, blood spurts out, rendering the shuddering body still. Beheadings are believed in the Hindu culture to induce ultimate humility or even transform the opponent into a devotee. British historian AL Basham argues that the tradition of animal slaughter was justified by the doctrine that the soul of the victim, like that of the buffalo, went straight to heaven.

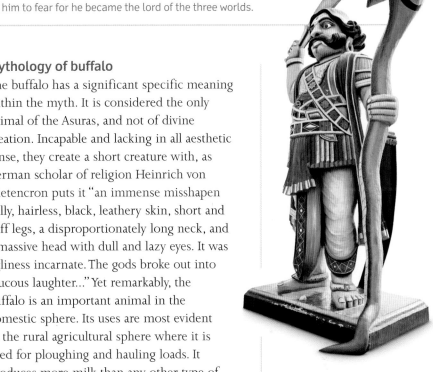

△ **Made of brick, plaster, and paint**, this statue of Mahisha in human form is located near the Chamundeshwari Temple in Mysore, Karnataka.

Durga's imagery

The riveting images of Durga are incomparable to any other iconographic element in the subcontinent, both in popularity and prevalence. Every difference in her visual corresponds to a different interpretation of her being.

△ **This 19th-century gouache artwork** of Durga carrying all her weapons portrays her with a powerful, yet serene, expression. Conventional representations show her as fierce and warrior-like.

The name Durga conjures up an image of the many-armed goddess riding a large feline. In October, while being worshipped, she is depicted as ready for battle. Then, British historian AL Basham notes, her hands are in combat mode and her face belies tension, with an enigmatic smile. The buffalo-Asura lies at her feet, blood gushing, his chopped head lying on one side. From within the neck, the Asura emerges in his human form, carrying a sword and shield, eyes bulging in a terrified look.

Today, often, to soften this act of violence, her children – Sarasvati, Lakshmi, Ganesha and Karttikeya – flank her. There is even a small Shiva peeping over them from the top.

This is Durga as perceived today. One could say she is domesticated since she is depicted with her children and handsomely turned out in silken clothes and jewellery. It is indeed a great transformation from her early depictions.

Standardized depiction

The didactic canonical literature, such as the *Brihat Samhita*, and the *Vishnudharmottara Purana*, prescribe how an image of Durga should be created. According to the *Shilparatna*, an ancient treatise on iconography, Durga should have three eyes and on her head a *jatamukuta* and in it should be the *chandra kala*, or the crescent moon. Moreover, she should have multiple hands. She should wield a trident, a *khadga*, or sword, a *chakra*, or disc,

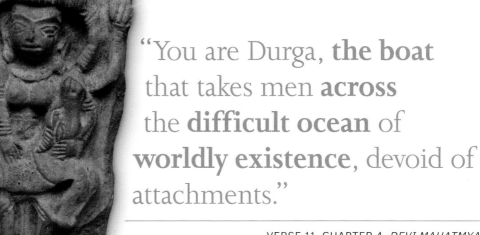

▷ **This 2nd-century terracotta sculpture** depicts Durga slaying the demon with sheer physical force instead of with weapons.

and a stringed bow in her right hands. In the left hands, she should bear a *pasha* or noose, an *ankusha* or goad, a *khetaka* or shield, a *parashu* or battle axe, and a bell. Durga's right leg should be placed on the back of her lion and her left leg should touch the buffalo body of the Asura.

"You are Durga, **the boat** that takes men **across** the **difficult ocean** of **worldly existence**, devoid of attachments."

VERSE 11, CHAPTER 4, *DEVI MAHATMYA*

Visuals in the Kushana period

It is possible to trace Durga as Mahishasuramardini ("She who kills the Asura Mahisha) in artistic representations to the 1st century. From this period till about the 3rd century, the period of the Kushana dynasty, one encounters small plaquettes in terracotta or sandstone, in shallow relief, showing a four-, six-, or eight-armed Durga killing the buffalo without the use of weapons. Mathura and nearby Sonkh in Uttar Pradesh have yielded a large number of small rectangular stone reliefs and terracotta figurines of Durga. Her popularity at least in North India, is well-attested by a number of images in stone. In these, the buffalo is shown kicking his forelegs up with upturned head while Durga with one hand around the neck and with her lower left arm pressed down on the buffalo's back. The remaining hands are holding weapons.

KUMARTULI

A small neighbourhood in Kolkata, West Bengal, Kumartuli is famous for its potters, known for their prowess in making life-sized sculptures of Durga. Engaged in this craft for generations, they combine soil, clay, straw, and paddy husks to fashion thousands of figurines. Each stage of the idol-making process is done dexterously by hand. Devotees gaze at their creation for emotional and spiritual succour. At the end of the nine-day Durga Puja celebrations, these images are submerged in water.

Further modifications

It appears from this period onwards there is an unbroken tradition of her representations, with some minor changes. Subsequently, a lion appears on her left and Durga places her left foot on the back of the lion with one hand in the process of pulling out the buffalo's tongue.

An increase in the number of Durga images may be seen by the time of the Gupta rulers, who ruled from the 4–6th century. Three large relief panels from the early 5th century have been found in Udayagiri caves of Madhya Pradesh. They mark a clear break with smaller stone reliefs and small terracotta figurines. These later pieces show her using the trident.

Different types of representations abound. Sometimes, Durga is shown raising the buffalo by its hind legs as she pierces the back with the trident or she is shown holding the tail instead of its hind legs. These images can be dated from the 5th to the 8th centuries. In South India, the oldest image is from the 3rd century, found in Sannati, Karnataka, where Durga is seen standing on the severed head of the buffalo, accompanied by a *gana* on the right side.

One of the most beautiful depictions is a large relief from Mahabalipuram, Tamil Nadu. The goddess is youthful and poised with her string bow outstretched. A host of female warriors and *ganas* stand by to aid her. Mahisha is a human figure here with a buffalo's head. He is larger in size than Durga. What is remarkable is his expression, which is one of dazed hurt as he recoils from her attack.

Navadurga

Navadurga is a collective term to refer to the nine manifestations of Durga. Each form is celebrated during Navaratri, a nine-day festival and represents a different facet of the goddess.

▽ **SHAILAPUTRI**
Worshipped on First day
Governing planet Moon

She is the daughter of the Mountain King Himavat. Also known as Sati or Parvati, she embodies the power of the Trinity – Brahma, Vishnu, and Shiva.

Lotus in the right hand

△ **CHANDRAGHANTA**
Worshipped on Third day
Governing planet Venus

She is Sati in her married form, and embodies the feminine spirit accompanying Shiva in his Chandrashekhar manifestation. The sound of the moon-bell on her forehead is believed to drive away evil forces.

Amrit Kalash, or the pot of nectar

Kamandalu in the right hand

▷ **BRAHMACHARINI**
Worshipped on Second day
Governing planet Mars

She is Sati (See pp 98–103) in her unmarried form and embodies consciousness. It is in this form that Sati practised asceticism to fulfil her resolve to marry Shiva.

△ **KUSHMANDA**
Worshipped on Fourth day
Governing planet Sun

Also known as Ashtabhuja Devi, she is considered the source of the Sun god's power. It is believed that she bestows *siddhis*, or supernatural powers, and *nidhis*, or wealth.

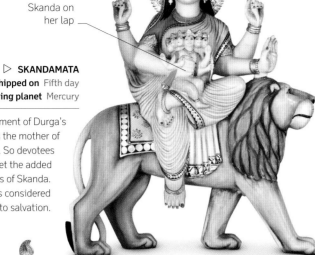

Skanda on her lap

▷ **SKANDAMATA**
Worshipped on Fifth day
Governing planet Mercury

The embodiment of Durga's maternal spirit, she is the mother of Skanda or Karttikeya. So devotees who worship her get the added benefit of blessings of Skanda. Her worship is considered conducive to salvation.

◁ **KATYAYANI**
Worshipped on Sixth day
Governing planet Jupiter

Daughter of a sage, she embodies the cumulative anger of the gods at the Asura Mahishasura. Katyayani is the fierce form of Durga, and is known for her anger, vengeance, and ultimate victory over the Asuras.

▽ **MAHAGAURI**
Worshipped on Eighth day
Governing planet Rahu

She represents all that is pure and resplendent. It is believed that the flaws and faults of all who please her are reduced to ashes. Her grace redeems them.

Ox, her mount

▷ **KALARATRI**
Worshipped on Seventh day
Governing planet Saturn

Also known as Chandi, Chamunda, and Kali, she is considered as one of the most destructive forms of Durga. A manifestation of all that is terrifying and devastating, she is the death of time and is greater than *kala*, or time, itself.

Donkey, her mount

Fully bloomed lotus

△ **SIDDHIDHATRI**
Worshipped on Ninth day
Governing planet Ketu

Said to have originated when Shiva worshipped the non-manifest form of the goddess Adi Parashakti for creation, she appeared from the left half of Ardhanarishvara. She removes ignorance and bestows all types of *siddhis* on her devotees.

A vigil in Her name

In some parts of northern India, Durga metamorphoses into the gentler goddess Sheranvali. In this form, she is often revered in grand communal affairs called *jagaranas*.

When there is an announcement of a *jagarana* in a neighbourhood, there is a wave of anticipatory excitement for days, for it involves night-long music, singing of bhajans, reciting and listening to the stories of the Goddess, and communal feasting. The word *jagarana* means wakefulness and the carnival-like celebration, popular in Punjab, Haryana, Himachal Pradesh, and Delhi, especially during the nine-day festival of Navaratri, is believed to awaken the mind to higher spiritual goals.

The Goddess in the *jagaranas* is Sheranvali, meaning female lion rider. American scholar of religious studies Kathleen M Erndl notes that she is often identified with Durga. She is like all the great male gods in her power and universality, but also has the accessibility, immanence, and intimacy of lesser deities and saints.

A community comes together

Jagaranas are essentially ritualized community celebrations. Devotees gather at a designated space, often a pandal, decorated with elaborate flower arrangements and lights. The aura in these pandals is much like a Hindu wedding. A giant idol of Sheranvali, surrounded by idols of other deities, takes up much of the space on the stage. The goddess resembles a bride, with silk clothes, a red and gold *chunni*, or scarf, and ornate jewellery. Like a rani in her majestic court, she is ready to witness the unwavering devotion of her devotees.

People sit before her, their hands clasped in devotion. The music and the cry *Jai Mata Di*, or Praise the Mother, rings out through the night, dispelling its darkness. More elaborate celebrations have performances by specialized bhajan *mandalis*, or music troupes.

△ **Oblations to the goddess**
An assortment of offerings is made to the goddess, ranging from flowers and fruits to cooked food and clothes.

△ **Seeking her blessings**
A devotee bows before the goddess at a *jagarana*. Several male gods from the pantheon, such as Hanuman, Ganesha (left), and Shiva (right) flank the main idol.

Union with the goddess

As the songs tell her story to the lively beat of drums, the goddess often starts *khelna*, or playing, in a woman, that is she possesses the woman. The state is often characterized by glazed eyes and a change in voice, as the possessed rotates her head. It is the complete, but temporary, domination of the body and the blotting out of consciousness by the power of the goddess.

Erndl views *jagaranas* as a ritual performance in which a woman acts like a *savari*, or vehicle, for the goddess to appear in person and reveal herself to her devotees.

While possessed, the woman embodies the Shakti of the goddess and participates in her powers. People witnessing the woman or "Goddess in woman" go and touch her/Her feet in respect, just as though she/She is the goddess and ask her/Her questions. Her role is like that of an oracle. Erndl asks a pertinent question – Is it the goddess who is possessing the woman or is it the goddess who gets possessed?

The legend

The ceremonies often end with the recitation of *katha*, or story, of Queen Tara, who is credited with introducing the practice of

"The **mightiest** is your name, O Sheranvali! You, who **resides** in the **highest mountains**, restore all my ruined endeavours."

SONG IN PRAISE OF SHERANVALI FROM THE HINDI FILM *SUHAAG* (1979)

the *jagarana* thousands of years ago. In the tale, Queen Tara and her husband King Harishchandra sacrifice their son so that they may receive a *darshana,* or catch sight, of the goddess. She grants their wish and, happy with their devotion, also brings their son back to life.

This *katha*, believed to bring a shower of blessings to all who listen to it, is only recited during a *jagarana*. It is difficult to determine the tale's antiquity as it is a part of oral traditions. It has also, only recently, been published in pamphlets sold at pilgrimage centres.

△ **Live production**
The modern form of *jagaranas* are like a stage performance, involving professional singers, bands, and sophisticated music systems.

△ **In the image of Durga**
Sheranvali bears all the marks of Durga, such as the many arms holding weapons and a feline vahana, but is devoid of her violent exploits.

A devotional dance
Durga Puja evenings across the country are often incomplete without the Dhunuchi dance. Women, men, and children dance to rhythmic beats of the *dhol*, or drums, while holding lit frankincense in an earthen pot. The swirling smoke and earthy scent creates a sensory experience and a beautiful sight for the beholder. In this image, devotees in Kolkata, West Bengal, perform the dance as they take the Dugra idol for immersion.

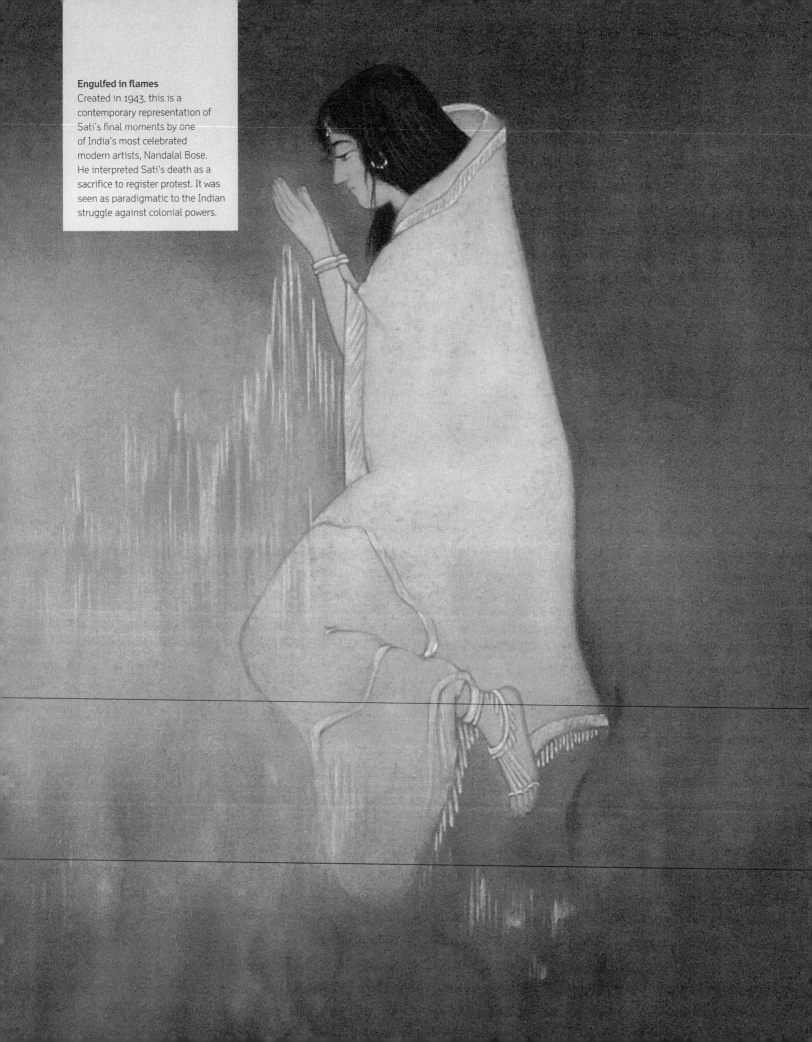

Engulfed in flames
Created in 1943, this is a contemporary representation of Sati's final moments by one of India's most celebrated modern artists, Nandalal Bose. He interpreted Sati's death as a sacrifice to register protest. It was seen as paradigmatic to the Indian struggle against colonial powers.

Sati

The righteous one

> "Since you **insult** me... **pure** in speech, mind, and acts, I **cast** off **this body**, O father, born of you."
>
> VERSE 53, CHAPTER 30, *VAYU PURANA*

Sati is the first manifestation of all of Shiva's spouses. She is his beautiful, gentle, intellectual, *tapasvini* or ascetic wife. Unable to bear her irascible father, Daksha's scorn and insults towards her beloved Shiva, she jumps into the holy fire and gives up her life.

Many people view her as a synonym for Parvati because the latter was her reincarnation, and both were wives of Shiva. Though there are some similarities, they are different from each other. The word "Sati" has since come to mean virtuous and was later used to denote a wife who commits self-immolation on her husband's funeral pyre.

Textual references

While Sati does not make an appearance in the Vedic texts, there are ample references to her by the time of the Epics. The *Ramayana* and the *Mahabharata* present her as Shiva's wife, while the latter describes the destruction of Daksha's sacrifice as well. Her identity becomes consolidated post this period and, from the 4th century onwards, there is the presence of Sati myths in the Shaiva Puranas.

The story behind Sati's birth

Stories within the *Shiva Purana* indicate that there are two main reasons behind Sati's birth. According to one story, Sati came into being as a result of the creator god Brahma's desire to take revenge on Shiva. This was because the god had laughed at Brahma's feelings towards his own daughter. According to the other, Sati took birth in order to distract Shiva from excessive asceticism. The gods believed that it was detrimental to all creation as the tremendous amount of energy he released in his meditative state could not be absorbed by the universe.

Brahma and the wandering celestial sage Narada pleaded with the Great Goddess to take birth in order to become Shiva's spouse. The Goddess, however, needed a medium to be born. They approached Daksha, Brahma's son and a learned Prajapati, to meditate on the Great Goddess so she would be born as his daughter. The Great Goddess granted their wish and took birth as Daksha's daughter Sati.

Her birth was marked with the auspicious omens befitting one with such a momentous task ahead of her. To celebrate, her father performed all the conventional ceremonies and rites of the Vedas, and her mother Prasuti took part in the great festivities of music and song.

▷ **Granite sculpture** of Brahma, the creator, in Chola art style, from the 10th–11th century

Sati's love for Shiva

An entire section of the *Shiva Purana,* called "Sati Khanda", is replete with the wonderful tales of Sati. She came into being to beguile and compel Shiva to fall in love with her. From the moment she was born, she was in love with Shiva. As a small girl, while engaged in various sports with her sisters and girlfriends, she drew Shiva's pictures and sang sweet songs in his memory.

Sati grew to be a young woman and her central pursuit was to get Shiva to feel for her the same way she felt for him. In order to appeal to him, a woman would have to possess much more than physical beauty. Realizing this, she chose the path most familiar to him, that of asceticism.

Her unflinching resolve

She embarked on the arduous path of severe austerities. She meditated with unwavering concentration for 100,000 years, her mind firmly fixed on nothing, but only complete and unadulterated devotion to Shiva. In the month of Ashvin (September–October), she did the rituals of offering rice. Then again on Chaturdashi, the 14th day of the waning phase of the Moon, she did the prescribed rituals. In November–December, she cooked what was required and practised strict dietary abstinence, eating only specific food on prescribed dates of the holy calendar. She stayed awake all night and performed special worship. Sometimes, on the coldest days from January to February, she remained in wet

△ **King Daksha sits** before the holy fire as the great sacrifice begins in this miniature painting, with gouache on paper, from the Kangra school, dated 1850.

clothes on the banks of the river. She was so firm with her penances that she refused to eat even dry leaves to sustain herself and got the appellate "*Aparna*", meaning "without leaves".

Her mother, unable to see her dear daughter perform such rigorous penance tried to persuade her, but Sati continued to forge ahead. She repeated various mantras with fruits and flowers. She was steady and never thought of anyone else. At times, Shiva or one of his agents tested her, but she remained steadfast.

Fruits of her labour

Eons passed and she acquired the enlightenment that only seers possess. Finally, Shiva was pleased, for he specifically wanted a wife who not only had comely features, but was also familiar with yogic practices. When he asked Sati what boon she wanted, she shyly asked him to marry her, and he agreed without hesitation. The wedding took place with all the rituals. After they were married, Shiva's love enveloped her and their lovemaking was long and passionate. However, a time came when Sati was satiated and desired something else from their union, for she was, after all, a cerebral goddess.

Sati's quest

Sati told Shiva, "After sporting with you, I wish to know the great pleasing principle whereby all living beings surmount worldly miseries in a trice." She wanted to know of the activity that enables people to obtain the supreme region and free themselves from worldly bondage.

Shiva explained it in great detail. He told her that it was achievable by his grace and that there was no difference between perfect knowledge and devotion. He talked about gyan, *vairagya* or detachment, the *yugas*, or any of the four ages of humankind. He then told her that he is always subservient to a devotee. She was delighted and bowed to him with much pleasure.

They continued to have long discussions about the shastras, virtue, and righteous living, and also about the lore of yantras and mantras. He told her about the duties of kings, wives, and sons. He also introduced her to the medical lore and the astral lore, palmistry, and the norms of people of different castes and stages of life. This glorious union of the two great divinities came to an end with Daksha's sacrifice and Sati's death (See pp 102–03).

> ## "**Fire came out** of all limbs of her **body** and was blown by the wind, from the Agneyi Dharana. It **reduced her to ashes**."
>
> VERSE 55, CHAPTER 30, *VAYU PURANA*

POPULAR DISCREPANCY

The goddess Sati has come to be associated with the now-illegal, death by suicide practice of *sati*, where a wife immolated herself on her husband's pyre. During the medieval period, this practise became an accepted act of devotion by a faithful wife. However, there seems to be no clear correlation between the goddess and this practice. The myth of Sati also does not seem to be in consonance with the practice of *sati*. In fact, the goddess serving as a mythological paradigm for *sati* is surprising because her death causes Shiva much grief.

△ **Stone hand prints** of queens who immolated themselves, from Mehrangarh Fort in Jaipur, Rajasthan

Grieving Shiva
This Pahari painting from the Kangra school of Himachal Pradesh, dated c. 1800, depicts an angry Shiva roaming the Earth while carrying Sati's body on his trident. The artwork was created with opaque watercolour and gold on paper.

Sati's cosmic end

The *Shiva Purana*, the *Kalika Purana*, and the *Devi Bhagavata Purana* tell the story of Sati's death. The underlying themes in all these tellings are of honour, love, and devotion. It epitomizes Sati's commitment towards her husband Shiva.

Sati's father Daksha had become the chief of all progenitors, that is a Prajapati. He decided to celebrate with a large Vedic *yagna*, or sacrificial offering. He invited the entire universe, including the great gods, Vishnu, the preserver, and the creator, Brahma, the Devas, and even the celestial and terrestrial sages.

His son-in-law, Shiva, the god of destruction, was the only exception. Daksha did not consider him worthy, as he was a *kapalin*, or a skull bearer, incorrigible, and not of nobility. Sati was once his favourite daughter, but, now it seemed like the king wanted to insult the couple by not inviting them to the *yagna*.

Back at her home in the Himalayas and ignorant of her father's intentions, Sati watched the guests leave for the *yagna*. Excited, she turned to Shiva and urged him to get ready as well. The great god refused. He believed that those who go to someone's home without an invitation attain disrespect, which is more serious than even death. Determined to discover why her father had not extended the invitation to them, Sati decided to go to the *yagna*.

She arrived at the hallowed grounds in Kanakhala, near Haridwar by the River Ganga, and confronted her father. The king, however, only insulted Shiva. He called him inauspicious, haughty, evil-minded, and the king of goblins and vampires. "Abandon this body of yours," Daksha told Sati. She tried to tell her father of Shiva's inner beauty and the philosophy behind his outward appearance. She was unable to convince him of her husband's power. Deeply anguished she jumped into the sacrificial fire.

Shiva heard of Sati's death and, as sorrow blanketed him, he took on the Virabhadra, or warrior, form. He reached the site and destroyed everything. Fierce and blazing, his anger threatened to scorch the world. Finally, as immeasurable grief consumed him, he cradled the dead Sati and walked away.

Shiva roamed the Earth carrying Sati's body. This threw the world into such disarray that Vishnu decided to intervene and restore order. He dismembered Sati's body, allowing the different parts to fall gently to the Earth.

Always together, Shiva joined her in the Bhairava form, united with her for eternity. Today, the places where her body parts fell are known as *Shakti pithas*.

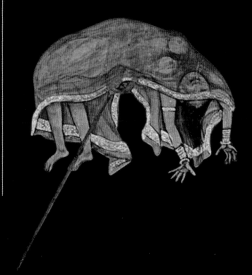

Shakti pithas

Each site, where a portion of Sati's body fell, became a place of magical potency, sanctifying the landscape. These locations are today called Shakti *pithas* or the "seats" of the Goddess. They are abiding spaces of the Goddess and a pilgrimage spot for all the Devi worshippers.

The myth of the dismemberment and distribution of Sati (See pp 102–03) comes from the *Kalika Purana* and the *Devi Bhagavata Purana*. In both the Puranas, the goddess is the main focus. Each, however, has a different account of Sati's death. In the *Kalika Purana*, she meditated for a moment, split the top centre of her skull, and gave up her life. In the *Devi Bhagavata Purana*, she burnt herself through the fire of her concentration, called *yogagni*. The common theme that runs through these Puranas is that she self-destructed and died.

After her death, a grief-stricken Shiva carried Sati's body on his shoulder and roamed the world. Vishnu used his *sudarshana chakra* to cut her body into many pieces, which fell in different regions across the Earth. The place where a part of her body fell became sanctified and is today known as a Shakti *pitha*, or seat of the Goddess.

American scholar of religious studies Diana L Eck in *India: A Sacred Geography* writes, "With her death, Sati has indeed made the sacrificial ground into a cremation ground, sacred to Shiva. The *Kalika Purana*, however, reverses the flow of affection at this point. Sati's devotion to Shiva is matched by his devotion to her…"

△ **Shiva carrying Sati**
This Kalighat painting shows lifeless Sati on Shiva's shoulders, as he balances her head with his trident.

△ **Tarapith**
This idol of Maa Tara, a tantric aspect of the Devi, is from a Shakti *pitha* in Rampurhat, West Bengal. It is believed that her third eye fell here.

The dismemberment and distribution of Sati is the dismemberment and distribution of the sacrifice. And it is distributed all over India."

Ancient origins

Eck further points out that while these Puranas may be dated from around the 8th to the 11–12th century, the emblematic context within which the idea of the parallel between the body and the cosmos exists is ancient. It is perhaps as old as the well-known "Purusha Sukta", or the hymn of creation in the *Rigveda*. Here, the gods divided the primordial cosmic being or *Purusha* to become the whole creation. By dismembering *Purusha* in the cosmogonic sacrifice, the gods fashioned a wide-ranging series of parallels between the body and the cosmos. For instance, His mind was the Moon, His eye was the Sun, His mouth was Indra and fire, and His breath was the wind. It is this allegorical image that the *Devi Bhagavata Purana* adopts to define the universe as numerous portions of the goddess.

The symbolic thinking that is the correspondence between the microcosm of the body and the macrocosm of the universe that was created with "Purusha Sukta" pervades the

> "All the **parts**... have been **expressed** at the various places of pilgrimage, the number of which are the most **excellent** and **foremost** on the earth."
>
> VERSE 85, CHAPTER 1, *DEVI GITA*

length and breadth of Hinduism even in contemporary times. In the religious landscape of India, the image of the body is frequently utilized to suggest the wholeness and interrelatedness of the land. Sati's sacrificial dismemberment is the most striking instance of the relation of sacred space to the body cosmos. It gave rise to the system of *pithas*.

Contentious number

The number of Shakti *pithas* in the subcontinent is not static. The *Kalika Purana* speaks of four *pithas* and the *Devi Bhagavata Purana* lists the

△ **Kamakhya Temple**
The holiest of all Shakti *pithas*, the Kamakhya Temple in Assam is where, it is believed, Sati's yoni fell.

△ **Arasuri Ambaji**
The Ambaji Mata Temple in Banaskantha, Gujarat, it is widely believed, is where Sati's heart fell.

"Whoever remembers or hears these excellent **one hundred and eight names** of the Goddess as well as of **Her places of pilgrimage**, will be **liberated** from all sins and will go to the **realms** of the Goddess."

VERSE 86, CHAPTER 1, *DEVI GITA*

auspicious number of 108. Another prevalent tradition is that there are 51 *pithas*. These are carefully enumerated in some tantric texts, such as *Pitha Nirnaya* of the *Tantrachudamani* from the late 17th century.

Beyond the myth of Sati's dismemberment, there are many textual traditions about the Shakti *pithas* in India. The earliest source is the 8th-century text, *Hevajra Tantra*, which speaks

of Jalandhar, Punjab, Odiyana in the Swat Valley, Purnagiri in the south, and Kamarupa in Assam as Shakti *pithas*. Therefore, the tradition of the *pithas* extends far beyond any list of 51 or 108, for there are thousands of goddesses all over India that people claim to be a part of Shakti's body.

A medium to permeate

One could perhaps even say that the distribution is a way of universalization. The myth of dispersal of Sati's body parts produces a theology of the omnipresence of Shakti. According to Eck, every goddess seems to participate since there are so many claimants in different parts of the country. It seems less significant to worshippers as to which parts fell where, with many overlapping traditions. Sati thus distributed is dead but alive, not fragmented but whole. The myth of the distribution does not create a cult of Shaktim, but a theology of the pervasiveness of Shakti. So the ankle at Kurukshetra, Haryana, does not betoken a mere fragment of the goddess. It signifies that the presence of the goddess is much wider than this or any local manifestation. It is a sense of the goddess that claims the entire land as her domain.

△ **A form of Parvati**
This idol of goddess Harsiddhi, painted in dark vermilion colour, is from her shrine in Ujjain, Madhya Pradesh.

△ **Narmada Temple**
The Shondesh Shakti *pitha* in Amarkantak, Madhya Pradesh, is where the Devi's right hip fell. Here, she is worshipped as Narmada.

American scholar of religious studies David Kinsley echoes the same thought when he says that the Earth is considered the body of the goddess Sati, and this way she has made herself available to all her devotees.

Unification

At the same time, there are many local goddesses and all are understood to be connected as manifestations of Shakti. The mythic imagination of Puranic mythographers and theologians brought together the local Goddess with the universal Goddess in a wonderful web. The myth provides a context for viewing the ideal one Goddess and the various local goddesses in the Indian subcontinent. The representation of the divided body weds the various others, rendering her both universal and yet local. This paramount belief is a universalizing myth that connects one goddess with another throughout the length and breadth of India. Through the modus operandi of the Sati myth many local goddesses are not only accommodated but also honoured.

Shiva by her side

In most Shakti *pithas*, Shiva follows the goddess wherever her body parts fell. In some places, he becomes the fierce Bhairava and in others, he takes on the phallic or lingam form. In this context, Kinsley points to how Sati's death was transformative. Through her death, she incites Shiva into a skirmish with the sacrificial cult and subsequently an accommodation within it. In this way, Shiva, considered to be a savage god, is brought within the sphere of dharma and the hierarchical normative religion.

All-pervasive

Shakti *pithas* are found all over the subcontinent. The most significant and which is common to all mythologies is Kamarupa in the northeastern part of India. This is where Sati's yoni or vulva fell and it become the site of the famous Kamakhya Temple (See pp 312–13). Then, there is Devi Patan in Uttar Pradesh, which is the location of her right hand. Jwalamukhi in Himachal Pradesh is said to be the place where her tongue fell, Labpur in West Bengal for her lips, while Janasthan in Maharashtra is for her cheeks, and Ujjain in Madhya Pradesh for her elbow. Of course, there are many more Shakti *pithas* scattered across India, each with its own culture and tradition.

△ **Anointed with red colour**
This idol of Maa Tarini, a form of Shakti, is from her shrine in Ghatgaon, Odisha. She is always depicted in red with two large eyes.

△ **Sanctified by Sati's hair**
Durga idol from Chamundeshwari Temple in Mysuru, Karnataka, where, it is said, Sati's hair fell.

The goddess who dares
This gouache painting of Parvati, from the 19th century, portrays the four-armed form of the goddess. She is seated on a throne in the *varada* mudra and painted green, possibly to show her association with fertility.

Parvati

The feisty challenger

"Listen to my vow, **dear mother**. Indeed, with **my great penance** I shall fetch that **clever (lord)** here itself and **woo him**… I shall **destroy** the **Rudratva (dreadfulness)** of Rudra."

VERSES 135–36, CHAPTER 21, *SKANDA PURANA*

△ **This sandstone sculpture** is a great example of Parvati's audacious nature as she has her arm around Shiva. It was created in the 10–11th century in Central India.

Every possible superlative for the divine feminine can be applied to Parvati, for she is the embodiment of Her most liberated form. She is Shakti, the earliest form of Shakti or *Adishakti*, the ultimate Shakti or *Parashakti*, and the greatest Shakti or *Mahashakti*.

As Parvati, however, she is often understood as the wife of Shiva, the destroyer, and mother to Ganesha and Skanda-Karttikeya. She is also the daughter of the eponymous mountain king Himavat and his wife Mena.

References in early texts

Although Parvati and her numerous manifestations are not found in Vedic literature, there are a few references to what appears to be her. One of her epithets "Ambika" (See pp 124–25) finds mention in a few later Vedic passages, along with a reference to Rudrani, wife of Rudra or Shiva. The *Kena Upanishad* also mentions a goddess called Uma Haimavati, which could be a reference to Parvati. The *Mahabharata* and the *Ramayana* tell her story in her Durga and Sati form. However, it is in the Puranas that her fascinating mythology (See pp 112–15) unfolds in all its beauty.

Her abode

Parvati is closely connected to the mountains. Her name literally means "of the mountains", which comes from the word "*parvat*" or mountains. Her epithets, such as Girija, Shalilasuta, Himalayaputri and Haimavati, link her to lofty peaks and the landscape scattered around them. It seems too that her origin was among the peoples living around the mountains. In this respect, she seems like an appropriate partner for Shiva who, it is believed, lives in the Himalayas.

Some Puranas, such as the *Shiva Purana*, indicate that her abode is in the Vindhyas. Her epithet Vindhyavasini (See pp 206–07) hints at this. She is also worshipped in this form near Mirzapur, Uttar Pradesh. Some legends state that Shiva and Parvati lived on Mandara, a mythical mountain, sometimes identified with a hill found to the south of Bhagalpur, Bihar.

Passionate yet autonomous

Parvati is perhaps the only spousal goddess who has an earlier avatara in the form of Sati (See pp 98–101). Though she has Sati's traits, she also has an intuitive awareness of Sati's travails and her

IN TODAY'S TIMES

HARIYALI TEEJ

In northern and western India, women participate in the festival of Teej to honour Shiva and Parvati's union. The festival, celebrated during monsoon, signifies fertility. The goddess's relationship with Shiva often influences married women who celebrate the festival for marital bliss. Single women perform the rituals seeking suitable husbands. Women adorn themselves as brides and sing and dance as a part of the festivities.

▷▷ primary objective of luring Shiva into a conjugal life. She is the loyal, loving wife who tolerates Shiva's peccadilloes. Yet, she is tolerant only till a certain point, after which she takes control as is befitting of a strong goddess. In one instance, her vestiges of a mighty goddess became apparent when her words, replete with sarcasm, reminded Shiva of his tryst with the sages' wives.

At the same time, she was so deeply in love with Shiva that his proximity to the dripping, alluring Goddess Ganga caused her much heartburn. She was jealous and wary of Ganga seated atop Shiva's head. One of the reasons why she wanted to merge with Shiva's body as Ardhanarishvara (See pp 122–23) was to keep a close eye over his dalliances and Ganga's attempt to enter Shiva via his ear.

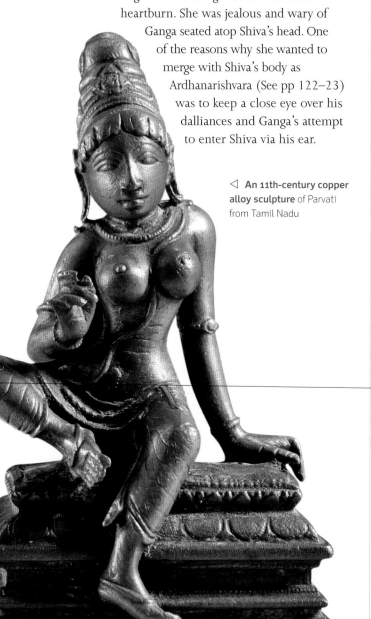

◁ **An 11th-century copper alloy sculpture** of Parvati from Tamil Nadu

Breaking norms

Parvati is steadfast in *tapas*, or penance, perhaps even more than Shiva. Unlike her husband – who once burnt the god of love Kama for disturbing his *tapas* – Parvati does not turn to violence. Her focus remains her penance, no matter what the distraction.

By insisting on the practice of *tapas*, she actively subverted the Shastras as "*stridharma*", or the normal mode of behaviour for a woman, and challenged normative social dictates. The Dharmashastras certainly do not prescribe that women leave home and hearth to retire to the wilderness and engage in *tapas*. Yet, Parvati's *tapas* advocates yoga as a higher form of love than sexuality. Ellen Goldberg, Canadian scholar of religious studies, calls Parvati the "model yogini". American scholar of religious studies David Kinsley argues that the fire of her lust transmutes into the fire of asceticism, and that she represents the idea that passion has to be controlled, not denied.

Independent depictions

Indian art is replete with motifs of Parvati. In most icons, she is depicted as beautiful and the images are richly decorated. South Indian Chola bronze statues, created between the 9–13th century, show her standing in the *tribhanga* posture, with three bends in the body – at the knees, hips, and shoulders. These aesthetically pleasing images depict her as delicate.

Some independent representations have shown her with six hands. In these, she holds lotuses in her four hands. The other two exhibit symbolic hand gestures or mudras, particularly the *varada* mudra, which conveys beneficence, and the *abhaya* mudra, which portrays fearlessness. There is a profusion of temple art depicting Parvati in *tapas* from the 7th century onwards. Scholars noted the presence of earlier representations from 2nd-century Mathura, Uttar Pradesh.

Familial depictions

Another conventional representation is of Parvati with Shiva. Most of the time they are a very amorous couple and their passionate

△ **A blackstone sculpture** of Parvati from Rajasthan, created in the 8th–9th century, depicting the goddess performing the *panchatapas*, or the ritual of five austerities

"When the goddess… **manifested herself**… everything, the entire unit of the three worlds **became delighted**… The groups of Devas, the great Sages, Charanas and the groups of Siddhas attained **great joy**."

VERSES 71–74, CHAPTER 20, *SKANDA PURANA*

a pastoral setting. Parvati can be sometimes seen threading a garland for Shiva, made up of severed heads or skulls called *mundamala*. Ganesha sits in her lap as Shiva is lost deep in thought. In other paintings, she can be seen nursing Ganesha as the six-headed Skanda sits, sulking nearby. All the vahanas or mounts, are also shown placed near the four deities. The *parivara* is studded with important deities and each one has a close mythological contact with the other.

body language has been captured beautifully in sculpture and other forms of art. Their divine wedding, for instance, is celebrated in an icon called Kalyanasundaramurti. It usually depicts the moment when Shiva accepts her as his bride by taking her right hand in his. Sometimes, they are accompanied by other divinities, such as Brahma, Vishnu, and sages, who are shown conducting the rituals. In the Umamaheshvaramurti or Gaurishankaramurti icon, Parvati is sometimes seen embracing Shiva. When depicted with him, she has only two hands, the right one holding a lotus and the left hanging loosely by the side.

Especially noteworthy is the conjoined image of the linga and the yoni and those showing *maithuna* or sexual intercourse. These images show that she is the *nari* or the female form as Ardhanarishvara and the yoni of Shiva's lingam.

In paintings depicting the Shiva *parivara* or family, Shiva, Parvati, and their two sons Ganesha and Skanda can be seen sitting in

THE STORY OF ANNAPURNA

Shiva and Parvati got into an argument one day. The god told her that everything materialistic, including food, was a mere illusion. This infuriated Parvati, who represented the material world. To show him her importance, she told him that she wanted to see how the world would survive without her, and disappeared. The world, deprived of food, went hungry, and there was a famine. As everyone begged Shiva for help, he discovered that there was only one kitchen on Earth, in the city of Kashi, where food was still available. Shiva, now a mendicant, went there and saw, to his surprise, Parvati who had taken the form of Annapurna. She held a ladle and a cooking pot and was distributing food to the gods and the inhabitants. Annapurna offered Shiva food as alms and made him realize her importance. Since then, her worship ensures that no household ever goes without food.

▷ **A chromolithograph** from Kolkata, West Bengal, showing Shiva seeking alms from Annapurna who holds a ladle and cooking pot.

Parvati's mythology

The extensive mythology around Parvati developed only after the 5th century, and it is almost completely associated with episodes from her life with her family, especially Shiva, the destroyer.

The mythology around Parvati invariably places her in a domestic sphere. But, she is not a goddess who can be tamed by domesticity. Instead, she revels in its power. All her stories portray her in sharp contrast to Shiva and yet, render their beautiful, complex union. In most of her myths, she comes across as a wonderful foil to the aloofness embodied by Shiva.

Parvati's birth

Most versions of her birth place her as someone who must lure Shiva into marriage with her. This became imperative because of Tarakasura, an invincible Asura, who tormented the Devas repeatedly. It was said that only Shiva's child could defeat him. The only solution was for Shiva to get into a conjugal relationship so that his son could annihilate the Asura.

The conundrum was that Shiva, after Sati's demise (See pp 102–03), returned to asceticism, and showed no sign of breaking his celibacy. Even Kama, the god of love and desire, was unable to lure him from his favoured way of being (See p 114). The gods realized that only someone with similar inclinations would be able to attract him. So, Parvati was born from Sati to help the world

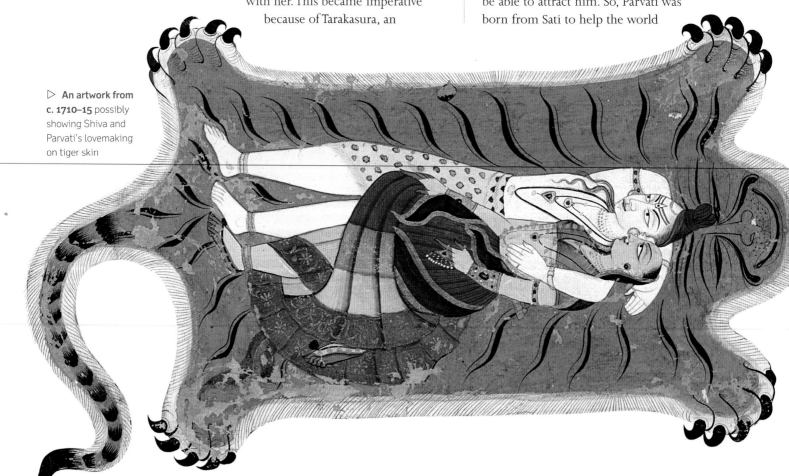

▷ **An artwork from c. 1710–15** possibly showing Shiva and Parvati's lovemaking on tiger skin

"O Lord of Devas, you are my **husband**… I am the same woman now **born of Mena** for the sake of the **accomplishment** the task of the Devas, regarding the **slaying of Taraka**, O lord of the chief of Devas. **A son** will be **born of me** to you."

VERSES 84–86, CHAPTER 22, *SKANDA PURANA*

in its time of crisis. The residual of a past must have existed, for Parvati displayed a keen interest in Shiva from the time she was young.

According to the Puranas, her birth saw great celebrations with the playing of divine drums and dancing by celestial damsels. There was singing and eulogizing of Parvati by all and even the grim sages took part in all this merriment. The Daityas, however, had a sense of grave foreboding and looked at the future with uneasiness and fright.

Breaking Shiva's resolve

Realizing Shiva's love for meditation, Parvati proceeded to do penance in order to gain his attention, not unlike her Sati form (See pp 98–101), who had done the same in a previous lifetime. She refrained from drinking water and ate only dried leaves, and eventually subsisted on air alone. She stood on one leg for a year and after some time on just her toe. She made her penance tougher. Sitting in the midst of fires during peak summers and exposing herself to the elements during the rainy season, she outdid all the Rishis as she entered the challenging world of the renouncer. She resorted to the noblest of mental feelings. The goddess, the cause of all auspiciousness, performed the greatest penance for the delight and pleasure of Shiva for 1,000 divine years. Once, her concerned father, Himavat, told her not to get afflicted and to not strain herself. He said, "Just as one cannot grasp the Moon stationed in the sky, so also it is difficult to attain Shambhu." He was right, it was not easy to wean Shiva away from asceticism. Parvati, however, continued to rival Shiva in her *tapas*, or penance.

Parvati's asceticism became even more difficult when Shiva, in disguise, tried to seduce her away from her *tapas*. He ridiculed himself in front of her and she castigated his manners and style of living. Parvati remained steadfast, until Shiva gave in and fell in love with her. He had found his match once again.

The ultimate divine wedding

Their marriage ceremony was very elaborate. The wedding procession included everyone from the celestial world and Shiva's own favoured Bhutas, or ghosts, goblins, and Pishachas, or flesh-eating spirits. There is a common leitmotif in the descriptions of Parvati's mother Mena's outrage when she first sets her eyes upon Shiva. Some versions talk about her outrage and horror, as she is unable to understand why her beautiful daughter would want to marry such an outrageous looking person. In others, she faints or threatens to kill herself. Such minor interruptions notwithstanding, all accounts talk of a grand wedding where even the great gods Vishnu, the preserver, and Brahma, the creator, participate.

Passionate intimacy

Once back in their abode in the mountainous region of Kailash, the lovemaking of Shiva and Parvati became legendary.

>> According to the Puranas, it went on for thousands of years, and shook the cosmos, frightening even the gods, who started to question the wisdom of their plan to bring the two great deities together. They started fearing the powers of a child born of such a union. The offspring could possibly consume all things in the three worlds – they feared for their own lives.

Sometimes, it is said that the gods became impatient and did the unthinkable, that is, they interrupted the two. Shiva being a *mahayogi*, or great ascetic, customarily retained the semen while making love to Parvati. When interrupted, the spilled semen took a circuitous route via a series of carriers, including Agni, the god of fire, goddess Ganga, and Vayu, the god of air. Parvati was so infuriated by this interruption that she cursed Agni and other gods that they would never bear children themselves.

Skanda and Ganesha

As for Parvati's children, neither was born parthenogenetically. Skanda was "created" of Shiva's seed, which was transported, ultimately, to the Krittikas. They acted as wet nurses, suckling the baby found among the bulrushes on the side of the River Ganga. In the *Shiva Purana*, there is an entire section called "Kumara Khanda", which describes Skanda's birth.

Another time, before the birth of Skanda, Parvati, feeling lonesome for too long, gave birth to Ganesha in Shiva's absence. It was from

the very dirt of her body that she created a *putla*, or doll, and infused it with the breath of life. She was delighted at her creation, but Shiva was unaware of this child. Unfortunately, not realizing who the child was and being stopped from entering his wife's inner chambers, Shiva decapitated him. On learning about his son's death, Parvati was distraught, and, in some versions, threatened mayhem of a cosmic nature, if her son was not brought back to life immediately. The head was then hurriedly replaced by one of an elephant.

These episodes reflect the perennial tension between the couple, with Shiva reluctant to be inducted into a householder realm. But Parvati is strong enough to domesticate Shiva, a kind of taming or leavening of his antinomian ways. The need for a progeny is also understood in this context. Parvati is, therefore, the active Shakti and *prakriti*, or materiality.

KAMA IN ASHES

In an attempt to get Shiva to fall in love with Parvati, the gods called upon Kama, the god of love and desire, who shot his arrow, replete with flowers and sugarcane, to arouse passion in the mighty god. However, Shiva, enraged at this disturbance in his great meditation, reduced Kama to ashes with a flash of his third eye.

△ **Titled "Madan-Bhasma",** this lithograph from 1890 encapsulates the dramatic moment when the ascetic Shiva turned Kama to ashes. Parvati can be seen kneeling before the angry god.

"Then they brought **Gauri** there… the **splendid lady of bright face** … She was as though a tank of the **nectar of beauty**. On seeing her even the Sages became deluded… having **splendid lustre**, they appeared to be stunned and crazy."

VERSES 21–22, CHAPTER 23, *SKANDA PURANA*

This sculpture of Shiva's *parivar*, or family, is from a temple dedicated to Shreenath Mhaskoba, a form of Shiva, in Pune, Maharashtra. It shows all the members – Shiva (left) and Parvati (right) as well as their sons Ganesha (bottom left) and Karttikeya (bottom right) – along with their vahanas.

A mesmerizing depiction
Theatrical renditions of the story of Shiva and Parvati are often extremely powerful and moving. Here, Indian actor Hema Malini portrays Parvati (right) in the dance drama, "Durga", performed in Thane, Maharashtra. In this two-act play, the actor effortlessly transforms from Sati to Parvati, and ultimately Durga. Standing alongside Shiva (left), her hand in the *abhaya mudra*, she presents a typical and beautiful image of the Goddess.

Parvati and Shiva

In Parvati's relationship with Shiva, one encounters a kind of chutzpah not seen in any other goddess. The mythology and iconography indicate that whether it is in the matter of lovemaking, offspring, or recreation, Parvati is very much his equal partner.

Amongst all the celestial couples, nothing can compare to the colourful and fulsome relationship that Parvati and Shiva share. It is an egalitarian bond where Parvati is not submissive, but emerges as a powerful parallel to Shiva, the supreme being.

Domesticating Shiva

Shiva has always been associated with destruction and liminal spaces, such as cremation grounds, and followers of unusual appearance and strange behaviour. Parvati changed this perception as she brought Shiva, the ultimate renunciant, into the fold of a householder, with a wife and two sons.

American scholar of religious studies David Kinsley notes that together, they represent the perennial tension between the ascetic ideal and the householder ideal. He says that Shiva's induction into the world of dharma took place through their union and extended his range of activities into the domestic sphere. Parvati orchestrated a semblance of normative order

THE CHARMING SHIVA

Once, Shiva went to the pine forest of Daruvana to bless the sages and demonstrate how they could reduce their sins. He appeared bizarre and shocking to the sages who were aghast at his behaviour as it was against dharma, as they understood it. Shiva went about naked, violating all restrictive conventions and social etiquette. He proved to be such a contrast to the austere sages that their wives found themselves enthralled by him.

▽ **An 18th-century painting** from Mandi, Himachal Pradesh, depicting Shiva and Parvati sewing a blanket, as their son Ganesh hugs his father from behind. Kartikkeya helps his parents with the task at hand.

into Shiva's life, albeit one based on Brahmanical principles. When Shiva is with Parvati, the conflict between asceticism and marital life yields to symbiotic harmony.

Cerebral exchanges

There is no doubt that Parvati, the intellectual goddess, is a match for Shiva par excellence. Their relationship was also a constant questioning of what was more relevant – *pravritti* or *nivritti*. While *pravritti* means being active, *nivritti* is a quiet withdrawal into one's own spiritual self. Shiva was the epitome of the latter. With his eyes closed, he seemed invested in the eternal truth of the soul, not worldly ephemeral notions. It is in continuation with this thought that the tussle between Shiva and Parvati over offspring took place. For Shiva, an ascetic, had no use for a son, but Parvati, representing the householder, insisted that living in the social world meant that one should perform familial duties of having children.

Interactions like these indicate that Parvati does not subscribe to the ideal image of a spousal goddess, such as Lakshmi, who is often rendered submissive to her husband.

Challenger to Shiva

It is also Parvati's quick wit and repartee that places her on an equal footing with Shiva. This can be clearly seen in their encounter when, as an eight-year-old, she accompanied her father to pay obeisance to Shiva. When the god disapproved of her presence during his *tapas*, or penance, she told him that though endowed with the power of penance, he too was a part

> "It was by **my grace** that Shiva was born… There is no doubt… that he has become well-established **through me**."

VERSES 94–96, CHAPTER 34, *SKANDA PURANA*

of *prakriti*, or nature. Shiva told her that he was destroying *prakriti* through his isolation and meditation. Parvati's response displays her flagrant boldness when she replied that his speech, whatever he hears, and whatever he eats, is also a part of nature.

This characteristic becomes apparent even during a game of *chausara*, or dice. When Shiva started losing, his allies accused Parvati of winning by unfair means. Unfazed and victorious, she instead told Shiva to remove his embellishments one by one. It was enough to shock all who were present, even Shiva. This was when she, rather sarcastically, reminded him of the time he walked through the forest of Daruvana, sans attire, and reduced the Rishis' wives to helpless swoons (See box).

In yet another episode, Shiva teased Parvati for her dark complexion. Her retaliation was quick, as she made a pun on the word "kala", meaning time or dark complexion. She told him that he was the one often called Mahakala and that he appeared fair only because he went about smearing himself with ashes.

Comfortable companionship

Shiva and Parvati seem to have a lovely, egalitarian relationship. The Puranas describe them as indulging in various activities together. They engaged in aquatic sports, played on the swing, gathered flowers, played the lute, painted, adorned each other, went on long rides, and even deliberated over the events of the world. For those who like to see them as a couple, Parvati is a key player, even as the spouse of a powerful male deity such as Shiva.

△ **This painting, dated 1694–95** shows Parvati arguing with Shiva after he cheated her out of a necklace in a game of *chausara*. The painting is a part of a series that illustrated the *Rasamanjari*, a 15th-century Sanskrit love poem.

The three-legged Rishi
Created in the 14–15th century in Vishnupur, Odisha, this sculpture in black schist shows Shiva and Parvati together. Bhringi is seen on the extreme right, standing upright with the help of his third leg. Between him and Shiva is Nandi, the bull.

Bhringi's foolish act

This story is a part of temple lore. Relying on humour and wit, it emphasizes the connection between Shiva and Parvati. Over the years, there have been a few versions, with minor alterations, but the premise remains the same – Bhringi's misdemeanour.

After their grand wedding, Shiva, the destroyer, and Parvati made Mount Kailash their home. Every day, the powerful divinities received utmost reverence from their devotees. The worshippers sang their praises and then paid homage by performing *pradakshina*, or circumambulation.

All was well until one day, Bhringi arrived. He was a well-known Rishi and a pugnacious *bhakta*, or devotee, of Shiva. While every devotee of Shiva revered Parvati with equal devotion, Bhringi refused. He instead focused on Shiva and performed the *pradakshina* only around him. Seeing this, an enraged Parvati asked, "Why do you worship only Shiva? We are two halves of the same truth." Bhringi ignored her.

Miffed, Parvati decided to teach him a lesson. She proceeded to do *tapas*, or penance, so that she could ask Shiva for a boon. Shiva, satisfied with her penance, said, "Parvati, you have pleased me with your arduous *tapas*. Tell me what you desire."

The goddess replied, "I want to be united with you as half your body, so I can always be near you." Shiva granted her wish and they become Ardhanarishvara (See pp 122–23). In that avatar, they stood as one body – one half bearing the form of Shiva and the other bearing Parvati's form. Triumphant, the goddess waited for Bhringi. When he arrived, he saw, to his horror, what had happened to his beloved Shiva. Unrelenting, he took the form of a beetle and pierced a hole between the two so that he could circumambulate only Shiva.

Seeing this, Parvati, infuriated, cursed the Rishi. "May Bhringi lose all those parts of his body that come from the mother," she declared, "for it is I, the mother, who has provided all the people of the universe with flesh and blood."

In an instant, Bhringi lost all his muscles and became a pathetic bag of bones. He retained only what he had received from the father – bones and nerves. He collapsed on the floor.

Shiva felt sorry for his fervent and foolish devotee. To help him stand upright, he gave him a third leg. Bhringi, realized his folly and apologized to Shiva and Parvati.

He began to understand that Shiva and Parvati together make up the whole, and that one exists because of the other. Bhringi, however, was denied flesh and blood forever.

The world is always a witness to his grave mistake. He is often seen lurking around the two great deities, his rib cage prominent and bearing a third leg. His expression is always a little melancholy.

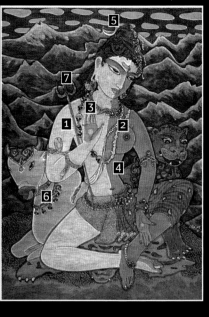

The perfect symphony

Indian artist S Rajam's vision of Shiva and Parvati as Ardhanarishvara

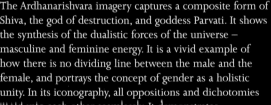

The Ardhanarishvara imagery captures a composite form of Shiva, the god of destruction, and goddess Parvati. It shows the synthesis of the dualistic forces of the universe – masculine and feminine energy. It is a vivid example of how there is no dividing line between the male and the female, and portrays the concept of gender as a holistic unity. In its iconography, all oppositions and dichotomies meld into each other seamlessly. It demonstrates interchangeability and flow, and advocates the need to look at both forms as equal and complementary.

1. The left half of the figure embodies Shiva. The blue-grey tint indicates that his body is smeared with ash, which is symbolic of him as the one who can destroy the world with fire.

2. The right half of the figure, where the heart lies, depicts Parvati. The female form is accentuated through feminine elements – prominent breast, precious metal jewellery, and a bindi on her forehead. Her well-combed hair is dressed up as *karanda mukuta*, or a basket-shaped crown, and her clothing is ankle length. She is depicted as manifesting normative and civilized behaviour.

3. In sharp contrast to Parvati, Shiva is shown with elements that emphasize his wild and free side. So he wears the *sarpa mekhela*, or serpent girdle, *jata mukuta*, or crown of coiled braids, *mundamala*, or necklace of skulls, *sarpa kundela*, or coiled serpent earring, and a short loincloth made of elephant skin.

4. Parvati is painted green, perhaps, to imply vegetation and fertility, a theme common to female forms.

5. The crescent moon, or *Chandrashekhara*, stands for time since measurement of time as days or months depends on the waxing and waning of the moon. Shiva wears it as a diadem, indicating that even all-powerful time is a mere ornament for him.

6. Nandi, the bull, Shiva's vahana, or mount, sits besides the god. He is symbolic of Shiva's virile nature. Shiva is seated in the *abhaya mudra*, or fear-not posture, a way to emphasize his strength. Parvati's vehicle, Dawon, a tiger or lion sits next to her.

7. Shiva is believed to be the master of three worlds, he is shown with many tripartite elements. The trisul, or trident, that he wields stands philosophically for the three *gunas*, or the three processes of creation, preservation, and dissolution. He has three eyes, with the *trinetra*, or the third eye, representing knowledge, wisdom, and omniscience. He also wears a *tripundra*, or three parallel lines of ash, on his forehead.

श्रंविका

The inner power
Ambika is represented in this c. 1725 painting in ink and opaque watercolour on paper from a *Devi Mahatmya* manuscript.

Ambika

Progenitor of all goddesses

"To that Ambika who is **worthy of worship** by all devas... who is the **embodiment** of the **entire powers** of all... we bow in **devotion.**"

VERSE 3, CHAPTER 4, *DEVI MAHATMYA*

The word *ambika* or "mother dear" is a common epithet in the *Devi Mahatmya*, and emphasizes the Goddess's maternal and nourishing character. It also refers to a distinct goddess who is the mother of the universe. As a goddess, Ambika finds mention in sections of the *Yajurveda*. In the *Vajasaneyi Samhita* and *Taittiriya Brahmana*, she is the sister of Rudra or Shiva the destroyer. In the *Taittiriya Aranyaka*, she is referred to as his consort. Later texts classify her as Parvati (See pp 108–11) and in some instances even Durga (See pp 80–83).

Indistinct features

Her characteristics are vague and she is not as specifically delineated as the goddesses Durga, Kali, or Parvati. This could be because, in the texts, the epithet *ambika* and the goddess Ambika are not clearly separated. Sometimes, she is depicted with eight arms wielding many weapons, and associated with the goddess Amba. Despite this, she is believed to embody all the goddesses, and hence, could be the all-powerful Great Goddess.

As a Great Goddess

Perhaps the most descriptive reference to Ambika is in the *Devi Mahatmya*. Her beauty, the text describes, was so striking that the Asura brothers Shumbha and Nishumbha wanted to possess her – a desire that inevitably led to their ultimate destruction. She took form when the Devas, defeated by the Asura brothers, fled to the Himalayas and sought the Devi's help. The Devas sang songs of high praise, and marvelled at the Devi who dwelled within all creatures, and in many forms, such as illusion, consciousness, power, sleep, and hunger. They praised her 24 characteristics. They ended each praise with the chant, "Hail to her! Hail to her! Hail to her!"

When the goddess Parvati heard Devas, she asked them, "Who are you praising?" Before they could reply, an auspicious goddess sprung forth from Parvati's sheath. "This praise is addressed to me," the goddess told Parvati. This was Ambika.

Chanda and Munda, generals of the Asura brothers, saw Ambika. Taken by her beauty, they told the Asura brothers about her. Shumbha sent his emissary Sugriva to woo her into marrying him or his brother. An unimpressed Ambika, told Sugriva, "Only he who conquers me in battle and is my match in strength, shall be my husband."

Angry, Shumbha sent Dhumralochana, the chieftain of the Daityas, to bring him Ambika. He was told to slay anyone who tried to get in his way. The chieftain reached the battlefield with an army of 60,000 Asuras. They showered the Devi with javelins, arrows, and sharp axes. However, the powerful goddess merely looked at Dhumralochana and uttered the sound "hum", reducing him to a pile of ashes.

The black goddess
This Madhubhani cloth painting from Bihar depicts Kali in her most common form, with a long, red tongue and a garland of skulls. The artist has added some unusual elements as well, such as flowers and jewellery, perhaps to make the image more accepted in modern society.

Kali

The brutal and aggressive force

"Bearing the **strange skull-topped staff**… **filling** the regions of the sky with her **roars**, and… **slaughtering** the great asuras… she **devoured** those hosts of the foes of the devas."

VERSES 7–9, CHAPTER 7, *DEVI MAHATMYA*

With a long, lolling tongue, dishevelled hair, an apron of chopped hands as a lower garment, upper body bereft of clothing, and a necklace of decapitated male heads barely hiding her drooping breasts, the goddess Kali is one of the most extraordinary and enthralling divinities of the Indian subcontinent. Everything about her proclaims her antinomian character. Everything about her instils awe, aroused by dread. When compared to the near perfect voluptuous beauty of other female divinities, it is almost as though Kali relishes her contrarian persona. She is indeed the most fierce of all.

Kali's precursors

Although there is no mention of Kali in early Vedic texts, some scholars believe that Kali may have antecedents in some of the goddesses in the *Rigveda* (See pp 40–43). So Nirrti, who is connected with death and destruction, Ratri who personifies night, and Aditi, the mother of many gods, especially Adityas, are often understood to be forerunners of such divinities as Kali. This is perhaps because she embodies, in one way or the other, some of their major characteristics.

Kali's ancestry can be traced to a reference in the *Jaiminiya Brahmana*, a part of the Vedic text *Samaveda* and dated to around 8th century BCE.

It has a verse celebrating the triumph of the Indra, the god of heavens, over the ogress Dirgha-jihvi. The words *dirgha* means long and *jihva* means tongue. So Dirgha-jihvi was one who had a long tongue and who thirsted for and liked to lick the divine drink soma. This ogress could be a predecessor to Kali. Over centuries, the fierce form of the Goddess assumed the form of Kali.

Rise to fame

The name Kali first appears in the text *Mundaka Upanishad*, composed in the 5th century BCE. In it, she is one of the seven black "flickering tongues" of flame that is Agni. These flames devour sacrificial oblations and transmit them to the gods. Through this early association, Kali is linked to fire and its destructive capacity as well as with the cremation ground.

In many texts of the early medieval period, Kali is the goddess of the tribes, such as the Shabaras, the Chandalas and the lower castes in wild places. American scholar of religious studies David Kinsley, points out that even Kali temples were built far from the settled areas of towns and villages. She, very much belonged to the periphery of Hindu society. According to Sanskrit scholar Sukumari Bhattacharji, Brahmanical religion was eventually

>> altered into a more popular religion. Regional stories entered the Puranas, which successfully wove together disparate elements. So with accommodation through scriptures and explanatory mythology, Kali moved from the periphery of the tribal and regional to the centre stage of the Brahmanical milieu.

With the compilation of the Puranas and Tantras from the 5th to 15th century, Kali's tales and invocations are found with great frequency. She rose to prominence in the literary tradition, first in the *Devi Mahatmya* (See pp 70–75) of the 6th century.

The ultimate ferocity

In the *Devi Mahatmya*, Kali's association with elements such as battlefields, destruction, and death is established. Several other Puranas, such as the *Agni Purana* and the *Garuda Purana*, also mention her in invocations that aim at success in war. Her description continues to be the same – gaunt and dancing madly as she crushes, tramples, and breaks the enemy.

Even when Kali is depicted in paintings, the background is either the cremation ground or a battlefield. She is often seen doing the dance of death in the ashes of the burning grounds. Kali's fierce identity is also reflected in her name. The word *kali* comes from *kala*, which means blackness. Seen metaphorically, Kali is the embodiment of *tamas*, or that aspect of energy which is responsible for dispersion. She thereby produces an immeasurable void, one that swallows up everything. She is therefore black, resonating with the mysteriousness of blackness. At the same time, the word *kala* can also mean time. So she is also the goddess of time, one who destroys everything, including the dissolution of the

▽ **A 14th-century Nepalese sculpture** of Kali as Chamunda shows her in her emaciated form, ready to drink blood from a vessel. An animal and two creatures can be seen at her feet. One of them has its hand raised, almost as if trying to collect the blood dripping from the severed head in her hand.

"By her this **universe is deluded,** and it is she who **creates** this universe… who takes the form of the **great destroyer**… all this cosmic sphere is **pervaded**."

VERSES 37–38, CHAPTER 12, *DEVI MAHATMYA*

universe. Time, like blackness, also devours everything and waits for none. Her "hunger" swallows every second, thereby transforming it into the past. Indian author and monk Swami Harshananda has rightfully said, "a power that destroys has got to be depicted in terms of awe-inspiring terror."

As the mother

Despite the violent power often connected with Kali, she is also the great mother, the source and protector of every being. Life comes from her and every experience, including that of death, which is her gift, is an experience of her. Anthropologist Sarah Caldwell writes, "She is both the ground of earthly existence and the means to salvation."

Kinsley suggests that she is the mother because "she gives birth to a wider vision of reality than the one embodied in the order of *dharma*." Sometimes, the dharmic order is insufficient, and Kali presents an alternative model to this order, which has elements "out of place" and "out of control".

Manifestation of Sati and Parvati

Kali is mainly a part of the god of destruction Shiva's arena, and is understood to have come forth from either of his wives Sati or Parvati. Kinsley draws attention to the *Skanda Purana*, composed in 8–9th century, where Kali manifests when Daksha infuriates his daughter Sati by ignoring her and her husband Shiva from the invitation to the great sacrifice (See pp 102–03). Enraged, Sati rubs her nose and Kali appears.

Being a manifestation of Parvati, Kali is also seen as Parvati's wrath and personified alter ego. Her association with Parvati is clear from the *Linga Purana*, which was composed in the 6–10th century and is one of the central texts on Shiva. In one episode, Shiva requests Parvati to slay the Asura Daruka, who has been granted the boon that only a woman can kill him. Parvati enters Shiva's body and, remaking herself from the poison in his throat, re-emerges as Kali. Then, with the help of Pisachas, or the flesh-eating spirits, Kali destroys Daruka. Shiva and Parvati's married life is replete with references to Kali, especially her skin colour. Kinsley points to an instance in the *Vamana Purana*, a Shaiva text composed in the 9–11th century. In it, Shiva playfully addresses Parvati as Kali, alluding to her dark complexion. Irked by this reference, Parvati, takes off to perform penance in order to transform her dark complexion. The dark skin she sheds, called *kausha*, gets transformed into a fierce goddess called Kaushiki, also known as Ambika (See 124–25), from whose anger appears Kali. Parvati's Kali-like nature is also reiterated in many other Puranas, such as the *Padma Purana*, composed in the 4–15th century, and the *Kalika Purana* composed in the 10–11th century. Therefore, as Kinsley says, "Kali plays the role of Parvati's dark, negative, violent nature in embodied form."

Diverse encounters

Today, across India, Kali can be experienced through many Kali-like goddesses, such as Chandi, Chamunda, Bhairavi, Alakshmi, Chinnamasta, Yellammma, and Korravai. Some scholars claim that Kali is Bhagavati and even the fiercer Bhadrakali in Kerala. These Kali-like goddesses seem to have originated from a common ancient religious, cultural, and psychological sphere. They share an association with blood, sacrifices, death, and nudity.

△ **This Basohli painting from Himachal Pradesh** was created in c. 1740. It shows the three divinities Shiva, Vishnu, and Brahma (left to right) revering Kali as she sits in a cremation ground, engulfed in flames.

KALI AS A DASAMAHAVIDYA

The Tantric cult of the Dasamahavidyas (See pp 270–71) arose in the late medieval period. Kali is usually mentioned and portrayed as the very first, or *adi*, Mahavidya in this cult of 10 goddesses. She is considered one of the most important of these goddesses and, sometimes, it appears that the other Mahavidyas are but veritable forms of her personality.

Kali's mythology

▽ **This c. 17th-century jackwood sculpture** of Kali from Kerala shows her with two rounded fangs instead of the usual long tongue and some jewellery instead of the garland of skulls.

Kali's tales are gory and brutal. When one encounters them, there is the stimulation of a myriad emotions and sentiments. There is primal fear, but also reassurance as she appears most capable of protection, once one becomes a part of her world.

In most of her mythology, Kali is recognized as a fierce goddess who is undefeatable on the battlefield. In all her stories, she is an autonomous goddess. However, through the course of her mythology, due to her wild and untamed character, she was accommodated into the Shaiva pantheon.

Role in the Devi Mahatmya

Kali makes her mythological debut in the *Devi Mahatmya* where her role is the most significant as she slays many gigantic Asuras, including Chanda and Munda. The story goes that the Asura Shumbha ordered Chanda and Munda to go to the peak of a golden mountain, where the goddess Ambika (See pp 124–25) sat, grab her by her hair, and bring her to him. The two marched in a fourfold array, their bows bent and swords drawn. Ambika saw them and became terribly angry and in a fuming state, her countenance became as dark as ink. From the surface of her fiercely frowning forehead issued Kali who took over the operation of decimation.

Her method of annihilation was unique. She snatched elephants with one hand and flung them into her mouth along with their rear men, drivers, and bells. She did the same to the cavalry, with their horses and chariots, and ground them with her teeth.

As she ate them, the crunching sound was most frightful. She roared, mounted her lion, and proceeded to sever the heads of Chanda and Munda. She held their heads, laughed, and turned to Ambika. These, she told the goddess, were like two great animal offerings to her. Ambika then declared that henceforth Kali would be known as Chamunda.

Shiva's untamed wife

Considered a manifestation of Parvati, Kali is, by association, Shiva's spouse as well. However, she is bolder and more powerful and mostly acts on her own.

An episode in the *Linga Purana*, a Sanskrit text composed in the 6–10th century, recounts Shiva's battle with Tripurasura or the Asura of the three cities. At the battlefield, Kali is fiercely attired in an elephant hide and whirls her trident, which is adorned with skulls. Her eyes are half-closed due to intoxication after drinking the blood of Asuras.

Although there are several instances that reiterate Kali's role as Shiva's wife, it is profoundly evident that her persona is much more than that of a consort. She is often depicted sans Shiva or when she is with him, he is in a submissive position, supine under her feet.

One of the best-known representations of Kali is one where she is dancing on Shiva. Known iconographically as Dakshinakali, it shows Kali standing or seated on a supine Shiva (See pp 142–43). American scholar of religious studies David Kinsley points to a myth pertaining to this image, recounted in many

> "Others we **admire**; others we **love**; to Her we **belong**. Whether we know it or not, we are Her children, **playing round Her knees**."

SISTER NIVEDITA, *KALI THE MOTHER* (1900)

---

versions of the Ramayana, including the *Adbhuta Ramayana* (See pp 26–31), the Oriya *Ramayana* by the 15th-century poet Sarala Dasa, and the *Jaiminibharata Ramayana* from Bengal.

The story goes that after defeating the Asura Daruka, Kali was immersed in a tempestuous dance of bloodshed. The ongoing massacre had brought about an apocalyptic spectacle of destructive frenzy. She relished the blood and gore of her victims and the entire battlefield bore evidence of this trail of terror. This revelry of violence may have destroyed evil elements, but now, the world was in danger as she danced out of control. The gods feared that the world would collapse with her irrepressible energy, and begged Shiva to stop this endless rampage. Shiva, acquiesced, lay among the other corpses on the battlefield so that when Kali stepped on her husband's body, she would stop.

The *Linga Purana* version of this story has Shiva taking the form of a weeping infant to arouse Kali's maternal and protective instincts. Overwhelmed by seeing the infant, Kali stops, lifts the baby up, and suckles him at her breast.

▽ **A street performer** in Kolkata, West Bengal, dressed as the ferocious goddess Kali, draws attention to the ill-effects of firecrackers and COVID-19 pandemic.

Leading to victory
This early 18th-century Nepalese folio depicts a scene from the *Devi Mahatmya*. Here, the Devi leads the Matrikas into battle against Raktabeeja, as Kali (in blue) drinks his blood and devours his clones with her long tongue.

Battle with Raktabeeja

Kali's encounter with, and the inevitable destruction of, the Asura Raktabeeja, as told in the *Devi Mahatmya*, establishes her fierce and bloodthirsty identity.

The gruesome battle to rid the universe of the wicked Asuras, Daityas, Danavas, and other demons of yore, raged through the day and the night. Chandika, the Devi, faced all kinds of foes. Some changed their shape, others looked terrible, and they all wielded weapons of different shapes and sizes.

She expunged them all until she came face to face with the most unimaginably dreadful Asura Raktabeeja. Every time a drop of his blood touched the ground, he recreated himself.

Chandika attacked him and as streams of blood flowed from his wounds, thousands of combatants, all in Raktabeeja's form and valour, came into being. They filled the battlefield and pervaded the world.

First, the Matrikas (See pp 144–47) faced him, each wielding a weapon of her choice. Vaishnavi struck him with her discus, Aindri with her thunderbolt, Kaumari with her spear, Varahi with her sword, and Maheshvari with her trident. The Devas grew alarmed as Raktabeeja guffawed at the face of the attack. He used his club and fought off the Matrikas. He seemed invincible.

Chandika seemed unfazed. She laughed and summoned Kali. "Roam the battlefield and open your mouth wide," she told the fiery goddess, who wore a necklace of skulls. "Drink the blood that flows when I pierce Raktabeeja with my weapon. Eat the many Asuras that spring from his blood," she proclaimed. Chandika knew that with his blood emptied, Raktabeeja would perish.

She struck the Asura. Kali, her mouth wide open, drank his blood and devoured all the clones that his blood had birthed. Desperate, the emaciated Asura struck Chandika with his club, but the blow glanced off her. She did not feel the slightest pain. She hurled weapons at him and Raktabeeja grew weaker, until he fell to the ground, dead.

The Devas rejoiced. The battleground became a place of celebration as the Matrikas danced, intoxicated by the blood they had consumed.

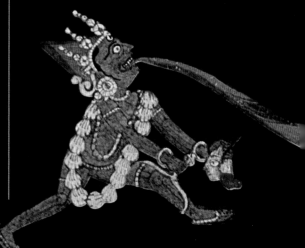

The worship of Kali

There is much more to the worship of this dark goddess than esoteric rituals, offerings, and mantras. The devotee must undertake a difficult journey to reach her – one that will deconstruct all perceptions of the material world.

Kali is worshipped everywhere – homes, temples, cremation grounds, and in the mind of the practitioner. There are different types of devotees as well. There are those who worship Kali through bhakti practices, much like other divinities, with offerings of flowers, food, incense, clothing, and the chanting of prayers. Here, the emphasis is on the emotional depth of the worshippers. Then, there is the Tantric order, with elaborate and radical rituals and the deliberate dismantling of social conditioning.

The Tantric worship of Kali

There is a belief that violations of social conditioning draws the devotee closer to the goddess. In the *vamachara*, or left-handed Tantrism, this "spiritual endeavour", notes American scholar of religious studies David Kinsley, takes a "particularly dramatic form". The ritualist worshipper, or *sadhaka*, undertakes Panchatattva, or the ritual of five

forbidden things. This includes wine, or *madya*, meat, or *mansa*, parched grain, or *mudra*, and illicit sexual intercourse, or *maithuna*. "In this way he overcomes the distinction (or duality) of clean and unclean, sacred and profane, and breaks his bondage to a world that is artificially fragmented," notes Kinsley. In doing so, the practitioner, "boldly confronts Kali and thereby assimilates, overcomes, and transforms her into a vehicle of salvation." The success ensures that the forbidden loses "its power to pollute, to degrade, to bind".

Community worship

All-night vigils, or *jagranas*, are also central to Kali worship. During these community gatherings, devotees tell stories of the goddess, accompanied by music and the chanting of holy mantras. Cases of possession are not uncommon and many believe that the aroma of burning incense and camphor, sounds, and movements can trigger this trance-like possession.

The mother

The devotee often approaches Kali as a helpless child. The mother may be fearsome, hostile even, yet, the child turns to her for protection, security, and warmth. However, her role as a mother did not emerge until early 18th century in Bengal. There is also little to no mythology or iconography of her as a maternal figure.

Of life and death

In West Bengal, the night of Diwali, the festival of lights, is important for Kali's worship. The *Kali Tantra* states that the goddess's worship

△ **This is a popular southern** representation of Kali, whose image finds a place even in a marketplace, such as here, in Madurai, Tamil Nadu.

THE RITUAL THEATRE OF MUDIYETTU

Every year, after the harvesting season, ahead of summer, the sound of drums and chants ring through the air in villages across Kerala. This is a part of Mudiyettu, a ritual dance in honour of the goddess Kali in her Bhadrakali form. The entire village participates in this performance. Devotees first make a *kalam*, or drawing, of the goddess on the temple floor to the sounds of the kalam pattu, a song in her praise. This is to ensure that the spirit of the goddess transcends and merges with the soul of the actor who will play her. The dance, which takes place before the entire village, is a re-enactment of the battle between Bhadrakali and the Asura Darika.

"**Mind** and **words** are **powerless**
To **encompass your glory** whose extent is
as **immeasurable as** that of **cosmic space**…
The **myriads of galaxies** you **set in motion**
move with precipitous speed… O beautiful One
I extol you as Kali."

SUBRAMANIA BHARATI, *MAHASHAKTI VAAZTHU*

must take place on Amavasya, the 15th day of the dark half of every lunar month. This happens on the darkest night of the month, in a cremation ground, full of skulls and bones of the dead and the charcoal of funeral pyres. American scholar of religious studies Diana L Eck notes that this helps the devotee achieve great power and perfect knowledge, which would, in turn, lead to peace, prosperity, and salvation. In his book, *Hindu Goddesses*,

Kinsley calls her the divinity who claims the terrain of life and death. Difficult as it may be to look death in the face, she signals that the fullness of life includes both the flowering and the finality. Life feeds on death and death is inevitable.

▷ **Goddess Kali's** icon is given its final touches at Kumartuli in Kolkata, West Bengal, ahead of Diwali.

The travelling impersonator
A Bahurupi (right), dressed as the goddess Kali, travels in a train in Kolkata, West Bengal. Often described as folk cosplayers, Bahurupis, or the one with many forms, are traditional storytellers and performance artistes who dress as different mythological characters or gods. They travel across villages and towns to perform in exchange for food and money. Today a dying art form, this tradition has been around for centuries in West Bengal.

In Kali's name

There is an inextricable link between the goddess Kali and the ruthless Thuggees or bandits who often find mention in records from the 1800s. It is a relationship bound in blood and violence.

The persistence of the leitmotif of Kali as being linked with blood, death, and danger gets corroborated in her rather tarnished association with the infamous Thugs or Thuggees, a band of supposed ruthless bandits who terrorized parts of Central India during the 19th century.

One of the earliest references to the Kali–Thug connection during this time comes up in the Superintendent of Thug Police Captain WH Sleeman's 1839 tome, *The Thugs or Phansigars of India*. In an interview, Sahib, a Thug, tells the officer, "She influences our fates in this world; and what she orders in this world, we believe that God will not punish in the next." The reference here is to Kali, also known as Bhowanee, their titular deity. According to records from British officials, the Thuggees, in disguise, befriended unsuspecting travellers and gained their trust before murdering and robbing them. Women, hermits, craftspeople, lepers, or those with disabilities were spared. They used a *rumal*, or knotted handkerchief, to strangle their victims. It is perhaps why they also got the epithet Phansigars, *phansi* meaning noose.

Sleeman noted that the Thuggees would begin their "expedition" by sacrificing a sheep, sometimes a human, before an icon of Kali. They would lay out the tools of their trade, such as the noose and pickaxe along with offerings, such as flowers and sweets. After the prayers, they would wait for a sign that Kali was happy with their plan. Only then would they set off in search of their next victim.

The Kali connection

The Thuggees trace their origin to Kali's battle with the demon Raktabeeja (See pp 132–33). Their mythology, as recounted in Sleeman's

△ **Celebrating the goddess**
A hand-coloured woodcut illustration from the 19th century titled "Kaleepoojah or Feast of the Thugs"

△ **Representations of a clan**
A photograph of a group of supposed Thuggees, dated 1865

Ramaseeana or A Vocabulary of the Peculiar Language Used by the Thugs, is a little different from the one told in the *Devi Mahatmya.*

In it, Kali, tired of drinking so much blood, creates two men from the sweat of her arms. She hands them knotted handkerchiefs and orders them to kill the Asuras by strangling them. Not a drop of blood must fall on the ground, she tells them. After the slaughter, the men return the handkerchiefs, but Kali tells them to use it to earn their living. They must strangle people the way they strangled the Asuras and use the loot to survive. She tells them that as long as they followed her rules, no harm would come to them.

Incidentally, Shiva, the destroyer, is also known as Vankeshavara, or the god of the vagabonds. This epithet led him to be also known as the deity of the bandits. Kali being the spouse of Shiva also shared the devotion of such marginalized people.

Historicity

The Thuggees and their relationship with Kali became an integral part of India's 19th-century cultural history as recorded by British officers. The stories of this fascinating cult and its bloodthirsty goddess have since made their way into popular fiction and cinema, even stereotyping an entire culture and its practices.

> "For **terror** is thy **name**, **Death** is thy **breath** And every shaking step **Destroys a world for e'er.**"

SWAMI VIVEKANANDA

Many scholars question this and wonder if the Thuggees were but an invention of the colonial regime, or a reflection of that regime's inability to understand a different culture and its traditions.

Scholars have also discussed several early accounts of a group, much like the Thuggees, and their goddess, some dated as early as 7th century. Among them is Buddhist traveller Hiuen Tsang's reference to an encounter with a similar group and his narrow escape, as he almost became a sacrifice to their goddess. Ziauddin Barani, a medieval historian writing in the 12th century, recounts a mass arrest of such a group as well.

Other scholars suggest that Thuggees could have been Hindu and Muslim soldiers raiding, robbing, and killing travellers for resources to fight the colonial powers. Kali was merely their, or their region's patron goddess.

△ **Rituals of propitiation**
A 19th-century gouache painting of "Cally poojah", or slaughter in Kali's name

△ **A sacrifice for her**
An engraving from 1888 depicting a supposed group of Thuggees conducting a human sacrifice

△ **At Her feet**
An illustration of devotees paying their respects to the goddess Kali

Weaponry

Hindu goddesses have been time and again called upon to defeat evil and protect the innocent. Though invincible, these deities wield an arsenal of weapons that contain immense power, some are even capable to end the world.

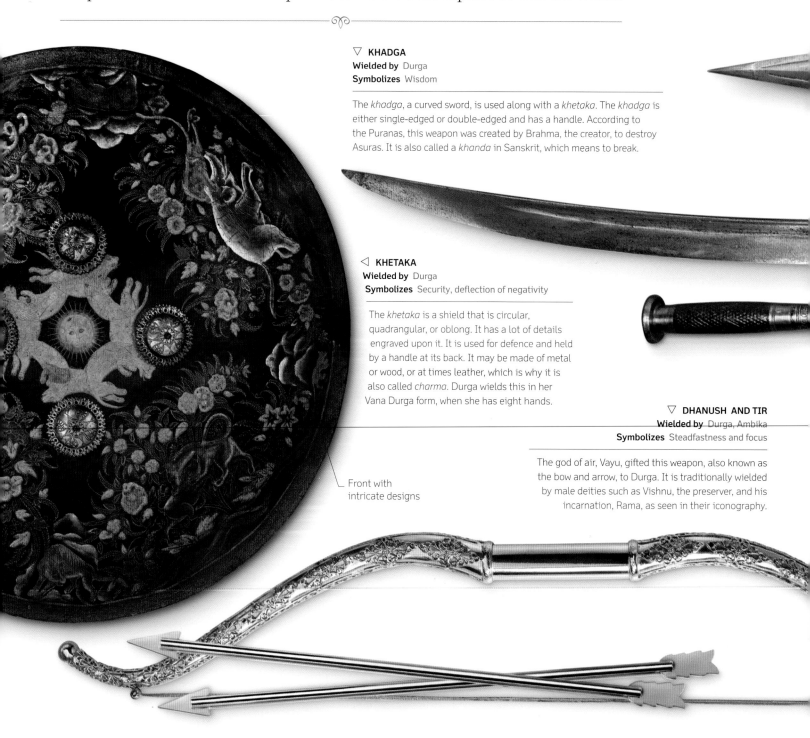

▽ **KHADGA**
Wielded by Durga
Symbolizes Wisdom

The *khadga*, a curved sword, is used along with a *khetaka*. The *khadga* is either single-edged or double-edged and has a handle. According to the Puranas, this weapon was created by Brahma, the creator, to destroy Asuras. It is also called a *khanda* in Sanskrit, which means to break.

◁ **KHETAKA**
Wielded by Durga
Symbolizes Security, deflection of negativity

The *khetaka* is a shield that is circular, quadrangular, or oblong. It has a lot of details engraved upon it. It is used for defence and held by a handle at its back. It may be made of metal or wood, or at times leather, which is why it is also called *charma*. Durga wields this in her Vana Durga form, when she has eight hands.

Front with intricate designs

▽ **DHANUSH AND TIR**
Wielded by Durga, Ambika
Symbolizes Steadfastness and focus

The god of air, Vayu, gifted this weapon, also known as the bow and arrow, to Durga. It is traditionally wielded by male deities such as Vishnu, the preserver, and his incarnation, Rama, as seen in their iconography.

△ ANKUSHA
Wielded by Ambika, Durga
Symbolizes Spiritual practice

The *ankusha*, or an elephant goad, is a weapon with a sharp hook made of metal attached to a short or long wooden stick. When paired with a noose, the two become tools of subjugation.

▽ SHAKTI
Wielded by Durga
Symbolizes Female energy

The *shakti* is a sharp-pointed metal spear with a long wooden handle. The handle is often studded with colourful jewels.

Curved blade ensures decapitation in a single stroke

△ RAM-DAO
Wielded by Kali
Symbolizes Sacrifice

Kali's iconography often depicts her wielding this weapon, which she uses to decapitate her enemies. Once used as a sacrificial sword, the carved eye represents Shakti watching over her devotees and their sacrificial offerings.

▷ TRISUL
Wielded by Durga, Kali
Symbolizes Trinities

Considered one of the most powerful weapons, the trisul, or trident, it is said, can nullify any supernatural weapon. Shiva, the destroyer, gifted this weapon to Durga before she went into battle with the Asura Mahisha. It represents the trinities of life – creation, maintenance, and destruction, the past, present, and future, and the mind, body, and soul.

▷ GADA
Wielded by Ambika, Durga
Symbolizes Sovereignty and cosmic order

The *gada*, or mace, has a rounded top and tapering end and is meant for close-range fighting. Though made partly or wholly of iron, some are made with gold or have gold ornamentation.

Ravi Varma

Untamed fury

Indian artist Raja Ravi Varma's rendition of Kali trampling on Shiva

Kali's form strikes awe and fear. To see her, to get her blessed sight, that is *darshana*, is to get stunned. She is firmly ensconced as Shiva's consort, and both divinities embody wildness, complementing each other. In all her representations with Shiva, she is never meek or docile. Unlike Parvati, who injects calmness in Shiva, Kali stirs up his destructive behaviour. Ironically, it is Shiva who attempts to tame her. This image is an example of that dynamic between them.

1. Kali's dark blue skin tone emphasizes her association with Shiva who is often portrayed in blue. One legend tells of an incident when the god swallowed *halahal* or *kalakuta*, or poison, that turned him blue. This association is reiterated through the *chandra kala*, or crescent moon, on Kali's crown, which is a prominent symbol in Shiva's image as well. The crescent moon could also indicate Kali's association with the passage of time.

2. She brandishes a *khadga*, or scimitar, stained with the blood of the Asura Daruka, in one of the left hands. In one of the right hands, she holds the Asura's freshly decapitated head. The other right hand holds a plate to collect the blood dripping from the Asura's head, so that she can devour it.

3. Her consort Shiva is shown lying down like a corpse on the ground. He adopted this strategy to calm Kali down as she wreaked havoc on the battlefield.

4. The lolling, protruding tongue signifies her shock, perhaps also embarrassment, at stepping on her husband. Its red colour shows that it is stained with blood, indicating how she laps up blood of various Asuras.

5. She is nude, called *digambari*, meaning sky clad. She wears a skirt or girdle of dismembered arms around her waist. It is a reminder of her association with death and destruction. It is believed to be a later addition by artists who probably found Kali's nakedness too discomfiting. Nationalists saw it as the hands of those who laid down their lives for the liberation of the motherland.

6. A garland of decapitated heads or *munda mala* adorns her neck. This is invariably made of heads of mustachioed men, who were probably sacrificed to her. It never constitutes females as they create life and killing one would tantamount to blocking the cycle of life. Sometimes, the heads are 51 in number, just like the 51 letters of the Devanagari script. Each represents a form of energy or a form of Kali.

7. Her hair is unbound, wild, and disheveled, called *jvalakeshi* or *jvalitashikha*, meaning flaming hair. It signifies her untrammelled freedom and her liberation from societal norms. That's why she is also called *muktakeshi*, meaning one with free-flowing hair.

Matrikas

The wild mothers

> "… great asuras **perished**… **pierced** through by the spear of **Kaumari**… **repulsed** by (sprinkling of) the water purified by the **incantation of Brahmani**… **powdered** on the ground by the **blows** from the snout of **Varahi**."
>
> VERSES 38–39, CHAPTER NINE, *DEVI MAHATMYA*

Matrikas, meaning mothers, are an early assemblage of goddesses depicted and worshipped together. Sometimes, the term Matrigana, meaning a band of mothers, is also used.

This inclination to venerate goddesses collectively is a feature within Hinduism. It is significant that grouping is prevalent among female divinities and not among the male ones. Other goddess clusters include Ashtalakshmi, Navadurga (See pp 92–93), Dasamahavidyas (See pp 270–71), Nityakala Devis, and Chaunsatha Yoginis (See pp 316–323). The Matrikas, however, are the oldest of them.

References in text

Scholars have found the earliest references to the Matrikas, also called Matas or Matris, in the epic *Mahabharata*, in a section dated about 1st century CE. While their number is not specified, the passages seem to show that there were many, notes American scholar of religious studies David Kinsley. The references made to them in the epic seems to signify their inauspicious and dangerous qualities. In one instance, Indra, god of the heavens, sends them to kill Karttikeya, the god of war, when he is born. However, their maternal instincts emerge when they see the child and they request him to adopt them as his mothers, and come to be known as Krittikas.

Their physical description, such as long nails, protruding lips, and sharp or large teeth, only drives home their menacing facets, notes Kinsley. He adds that they dwell in burning grounds, trees, crossroads, caves, and mountains. They speak different languages and this could indicate that they were from different regions, at first, associated with non-Brahmanical traditions prevalent in the peripheral areas. They may have also represented village goddesses associated with disease. Indian scholar of Tantra NN Bhattacharyya suggests that they came from a Tantric complex.

By the early medieval period, the names and numbers of the Matrikas become standardized. Besides the Puranas, they are mentioned in the Tantras. Major mutations in their inherent character also take place. Among these are their associations with the male gods and their more protective role. They are also considered emanations of the great Devi.

»

IN TODAY'S TIMES

IN MODERN LITERATURE

Author Anuja Chandramouli gives the Krittikas or the Matrikas a feminist twist in her novel titled *Kartikeya: The Destroyer's Son*. In one version of the myth, the Krittikas are accused of infidelity by seven sages and cursed for giving birth to illegitimate children. However in Chandramouli's retelling, they stand their ground and fight for their rights.

The Ashtamatrikas
This late 18th-century painting in opaque watercolour with gold on paper is from Bikaner, Rajasthan. It depicts the Matrikas as the Ashtamatrikas, or eight mothers. It is significant that each of them displays the physical characteristics of the male god from whom they emerged.

The *Devi Mahatmya* references this in the episode where Durga, as she grapples with the Asura Raktabeeja, calls upon the Saptamatrikas, or seven mothers, to assist her (See pp 132–33). They then emanate from the Devi to perform protective functions on her behalf. They also appear in the third episode (See pp 150–51) of the text when they help kill Shumbha and Nishumbha. After killing the two Asuras and drunk on their blood, they dance with wild abandon.

The 11th canto of the *Devi Mahatmya* contains detailed descriptions of the Matrikas. Brahmani rides a heavenly chariot yoked with swans and Maheshvari carries the trident and the serpent, and rides a bull. Kaumari, who is sinless, has a peacock by her side and wields a large spear, while Vaishnavi holds the great weapons, such as conch, discus, club, and bow.

The Shaktis

The Matrikas are seen as the Shaktis of male gods with similar names. For example, Brahmi or Brahmani has an association with Brahma, the creator, Maheshvari with Maheshvara, another name for Shiva, the destroyer, and Vaishnavi with Vishnu, the preserver. They have the same forms, weapons, and vehicles as their male counterparts. Since the Devi manifested from the combined energies of the gods, this theory of Saptamatrikas origin is not surprising. The weapons they gave the Devi to defeat Asuras were not copies, but empowered with the goddess's force – Shakti. So the created is also the creator.

In another myth, the Saptamatrikas come to Shiva's aid in his battle with Andhaka, the ferocious Asura. As with Raktabeeja, the Asura simply duplicated himself with every drop of blood. Seeing Shiva faced with thousands of Andhakas, the male gods sent the Saptamatrikas to stop the blood from falling.

Indian author and monk Swami Harshananda in his study has noted that the followers of *Tantrashastra* have given an esoteric interpretation to the Matrikas. According to him, Brahmi represents the *nada*, or the energy in "which even the first throb has not appeared". This is known as "the unmanifest sound" or the "the origin of all creation".

△ **Lotus mandala** with eight mother goddesses

"**Worship** of the Matrikas is aimed at... **keeping** them **away**. To **make much** of one's children might **attract** the Matrikas' **attention** and **risk** incurring their **dread afflictions**."

DAVID KINSLEY, *HINDU GODDESSES: VISIONS OF THE DIVINE FEMININE IN THE HINDU RELIGIOUS TRADITION* (1988)

The power of Vaishnavi gives the universe its definite space, the symmetry, beauty, organization, and order. Maheshvari signifies the power that provides individuality to the created beings. She lives in the hearts of all and makes them play. Kaumari is described as "the ever-youthful deity" by Harshananda, and denotes the "force of aspiration of the evolving soul". Guru Guha is one of her names, guru meaning teacher and *guha* meaning cave.

Varahi "is the all-consuming power of assimilation and enjoyment". She is the one because of whom living beings have "food and physical enjoyments". Aindri signifies "the terrible power that destroys all that is opposed to the cosmic law". Finally, Harshananda explains that "Chamunda is the force of concentrated awareness, the power of spiritual awakening in the heart that devours the ceaseless activity of the mature mind."

Iconography and purpose

The Matrikas are depicted in human form mounted on the vahana of their male counterpart. Narasimhi and Varahi have the faces of a lion and a boar. Grouped with Ganesha, the son of Parvati and Virabhadra, a fierce form of Shiva, on each side, they are seen on panels in temples dedicated to Shiva. They also have shrines built only for them. In fact, their arrangement depends on what type of an "effect is desired", as per Harshananda. In case the safety of a village is a concern, then Brahmi is in the centre. In case an increase in population is the requirement, then Chamunda is depicted as standing on a corpse. Sometimes the Matrikas are shown sitting upon lotus thrones as well. Their attendants and mounts accompany them.

Association with children

There are several references that link Matrikas with children. Initially, their relationship was not maternal. Instead they were fierce goddesses who attacked children. Scholars note that this was probably attributed to the superstition that women who died either without a child or while birthing become angry spirits intent on attacking other people's children.

They later took on the role of protectors and this is reflected in their iconography as well, where they are shown with children either standing nearby or on their laps. Early sculptures show a variety of women with either animal or bird heads, holding or surrounded by children.

▽ **This 9th-century sculpture** in red sandstone from Madhya Pradesh depicts the seven Matrikas. Ganesha, the god with the elephant head, is seen on the extreme right.

Saptamatrika

The fierce and destructive Matrikas, or mother goddesses, have a varied origin story, depending on the text being studied. In the *Devi Mahatmya*, however, they are the feminine counterparts of the male gods and personify their Shakti or energy.

Trident

◁ MAHESHVARI

Male counterpart Maheshvara, an epithet of Shiva
Symbolizes Power that gives individuality to beings

Like Shiva, the destroyer, Maheshvari can be seen seated on Nandi, her vahana. She has four arms and carries a trisul, or trident, *akshamala*, or a string of prayer beads, and *damaru*, or pellet drum. On her head, she wears the *jata makuta*, or hair twisted into the shape of a crown. She also has the *trinetra*, or the third eye, on her forehead.

Nandi, the bull

△ AINDRI

Male counterpart Indra, god of the heavens
Symbolizes Power that destroys the cosmic law

Aindri, or Indrani, has four arms and three eyes. Some texts describe her as the one with 1,000 eyes. She holds the vajra, which is the thunderbolt of Indra, and lives in the Kalpavriksha, or the wish-fulfilling tree. Her vahana is a white elephant similar to the one Indra rides.

Brass nut cutter from Tamil Nadu, 18–19th century

▷ KAUMARI

Male counterpart Kumara or Karttikeya, god of war
Symbolizes Valour and courage

With the peacock as her vahana, the goddess Kaumari is often depicted with four hands, wielding weapons such as spear, axe, and bow. In some of her iconography, she is shown with six heads, just like her consort Karttikeya.

▷ **BRAHMI**
Male counterpart Brahma
Symbolizes Symmetry, beauty, organization, and order in the universe

Like Brahma, the creator, she has four heads, and holds a *kamandalu*, or a water pot, and a rosary in her hands. Also known as Brahmani, her mount is a white swan, though she is usually seen seated on a lotus.

Basket-shaped crown

◁ **VARAHI**
Male counterpart Varaha, a form of Vishnu
Symbolizes Power of assimilation

With the face of a boar and a skin tone similar to a storm cloud, Varahi is the Shakti of Varaha, the third and boar avatar of Vishnu, the preserver. She wears the *karanda mukuta*, or a basket-shaped crown, and rides an elephant.

△ **CHAMUNDA**
Male counterpart Shiva
Symbolizes Spiritual awakening

The most ferocious of all the Saptamatrikas, Chamunda is often portrayed totally emaciated with prominent ribs, sunken belly, drooping breasts, socket eyes, protruding fangs, and skulls in her matted hair. In this representation, she also has a scorpion, a symbol of death and disease, sitting like an ornament near her navel.

▷ **VAISHNAVI**
Male counterpart Vishnu
Symbolizes Protection and maintenance

Just like her consort Vishnu, Vaishnavi can be seen seated on Garuda, the king of birds. Some of her typical iconography shows her holding a *chakra*, or disc, which is the preferred weapon of Vishnu, and a *shankha*, or conch, which is indicative of Vishnu's oceanic connections.

Unbound wrath

This painting from the middle of the 19th century shows scenes from the Devi's encounter with Shumbha and Nishumbha. (Clockwise from the top left) The Devi fights the two Asuras, Kali (in black) strikes the ground, and the Devi blows the conch, as eight-armed Shumbha fights from his chariot.

Shumbha and Nishumbha's end

The Devi's battle with Asura brothers Shumbha and Nishumbha marks the end of the great battle as well as the mythological portions of the *Devi Mahatmya*. It also alludes to the singular identity of the Goddess, who is the world herself.

Raktabeeja and his army of Asuras lay dead, slaughtered at the hands of the Devi (See pp 132–33). When the Asura brothers Shumbha and Nishumbha heard the news, they rushed to the battlefield where they faced Chandika, the Devi.

Like two dark thunderclouds, they first attacked her with a tempestuous shower of arrows. Then Nishumbha attacked the lion, her vahana, with a sharp sword. She sliced some of their weapons with her discus and smote the others.

Nishumbha, enraged, threw a spear at her, but her punch turned it to dust. He brandished his club and she smote it with her trident. Then she cut Nishumbha to the ground with her battle axe.

Incensed, Shumbha stood tall on his chariot and faced the Devi. In response, she blew her conch, pulled at the bowstring with a thundering twang, and rang her bell. The sound destroyed the strength of the Asuras and their army. She then smote Shumbha with her trident, who fainted.

Nishumbha regained consciousness and attacked Kali and the lion with his bow and arrow, but Chandika pierced his heart with her spear. As he fell, another person of great strength emerged from him. "Stop," he exclaimed. But, the Devi laughed and struck him with her sword.

Her lion devoured the Asuras, while Kali and Shivaduti devoured the others. Asuras drowned in the water that Brahmani had purified. Maheshvari killed them with her trident, Aindri with her thunderbolt, and Vaishnavi with her discus. Varahi powdered the others to the ground with her snout.

Shumbha regained consciousness and saw his dead brother. He turned to the goddess and taunted, "You are merely relying on others to win this battle." She laughed and replied, "I am the only one who exists in this world." As she spoke, all the other goddesses merged into her body, until Chandika stood there alone.

The Devas and heavenly sages watched in awe as they battled each other. He leapt into the sky and she grabbed him and threw him to the ground. He jumped up to attack her, but the goddess was quicker. She leapt up and drove a spear into his chest, killing him instantly.

The Devi's incarnations

There are more than 200 epithets for the Goddess in the *Devi Mahatmya*. Many of them have been delightfully delineated and at once bring to mind the characteristics and the raison d'etre that have provided Her the nomenclature.

△ **These pair of wooden covers** of a *Devi Mahatmya* manuscript, created in the 18th century in Nepal, show the goddess Durga killing the Asura Mahisha.

In the last 14 verses of the 11th chapter of the *Devi Mahatmya*, the Goddess declares Her future manifestations in different ages and one comes across more of Her names – Raktadantika, Shatakshi, Shakambhari, Durga, Bhimadevi, and Bhramari. Likewise, the text also lays out names of the future Asuras.

In times to come

In a reassuring statement, evocative of the *Bhagavada Gita*, which is a part of the epic *Mahabharata*, the Goddess announces that She will come forth time after time to extinguish all evil. The Goddess, however, does not just proclaim that She will return to purge the Earth of foes. She also asserts, in a futuristic way, how and when She will appear and the form She will take.

She will appear because of the treachery of Asuras but also present Herself in case of natural disasters – droughts, floods, and forest conflagrations. Devotees can also expect Her presence in times of attacks by virulent snakes and even in areas where foes and hosts of robbers exist.

Devi's monologue

After the Devi slays the great Asura Shumbha (See pp 150–51), Indra, the god of the heavens, and other deities led by Agni, the god of fire, with their objective fulfilled and their cheerful faces illuminating the quarters, praise the Goddess. They laud Her for removing the sufferings of Her supplicants. They call Her the ruler of the moving and the unmoving, the power of Vishnu, the preserver, and the primeval maya. They address Her gracious form, in which She becomes the final cause of emancipation in the world. They laud Her as the embodiment of all beings and in many other ways. The Devi begins Her monologue on hearing this praise to Her name.

Her future forms

She says She will be called Raktadantika, or red toothed, when She will devour the fierce and great Asuras descended from Viprachitti, the king of Danavas. In this encounter, Her teeth shall become red like the flower of the pomegranate. Therefore, when Devas in

heaven and people on the Earth praise Her, they shall always talk of Her as the one with red teeth.

When there will be no rain continuously for a period of 100 years, the sages will appease Her and She will be born on a drought-ridden Earth. She will then be exalted as Shatakshi, or the one with 100 eyes.

As the goddess Shakambhari, the Devi says, She will support the entire world with life-nourishing vegetables, which She will beget from Her own body. Her body will be the Earth, the source of plant life, and She will be a vital force concerned with the growth of crops – the nourishing sap of all beings. She will then be revered on the Earth as Shakambhari, or the provider of fruits and vegetables.

THE DEATH OF ARUNA

The Asura Aruna once performed a difficult penance to please Brahma, the creator. The god granted him a boon that no two- or four-legged creature woud be able to kill him. Armed with the boon of immortality, Aruna inflicted utter destruction upon the gods, who sought refuge in Brahma, Vishnu, the preserver, and Shiva, the destroyer. They suggested that the Devas seek help from the supreme Goddess. In Her presence, they heartily sang Her praises. Pleased with their ardour, the Goddess appeared as Bhramari. She went to Aruna's kingdom and summoned him for a fight. She then unleashed an army of bees, which stung the Asura and brought about his end. Therefore, the Asura was killed not by any two or four-legged creatures, but by the six-legged bees.

> "This slaughter that you, O Devi, **multiplying your own form into many**, have now **wrought on the great asuras** who hate righteousness, O Ambika, which other (goddess) can do that work?"

VERSE 30, CHAPTER 11, *DEVI MAHATMYA*

When She slays the great Asura Durgama, She will have the famed name of Durgadevi. Again, taking Her fierce form on the great mountain Himalaya, She will destroy the Rakshasas to safeguard the sages. All the sages will then eulogize Her and She will have the renowned appellation of Bhimadevi, or the one who is formidable.

When the Asura Aruna wreaks mayhem across the three worlds, the Goddess will take on a form consisting of a large number of bees. She will then sting him for the good of the people and the world. She will be lauded as Bhramari, or the one with the sound of the bees (See box).

Thus, whenever trouble arises due to the advent of Danavas, Rakshasas, and Asuras, the Goddess shall incarnate Herself and destroy the foes to restore cosmic order.

To defeat obstacles
A group of women gathers along the banks of River Burigonga near Dhaka, Bangladesh, to break their fast as a part of the Bipodtarini Vrata. They hold *thalis*, or plates, decorated with lamps. Women worship the goddess Bipodtarini, a manifestation of Durga, during times of crises and to remove obstacles. She is popular in Bangladesh and the Indian states of Assam, West Bengal, and Odisha.

Emergence of the Devi Bhagavatam

The inspirational seed of the *Devi Bhagavata Purana* was clearly the *Devi Mahatmya*. But, it is in the former that one encounters a grander, more magnificent theological vision of the Goddess.

One of the most important works in Shaktism, besides the *Devi Mahatmya* (See pp 70–75), is the Sanskrit text, the *Devi Bhagavata Purana*. It celebrates the divine feminine as the primary divinity, the origin of all existence, the preserver and the destroyer of everything, and the one who empowers spiritual liberation.

The title, composed of two words, means a devotee of the blessed Devi, and is also referred to as the *Devi Bhagavatam* or the *Srimada Devi Bhagavatam*. Just like the Vedas, the other Puranas, and the epic *Mahabharata* (See pp 18–19), its composition is attributed to the sage Veda Vyasa. Some scholars suggest that it may have been composed as early as the 6th century, while others date it between the 9th and the 14th centuries. The text has 318 chapters spread across 12 *skandhas*, or books. While it is not the earliest text that celebrates the divine feminine, the *Devi Bhagavatam* is definitely one of the first to forcefully assert the ultimate supremacy of the Goddess.

Context for composition

Scholar of religious studies C Mackenzie Brown in *The Triumph of the Goddess: The Canonical Models and Theological Visions of the Devi-Bhagavata Purana*

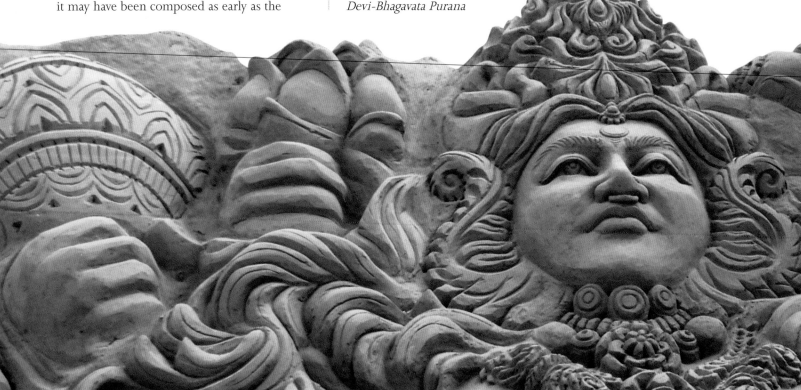

ASSIMILATION IN THE PURANAS

The Puranas were always involved in a process of remodelling and recasting. Indian scholar of Puranic literature RC Hazra points to an episode in the *Devi Bhagavata Purana* where the king Sudarshana is said to have consecrated an icon of the Goddess through Vedic Brahmans. During this ritual, Vedic hymns were chanted along with the performance of Homa, or fire ritual. At the same time, although Tantric elements, such as animal sacrifice, worship of kumaris, or virgins, and music and dancing were introduced, they were made optional. This system of worship reflects that in the Puranas, Tantric deities and rites were often retained but refined and mixed judiciously with Vedic rites and customs thereby giving birth to a syncretic whole.

notes that the Shakta movement gained momentum with the appearance of the *Devi Mahatmya*. However, over time, it was pulled into a dynamic race amongst the various theistic schools, particularly the Vaishnavas. Meanwhile, Brown writes, the Brahmanical social landscape was riddled with "growing threats to its sense of proper social order both from within, through internal corruption" as well as external forces such as Muslim invasions. The resultant societal anarchy was perceived as mirroring the decaying of the cosmic order. Therefore, it was through the composition of the *Devi Bhagavata Purana*

that the Goddess was revealed as succeeding over diabolic forces that endangered the harmony in the cosmos.

Absorption into the mainstream

From the time of its composition, in order to give it authenticity and legitimacy in the Brahmanical traditions, there were attempts to integrate the *Devi Bhagavata Purana* into the list of *maha*, or great, Puranas. This is most evident in the process of associating the Devi with cosmology. She is inserted into the Puranic scheme by recounting how She destroys evil forces in every cosmic cycle.

As is common with most later texts, the *Devi Bhagavata Purana* also tries to draw legitimacy by recognizing the authority of and tracing an association with the Vedic literature. Therefore, the Goddess is conceptualized as the source of the Vedas and the very core of the Gayatri Mantra – today believed to be one of the most important mantras in the Vedas.

The text, perhaps to widen its popularity, also upholds the importance of Tantra, but asserts that Tantric ideals should be seamlessly juxtaposed with the Vedic ones (See box).

At the same time, the composition of the *Devi Bhagavata Purana* is tantamount to a re-envisioning process, in which She undergoes a transformation, from a martial and erotic goddess into a universal mother with infinite compassion.

"The Goddess… becomes **less of a warrior goddess**, and more a **nurturer** and **comforter** of her devotees, and a **teacher of wisdom**."

C MACKENZIE BROWN, *THE DEVI GITA: THE SONG OF THE GODDESS: A TRANSLATION, ANNOTATION, AND COMMENTARY* (1998)

Philosophy of the Devi Bhagavatam

The *Devi Bhagavata Purana* exhilarates in the apotheosis of the Goddess. Apart from delving into mythology, this treatise presents itself as a significant theological underpinning in the Goddess tradition.

Even though Mahadevi, or the Great Goddess (See pp 60–61), was first formulated in the *Devi Mahatmya*, the *Devi Bhagavata Purana* is the first instance where one encounters her complete and composite theology.

Central idea

The underlying philosophy of the text is Advaita Vedanta (See box). The ideas are, however, reformulated and centred around the Goddess, who not only encapsulates Brahman and Atman and their interconnected oneness, but She is also the ever changing empirical reality, that is maya.

The central theme of the *Devi Bhagavata Purana* is the over arching reality of the Mahadevi (See pp 160–61) and it attempts to establish Her sectarian supremacy. She is conceived as *Adya*, or primordial, Shakti – the highest principle in the universe. Mahadevi is said to reside in Brahma,

---

ADVAITA VEDANTA

First expressed in the Upanishads and later popularized by different philosophers, including Adi Shankaracharya in the 8th century and Vivekananda in the 19th century, the concept of Advaita Vedanta advocates that there is only one eternal and unchanging reality, that is Brahman. This school of thought also emphasizes that Atman, or individual soul, is identical to Brahman. Essentially, it stresses on the synthesis of Brahman and Atman.

> "Seeing that **beautiful form**, all **distress was removed**. With all **Consciousness** filled with Peace, the **Gods bowed down to Her** with great delight."

VERSE 56, CHAPTER 5, *DEVI GITA*, TRANSLATED BY SWAMI SATYANANDA SARASWATI

the creator, as the creative principle, in Vishnu, the preserver, as the sustaining principle, and in Shiva, the destroyer, as the destructive principle. American scholar of religious studies John Stratton Hawley states that the *Devi Bhagavata Purana* delineates the "high theology" of the Goddess.

Change in orientation

The text also describes in new ways the manifold nature of the Goddess. It demonstrates the superiority of the Devi over competing masculine theologies. There is almost an insouciance as it goes about unseating authoritative male centred and male oriented theologies. For example, the Prakriti Kanda of the *Brahmavaivarta Purana* has several verses eulogizing Vishnu in his manifold incarnations. Interestingly, the same kind of description reappears in the Book 9 of the *Devi Bhagavata Purana*. Strategically, the nomenclature related to Vishnu is replaced with epithets for Devi.

Scholar of religious studies C Mackenzie Brown in his introduction to *The Devi Gita: The Song of the Goddess: A Translation, Annotation, and Commentary* says, "The *Devi-Bhagavata* was thus, in part, a response to the growing popularity of the devotional movements centred on the great male gods, and to the increasing prominence of the great Puranas extolling Vishnu or Shiva… The *Devi-Bhagavata* is modelled in many ways on the *Bhagavata*, and substitutes itself in place of the Vaishnava Purana in the traditional list of eighteen Maha-Puranas. It takes over many

motifs from the *Bhagavata*, but reinterprets them in such a way as to belittle Vishnu and to glorify the Goddess."

Hierarchy in the feminine pantheon

As with most Shakta texts, the recurring theme in the *Devi Bhagavata Purana* is also that the Goddess multiplies in different forms as and when the need arises. Indian scholar of Tantra NN Bhattacharyya in *History of the Tantric Religion: A Historical, Ritualistic, and Philosophical Study* writes, "In every creation of the universe, it is said, the Mula-Prakriti assumes the different gradations of *ansharupini*, *kalarupini*, and *kalamsharupini*, or manifest herself in parts, smaller parts, and further subdivisions. In the first grade, she is represented by Durga, Lakshmi, Sarasvati, Savitri and Radha; in the second by Ganga, Tulasi, Manasa, Shashthi, Mangalachandika and Kali; and in the third by the Grama-devatas or Village Mothers and by womenfolk in general."

Bhattacharyya points out that even women on the Earth are appearances of Her and hence should also be treated reverentially. Whoever insults them invites the fury of the Goddess.

The feminine theme also appears in a myth in the *Devi Bhagavata Purana* in which the mighty male gods, Brahma, Vishnu, and Shiva, are metamorphosed into women prior to being permitted to see the Devi in Her highest form. These traditional stories of sex alteration may be the antecedents of a prevalent practice, where it is customary for the priest to don female clothing while performing priestly functions.

Mahadevi

The Supreme Goddess

> "I alone **existed** in the **beginning**; there was **nothing else** at all… My **true Self** is known as **pure consciousness**, the highest intelligence, the one **supreme Brahman**."
>
> *THE DEVI GITA*, TRANSLATED BY C MACKENZIE BROWN, *THE SONG OF THE GODDESS: A TRANSLATION, ANNOTATION, AND COMMENTARY* (1999)

She first appears as a stream of light, brighter than the sun and the moon, blinding the gods who have sought her presence. When She takes form, she becomes a four-armed, three-eyed Goddess, adorned with jewellery, dressed in red, with flowers in the hair, and the crescent moon on the brow. She is beautiful and gentle, and always keeps a watch over Her children.

This is Bhuvanesvari or the World Mother, as scholar of religious studies C Mackenzie Brown calls her. She is first described in the *Devi Gita*, from the *Devi Bhagavata Purana*, which explores the philosophy of the Great Goddess.

The world of the Goddess

The *Devi Bhagavatapurana* describes in great detail, the Goddess's abode, the Jewelled Island or Manidvipa, nestled in the ocean of nectar. From here, she keeps a watch over her devotees. She sits on a throne made of five corpses and its legs are Brahma, Vishnu, and the two forms of Shiva, Rudra and Isana.

Emergence of a mythology

The idea of "The" Goddess who brings under her wing all the other goddesses is first seen in the *Devi Mahatmya*. The mythology becomes expansive by the time of the *Devi Bhagavata*

Purana. It is here that she becomes, notes scholar of religious studies David Kinsley, the "mother of all, to pervade the three worlds, to be the support of all, to be the life force in all beings… to be the only cause of the universe."

The texts emphasize this cosmic nature and identify her as the ultimate power or shakti. Kinsley writes that here she is described as a "powerful, active, dynamic being who pervades, governs, and protects the universe", much like the three male gods within the Hindu pantheon – Brahma, the creator, Vishnu, the preserver, and Shiva, the destroyer.

 Of course, when the desperate gods propitiate her and seek her assistance, she helps them, her many manifestations ridding the earth of all evil. So, she demonstrates not just her peaceful, motherly side, but also the ferocious, often frightening, form.

Within the texts from the Shakta tradition, She is higher than the other gods. "The world is said to be destroyed when she blinks her eyes and to be recreated when she opens her eyes," writes Kinsley. So, the *Lalitasahasranama* discusses how the 10 forms of Vishnu emerged from her fingernails, while the *Saundaryalahiri* tells of the creation of the universe from a mere speck of dust from the Goddess's body.

IN TODAY'S TIMES

DIFFERENT REPRESENTATIONS

Scholar Kathleen M Erndl in an essay wrote, "Devotees are not usually concerned with a general explanatory model, but rather with the specifics of their experience in a particular context." It is perhaps why devotees would consider the goddess of their choice as the Mahadevi or the Supreme Goddess. So, while She is not worshipped as one goddess, her many manifestations are. It does not matter if she is a popular goddess from the Hindu pantheon or a village or town goddess. Whether it is Vaishno Devi in the North, Kali in the East or Bhagvati in the South, for the devotee, they are all Mahadevi.

The Great Goddess
The 20-armed Mahadevi wields weapons, while standing on a lotus in this watercolour from Bikaner, Rajasthan, dated c. 1725. In this image, she has alternatively been called the dancing goddess. This painting seems to be a significant representation as she was also the protector deity of the Bikaner royalty.

Devi Gita

The *Devi Gita* is a significant philosophical treatise on the Shakta tradition. It gives the worshipper an insightful gaze into the many forms of Devi, and portrays Her as powerful yet compassionate, benign, and beautiful.

The *Devi Gita*, literally "Song of the Goddess", is part of the larger text, the *Devi Bhagavata Purana*. At the same time, it is also an independent text, perhaps, a later interpolation that was composed by the 13th century.

The context for this text can be traced to the 6th century, when, following the rise of several male deities to prominence, a new theistic movement began in which the supreme divinity was envisioned as female. Appearing first as a violent deity in the *Devi Mahatmya* (See pp 70–75), the Goddess gradually evolved into a more benign figure. It is in this beneficent mode that the Goddess appears in the *Devi Gita*.

Many scholars have drawn parallels between the *Devi Gita* and the *Bhagavad Gita*. Indian historian R Mahalakshmi notes that "just as in the *Bhagavad Gita*, Krishna delivers a sermon to his disciple/friend Arjuna, in the *Devi Gita*, the Devi herself presents her song to the king of mountains, Himalaya."

The text is like a manual that instructs the devotee on how to experience Devi's magnificence. It enunciates a doctrine of holistic spirituality. It propounds *bhakti yoga*, or devotion, and puts forth *para bhakti*, or transcendental devotion. In this form of bhakti, the devotee is not concerned with personal benefits, rather, the worship is wholly focused on the Goddess.

Song of the Goddess

The seventh chapter in the *Devi Gita* is preceded by an explanation of devotion and its varieties. Here, Himalaya, the king of mountains, asks the Goddess to list the places and times that are particularly beloved to Her, and which devotees should visit or observe. The Goddess responds by saying that since She is the essence of all things, all places and times are sacred. Even so, She lists some of them.

हिमालय उवाच -

कति स्थानानि देवेशि द्रष्टव्यानि महीतले ।

मुख्यानि च पवित्राणि देवीप्रियतमानि च ॥

Himalaya said: "Best of Goddesses! How many are the primary abodes dear to you, which are sacred and should be seen?"

श्रीदेव्युवाच -

सर्वं दृश्यं मम स्थानं सर्वे काला व्रतात्मकाः ।

उत्सवाः सर्वकालेषु यतोऽहं सर्वरूपिणी ॥

The Goddess said: "Everything which is perceptible is my abode, all times consist of vows, and there are celebrations at all times, because I comprise everything."

तथापि भक्तवात्सल्यात्किञ्चित्किञ्चिदथोच्यते।
शृणुष्वावहितो भूत्वा नगराज वचो मम ॥

"Even so, because of my affection for devotees, I shall now speak of some. King of Mountains, listen to my words with care."

———————————— ⚭ ————————————

कोलापुरं महास्थानं यत्र लक्ष्मीः सदा स्थिता ।
मातुःपुरं द्वितीयं च रेणुकाधिष्ठितं परम् ॥

"Kolapura is the great abode where Lakshmi is always present. The second abode is Matripura, where Renuka presides."

———————————— ⚭ ————————————

तुलजापुरं तृतीयं स्यात्सप्तशृङ्गं तथैव च ।
हिङ्गुलायां महास्थानं ज्वालामुख्यास्तथैव च ॥

"The third is Tuljapura, and then Saptashringa. There is a great abode in Hingula and there is the abode of Jvalamukhi."

विन्ध्याचलनिवासिन्याः स्थानं सर्वोत्तमोत्तमम् ।
अन्नपूर्णामहास्थानं काञ्चीपुरमनुत्तमम् ॥

"The abode of the one who lives in Vindhyachal is the very
best of the best. There is the great abode of Annapurna,
and Kanchipura, which is unsurpassable."

नीलांबायाः परं स्थानं नीलपर्वतमस्तके ।
जांबूनदेश्वरीस्थानं तथा श्रीनगरं शुभम् ॥

"There is the great abode of Nilamba on the top of the Nila mountain,
the abode of the Jambunadeshvari, and the auspicious Shrinagara."

गुह्यकाल्या महास्थानं नेपाले यत्प्रतिष्ठितम् ।
मीनाक्ष्याः परमं स्थानं यच्च प्रोक्तं चिदंबरे ॥

"There is the great abode of Guhyakali, which is established in Nepal, and
the best abode of Meenakshi, which is said to be in Chidambaram."

वैद्यनाथे तु बगलास्थानं सर्वोत्तमं मतम् ।
श्रीमच्छ्रीभुवनेश्वर्या मणिद्वीपं मम स्मृतम् ॥

"The abode of Bagala in Vaidyanatha is agreed to be the best of all. My abode – the abode of the glorious Bhuvaneshvari (goddess of the world) – is remembered to be the auspicious Jewel Island."

श्रीमत्रिपुरभैरव्याः कामाख्यायोनिमण्डलम् ।
भूमण्डले क्षेत्ररत्नं महामायाधिवासितम् ॥

"The genital organ of the glorious Tripura-bhairavi in Kamakhya is a jewel of abodes on the Earth, and is inhabited by Mahamaya."

नातः परतरं स्थानं क्वचिदस्ति धरातले ।
प्रतिमासं भवेद्देवी यत्र साक्षाद्रजस्वला ॥

"There is no place greater than this on the Earth, where the Goddess Herself resides each month during menstruation."

Adorned with flowers
The lotus is most often associated with Lakshmi. Here, the goddess she is represented as a silver idol in a sea of lotus petals.

Lakshmi

Goddess of wealth and fortune

△ **A c. 18–19th century** *deepa*, or a votive lamp in bronze from Chingleput district in Tamil Nadu, depicting Lakshmi

> "… O Daughter of the **Ocean of Milk**. … **O Support** of the Three Worlds. **Salutations** to you of the **propitious glance**. Protect me, for I come **seeking refuge**."

A PURANIC SONG DEVOTED TO LAKSHMI, CONSTANTINA RHODES, *INVOKING LAKSHMI* (2010)

Her radiant visage reflects grandeur, richness, splendour, and lustre. She wears a brightly coloured sari and gold jewellery adorns her. Coins flow from her palms as she stands or sits on a full-blown lotus, lustrated by a pair of elephants. This is the goddess Lakshmi who bears gifts of affluence for one and all.

Worshipping Lakshmi

Today, it is not uncommon to see a small image of Lakshmi in silver, a photograph, or calendar grace millions of homes, shops, and offices. By placing her in a setting, it is automatically understood that she will bless the surroundings. Every morning, on entering the establishment, the devotee initiates direct communication with her by lighting incense sticks and an oil lamp and by uttering a short invocation to Lakshmi.

The goddess requires just this brief obeisance, for she does not insist on onerous fasts, nor does she have wrath that needs appeasing. She does not have the mythological, triumphant force of Durga (See pp 80–83) or the visually compelling aura of Kali (See pp 126–29). Unlike Sarasvati (See pp 186–89), she does not represent a human quality of intelligence or a propensity towards music.

Singled out by devotees, Lakshmi's importance lies in the fact that she represents something that almost everyone craves for but may not always have – wealth.

The notion of Lakshmi

Lakshmi has always been a popular goddess in the Hindu pantheon, equally loved in different parts of the country, and adored for thousands of years.

A combination of two main notions was responsible for bringing forth the composite goddess Lakshmi. In the *Rigveda*, the appellative "lakshmi" was used as a sign, as the original connotation of Lakshmi was with luck or fortune, as it, almost churlishly, waxes and wanes.

There was a connection between luck and material prosperity in the Vedic period. It is no surprise, therefore, that Lakshmi eventually became the goddess of signs of good fortune.

As Shri

The second stream that merged with the evolution of Lakshmi is the connotation of Shri. For the longest time, the goddess's name has the prefix "Shri", or just Shri in southern India. The word is sometimes translated as a concept rather than a goddess.

IN TODAY'S TIMES

GANESHA AND LAKSHMI

In different Hindu traditions, it is a common practice to worship Lakshmi along with Ganesha. According to mythology, Lakshmi was childless and adopted Ganesha from Parvati with the promise that her worship would be incomplete without reverence to the elephant-headed god. It is believed that invoking him removes obstacles in the path to achieve wealth and prosperity. At the same time, he blesses the devotee with intellect to use that wealth in judicious ways.

» It evokes many things – grace, prosperity, affluence, abundance, auspiciousness, authority and well-being.

In the "Shri Sukta", a late 5th-century BCE hymn, appended to the *Rigveda*, Shri is used in the sense of plenitude. The belief is that Shri was a pre-Vedic deity connected to fertility, water, and agriculture. It does seem that Lakshmi and Shri were different goddesses since in the "Shri Sukta" they are, sometimes, mentioned separately. Over time, these two goddesses fused. Though, there does not seem to be a myth connecting the two. Their merging may have been because land and agriculture was the main source of wealth. Lakshmi became anthropomorphized as well and became affixed to the idea of material wealth. She became the embodiment of earth's wealth and bounty.

As a single goddess

As early as the 2nd century BCE, Lakshmi was a single, standalone goddess, who symbolized several important markers. Over centuries, this has changed and she has, today, taken on the role of a model wife to Vishnu, the preserver. She, however, had a chequered past. In the centuries before and after the Christian era, she remained unaligned to any specific male god. In fact, in the early stages of her history, she had several alliances with different male deities and appeared quite liberal.

She also quite successfully toppled a common belief around single goddesses that drew a significant connection between their unmarried status, lack of conjugal relationships, and their association with danger and anger. Such goddesses were not considered as auspicious as those who were married. Lakshmi's depictions in material form and literature flagrantly toppled this idea of auspiciousness being tied to married or unmarried goddesses.

△ **Varalakshmi Vratam** is a popular festival that is celebrated across many states in southern India. On this day, devotees worship the eight manifestations of Lakshmi. Instead of an idol, families create the goddess using a coconut mounted with an icon of Lakshmi, often in silver, who is dressed in silk and adorned with jewellery.

"O **Lady of the Lotus**! Because of your touch, the Lord is **filled with auspiciousness**. Your auspiciousness is not caused or conditioned – it **exists on its own**, for is not your name not **Shri**?"

VEDANTA DESIKA'S PRAYER, VIDYA DEHEJIA, *DEVI, THE GREAT GODDESS: FEMALE DIVINITY IN SOUTH ASIAN ART* (1999)

Vishnu's consort

The transition to Lakshmi's status as Vishnu's spouse came around 400 CE with the emergence of the myth of the churning of the ocean (See pp 174–75). One of the most celebrated stories in India, this is the earliest myth connected to the birth of Lakshmi and is told in the Adi Parva of the *Mahabharata*, the *Vishnu Purana*, the *Padma Purana*, and the *Devi Bhagavatam*.

In it, as the Devas and Asuras churn the ocean seeking the nectar of life, Lakshmi emerges from its depths seated on a full-blown lotus. It is perhaps why she is also called Jaladhija, or the one who is born of the ocean.

It is also said that she is content with Vishnu only because he is the god who has so many avatars. He, himself, is prone to changing form, notes Indian historian R Mahalakshmi. His different avatars satisfy her restless spirit, for she is Chanchala, a transitory, almost fidgety and flickering personality.

Ultimately, one can view the capriciousness of Lakshmi as an allegory for the inherent quality of fortune, that is uncertainty. It is made clear through the embodiment of this goddess that good fortune may come and go. Keeping her pleased is one way of feeling less insecure about this truism of life.

The goddess of all

Lakshmi is not a sectarian goddess, for she belongs to everyone – Buddhists, Jains, and Hindus. Her importance is clear even in today's mundane world. In India, the birth of a daughter or even the arrival of a daughter-in-law is greeted with the phrase "Lakshmi has arrived in our midst." She is, after all, the goddess who attracts and bestows good fortune upon the whole family.

▷ **Lakshmi is often** portrayed on coins, an allusion to her status as the goddess of wealth. Here, she is depicted on a silver coin, which is typically purchased on Diwali, the festival of lights.

Lakshmi and Vishnu

The embodiment of good fortune, the sovereign goddess Lakshmi is much more than the wife of Vishnu, the preserver. She also acts as the mediator between the god and his devotee.

Almost every depiction of Vishnu, the preserver, has the goddess Lakshmi in his vicinity. As a couple, they are responsible for sustaining and enhancing the cosmic order and the life of the householder. Lakshmi, however, is not the actualizer of Vishnu's power. She is the spouse and a symbol of auspiciousness and prosperity in the domestic sphere.

Iconography

Lakshmi is often seen residing on Vishnu's chest or seated beside him on his lap or between his feet. Some images have her massaging his feet,

perhaps, it is believed, to invigorate his limbs, tired after fighting the unrighteous and evil. Indian mythologist Devdutt Pattanaik notes that Vishnu, knowing the power of wealth to corrupt, does this to keep Lakshmi in check. At times, the visual representation also shows her as disproportionately smaller to Vishnu in size, perhaps a way of expressing her subordination to him.

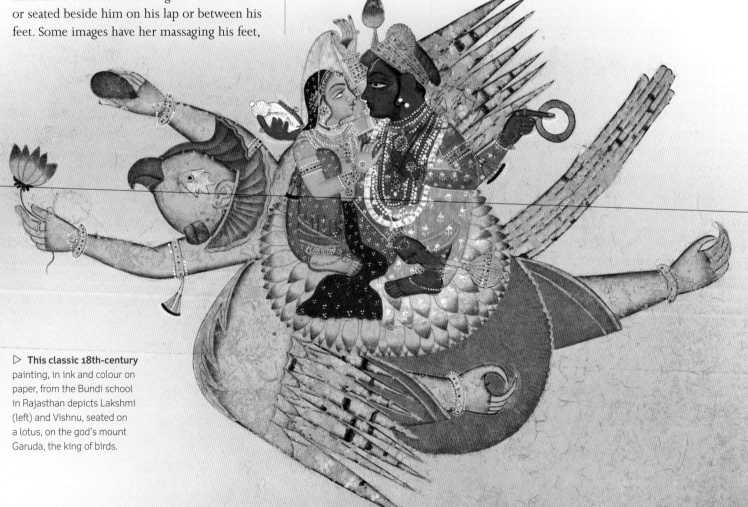

▷ **This classic 18th-century** painting, in ink and colour on paper, from the Bundi school in Rajasthan depicts Lakshmi (left) and Vishnu, seated on a lotus, on the god's mount Garuda, the king of birds.

"May the eyes that are **spellbound by the beauty** of Vishnu **Fall on me** and bestow upon me prosperity and happiness… Fall upon me and **grant me welfare**."

ADI SHANKARACHARYA, KANAKDHARA STOTRA, DEVDUTT PATTANAIK, LAKSHMI, *THE GODDESS OF WEALTH AND FORTUNE* (2002)

A crucial bond

Vishnu temples are rare in North India though those dedicated to his two avatars, Rama and Krishna are widespread. The situation is different in peninsular India. By the 12th century, Shrivaishnavism, a form of Vaishnavism or worship of Vishnu and his incarnations, evolved in South India, mostly in Tamil Nadu and parts of Andhra Pradesh and Karnataka. The name was especially meaningful as the prefix "Shri" is an epithet of Lakshmi, and means sacred and revered. It also visualized Vishnu as the embodiment of the supreme divine principle.

Scholar of Hinduism, Vasudha Narayanan notes that the Shrivaishnavas distinguished themselves from other Vaishnav groups as they insisted that the intimate bond between Lakshmi and Vishnu was crucial to the life of faith and the logic of salvation, as without Shri there is no deliverance.

BHU DEVI

Often, as Vishnu descends to earth in one of his many incarnations, so too does Lakshmi. One such instance is of Lakshmi, as Bhu Devi representing the earth. Once, Vena, a king, plundered the earth so much that the sages intervened and killed him. They created a new king named Prithu, from his remains. This was an incarnation of Vishnu. Meanwhile, tired of being persecuted, Bhu Devi escaped in the form of a cow. Prithu gave a chase and caught her. He then threatened to kill her unless she allowed people to milk her for their sustenance. She in turn told him that if he killed her, the world would cease to exist. When Prithu gave her his assurance, she finally agreed to give the people milk for their survival.

The mediator

This divine sharing of the feminine and the masculine, scholars note, was the ultimate truth. Lakshmi and Vishnu are inseparable and essential to each other and to the act of mutual loving devotion. By helping devotees achieve prapatti, or self-surrender to god, Lakshmi also enhances the *saulabhya*, or accessibility of the divine.

Lakshmi also takes on an active role as the mediator or *purushkara* between the Vishnu and his worshippers. Her accessibility is analogous to a mother's love or *vatsalaya*, notes scholar Ranjeeta Dutta. She is the medium for salvation, the kind mother who acts as a mediator between a stern father, Vishnu and an errant son, the devotee. Indian art historian Vidya Dehejia notes that devotees often beseech her to speak to their lord for them. She recommends to Vishnu and thereby helps living beings in their desire for redemption and salvation.

Dehejia writes that the 13th-century philosopher Vedanta Deshika considered Lakshmi "as the ultimate source of all auspiciousness, thereby, in a way, indicating her superiority to Vishnu". However, she is not the creative power behind the universe. That responsibility rests with Vishnu who is the sole creator, preserver, and destroyer of it, as Shri watches. He, however, shares this with her as well. For Deshika, Lakshmi is indispensable while approaching Vishnu for if he represents righteousness, she is compassion. Dutta notes that "the notion of a universal divine couple, with Vishnu as supreme, emerged as the symbol of integration and imparted a stable and uniform character to the community."

△ **This c. 11th–12th century** carved conch from the Bengal region features Vishnu (centre left) with Lakshmi, as his consort, seated next to him.

The churning of the ocean

There are many versions of the Samudra Manthan, as the popular churning myth is called, in the Puranas and even the epic *Mahabharata*. This version tells of Lakshmi's emergence and her union with Vishnu.

The universe was listless. Amrita, the ambrosia, the very nectar of immortality, along with everything that made life worth living, had sunk deep, to the very bed of the ocean.

The Devas and the Asuras agonized over the loss of their vigour. Churning of the ocean was a dire necessity. They realized that they would not be able to accomplish the task on their own, so they combined their strength.

It was an epic task, indeed. To help them, the mountain Mandara became a massive churning stick and Vasuki, the king of snakes, agreed to become the rope. Vishnu, the preserver of the universe, became Kurma, or the tortoise form, and his hard and strong back provided the foundation.

The Devas and the Asuras stood facing each other and each party grabbed one end of the snake rope. They began churning the ocean, until treasured items began emerging from its floor.

Among the first to appear was Kamadhenu, the cow of abundance. Soon, the celestial flower Parijata came up as did the Kalpavriksha, the tree that fulfils all desires, Rambha, the Apsara, and Chandra, the Moon.

Then, finally, the resplendent Lakshmi appeared, carrying a bowl of amrita in her hands. She was glorious and everything that came before her paled in comparison. An argument broke out between the Devas and the Asuras as both sides had exerted themselves for the amrita but the Devas were not willing to share it with the Asuras. So Vishnu took on the form of the beguiling Mohini, who used her powers of illusion to enchant the Asuras while the Devas quickly drank the amrita.

Vishnu, when he saw the beautiful, alluring, and captivating Lakshmi, claimed her as his consort. There are different versions of this story, but the *Vishnu Purana* states that Lakshmi chose Vishnu as her consort of her own accord. It also tells how she arose from the ocean, with elephants sprinkling her with waters from the River Ganga and other sacred rivers.

In search of nectar
This painting from South India, dated 1825, depicts Lakshmi's emergence from the ocean. Seated on a lotus, she is draped in a golden sari. The Devas are on the right and the Asuras on the left. The various precious objects from the ocean are depicted along the top of the painting.

By Lakshmi's grace

The many myths around Lakshmi tell of a goddess who favours her true devotee with fortune, power, wealth, and prosperity. She is the power behind the king, and she fulfils the desires of those who are in need.

The melding of concepts from the Vedic Shri and the Puranic Bhu Devi led to the emergence of a composite form of Lakshmi. She became a symbol of fertility, wealth, and the existential characteristic of fortune – both good and bad that awaits each individual in a lifetime.

The power behind the king

Lakshmi has early associations with several male deities, Indra, the king of gods, being the most prominent. Several myths tie the two together, notes scholar of religious studies David Kinsley. Indra often loses and regains Lakshmi, however, "what is lost, acquired, or restored in the person of Sri is royal authority and power". The goddess's association with monarchy and power is also evident in her Rajyalakshmi form.

She protects only the virtuous ruler who is steadfast in the performance of his duties, and is quick to forsake the unworthy. Kinsley recounts the myth of the Asura Prahlada who was righteous as long as she was by his side. When she leaves him on Indra's request, "Prahlada is left emptied of his royal might and his predilections towards virtuous conduct".

△ **This painting** of the eight manifestations of Lakshmi or Ashtalakshmi is typical of the Kerala murals that use colours made with mineral pigments and vegetables. The goddesses, with Ganesha, the elephant-headed god (centre), represent prosperity, fertility, good fortune, good health, knowledge, strength, progeny, and power.

The Vishnu connection

It is only towards c. 400 CE that different mythologies build a clear connection between Lakshmi and Vishnu. The most well-known story is of her origin from Samudra Manthana or the churning of the ocean (See pp 174–75). It is during the course of this tale that Lakshmi chooses to be with Vishnu and not the other gods, including Indra.

Kinsley calls this link "fitting". He is, after all, the "supreme divine king". As Vishnu's avatars take their place as rulers or people of power on earth, Lakshmi showers them with fortune. Over time, her connection to Vishnu becomes so firmly established that she is born as his wife or consort to all his avatars.

The *Vishnu Purana* lists her different avatars that manifest alongside Vishnu. So, his Vamana or dwarf avatar finds his consort in Kirti, also known as Padma or Kamala. As Rama, he finds Lakshmi in Sita, and in Rukmini as Krishna.

The *Devi Bhagavata Purana* tells an interesting account of Lakshmi and Vishnu. Once, Lakshmi is born as a mare on earth as a result of a curse from Vishnu. He tells her that she will only be able to return to their home, Vaikuntha, when she gives birth to a colt. Lakshmi, as a mare, roams the earth in despair until she comes to the confluence of the rivers Yamuna and Tamasa. Here, she worships Shiva, who pleased at her devotion appears. He asks her why she is praying to him when she is the wife of the great Vishnu himself. Lakshmi tells him of the curse and asks him for help. After all, she tells Shiva, there is no difference between him and Vishnu. They are the same. Surprised and pleased that Lakshmi is aware of this secret,

LAKSHMI–ALAKSHMI

If Lakshmi is everything good and prosperous, her sister Alakshmi is hardship and misfortune. She was also born during the churning of the ocean, emerging earlier and along with the poison caused by the process. Also known as Jyeshtha, her depiction is that of an old hag, riding an ass and wielding a broom. Scholars indicate that the two sisters are two sides of the same coin, and one cannot be without the other.

> "**Victory** to thee O mother Lakshmi! It is only by **your grace** that even a … miserable pauper **also becomes supremely rich** and gets all kinds of wealth."
>
> *SHRI LAKSHMI CHALISA*

Shiva grants her a boon. Vishnu manifests as a stallion and the two have a child named Haihaya, who, legend has it, becomes the progenitor of the dynasty of the same name.

The practical wife

The relationship between Vishnu and Lakshmi is interestingly explored in a folktale. Vishnu would sleep for centuries, comfortable in his serpent bed, refusing to wake up for anyone, even the deities and sages who would be waiting to meet him or seek his help. Lakshmi is troubled and tells him that he must cast his glance towards the earth more often. As he sleeps, she says, negative forces arise. The only way he can resolve them is by descending to earth as an incarnation. Vishnu realizes what his wife is saying and decides to limit his sleep to four months in a year.

The wish fulfiller

There are several stories of Lakshmi blessing poets as well. There is the tale of the Indian philosopher Adi Shankaracharya, who as a student would often go house to house seeking alms. One home was so poor that the woman could only offer him one berry. Out of compassion, Shankaracharya composed the *Kanakdhara Stotra*, praising Lakshmi. She was so pleased that streams of gold berries fell from the heavens, covering the woman's courtyard.

The Shrivaishnava community in South India tell a story of the 13th-century philosopher Vedanta Deshika who composed and sang the *Shri Stuti* in praise of Lakshmi to help a poor, young man. Pleased with the beautiful hymn, Lakshmi blessed the man and showered him with gold coins.

Portrait of prosperity

A rendition of Gaja Lakshmi from South India

When Lakshmi manifests herself in her Gaja Lakshmi form, she becomes associated with *gaja*, or elephant. One of the most popular Ashtalakshmis, a group of eight manifestations of Lakshmi, her motif is common in Indian iconography from around the 2nd century BCE. It is widely prevalent in the reliefs of Bharhut and Sanchi in Madhya Pradesh, Bodh Gaya in Bihar, Manmodi and Ellora in Maharashtra, Badami in Karnataka, and Udaygiri and Khandagiri in Odisha. As is obvious for a goddess of fortune, one also encounters Gaja Lakshmi on many coins, including those from Ujjain in Madhya Pradesh, and Kaushambi, Ayodhya, and Mathura in Uttar Pradesh, as well as seals beginning from the Gupta period.

1. Two caparisoned elephants stand on both sides. Elephants are symbolic of royalty and emphasize Lakshmi's association with affluence.

2. The elephants are in the process of anointing the goddess with water from the *purna gatha*, or full vase, believed to be the sacred container from where life arises. A significant ritual in consecration and coronation ceremonies, this act of *abhisheka*, or sprinkling of holy water, gives her royal and cosmic authority.

3. The left hand is in the *abhaya mudra*, which indicates that she dispels fear. The right hand, in the *varada mudra*, indicates the bestowing of fortune, symbolized through coins emanating from her palm. This theme is reiterated through depiction of a coin-filled gold vessel and her elaborate jewellery.

4. Called *padmahasta*, or one with lotus in hand, she holds two lotuses in her upper hands. The lotus is often seen as a metaphor for the created universe, with blossoming life, and it shows her association with creation and life. Through the lotus motif, she is also connected with her consort Vishnu, the preserver, as he is often depicted with a lotus emerging from his navel.

5. She is seated in *padmasana*, a cross-legged meditation position mirroring the lotus, on which she is also seated. This represents her spiritual purity as lotus remains untainted despite emerging from murky waters.

6. She is surrounded by water, which suggests her origin from the Samudra Manthan, or the churning of the ocean (See pp 174–75). Water is also life-sustaining and it indicates her connection to fertility.

Tulsi Vrindavan
It is a common practice to plant Tulsi in a pillar-like rectangular pot called Tulsi Vrindavan, which is also perceived as the shrine of the goddess.

Tulsi

The sylvan form of Devi

"**No plant** in the world **commands** such… respect, **adoration**, and **worship**… as does *tulsi*."

KD UPADHYAYA, "INDIAN BOTANICAL FOLKLORE" (1964)

Blossoming in the centre of the *angana*, or courtyard, of many Indian households, Tulsi, a species of basil, is an important sacred plant in Hinduism. Worshipped as a goddess in her own right, one could say that Tulsi is a plant embodiment of Devi.

Origins

The rise of Tulsi from a mere plant to one representing sacrality can be traced to the period between 200 BCE to 300 CE. During this time, Brahmanism was assimilating an assortment of popular and widespread cults. In the process, animals, trees, mountains, and rivers came to acquire deific connotations. Tulsi was one such natural entity that became a part of the religious matrix. American cultural geographer Frederick J Simoons notes, "Hindus sometimes call the tulsi plant *tulsi-mata* ("mother tulsi"), which is in accord with the way they address the sacred cow as *go-mata* ("mother cow") and the sacred Ganges River as *Ganga-mata* ("mother Ganges")."

Part of the Vaishnava pantheon

The process of deification often draws its legitimacy by inserting the deity in the wider mythological framework. So Tulsi became a part of the Vaishnava myths (See p 183). Sometimes considered a manifestation of Lakshmi, she is often referred to as Shri Tulsi,

Shri being another name for Lakshmi, and *Lakshmi Priya*, which means Lakshmi's beloved. To further embed Tusli firmly in the Vaishnava system, she is also connected to Vishnu, the preserver, and his avatars. Scholars draw attention to how she is *Vaishnavi*, or one who belongs to Vishnu, *Vishnu Vallabha*, or Vishnu's beloved, and when seen as Rama or Krishna's wife, Rama Tulsi and Krishna Tulsi, respectively.

Tulsi may also have associations with other deities, including Shiva, the destroyer. Some scholars have pointed out that sometimes Shiva's image is created from the soil that nurtures the Tulsi plant. Select communities in Odisha and Kerala link her with their local deities and supernatural beings. Even so, as Indian anthropologist RS Khare, writes, she is the "central sectarian symbol" of Vaishnavism.

Auspicious nature

The *Padma Purana* says that every part of the Tulsi plant has purifying powers. If Tulsi wood is use to cremate the dead, they are freed from all sins and go to heaven. Bathing with the clay in which Tulsi grows is equal to bathing in a holy place. An important part of many Vaishnava rituals is the offering of garlands made of Tulsi leaves or Tulsi-infused holy water to deities. They also use the wood of the plant stem to make beads for the string used to do *japa*, or meditative mantra repetition.

IN TODAY'S TIMES

REVERING TULSI

The common practice is to plant Tulsi on an auspicious day, particularly on *Sankranti*, or days when Sun transmigrates from one constellation to the next, or during the Hindu month of Shravana (July–August). Traditional Hindu homes usually have the plant in the courtyard of their homes. Women mostly worship the Tulsi plant early in the morning after their bath, and then in the evening.

The wedding of Tulsi

During the Hindu month of Kartik (October–November), many homes and temples across India play host to a celestial wedding. Called Tulsi Vivah, or Tulsi's wedding, it is the union of Vishnu, the preserver, and his beloved Tulsi.

In Hindu traditions, *kanyadaan*, or giving away a daughter, is believed to be the biggest offering one can ever make to the divine. It has the power to free one of all sins, no matter how extreme. So every year, many daughterless couples perform Tulsi Vivah where they marry the Tulsi plant, as their daughter, to Vishnu.

Imitation of a Hindu wedding

In terms of its scale, the Tulsi Vivah can range from a close-knit homely affair to a grand celebration, but in its essence, it resembles a traditional Hindu wedding. The setting includes a *mandap*, or a marriage pavilion, with *agni*, or sacred fire, at its centre. The Tulsi plant, believed to embody the goddess, is wrapped with a traditional red sari and embellished with jewellery to look like a bride.

Sometimes, a paper face with a nose ring, earrings, and a bindi is placed on it to give anthropomorphic connotations. The groom Vishnu, or his avatar Krishna, appears as a brass statue, a picture, or a shaligram stone. Dressed in dhoti, he is offered sandalwood paste and the *janeu*, or sacred thread.

A Brahman priest is called upon to recite the mantras and conduct the rituals. The bride and the groom are connected through a *mala*, or cotton thread, in a re-enactment of the ritual of *gathbandhan*, or alliance. The bride is offered a *mangalsutra*, or auspicious necklace, to confer marital status upon her. Throughout the ceremony, and especially in the end, the participants shower puffed rice, mixed with turmeric and *kumkum*, or vermilion, on the couple to celebrate their union.

△ **Carrying the plant**
A decorated Tulsi plant is carried on the head as a part of a religious procession.

△ **Decorating her home**
Tulsi Vrindavan and its surrounding area is often decorated with traditional motifs.

△ **In Vishnu's avatar**
Sometimes, in Tulsi Vivah, Krishna replaces Vishnu. This image shows Krishna's brass statue being presented to Tulsi.

Mythological context

The antecedents of this ritual can be traced to mythology. There are several stories of Vishnu's union with Tulsi. American cultural geographer Frederick J Simoons recounts the most popular version. In it, Vishnu was once drawn to the beautiful and faithful Vrinda. Owing to the intensity of her fidelity, her husband, Jalandhara, an ordinary, low-caste man, mutated into an invincible Asura. Meanwhile, Vishnu tried to seduce Vrinda who evaded his advances and disregarded him in favour of her husband. Not being able to get Vrinda this way, the god disguised himself as Jalandhara and managed to trick her. Vrinda fell into the trap.

No longer shielded by the fervour of her fidelity, Jalandhar died. Vrindra, shocked at Vishnu's misdemeanor and heartbroken at her husband's death, cursed the god so he would turn into a stone. Vishnu retaliated and turned her into a plant. Over time, she became Vishnu's beloved.

In another version, Vrinda threw herself on the pyre of her husband, but Vishnu could not let go of her and transformed her into the Tulsi plant. In the *Devi Bhagavata Purana*, the goddess performs a difficult penance to be reunited with her husband Vishnu.

> "Krishna's marriage to Tulsi… reflects the world of **values** and **conventions** that shape and inform **human conjugal relations**."

TRACY PINTCHMAN, "THE MONTH OF KARTIK AND WOMEN'S RITUAL DEVOTIONS TO KRISHNA IN BENARES" (2003)

Modern-day rationale

There are also practical implications of this ritual. It is believed that on Shayani Ekadashi, or the 11th day of the bright fortnight of the Hindu month of Ashada (June –July), Vishnu retires to sleep in his abode in Ksheersagar, the ocean of milk. His slumber lasts for four months, a period traditionally known as Chaturmas. Since Vishnu's consciousness is practically absent in the universe during this period, Hindus are prescribed to stay away from auspicious ceremonies, such as weddings. When Vishnu rises from his long and deep slumber on Prabodhini Ekadashi, the 11th day of the bright fortnight of Kartik, it signals the commencement of the marriage season in India. Tulsi Vivah is celebrated to commemorate this.

△ **Recitation of "Mangal Ashtaka"**
In Maharashtra, just before the final mantra, a cloth screen is placed between the deities. It is taken off after the completion of the mantra.

△ **Accessorizing the goddess**
In this Tulsi Vivah in Punjab, women can be seen decorating the Tulsi plant. The goddess is presented with *choora*, or traditional bridal bangles in Punjab.

Omnipresent
In India, the Goddess does not always remain hidden in the sanctum sanctorum of shrines and temples. Her presence can be felt in every nook and cranny of the Indian cultural landscape. She can reveal Herself in the most unlikely of places. Pictured here is an idol of the goddess Lakshmi casually placed on a wall somewhere in India.

Rich tapestry
The Thanjavur style artworks are famous for sacred and devotional subjects, such as this painting of Sarasvati. With intricate details and gold embellishments, it presents the goddess in her typical form – four-armed, carrying a lute and a manuscript.

Sarasvati

The goddess of speech and wisdom

"Wealthy in spoil, **enriched with hymns**…
Inciter of all **pleasant songs**, **inspirer**
of all **gracious thought**,
Sarasvati accept our rite!"

VERSES 10–11, HYMN 3, BOOK 1, *RIGVEDA*

Lakshmi may dazzle and lure with golden material riches, playing truant with her worshippers. Durga may intimidate or even alienate with her raw pleasure in war, and Kali may frighten with the sheer weight of her antinomian symbolism, but Sarasvati is the complete opposite.

Clad in white, accompanied by a swan with a lute and manuscript in her hands, she has a comely mien, and graceful figure. Sarasvati embodies peace, positivity, and purity and has noble associations, those of knowledge, creativity, and speech.

As a river goddess

Sarasvati is one of the few Puranic goddesses whose first appearance can be traced to the oldest and most important Vedic text, the *Rigveda*, dated circa 1500 BCE. There are many mentions of her and four hymns, in particular, invoke her.

She is intimately yoked to a remarkable seminal idea in the Indic culture that is revering rivers. In the third hymn, Sarasvati finds representation as the goddess of the eponymous river. As a flowing river, she has fertilizing and purifying powers. Perhaps, she can be credited for the introduction to the

abiding belief in the sanctity of rivers as she is the earliest example where a river and a goddess melded into one. This phenomenon renders her the prototype of other later river goddesses, such as Ganga, Yamuna, Narmada, Godavari, and Kaveri (See pp 348–63). In this context, British translator of Sanskrit Ralph TH Griffith says, "The Sarasvati thus appears to have been to the early Indians what the Ganges… became to their descendants."

As goddess of speech

The word *sarasvati* is of Sanskritic origin and etymologically, denotes *saras*, or anything flowing or fluid. In a figurative manner, all things that are fluid or free-flowing in nature have had their associations with Sarasvati. For example, she is the goddess of the "stream of speech".

One could attribute the river's association with speech to the poets of the *Rigveda* who wrote their inspiring verses by the banks of the River Sarasvati. This connection gave rise to the belief that the river helped in the emergence of a sense of calm, euphoria, and wellbeing, which, in turn, led to great eloquence. The *Rigveda* also contains hymns to the power of speech, divinized in

"I sing a lofty song, for she is **mightiest**, most **divine of Streams**.
Sarasvati will I exalt with hymns and lauds, and, O Vasishta, Heaven and Earth."

VERSE 1, HYMN 96, BOOK 7, *RIGVEDA*

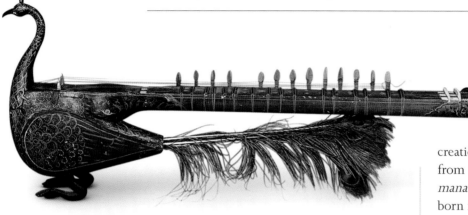

△ **A 19th-century** *mayuri veena*, a form of lute, which draws inspiration from *mayur*, or peacock, considered to be Sarasvati's vahana

another goddess called Vac. By the time of the Brahmanas, which form a part of the Vedas, and the epic *Mahabharata*, Sarasvati is equated with Vac and the concepts associated with her, especially her power to make human beings wise through speech – the prime medium for the Vedic seers.

In this merging, there is lesser emphasis on Sarasvati's nature as a river and she comes to fundamentally embody the power of speech. This amalgamation of the two aspects of this goddess is recognized in the Shatapatha Brahmana, where there is a clear reference to "Vacvai Sarasvati", which means Sarasvati is Vac.

A medium to divine truth

It is possible that Sarasvati's association with a concept as important as speech is the reason why, unlike many Vedic goddesses (See pp 40–43), she has not passed into oblivion. She exists today as a widely acknowledged goddess.

After all, the idea of sound and speech in Hinduism is extremely important. The kernel of sound is speech, which is not just sound, but lucid sound. In the cultural and religious sphere, speech is the prime means for the

dissemination of poetry, holy invocations, and exaltations. There is the perception that creation can take place from parents, that is from coitus, or from the mind, such as the *manasa purusha*, or the first human being born from the mind of Brahma, the creator, or from sound, that is *vac*. There is also an idea that the ultimate reality is encountered in the form of sound.

According to British scholar of comparative religion Gavin Flood, Hindu philosophy emphasizes that the potency of speech and the sound is best realized in the centrality and the power latent in words, particularly mantras. In many religious traditions of the subcontinent, as elsewhere in the world, the deities are pleased by singing hymns or reciting mantras. Perhaps, ritual recitation emphasizes the magical efficacy of sacred sound. American scholar of religious studies David Kinsley writes, "to pronounce a mantra is to make the deity present."

One could relate this idea to popular culture, where it is often said that anyone eloquent in speech is gifted with Sarasvati dancing and residing on their tongue.

It is also referenced in an episode in the epic *Ramayana*. Scholar of religious studies George M Williams refers to an incident where the Rakshasha Ravana's brother seeks a boon from Brahma. He asks for the annihilation, or *nirdevatvam*, of the Devas. However, Sarasvati, on the Devas's request, dances on his tongue, and he instead asks for *nidradevatam*, or sleep.

Association with Brahma

Sarasvati is often presented in relation to Brahma, the creator. In the Puranas, she is his consort and in the epic *Mahabharata* his daughter.

Although she is Brahma's wife, she is rarely depicted with him. There are also hardly any well-known, overarching mythological episodes that illustrate this association. She is, typically, shown alone (See pp 194–95) and has an autonomous role to play in the minds of her believers.

Scholar of religious studies Catherine Ludvik points to an interesting episode in the *Matsya Purana*, composed between the 3rd and 5th centuries. In it, Brahma creates Sarasvati from his own effulgence, and in that very moment, develops an incestuous attraction toward her. In spite of his disapproving sons, all he sees is her lovely face. As she circumambulates him, he grows ashamed of his ardour. To hide his feelings, especially in front of his sons, he makes his face appear on all sides, including the back of his head. Sarasvati makes a futile attempt to evade her father's advances by flying up, but a fifth face springs up atop his head so that he can continue taking in her lovely form.

Williams notes that, in some texts, such as the *Bhagavata Purana*, Brahma is often mocked for lusting after his own daughter. He adds that in countless versions of this myth, Brahma holds Kama, the god of love and desire, responsible for stimulating him with his magical projectiles, leading to his creation of and marriage to Sarasvati. This results in Brahma's curse according to which, Shiva, the destroyer, reduced Kama to ashes with fire from his third eye.

◁ **This illustration in black and white**, first published in 1875, depicts the two-armed form of Sarasvati (right) with her consort Brahma.

The three wives of Vishnu

The most fascinating mythological narratives related to Sarasvati are embedded in those of her consort Vishnu, the preserver. In most of these accounts, Sarasvati shares space and mythology with fellow goddesses Lakshmi and Ganga.

Compared to other goddesses, such as Parvati and Durga, the Puranas do not recount many individual myths about Sarasvati. One of the possible reasons for the absence of elaborate mythology around her is that most mythologies around goddesses are composed of adversarial or demonic conflict. Since Sarasvati is not a fierce goddess, representing only benign dimensions of life, such as music and education, she doesn't quite dovetail into mythological stories.

Quarrelling myth

Even so, some Puranas make a reference to her in the context of Vishnu and his marital life with his three wives – Sarasvati, Lakshmi (See pp 168–71), and Ganga (See pp 352–55). Scholars point to the *Devi Bhagavata Purana* and the animosity between the three goddesses that it details.

It tells of Sarasvati's growing anger as she watches Ganga's love play with Vishnu. She tells Vishnu that he should not have married three wives if he was going to spend all his time with just one. On hearing this, Vishnu leaves his abode Vaikuntha. A fight breaks out between Sarasvati and Ganga. Lakshmi tries to intervene, but without success.

Sarasvati, enveloped by jealousy, curses Ganga that she would have to descend to the Earth in the form of a river, carrying the bones and tendons of dead bodies. Vishnu returns and

▽ **This Kalighat painting shows** the goddesses Lakshmi (left) and Sarasvati (right) dancing on lotus flowers and playing castanets and tambura, respectively.

"… O Goddess **bestowing boons liberally**… O **white visaged** Shambhavi! O mother deft in **playing the lute**! O super goddess seated upon the lotus – you are **my only support**."

SHRI SARASVATI CHALISA

△ **This painting of goddess Ganga** sitting on her vahana, the crocodile, was created in c. 1890 in Kolkata, West Bengal.

learns of the brawl. He decides to live with Lakshmi and sends the other two to the Earth. He prophesied that Sarasvati would be a river that would appear and disappear, so would Ganga, but she would score more merit than the former. Lakshmi would have to become the Tulsi plant on the Earth eventually due to her participation in the fracas.

Version in the Bhagavata Purana

Scholar of religious studies George M Williams points out another rendition of this myth is given in the *Bhagavata Purana*. In it, while Vishnu is speaking to his three wives, Ganga passes him a seductive look. Sarasvati sees this and becomes angry. She charges at Ganga and a stormy exchange ensues, even as Lakshmi tries to play the mediator. Resenting her intrusion, Sarasvati curses Lakshmi to take birth on the Earth. Ganga then curses Sarasvati to be born as a river on the Earth. Sarasvati in turn curses Ganga that she would be born as a river as well.

Vishnu appeased the wives, but curses once pronounced cannot be reversed. So Lakshmi is born as the Tulsi plant in a sage's hermitage, king Bhagiratha's prayers bring Ganga to the Earth as a powerful river, and Sarasvati becomes a river as well. She, later, leaves her mortal form and goes to Brahmaloka, the creator Brahma's abode, to be his spouse. British scholar of Hinduism John Dowson says that the Vaishnavas of Bengal popularized another version of this myth. The goddesses clash roundly in this version as well, but Sarasvati's character is far more domineering. Vishnu decides to then foresake his relationships with Sarasvati and Ganga, who eventually come to be associated with Brahma and Shiva, respectively.

Separate existence

No matter what the version, this popular myth clearly indicates that Vishnu's companions are in constant competition with each other. They can hardly tolerate each other's presence. German scholar of South Asian art Heinrich Zimmer notes that it is believed that when Lakshmi or Sarasvati bestow a boon on a believer, the other stays away. The result is, as Zimmer puts it, "the wise are not wealthy and the wealthy are not wise". But, at Vishnu's feet, the two are submissive and relegated to a position of "antagonistic co-operation".

KAVYA

Starting from around the early centuries of the Common Era, one encounters Kavya, which is an ornate Sanskrit literary style employed in courtly writings. It involves elaborate figures of speech, among which metaphor and simile predominate. There is also the adroit use of varied and complicated metres. Often, traditional subjects and themes, derived from popular epics, are idealized. The Kavya literature, therefore, aestheticizes the life and deeds of its protagonist and thereby transcends the foibles of human conditions.

The deity of culture

Many dancers, musicians, painters, students, and people engaged in the pursuit of arts and learning regard Sarasvati as their patron goddess. Representing the finesse of culture, she is often the presiding deity during stage performances and in educational institutions.

In Sarasvati's persona, one encounters the amalgamation of two central theological concepts – the worship and sacrality of rivers (See p 187) and the worship of creativity and wisdom. Over the centuries, it is her role as a deity of knowledge and culture that has acquired more prominence in the popular imagination. She is widely revered by poets, musicians, and students all across the Indian subcontinent.

Embodiment of learning

Sarasvati's calm and composed nature kindles a sense of serenity, one associated with the accomplishment of and a surrendering to learning. In a milieu where knowledge is exalted enough to be deemed one of the major paths to omniscience and ultimately to salvation, Sarasvati embodies a crucial arena. After all, she is the goddess, not just of education, but of wisdom that liberates.

She is also the patron deity of the arts, and devotion to her is seen in striving for inspiration to create literature, poetry, and music. In Hindu tradition, most goddesses wield powers linked with fertility, protection, and materiality. Sarasvati, however, appears unique because her power encompasses an entirely different domain, a far gentler cerebral realm – one of the arts and refinement.

Anyone familiar with the everyday lives of people in the Indian subcontinent can witness the relevance of *shiksha*, or learning,

△ **Divine light**
Almost every function in India begins with a ceremony of lighting the lamp. The *jyoti*, or flame, is believed to dispel darkness and evil energies, and bring auspiciousness.

△ **Unbound reverence**
Musicians of all ages and religions look up to Sarasvati as the epitome of their art. Seen here is a man playing a sitar.

and *kala*, or art, both of which permeate every aspect of life. It is perhaps why Sarasvati, closely embodying both, has, over the passage of time, not only survived but thrived.

Secular worship

Since culture has no religious boundaries, the three major Indic faiths, Hinduism, Buddhism, and Jainism, all venerate Sarasvati. There may be many reasons why she appealed to denominations other than Hinduism. The most obvious one, Indian art historian Vidya Dehejia points out, is that Buddhism and Jainism probably adopted her because of the emphasis on knowledge as the means to liberation in their theological discourse.

Unlike other goddesses, Sarasvati is not restricted to a specific geographical location. She is rarely seen in personal home altars or in isolated shrines in the mountains or even in the dark interiors of a dense forest.

The follower is most likely to chance upon her in the "secular" environs of educational institutions. Most schools, colleges, and libraries in India have a representation of Sarasvati. Often, students, as they enter the portals of learning, pay obeisance to her by touching her feet.

> " … When other ornaments are ruined, the **ornament** of **speech** is an **enduring jewel**."

BHARTRIHARI, VERSE 76, NITISHATAKA, *SHATAKATRAYA*

Revered by performers

The image of the Nataraja, the dancer form of Shiva, the destroyer, is ubiquitous on performance stages. Sarasvati too, in a similar fashion, is recalled regularly during staged functions that begin with a Sarasvati *vandana*, or an ode to Sarasvati. It is either sung by a group of performers or by an individual or is rendered by the performance of a short dance where the goddess is invoked. In this manner, she is an integral part of the lives of students, regardless of their religious affiliation and background.

Dehejia also notes that interestingly, musicians, both Hindus and Muslims, worship her and display garlanded images of her in their music rooms. This illustrates her connection to the universal cultural roots of the Indian traditions and render her far less parochial. The goddess Sarasvati is, therefore, open to all.

△ **Dancing to the beats**
Classical Indian dancers often wear anklets made of *ghungroos*, or small metal bells. The sound from the *ghungroos* provides a rhythmic accompaniment to foot movements.

△ **Before the written word**
It is common practice in India to invoke goddess Sarasvati before commencing any literary pursuit.

Eloquence personified

An oleograph from Indian painter Raja Ravi Varma's portrayal of Sarasvati

Most Hindu goddesses in their representations are linked to cosmic ideas of creation, sustenance, and destruction. The images of Sarasvati are unique as they present her as an embodiment of culture and civilization. She is a goddess associated with the mind, with one of its objectives of attaining peace. This theme is unmistakable in all her portrayals through the abundant use of white. Her representations are serene and emanate calmness, but at the same time, are majestic.

1. With the two front hands, she holds a *veena*, a stringed instrument, diagonally across her chest. This musical accoutrement gives credence to her popular epithet *Veenavadini*, or one who holds a *veena*. It is indicative of artistic inspiration and the need for the cultivation of fine arts.

2. The right hand has a palm leaf manuscript, symbolic of knowledge and intellectual excellence. It is emblematic of her association with learning and education.

3. In the rear left hand, she holds an *akshamala*, or prayer or memory beads, which represent the power of concentration leading to creativity.

4. Her raiment is of white silk, and it represents the *sattva guna* in her. It is one of the three qualities or modes of existence, that is *gunas*. This quality is one of subtlety and purity as compared to *rajas*, representing passion, or *tamas*, representing laziness.

5. As is auspicious for any divinity, she is shown wearing a jewelled crown over her head and bedecked with pearl ornaments, associated with water and white colour. This reflects her tranquil yet resplendent nature.

6. The presence of the water in the background indicates her form as the river. It emphasizes her sacrality and purifying powers.

7. With its stunning plumage, the peacock, her vahana, communicates subtle veracity. It does not always spread its feathers to display its beauty. Instead, its tail, lowered seemingly with apparent humility, surprises the viewer with its actual beauty, when it is displayed while dancing.

Sacred animals

Many deities of the Hindu pantheon are seen alongside or seated on an animal in their iconography. These companions, often called vahanas or mounts, form an important part of the god or goddess's character and mythology.

Often seen in bright shades of green

▽ **PARROT**
Seen with Meenakshi and Matangi
Symbolizes Wisdom and speech

The goddess Meenakshi (See pp 344–45) is almost always shown with a bright green parrot sitting on her shoulder. The Mahavidya, Matangi (See pp 308–09) is also associated with the bird. She is called Shukapriya, or the one who is fond of the parrot.

△ **MAKARA**
Seen with Ganga
Symbolizes Protection

A mythological sea creature, it has the tail of a fish and the head of an elephant. It is believed that the *makara* symbol is used to protect against the terrors of the sea. Associated with Ganga (See pp 352–55), some texts refer to it as a *magar*, or crocodile.

Tail of a fish

▷ **CRANE**
Seen with Bagalamukhi
Symbolizes Long life and love

Bagalamukhi (See pp 306–07) uses the crane as her vahana. It attacks evil beings with its beak and claws. The goddess is sometimes depicted with the face of a crane in her imagery.

◁ **ELEPHANT**
Seen with Indrani
Symbolizes Strength, abundance, and intelligence

One of the Saptamatrikas, Indrani (See p 149) has the same vahana as her consort and the lord of the heavens, Indra. This elephant is also at times described as one with six trunks or with three heads.

▷ PEACOCK
Seen with Sarasvati
Symbolizes Wisdom

The peacock the most majestic of the birds is believed to be best suited to Sarasvati, (See pp 186–89) the goddess of knowledge and arts. It is believed that Krishna, an avatar of Vishnu would wear peacock feathers on his head so that Sarasvati would guide and give him good counsel.

△ ULUKA
Seen with Lakshmi
Symbolizes Wisdom and intelligence

The white owl or uluka is goddess Lakshmi's vahana. Not much is known about the origin of this association except that the owl keeps watch over homes and people, carrying reports of misdemeanours to the goddess. (See pp 168–71).

▽ LION
Seen with Durga
Symbolizes Strength and fearlessness

Much of Durga's iconography depicts her mounted on a fierce lion (See pp 80–83). The animal was gifted to her by Himavat, the mountain king, so that she could ride him into her battle with Mahisha, the Asura (See pp 86–87).

▽ NANDI
Seen with Shiva and Parvati
Symbolizes Waiting

Primarily associated with Shiva, the destroyer, the bull Nandi often doubles up as Parvati's vahana. A guardian deity, of Kailash, their home, Nandi is believed to have received spiritual knowledge from Shiva and Parvati.

Radha

The embodiment of devotion

"If I go [to Krishna] I **lose my home**
If I stay I **lose my love**."

DEBEN BHATTACHARYA, *LOVE SONGS OF VIDYAPATI* (1963)

The favourite mistress and consort of god Krishna, the eighth avatara of Vishnu, Radha is much more than Krishna's divine lover. She is an equal partner. She appears daring and always emerges triumphant by virtue of her ingenuity. In one particular episode, she dares to meet Krishna in the middle of the night, despite being married to the cowherd Ayana Ghosha. Therefore, she is venerated for her dedication and for the power of her love for Krishna.

Some consider Radha an incarnation of goddess Lakshmi (See pp 168–71). Others have discovered a mystical character in her and consider her as the human soul drawn to God.

Transformation into a goddess

It is interesting to note that the *Bhagavata Purana*, considered the oldest Purana and dedicated to Krishna, does not make any specific reference to Radha. There are just a few lines about a gopi who accompanies Krishna into the forest. Later works consider this to be a reference to Radha who started to appear in the later Puranas.

In the *Padma Purana*, there's a reference to *bhumi kanya*, or earth girl. Indian artist and writer Bulbul Sharma interprets this as a reference to Radha. According to Indian art historian Vidya Dehejia, Radha transforms from a humble cowherd girl to the highest goddess in the heavenly world of Krishna, only in the *Brahmavaivarta Purana*.

Regional references

Apart from Puranic references, there is ample regional literature around Radha. This also indicates her widespread popularity. American scholar of religious studies Donna M Wulff points out that Radha's roots are humble, appearing in the songs of the Abhirs, a cattle-herding community in North India, and some stray verses in Sanskrit, from about the 3rd century. She is also referred to in the texts from the 9–10th century.

Wulff also draws attention to the works of Rupa Gosvami, an Indian poet and philosopher, who lived and wrote in Vrindavan during the first half of the 16th century. According to her, Radha inspired devotees by the power of her feelings. Gosvami, who is a part of the Bengali Gaudiya Vaishnavas sect, also asserted that Radha was Krishna's *hladini shakti*, or blissful energy, which is the ultimate form of his energy. However, one sees her fully developed personality for the first time in the 12th-century poetic masterpiece *Gita Govinda* (See 208–13), and then in a series of poems and songs, both in Bengali and Hindi.

The hub of Radha–Krishna

Several Vaishnava sects worship Radha as well. She is celebrated mainly in the region north of the River Yamuna, called Braj, around the towns of Mathura and Vrindavan, Uttar Pradesh. Vrindavan has many Radha–Krishna temples that hold elaborate pujas for the divine lovers.

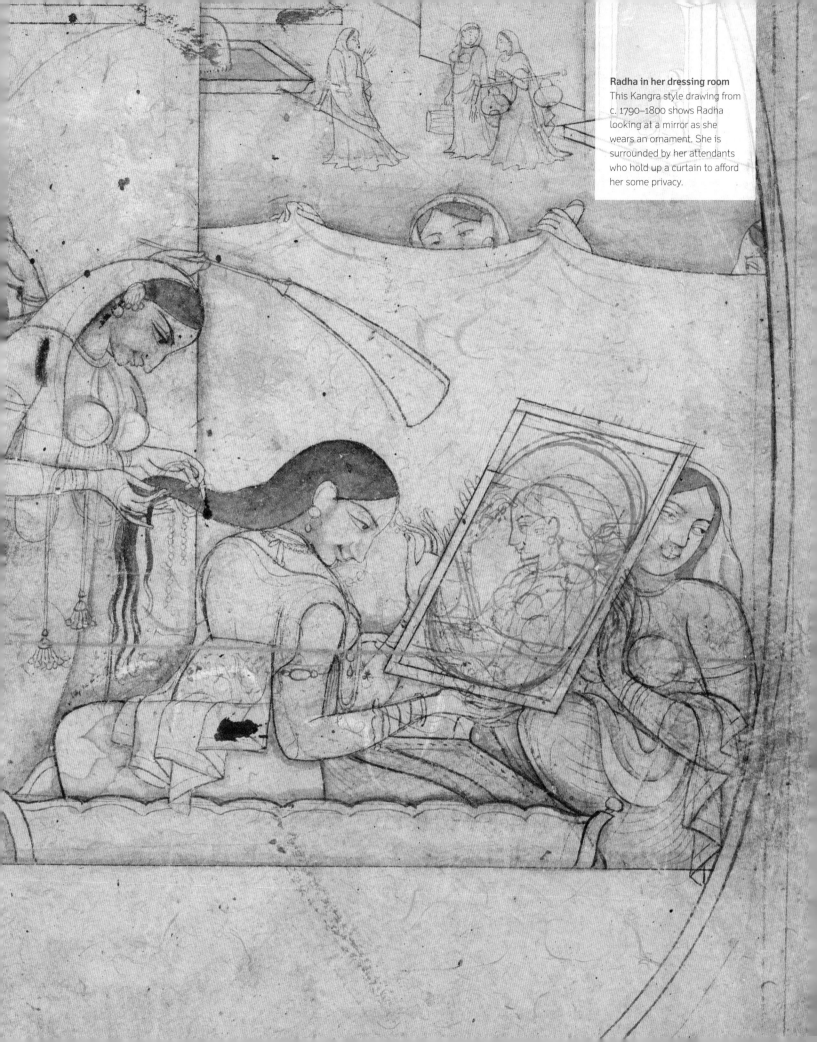

Radha in her dressing room
This Kangra style drawing from
c. 1790–1800 shows Radha
looking at a mirror as she
wears an ornament. She is
surrounded by her attendants
who hold up a curtain to afford
her some privacy.

The colour of flowers
Radha and the god Krishna share a deep and intimate relationship with Holi, the festival of colours. During this time, festivities often include a reenactment of the mythical celebration between the two lovers. Some of the most dramatic renditions take place in Vrindavan, Uttar Pradesh, as seen in this image. Here, artistes dressed as Krishna and Radha (right) take centre stage as their companions shower them with flower petals during Holi.

The women in Krishna's life

The most captivating of all Hindu mythological tales are those of Krishna's relationships with women. Unmasking simple joys of youth, these stories evoke the mood of romantic and erotic love that forms the base of the Radha–Krishna tradition.

In the woods of Vrindavan, a village of Braj, in present-day Uttar Pradesh, a love story unfolded like no other seen in the divine and earthly worlds. It was of Radha and Krishna, lovers nonpareil. Today, they are worshipped side by side, in reverence to their strong bond, and Radha's name has become inseparable from Krishna's.

Emergence of their combined mythology

Over the centuries, wonderful tales have been woven around

◁ **Radha and Krishna enjoy** each other's company in a flowering grove in this classic c. 1720 painting from Kota, Rajasthan.

Radha and Krishna's passion for each other. Their relationship was firmly established in the mythology by the close of the 1st millennium. From the 12th century onwards, after the composition of the *Gita Govinda* (See pp 208–13), there is abundant evidence that Vaishnava devotees perceived and worshipped Radha as Krishna's divine consort.

Radha's devotion

Radha's love for Krishna was obsessive, which made her break all norms of society and disregard her family. She was a married woman, hence, a *parakiya*, or one who belongs with another. According to some Puranas, she was also older than Krishna.

Radha's illicit love for Krishna and its power as a religious metaphor fascinated many poets in the 13th and 14th centuries. Bengal Vaishnavas held it in the highest esteem. In their works, Radha was a tragic heroine torn between her overwhelming love for Krishna and her reputation as a devoted wife. She indulged in this secret love play despite knowing how dangerous it was for her.

Yet, her love is praised as the purest of loves as it is selfless and hopes to gain nothing. This love is sometimes seen as a metaphor for the divine–human

> "When spring came, **tender-limbed** Radha wandered
> **Like a flowering creeper** in the **forest wilderness**,
> **Seeking Krishna** in his many haunts…"

JAYADEVA, VERSE 26, CHAPTER 1, *GITA GOVINDA*

relationship, with Radha representing the human devotee, who gives up her entire being to be one with god. It also allows for a metaphorical interpretation of the *Gita Govinda* as the longing of the human soul for the divine.

The passionate gopis

Krishna's divine exploits are celebrated in all parts of India in devotional poetry, scriptures, theological doctrines, visual arts, and dramatic performances. American scholar of religious studies David Kinsley throws light on the narrative in the *Bhagavata Purana*. In it, Krishna's father took him away from Mathura, where he was born, to Braj in order to escape the threat of his uncle Kamsa (See pp 204–05). The village women doted on him as a child and then, once he became an adolescent, moved to passionate longing. He played his flute arising passion in the women.

Kinsley points out that although the role of the gopis (See box) in the context of devotion is made fairly clear in this Purana, Radha, however, is not mentioned, in fact, no gopi is mentioned by name. In their deep and passionate devotion, their (body) hairs stand on end, they cry, and they become excited and animated. In fact, the devout believe that those who love Krishna would truly behave like the gopis. Kinsley also puts a time frame to this relationship and notes that this took place during Krishna's youth and before his part in the *Mahabharata* war.

Rukmini in Krishna's life

Subsequently, Krishna married Rukmini, who, according to the *Mahabharata*, was the daughter of Bhishmaka, king of Vidarbha, now in Maharashtra. According to the *Harivansha*, the appendix to the *Mahabharata*, they fell in love with one another and Krishna proposed marriage to her. But her brother Rukmin was a friend of Kamsa, the Rakshasa-king of the Vrishni kingdom, whom Krishna had killed. He, therefore, opposed him and thwarted the match. She was then betrothed to Shishupala, the king of the ancient kingdom of Chedi, now in Madhya Pradesh. But as she was going to the temple, Krishna saw her, took her hand, and carried her away in his chariot. Her intended husband and brother pursued them, but Krishna defeated them. He then took Rukmini safely to his kingdom of Dvaraka, now in Gujarat, where he married her. She became his chief wife and bore him a son named Pradyumna.

There is a real dearth of material to fully understand Rukmini's identity. Whatever one knows about her is through this episode of her marriage to Krishna. Even so, today, she is worshipped as a deity along with Krishna in some temples, particularly in South India.

△ **A sculpture of Rukmini** from Tamil Nadu belonging to the late c. 12–13th century

THE MILKMAIDS OF VRINDAVAN

Gopis were the female cowherds, the milkmaids of Vrindavan, who flocked around Krishna, and with whom he had an erotic relationship in his youth. The gopis are devotees and encapsulate bhakti, which is a selfless love of God beyond consideration of social norms. The relationship between Krishna and the gopis is described in many texts. They are representations of the individual soul's intense love of God.

▷ **A Rajput painting** of Krishna and the gopis, from c. 1720–30

Lathmar Holi

The historical town of Barsana in Uttar Pradesh, and the home of the goddess Radha, celebrates Holi in a unique way. A week before the festival of colours, the women welcome the men of the nearby Nandgaon village with lathis, or sticks, echoing a famous Radha-Krishna myth.

Every March, one week before Holi, the spring harvest festival of colours, Barsana, in Uttar Pradesh comes alive. The men from the neighbouring Nandgaon, said to be the god Krishna's home, descend on the small town. Armed with different hues of coloured powder and improvised leather shields, they walk through Barsana singing provocative songs and trying to get the women's attention.

The women are prepared. Dressed as gopis, or cowherds, wielding long, wooden lathis, they stand outside their homes. Amidst a swirl of colours, the women chase the men with the lathis, beating them in a playful manner, and even capture some of them. The prisoners are then dressed in colourful outfits and made to dance.

This celebration, Lathmar Holi, or "Holi of lathis", has become a popular tourist destination with thousands of people making their way to Barsana annually to take part in the merriment.

Grounded in mythology

According to the myth, Holi began in the Braj region of Uttar Pradesh, which includes the towns of Vrindavan, Mathura, Nandgaon, and Barsana. It is believed that Krishna lived in Nandgaon and once visited Radha's hometown. There, he teased Radha and her friends. Offended by his advances, they drove him out of Barsana with lathis. He returned soon after and retaliated with colours. So Krishna celebrated this festival with Radha and the gopis. They mixed flowers and leaves of the

△ **The gopis in waiting**
A group of women, clad in vibrant saris, hold lathis in Nandgaon, Uttar Pradesh, ready to charge at men.

△ **Lathmar Holi in action**
Drenched in Holi colours from head to toe, women playfully hit men with lathis, who in turn protect themselves with leather shields.

forest to create coloured water and poured it on each other. Since then, the festival is celebrated in Barsana as a reenactment of the eternal love of Radha and Krishna. It has a strong rural flavour, full of bawdy lyrics, and reflects the spirit of Krishna's love for Radha.

The festival of colours

Holi, as a festival, is celebrated in the northern parts of India. It occurs on Poornima, or the full Moon day, in the *phalgun*, which is the month of March according to the Gregorian calendar. It relates to the renewal of time and tracing a dramatic progression from chaos to order.

During this time, people douse each other and other hapless passersby with coloured water or powder in complete impunity. Scholars believe that the red water and powder could signify blood, one of the most important elements of life.

For some days preceding Holi, villages, towns, and cities witness merrymaking without restraint. There is a veritable orgy of colours, the playing of dhol or drums, raucous singing, and dancing. There is the consumption of sweets and *thandai*, a traditional drink made with cold milk, nuts, and *bhang*, or cannabis leaves, all synonymous with this festival. Holi also captured the imagination of

> "And the **Holi of Krishna** is no mere **doctrine of love;** rather, it is the **script for a drama** that must be acted out by **each devotee passionately, joyfully**."
>
> McKIM MARRIOTT, "HOLI: THE FEAST OF LOVE" (1966)

the Mughal emperors, who patronized it from the 16th century onwards. Their Rajput queens probably introduced them to the festival.

A state of mind

The idiom of Holi differs vastly from daily life. It is like a psychological release. Things that would not be expressed in the otherwise elaborately stratified society, with the proper structures of patriarchy, are completely inverted. Holi is about letting your guard down and breaking down socially constructed barriers and hierarchies. It is an exuberant, even raucous, period, during which all social formalities are overturned.

△ **A burst of colours**
The most distinct aspect of Holi is its colourful festivities wherein people drench each other in colours as part of celebrations.

△ **The celebratory dance**
A man dressed as Krishna playing an imaginary flute and taking *chakkars*, or spins.

Vindhyavasini

The exaltation of regional identification

"Salutations to **Her** whose **abode** is in the Vindhya Mountain."

VERSE 336, NAMAVALI, *LALITA SAHASRANAMA*

The goddess Vindhyavasini dwells in the mountainous Vindhya Range, from where she gets her name. She is a manifestation of Durga (See pp 80–83), and is considered her avatara. She is also known as Yogamaya or Ekanamsha. She was the sister of the deities Krishna and Balarama. Some believe that she is the reincarnation of Subhadra (See pp 66–67).

Saviour of Krishna

American scholar of religious studies Cynthia Ann Humes recounts the best-known myth. She describes how Vindhyavasini saved baby Krishna from being killed by his uncle Kamsa, the Rakshasa-king of the ancient kingdom of Vrishni. It was prophesied that Kamsa would die by the hands of his cousin Devaki's eighth child. Afraid, he imprisoned Devaki and her husband Vasudeva, and killed all their children. However, nobody could alter the divine plan.

Vishnu, the protector, incarnated as Krishna. He exhorted Mahamaya (See pp 78–79) to cast a spell on Kamsa and take birth as Vasudeva's cousin Nanda and his wife Yashoda's child. After the birth of his eighth child, he carried Krishna to Nanda's home and returned with the girl.

When Kamsa learnt that Devaki had given birth, he rushed to the prison with the intention of killing the child. He reached for the baby to smash her against a stone, but she escaped and took her eight-armed form. She flew to Vindhyachal (See box), which she made her abode, and became revered as Vindhyavasini.

Part of the Great Goddess sect

This myth suggests that Vindhyavasini had an independent force and identity before she was incorporated into the worship of Krishna. American scholar of religious studies David Kinsley suggests that the Prakrit drama *Gaudavaho* of the late 7th–8th century shows Kali as a manifestation of Vindhyavasini. She is worshipped by the tribal group Shabaras, is clothed in leaves, and venerated through human sacrifices. Kinsley points out that in *Gaudavaho*, Yashovarman, the king of Kannauj during his military service, reaches the Vindhyas and worships Vindhyavasini. Therefore, scholars accept that she is among the more ancient of Hindu goddesses and that her sect contributed to the rise of a Hindu theology of the Great Goddess.

Disparate characteristics

The attributes of Vindhyavasini rely heavily on her association with mountains. Kinsley argues that mountainous regions are geographically on the fringes of civilized society and extremely difficult to reach. He says that the Vindhyas, are very dangerous because it is home to violent and hostile tribes. Vindhyavasini is also believed to enjoy meat and blood, both of which are regarded as "highly polluting" by the Aryan culture. Humes, however, notes that the local people deny these seemingly Tantric roots of Vindhyavasini and prefer to view her as a milder Vedic vegetarian goddess.

IN TODAY'S TIMES

VINDHYACHAL

Between the cities of Prayagraj and Varanasi, Uttar Pradesh, where the Vindhya Range touches the southern bank of the holy River Ganga, is the town of Vindhyachal. This bustling pilgrimage centre has grown around the ancient temple complex devoted to the goddess Vindhyavasini. It is also one of the most significant *Shakti pithas*, or the seats of the Goddess, in India.

Gita Govinda

The *Gita Govinda* celebrates Krishna's youth as Govinda, the cowherd boy in the forest of Vrindavan, Uttar Pradesh. Since he was preoccupied with Radha through a large part of his youth, the prime focus of this work is the divine love between the two.

Krishna yearns for Radha
An anxious and restless Krishna waits for Radha (top right, in yellow), who is busy talking to her confidante. He is shown in different moods and points of time. This Pahari painting of a scene from the *Gita Govinda* was made in Kangra, Himachal Pradesh, in c. 1820–1825.

The *Gita Govinda*, or the "Love Song of the Dark Hero", is a 12th-century lyrical Sanskrit text in verse, written by Jayadeva, court poet to the Bengali king Lakshmanasena. It is an erotic work asserting the love between Krishna and Radha and lays the foundation for the further poetic descriptions of Radha's complex relationship with Krishna.

The text is divided into 12 chapters, which are subdivided into 24 divisions called *Prabandha*, each of which contains couplets grouped into eight, called *Ashtapadis*, literally "eight-steps".

Radha's love for Krishna is obvious in the Radha–Krishna paradigm. But one striking element that is different in *Gita Govinda* is its emphasis on the mutuality of their love, or the reciprocity of Krishna's love for Radha. Indian art historian Vidya Dehejia points out that "even though Jayadeva was writing in a heavily patriarchal society, in which Krishna was the lord supreme, he dramatically concludes his poem with Krishna, a total slave of Radha, pleading with her to place her foot upon his head."

Instead of metaphysical dogmatism, the *Gita Govinda* uncovered in Vaishnavism love, devotion, and absolute submission. It was an instrument that completely revolutionized, or rather revitalized, Vaishnavism.

Love song of the dark hero

The following selection of verses from the *Gita Govinda* focuses on Krishna, himself the god of the three worlds, pining for Radha amd unable to live without her. The verses capture the very specific locale of the sport of Radha and Krishna along the banks of the River Yamuna.

Chapter I: Damodara, Glad

मेघैर्मेदुरमम्बरं वनभुव: श्यामास्तमालद्रुमै-
र्नक्तं भीरुरयं त्वमेव तदिमं राधे गृहं प्रापय ।
इत्थं नन्दनिदेशतश्चलितयो: प्रत्यध्वकुञ्जद्रुमं
राधामाधवयोर्जयन्ति यमुनाकूले रह:केलय: ॥

> "The sky is thick with clouds, the forest earth is darkened by the Tamala trees, it is night-time, and this one is scared. Therefore, Radha! You get him home yourself!" Let the secret sport of Radha and Madhava, who were sent away with these words of Nanda, on each arbour and tree along the way on the banks of the River Yamuna, be victorious.

Chapter III: The Destroyer of Madhu, Infatuated

कंसारिरपि संसारवासनाबन्धशृङ्खलाम् ।
राधामाधाय हृदये तत्याज व्रजसुन्दरी: ॥

> The foe of Kamsa, too, placing in his heart Radha, who was verily the chain which held the desire for the world, abandoned the beauties of Braj.

इतस्ततस्तामनुसृत्य राधिका-
मनङ्गबाणव्रणखिन्नमानसः ।
कृतानुतापः स कलिन्दनन्दिनी-
तटान्तकुञ्जे निषसाद माधवः ॥

Having followed that Radhika here and there, his mind pained by the
wound of Cupid's arrow, with sorrow in him, Madhava sat in an
arbour on the banks of the Yamuna.

Chapter V: The Lotus-eyed One, Expectant

अहमिह निवसामि याहि राधामनुनय मद्वचनेन चानयेथाः ।
इति मधुरिपुणा सखी नियुक्ता स्वयमिदमेत्य पुनर्जगाद राधाम् ॥

"I am waiting here, go to Radha, plead with my words and bring her here."
So employed by the foe of Madhu, the same friend went and said to Radha:

तव विरहे वनमाली सखि सीदति ॥

"In separation from you, friend, the one with a
forest-flower-garland has become feeble."

दहति शिशिरमयूखे मरणमनुकरोति ।
पतति मदनविशिखे विलपति विकलतरोऽति ॥

"He burns up under the cool-rayed Moon, seems to be enacting death,
he falls at the arrow of Cupid, and exceedingly agitated, weeps."

वसति विपिनविताने त्यजति ललितधाम ।
लुठति धरणिशयने बहु विलपति तव नाम ॥

"He stays in the extensive forest and abandons his beautiful house. He lays on the bed of the earth and repeatedly cries out your name."

नामसमेतं कृतसंके तं वादयते मृदु वेणुम् ।
बहु मनुते ननु ते तनुसंगतपवनचलितमपि रेणुम् ॥

"He gently plays the flute, signalling your name, and greatly regards even a grain of dust blown by wind touching your body."

Chapter X: The Four-armed One, Charming

त्वमसि मम भूषणं त्वमसि मम जीवनं
त्वमसि मम भवजलधिरत्नम् ।
भवतु भवतीह मयि सततमनुरोधिनी
तत्र मम हृदयमतियत्नम् ॥

"You are my ornament, you are my breath, you are my gem in this ocean of life. May Your Reverence be ever gracious unto me — it is to this end that my heart greatly endeavours."

स्मरगरलखण्डनं मम शिरसि
मण्डनं धेहि पदपल्लवमुदारम् ।
ज्वलति मयि दारुणो मदनकदनारुणो
हरतु तदुपाहितविकारम् ॥

> "Place on my head your gracious foot-blossom as ornament, which destroys the poison of Cupid. The sun of Cupid's strike is terrible to me, who am burning up – may it (your foot) remove the disease that is caused by it."

Chapter XII: The Yellow-Robed One, Well-Delighted

गतवति सखीवृन्देऽमन्दत्रपाभरनिर्भर-
स्मरपरवशाकूतस्फीतस्मितस्नपिताधराम् ।
सरसमनसं दृष्ट्वा राधां मुहुर्नवपल्लव-
प्रसवशयने निक्षिप्ताक्षीमुवाच हरिः प्रियाम् ॥

> When the group of friends left, Hari said, seeing his beloved Radha, her lips drenched in a smile broadened by an intent which was under Love's hold, her glance repeatedly moving to the bed of soft leaves and flowers, his heart filled with *rasa*.

किसलयशयनतले कुरु कामिनि चरणनलिनविनिवेशम् ।
तव पदपल्लववैरिपराभवमिदमनुभवतु सुवेशम् ॥
क्षणमधुना नारायणमनुगतमनुसर राधिके ॥

> "Beautiful one! Place your foot-lotus on the surface of the bed of leaves. Even well-adorned, let this competitor of your foot-bud experience defeat. Radhika! For a moment, now, follow Narayana, who am your follower."

BUDDHIST AND JAIN ❋4
GODDESSES

The ascetic traditions of Buddhism and Jainism bowed to the grace of the Goddess and accepted Her into their fold. Through syncretic theology and mystical symbolism, the goddesses of Buddhism and Jainism combined their unique principles with nature, the cultural milieu, and old, familiar cults to formulate new additions to their existing canon.

The goddesses of Buddhism

There are a vast number of female divinities within Buddhism as powerful and commanding as those within the Indic religions. These goddesses also reveal an intrinsic connection with their Hindu counterparts.

Goddesses preside over many aspects of everyday living within the Buddhist culture. They are nature spirits and lofty cosmic divinities. Their dominion is expansive – across agriculture, childbirth, art, learning, the occult, truths of a high order, search for salvation, and even protection from epidemics and untimely death. They could be kind, generous, angry, and dreadful. However, they are definitely not on the periphery and have played a prominent role across different milieus.

Transformation

One of the biggest changes in the development of Buddhism was during the 1st century CE. It was almost a turning point on the way to salvation, notes American art historian Stella Kramrisch. It was a movement away from the Buddha to the Bodhisattva. A religion of faith and devotion replaced the philosophy of the ideal of personal nihilism. The trait of leaning towards the Bodhisattva and the goddesses was present, but at an almost nascent stage.

"This deviation," Kramrisch writes in her book *Exploring India's Sacred Art*, "that had begun about 600 years after the parinirvana of the Lord, once more after six centuries, was reinforced… and… directed toward Tara and Sakti." Indian scholar of Tantra NN Bhattacharyya, however, believes that though "early Buddhism or Jainism had nothing to do with the cult of the Female Principle, the reason for its

acceptance by the Buddhists and Jains evidently lay in its functional role in the religious history of India".

The goddesses

There is a dazzling gamut of Buddhist goddesses in the texts and art. For instance, Prajnaparamita (See pp 222–23) is golden and serene in her understanding of reality. Tara, the green goddess (See pp 232–35), is redolent of the medicinal forest of lush landscapes. Vajrayogini (See pp 244–47) dances in glee and devours all negativity for the supplicant, for she is the female Buddha, strengthened by yoga.

△ **Flower garlands** for Buddhist worship from Thailand

▽ **Buddhists**, especially those in and near the Himalayan region, attach spiritual and metaphysical powers to turquoise. They wear it as a ring, as in this image, or in a necklace.

"… **goddesses** can bring rain, create wealth, increase fertility, or **cure disease**… Goddesses are **ritually honoured** with… tender regard in hope they will **grant favours** to their devotees."

RICHARD S COHEN IN THE ARTICLE "GODDESSES IN BUDDHISM", EDITED BY YUDIT KORNBERG GREENBERG, *ENCYCLOPAEDIA OF LOVE IN WORLD RELIGIONS* (2008)

A symbiotic relationship

The number of goddesses only expanded during the Mahayana and Tantric movements. They represented what seems to be a happy, synergetic relationship between Hinduism and Buddhism.

For instance, within Mahayana (See pp 228–29), Vasudhara, the grain-bearing goddess of cornucopia, represents abundance, similar to her precursor, the Vedic goddess Prithivi (See pp 48–49). Tara and Vasudhara share traits with the Hindu goddess Lakshmi (See pp 168–71).

Marichi bears similarity with Ushas, the goddess of dawn. She is also the slayer of demons and evildoers, as, over the years, the concept of a warrior goddess, much like Durga (See pp 80–83), became grafted on to her personality. Texts indicate that Marichi was often invoked by devotees seeking her protection. However, there is no evidence that she is still worshipped.

Believers look up to Parnashavari, who is similar to Shitala (See p 377), for cures from diseases and epidemics. Janguli served the crucial function of protecting devotees against snake bites. Her counterpart in local Hinduism is Manasa, the goddess of snakes.

There was little change in the goddess Sarasvati (See pp 186–89) after her assimilation into the Buddhist pantheon. Her main trait as the Hindu goddess of learning remained the same.

American scholar of religious studies Miranda Shaw notes that the Tantric Buddhist goddess Simhamukha, with a striking lion face, seems to have visual parallels with the Yoginis in Tantric Hinduism (See pp 316–23). She also notes definite similarities between Chinnamunda, or the goddess with a severed head, and the Hindu Mahavidya Chinnamasta (See pp 300–01), noting that the former preceded the latter.

TANTRIC BUDDHISM

Tantric Buddhism became popular in the Indian subcontinent at a time when female deities had been emerging in Hinduism and Buddhism. According to Miranda Shaw, these goddesses got their full status as cosmic figures and supreme beings between the 6–7th century. It helped advance many female Buddhas who represent complete enlightenment. In India, it was the Vajrayana form of Tantric Buddhism that became popular from the 6–11th century.

The sacred mothers

Besides the Mother Earth, two human figures feature among the earliest goddesses in Shakyamuni Buddhism. They played an important role in Buddha's journey towards enlightenment.

For the longest time, scholars overlooked Buddhist goddesses. If mentioned, their descriptions often rendered them almost immaterial. In reality, however, texts, from as early as the 1st century, describe them as lively, multifaceted divinities with an array of powers.

There are an assorted range of goddesses, from arboreal spirits, frolicking female Buddhas, maternal and compassionate healers, and wisdom figures holding forth on concepts of liberation to commanding protectors. They often preside over actual occurrences in one's life, such as childbirth, and even dole out safety measures for diseases, epidemics, or curses. They cover almost the entire gamut of worries that besiege humans in one lifetime. However, three stand out the most.

Mayadevi, the birth mother

Lumbini, Buddha's birthplace in southern Nepal, once served as a mother goddess shrine. Its association with Buddha's nativity lay buried until, sometime following the 13th century, local women venerated the images of the mother goddess. Almost by default, the memory of Mayadevi, Buddha's mother, was also awakened and acknowledged.

However, her inclusion into the Buddhist goddess pantheon is debatable, even though there are lavish eulogies to her. She was, after all, a human. American scholar of religious studies Miranda Shaw writes in *Buddhist Goddesses of India*: "Mayadevi possesses the mythic overtones of an independent mother goddess by virtue of the fact that she conceived Shakyamuni Buddha through parthenogenesis,

▽ **This rare Nepalese mosaic** panel made with precious stones, from the 18–19th century, depicts Mayadevi (bottom right), the gods Indra and Brahma (bottom left), and the Buddha (centre) standing on a stack of lotus flowers.

without the help of a male." It seems clear that Mayadevi's veneration was not because of any overt or covert quality, but due to the deep reverence people had for the Buddha, her son.

The foster mother

Mayadevi did not live to raise her son and so her sister, Gotami, fostered Buddha. There is not much mention of Mahapajapati Gotami who appears only after Gautama attains Buddhahood.

His foster mother, she was the founder of the female contemplative renunciant monastic order. She was one of the first 10 to seek this calling and the first to take difficult monastic vows and become a Buddhist nun. Her career and enlightenment provide the embryonic concept of female Buddhahood. Her biography, *The Glorious Deeds of Gotami* or the *Gotami Apadana*, composed in the Pali language in c. 2nd–1st century BCE, provided a text for the Theravadin nuns.

Mother Earth

The first goddess to appear in Buddhism is Prithivi, the Mother Earth. It is undeniable that the mythographers drew upon fully established cultural motifs and almost borrowed the concept of the Vedic Prithivi (See pp 48–49).

She was also present at the moment the Buddha attained enlightenment. Shaw writes of a legend where Mara, the king of demons, challenges the Buddha, demanding that he provide his worshippers with a witness of his claim and worthiness to attain enlightenment. Buddha, in turn, touches the Mother Earth and invokes her. After all, she is

FEMALE BUDDHAHOOD

The question of female Buddhahood was raised only by Mahayana Buddhists particularly, those who proclaimed one path to universal Buddhahood that is Ekayana. For them, all men and women equally had the nature of the Buddha. The teaching of a sexual transformation from female to male, a popular theme in the Lotus Sutra, provided a means by which women become irreversible Bodhisattvas.

omnipresent and privy to everything that occurs on her voluminous being. Prithivi also provides the throne, the Prithivi *nabhi*, or the navel, metaphorically the centre of the universe, upon which the Buddha attains liberation.

There is also a delightful allusion to the everyday life of the monk connected to Prithivi. According to the Vinaya tradition, Buddha instructed his chief disciple, Ananda, to piece together the monastic robes in a patchwork pattern reminiscent of the troughs of tilled fields, in honour of Prithivi.

The earliest portrayals of Prithivi are found among the Gandharan reliefs, which date from the Kushana period, from the 1st to the 3rd century. Prithivi appears at the base of the Bodhi tree, or the tree of awakening. Her head and upper torso emerge dramatically from the ground surrounded by foliage. Often, the iconography depicts Buddha almost beckoning Prithivi by touching the fingertips of his right hand to the earth, demonstrating the *Bhumisparsha mudra*, or the earth-touching gesture.

△ **This stone sculpture** from c. 4–5th century depicts a Bodhisattva with an elaborate tasselled headdress. Such attire was worn by those who attained enlightenment. Similar looking sculptures have been excavated from the Gandhara region of modern-day Pakistan, Afghanistan, and western China.

"The **goddess of the earth**…
Spoke thus to the **Bodhisattva**; … 'Great Being,
It is **indeed** as you have declared!
In truth you are the **purest of all beings**.'"

LALITAVISTARA SUTRA, TRANSLATED BY MIRANDA SHAW, *BUDDHIST GODDESSES OF INDIA* (2006)

The goddesses in the sutras

Over the course of many years, several Mahayana sutras have been preserved across Mahayana Buddhist practices and traditions in India. These sutras, said to have originated in the 1st century, tell the story of the many goddesses within the Mahayana Buddhist pantheon.

△ **This painted wooden cover** from a palm leaf manuscript of the *Ashtasahasrika Prajnaparamita Sutra*, from the 10–11th century, shows Prajnaparamita being attended by two Bodhisattvas on either side.

The Mahayana school introduced goddesses into the Buddhist pantheon. The most important text documenting, through a story, the prominence of these divinities is the *Avatamsaka Sutra*, or the *Flower Ornament Scripture*, also called *Garland Sutra*, from the 1st–2nd century.

The Garland Sutra

The text tells the story of Sudhana, a pilgrim, who undertakes a voyage in his mission for enlightenment. During this, he encounters many goddesses who tell him of their personal search for spiritual awareness.

Each goddess leaves him with a teaching and he receives, with every meeting, a somewhat higher scale of knowledge. The goddess Prithivi, one of his mystical chaperons, forecasts his future Buddhahood. She tells him that being the Mother Earth, she gets to witness the enlightenment of every Buddha.

Mayadevi, as the mother of all Buddhas in the many worlds, tells her story to Sudhana as well. In it, as goddess Netrashri in another life, she helped Buddha attain enlightenment by defeating a hostile demonic army known to assault each Bodhisattva on the threshold of Buddhahood. The goddess swore to give birth to the Buddhas until he achieved perfect Buddhahood. This makes Mayadevi the quintessential mother. From her magical powers originated countless bodies by which she could appear as the mother of every Buddha in all the worlds of the universe.

The text of wisdom

The sutras are a category of Buddhist Mahayana texts. The oldest and most well-known among these that references goddesses is the *Ashthasahasrika Prajnaparamita Sutra,* or *Perfection of Wisdom in 8000 Lines*. Dated at perhaps 1st–2nd century, the text is not chronologically homogenous. As is the case with most ancient texts, certain portions display signs of antecedent leanings, compared to other parts. Though longer than other sutras, it is traditionally considered a kind of synopsis of a much lengthier work revealed by the Buddha.

The text reveals that in order for one to attain the Buddhist goal, one must realize the *paramitas*, or perfections, and *prajna*, or perfection of wisdom. The objective of this text appears to be to serve as a manual for the Bodhisattva in training. They are the earliest-known textual expression of the philosophy, marking the historical emergence of the goddess Prajnaparamita (See pp 222–23).

There is great fervour in the way she is eulogized as her very name reveals that she personifies wisdom and motherhood. What is interesting is the idea that the worship of Prajnaparamita surpasses that of the Buddhas.

> "She is the **Perfect Wisdom** who gives birthless **births** to all Buddhas.
> … It is mother Prajnaparamita alone Who turns the wheels of **true teaching**."

PERFECTION OF WISDOM IN 8000 LINES, TRANSLATION BY LEX HIXON, *MOTHER OF THE BUDDHAS* (2004)

This is because of the physiological truism that the Buddhas owe their existence to her as they cannot bring themselves into being.

It is remarkable to see the thought process giving pre-eminence to the very foundation, which is the allegorical originator, rather than to its products. This implies that even if the Buddha was to cease and his invaluable doctrine disappear along with him, the mother has the ability to reproduce such worthy offspring, again and again.

So, the original goddess Prajnaparamita, the embodiment of transcendent wisdom and the "Mother of all Buddhas", is within the human figure of Mayadevi as well.

Buddha's shrine

There is great reverence for the relics of Buddha, such as his teeth, robe, bones, and his ashes (See box). These were placed in a casket or reliquary and a stupa was built over it. Devotees circumambulate these stupas, wishing to be as close to the Buddha by this motion.

The Mahayana texts state that the relics of the Buddha receive their holiness from Prajnaparamita, for it is she who brought them into being. Without her, they would not be there, so the merit of worshipping her exceeds that of building stupas to enshrine Buddha's relics. She is the source of all sacredness. It is this philosophy that gives sanctity to the manuscripts that record the Buddha's teachings.

THE RELICS OF THE BUDDHA

Before his death, the Buddha left instructions regarding his mortal remains. After his cremation, his relics were to be distributed among his followers. His chief disciple, Mahakashyapa, completed his final rites before handing the relics to a group of disciples. When this happened, armed people from different clans arrived to claim the ashes. In order to avoid a violent clash, an unknown monk stepped in and the relics were divided into eight portions. Some of these were enshrined and placed in stupas.

Mother of all wisdom
This image, from an 11th-century manuscript of the *Shatasahasrika Prajnaparamita*, or *The Perfection of Wisdom in 100,000 Verses*, from Tholing Monastery, Tibet, depicts Prajnaparamita in a golden hue and wearing intricate jewellery and an elaborate crown.

Prajnaparamita

Mother of the Bodhisattvas

"She is **unstained**, the entire world cannot stain her... she **leads away** from **the blinding darkness**... She **cannot** be **crushed**. She **protects the unprotected**... She is the **antidote** to **birth-and-death**."

EDWARD CONZE, *THE PERFECTION OF WISDOM IN EIGHT THOUSAND LINES AND ITS VERSE SUMMARY* (1973)

Mahayana literature envisions the highest principle of enlightened wisdom as a goddess. While all Buddhist goddesses symbolize *prajna*, or wisdom, the goddess Prajnaparamita is perfection, the very epitome of wisdom par excellence. She has also, as a result, been elevated to the spiritual position of the "Mother of all Buddhas". The Prajnaparamita Sutras are key Buddhist philosophical texts composed by 4th-century scholar Asanga and named after the goddess. These are considered not only expressions of her wisdom, but personifications of herself.

Iconography

The goddess is most often depicted with a golden hue, with two or four arms. Her descriptions and iconography portray her as one adorned in lovely garments, gems, and as wearing a jewelled tiara, sometimes called a Buddha crown. This means she incorporates all aspects of divine enlightened knowledge.

Thangkas, or Buddhist paintings on cloth or silk, portray her with a deep orange hue. Here, she holds a palm leaf manuscript. In some sculptures, she displays a representation of it in her upper left hand as her most characteristic attribute. She also holds the vajra, or double-headed thunderbolt, in one of her rear hands, while her two hands in the front make the two-handed gesture of teaching.

As a deity

Prajnaparamita's advance as a deity in the Buddhist pantheon, from being on the periphery to coming right to the centre as the cynosure of all attention, is quite defined. This groundbreaking move takes place when under the guise of a female figure Prajnaparamita, the deification of wisdom, is achieved.

American scholar of religious studies Miranda Shaw writes, "The entire edifice or Prajnaparamita philosophy is based on the premise that the birth-giver is greater than the one who is born. The Buddhas receded in importance and devotion was directed to the maternal matrix of their omniscience – the inconceivably vast, magnificent, dazzling mother who brought them into being."

Ogress to protector
This slightly damaged silver roundel with gold foil of Hariti, dated 1st century, is from Pakistan, once a part of ancient Gandhara. One of the earliest representations of Hariti, it shows her on a throne, nursing a child. The auspicious symbol of a goose can be seen on the top left.

Hariti

Guardian of children

> **"The Lord** addressed her as follows: "Do you so tenderly **love your child**? But **you possess 500** such. How much more would persons with **one or two** love theirs?"
>
> SAMUEL BEAL, *BUDDHIST RECORDS OF THE WESTERN WORLD, TRANSLATED FROM THE CHINESE OF HIUEN TSIANG* (1884)

The creation of elaborate myths to make sense of certain ambiguous phenomena was a process common to all religious traditions. So too was the case with Hariti, a nurturing mother goddess, who was also greatly feared by those who worshipped her.

Hariti, believes American scholar of religious studies Miranda Shaw, is the first object of an independent cult within Buddhism.

The origin
Hariti was not always a goddess. She was malevolent and some myths even describe her as a Rakshashi. Over time, however, her status morphed and she rose to the stature of a Yakshi, or a nature spirit. Her popularity was due to her maternal, caring, and nurturing persona.

Her origin lies in quite a horrific legend set in the town of Rajagriha, Bihar. Hariti, in a previous life, has a miscarriage and promise to have her vengeance. Reborn as a Yakshi, she has 500 children. Determined to keep the vow she had made in her previous life, she eats Rajagriha's children and brings uncountable sorrow to the mothers. The residents ask the Buddha to help, so he takes Hariti's youngest child and hides him. Hariti becomes distraught and threatens to kill herself. The Buddha then tells her that her own personal grief is nothing in comparison to the enormity of pain she has brought to Rajagriha's people. He tells her to imagine the storm of sadness she brought on those who had but one child.

Hariti's transformation is immediate. She swears to mend her ways and becomes a follower of the Buddha. In turn, the Buddha promises her that she and her children will never lack food at the monasteries.

Her metamorphosis meant that she was now counted as one of the most loving, sincere, and faithful Buddhist goddesses. She became a benefactor granting wealth and children to those who offer her food and homage.

Iconography and associations
Unlike other Yakshis, Hariti's image often finds a place in monasteries, placing her at the centre of Buddhist institutional life. The Chinese monk Hiuen Tsiang makes references to this during his travels in India in the 7th century.

Her depictions vary but those from the Gandhara area seem more significant. She is almost always shown with one or more children either in her arms or around her. At times, she is with Panchika, a Yaksha, or a male nature spirit, as his consort, as in Maharashtra's Ajanta Cave 2 sculpture from the 5th century.

IN TODAY'S TIMES

ART

Some of the earliest sculptures of Hariti, dated as early as the 2nd–3rd century, were found in parts of Pakistan and Afghanistan. Various depictions of her can be seen in parts of North, West, and South India, Nepal, and Bali in Indonesia, too. Often, children surround her, or she accompanies the Yaksha Panchika as his consort. Indian artist Seema Kohli has given her own modern interpretation. A series of her paintings depict the goddess with dishevelled hair and lotuses, signifying knowledge, while her womb bears the wisdom of the Sun, Moon, and the stars.

In her image
King Jayavarman VII of the Khmer Empire commissioned the stunning Ta Prohm, a temple in Siem Reap, Cambodia, in honour of his mother and it held the statue of Prajnaparamita, the mother of all Buddhas. The goddess's statue was created in the likeness of the king's mother, as was the custom at the time. Ta Prohm's fame, however, stems from the trees that have taken over the complex, blanketing the structures with their thick roots.

The Mahayana pantheon

They protect, drive away nightmares, provide sustenance, guard against snake bites, and even heal. These goddesses, key to Mahayana thought, may have touches of the Hindu tradition, but are distinctly Buddhist in character.

The goddesses from the Mahayana pantheon may have drawn influences from Hindu deities, but they possessed singular Buddhist hallmarks. These were powerful goddesses whose primary role was that of protectors, replete with compassion and wisdom.

The protectors

Among the goddesses who play the role of guardians is Marichi, the goddess of the rays of dawn. She is a warrior and rides a chariot drawn by wild, fearsome boars. She has a golden banner and shoots arrows of light destroying all demons who trouble humans. Much like the *Rigveda*'s Ushas, Marichi too drives away the darkness every morning, and has the added role of a protector.

The goddess of the white parasol, Sitatapatra, protects her devotees from supernatural perils and astrologically fated calamities. She emerged from the crown of Buddha's head as he was deep in meditation while in Trayastrimsha, one of the heavens in Buddhist cosmology.

Snakes, so common in India, find a space in Buddhist faith, as they do in Hinduism as well. Such must have been the fear and awe of the reptile that most faiths worship or have a remedy for snake bites in the form of a goddess. In Buddhism, the goddess Janguli provides protection from snakes and immunity to poison. It seems like this was a case of assimilation as before the 9th century, in the areas that see the worship of Janguli, there is evidence of a female deity, who finds representation by earthen pots, stone, and clay effigies of snakes. Hinduism has a goddess of snakes as well, known as Mansa, while Jainism has Padmavati (See pp 254–55).

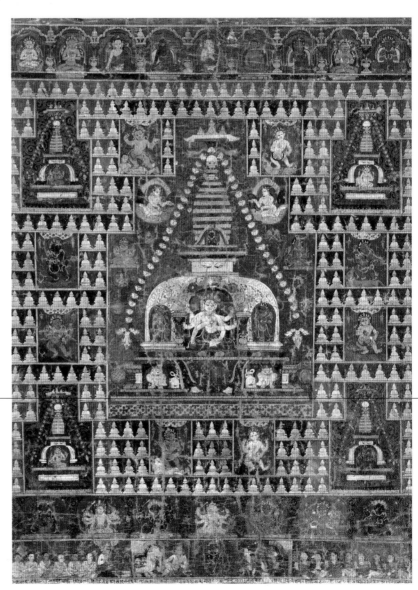

△ **Goddess Ushnishavijaya**
This c. 1510–19 painting on a cloth from Nepal depicts the goddess Ushnishavijaya (centre), the Buddha of longevity, who embodies *dharani*. She is surrounded by stupas, guardians, and Bodhisattvas.

"There is a **goddess** who travels **before the sun** and the moon.
She is **invisible**, indestructible, unbindable…
Unpunishable, unburnable and **unassailable**…
Her name is **Marichi**."

MARICINAMA DHARANI, TRANSLATED BY MIRANDA SHAW, *BUDDHIST GODDESSES OF INDIA* (2006)

For wellbeing and nurturing

Healing finds space within the pantheon by way of the goddess Parnasavari. Her name means tribal woman clothed in *parna*, or leaves and Savaras is the name of an ancient tribe. She lives in the forests in the high mountains and represents healing powers in herbs. Her attire, consists of natural produce – flowers, feathers, leaves and berries, which indicate her affinity to nature. She is envisioned exuberantly rambling through the forests.

A key goddess who emerged during the 9–12th century CE, Chunda is the boon-granting, saviour goddess who purifies negative karma. Her iconography shows her seated cross-legged in a meditative posture, a sure sign of renunciation. Her typical attribute is the vessel resting on the open palm of her hand, placed on the lap. She was the divine patron of the first Pala king, Gopala I who ruled the regions that cover Bihar and Bengal in c. 8th century. The Palas were a powerful dynasty that reigned in eastern India till the 12th century.

Sustenance, abundance, and wellbeing find representation in the goddess Vasudhara, whose name means "stream of treasure". Closely connected to wealth – material and by way of fertility – she finds parallels with Mother Earth and the Hindu deity Lakshmi. It is surprising to find a wealth-bestowing goddess like her within the pantheon, as Buddhism is mostly an atheistic religion. As American scholar of religious studies Miranda Shaw notes, "Buddhism has never really drawn a clear line between spirit and matter", having acknowledged the importance of basic human needs, such as food and medicine.

To defeat problems

The only Hindu goddess adopted into the Mahayana pantheon without a new name was Sarasvati. She continues the Hindu tradition for granting desired eloquence and oratorical expertise. However in Buddhism, she also helps with astrological matters, disharmony, or dreaded nightmares.

The goddess Ushnishavijaya, whose name means the victorious queen of crowning light, arose from the topmost portion of Buddha's head, or the *ushnisha*, which means crown or turban. This area of the head is regarded as one of inner vision and opening of doors of perception to a vaster cosmos. It can also mean the opening to a consciousness of complete awareness of truth. So, she is the goddess who bestows long life and grants rebirth in a Buddha paradise.

▽ **This brass sculpture,** created in the late 17th or 18th century, depicts Ushnishavijaya, who became a popular deity in Indian Buddhism during the 7th and 8th centuries.

DHARANI AND VIDYA

The word *dharani* refers to mantras that carry the essence of a deity. Miranda Shaw suggests that the goddess Ushnishavijaya's origin story, "underscores her character as a *dharani* goddess by describing her materialization from the light rays with which Shakyamuni Buddha etched her *dharani* in the sky."

Life of a Kumari
The *chakshu*, or fire-eye at the centre of the Kumari's forehead is a symbol of her power. Her divine status means that she is not allowed to touch the ground, and is carried in a palanquin. Her attendants, or Kumarimi, guide and dress her, but are not allowed to tell her what to do.

Kumari Devi

The living child goddess of Nepal

"She is believed to manifest a **powerful** Goddess who **protects** Kathmandu."

ISABELLA TREE, *THE LIVING GODDESS* (2014)

Deeply ensconced and long-enduring in Nepal's culture is the institution of the living Kumari, the physical incarnation of a goddess who inhabits the body of a child. The girl is regally dressed in red and gold, adorned in gold jewellery, with her hair in a neat topknot. A mere glimpse, it is said, brings the devotee prosperity and good luck. At any given time, there are 11 Kumaris across Nepal.

Selection process and life

The Kumari is chosen at the age of three or four from the Shakya clan of Buddha and must possess 32 similarities to the goddess. Her anointment takes place after she passes a series of spiritual tests, many of which remain shrouded in secrecy. Some reports indicate that one ritual involves leaving the girl alone in a darkened room. As a Kumari, she lives in the Kumari house and is carried on a golden palanquin when she ventures outside. She performs ceremonial duties and is expected to behave well. The Kumari retains her divine status until the first sign of puberty and before menstruation begins. Devotees believe that this is the moment that the Devi relinquishes the body and the goddess finds another child to live within.

Cultural crossover

It is believed that the Hindu goddess Taleju, a manifestation of Durga, inhabits the girl's body and mind for several years. This tradition, which merges Hindu beliefs with Buddhist ones, creates what Vidya Dehejia, Indian art historian, calls "a unique instance of religious syncretism".

Mythical origins

It is unclear how this practice originated, but Dehejia notes that the worship finds mention in manuscripts from the 13th century. Popular legends also credit the last king of the Malla dynasty, in power during the first half of the 18th century, with establishing this tradition.

There are several myths around its origin. In most of them, the last Malla king angers the goddess through his actions. When he pleads for forgiveness, the goddess tells him to find a child from the Shakya clan, to which Buddha belonged. She would manifest within that child's soul and allow him to worship her once again. This is how the belief in the world's only Living Goddess was born.

IN TODAY'S TIMES

CRITICISM

This tradition has come under severe criticism in recent times. Human rights activists argue that it impinges on children's rights as it subjects young girls to extreme practices and isolation. As goddesses, they are placed on the highest pedestal, which they have to give up suddenly on reaching adolescence. As former Kumaris, they may have to battle superstitions as well. However, things are slowly changing, as more emphasis is laid on their education and efforts are being made to help them transition smoothly into society.

▽ **The front view** of the Kumari Ghar, or the Kumari's home, in Kathmandu, Nepal

Tara

The one who nurtures and protects

"O holy Tara! You know **everything** that
I have done, my **happiness and suffering**,
my good and evil… think **lovingly** of me,
my only mother!"

A HYMN TO TARA, MIRANDA SHAW, *BUDDHIST GODDESSES OF INDIA* (2006)

Considered a Bodhisattva of compassion and action, Tara is one of the major Mahayana Buddhist deities worshipped as early as 4th century CE. She is also the most popular female divinity within Tibetan Buddhism.

Legends

There are several versions of her origin as a goddess. One of them refers to the Buddhist deity, Bodhisattva Avalokiteshvara. Once, he looked down on the Earth from his heavenly dwelling. He was so aggrieved by the misery he saw in the world that tears flowed down his face. The two streams of tears became the Taras — one white and peaceful, and the other green and fierce.

Tara's worship is most dominant in Tibet and Nepal. Indian art historian Vidya Dehejia, in fact, draws an association between Tara and the two queens of the first king who unified Tibet and introduced Buddhism to Tibet.

Understanding Tara

Tara is the female aspect of Avalokiteshvara, known variously as Eka Jata, Ugra Tara, Mahachinatara, and Nila Sarasvati. She occupies a central position in early Buddhist sources. Many Sanskrit texts, such as *Guhyasamaja Tantra* or the *Treatise on the Sun Total of Mysteries*, dated 8th century, were translated into Tibetan, and Tara's popularity spread in the region in the 9th century. As Indian historian Madhu Khanna observes, "Tara's reception and absorption into Hinduism was greatly facilitated via Tibetan Buddhism. The Hinduization of a Buddhist deity was mediated in literary sources, through the transmission of the celebrated narrative of Vasishtha from China to India, and by the assimilation of some Buddhist features in the iconography of Hindu Ugra Tara."

On a soteriological level, Tara's true character relates to her role as a saviour and as a natural concomitant to that function as a liberator. The saying *tarayati iti tara* echoes this principal purpose. This means that she saves her devotees from all types of calamities.

Tara is also designated *tarini*, or the one who helps beings cross over all forms of afflictions and the one who carries beings across the ocean of the repeated round of births and deaths, or *samsaratarini*.

In her green form
This section of a cloth painting from c. 1450–1500 depicts Green Tara. The painting is from Guge, an ancient dynastic kingdom in the western region of Tibet. Here, the goddess, seated on a lotus throne, displays the *varada mudra*, or the boon-giving gesture.

Forms of Tara

The goddess Tara manifests in several forms, each distinguishable by way of colour. While Green Tara and White Tara signify her peaceful and serene nature, her forms in red, yellow, blue, and black represent her anger and fierceness. What unifies each of them, however, is their role as a saviour.

▷ **GREEN TARA**
Other names Shyama Tara (Sanskrit), Jetsun Dolma (Tibetan)
Invoked for Protection

Perhaps the most popular in terms of worship, Green Tara is usually portrayed wearing ornaments made of gold and pearls. She is mostly seen in a standing pose and, at times, seated on a lotus with her right foot forward. Her green complexion symbolically depicts her connection with nature.

Green hue connects her to nature

△ **EMANATIONS OF TARA**
This 14th century stone sculpture from Tibet depicts 21 forms of the goddess Tara. Each form symbolizes different boons and characteristics, and some are known by their colour.

▷ **WHITE TARA**
Other names Sita Tara (Sanskrit), Sgrol-dkar (Tibetan), Saptalocana Tara (Nepalese)
Invoked for Longevity and healing

White Tara symbolizes purity and compassion. Her central pair of hands are cupped at the heart in the *manidhara mudra* and she is shown clasping the precious wish-fulfilling jewel, or *mani*. She also holds a lotus plant in different stages of flowering, which signifies that she nurtures a living being at every stage.

▷ **YELLOW TARA**
Other names Bhrikuti (Sanskrit)
Invoked for Wealth and prosperity

Yellow Tara is represented in her angry as well as
peaceful form. In her peaceful form, she is usually
standing, with a headdress and four arms. One
of the right hands is in the charity gesture
and the other holds a rosary. In the right hands,
she holds a trident and vase.

Four-armed form

▽ **BLUE TARA**
Other names Ekajati (Sanskrit)
Invoked for Transmutation of anger

In Sanskrit, her name Ekajati means one
who has a single *chignon*, or a knot of hair.
She is said to be one of the most terrifying
forms of Tara and is seen bearing a
chopper and skull cup. Her iconography is
perhaps meant to incite fear as she is
depicted with prominent teeth, a maniacal
laugh, and a protruding forked tongue.

△ **BLACK TARA**
Other names Ugra Tara (Sanskrit), Tro Nyer Chen Ma (Tibetan)
Invoked for Power and subduing evil

The fiercest form of the goddess, Black Tara is the one who
protects devotees from evil spirits, black magic, obstacles,
and negativity. She is wrathful and uses force to rid her
devotees of their obstacles. In her Tibetan form, she has
fangs like a tiger, which symbolize her ferociousness.

Typical standing
posture

Knot of hair

Terrifying expression
with protruding teeth

Dancing on
a male corpse

▷ **RED TARA**
Other names Kurukulla (Sanskrit),
Drolma Marmo (Tibetan)
Invoked for Subjugation

Red Tara is seen holding a red
lotus, the stem of which turns into a
noose. These signify her powers of
subjugation. She is said to have the
power to dramatically change lives.
Her left leg stands on a male figure,
which indicates controlling the ego.

Sragdhara Stotra

The *Sragdhara Stotra* is a Buddhist hymn composed by
Sarvagyanmitra of Kashmir who lived in about 8th century CE.
It is in praise of the Tantric goddess Tara who is described as the
mother of all Tathagatas, or the one who has gone.

The goddess of long life
This Nepalese Thangka depicts the white form of Tara. This manifestation is a symbol of longevity, calm, purity, and long life.

Jinarakshita, an ancient scholar, whose commentary on the stotra is popular, describes Sarvagyanmitra as a devout Bauddha *bhikshu*, or one who, having given away all he owns, wanders as a mendicant. This prayer was composed when Sarvagyanmitra's life was in danger and it miraculously protected him.

In the 37 verses, the author has communicated his sense of loss and hope that is generated by what he has heard and experienced of the goddess Tara.

The Buddha, as Sugata, is mentioned a couple of times as is Lokeshvara, a Bodhisattva. The gods, Brahma, the creator, Rudra or Shiva, the destroyer, Indra, the god of heavens, and Vishnu,

the preserver, are also mentioned. The goddess is not described in detail, although there is reference to her Tantras, her feet, and her colour that varies from red to green.

Her devotees believe that prayers to her lead to miracles. She is a saviour and a refuge for all those in deep distress, and the one who destroys all sin. She cures patients dying of disease and helps shipwrecked passengers reach the shore of the ocean. She also saves those who pray to her and are asleep in their beds when a fire breaks out. She can also save people from the brigands and their sharp swords. It is believed that one can defy death by praying to Tara.

A hymn to Tara

Using the metaphor of garlands of flowers to refer to praise, the poet makes a reference to *Sragdhara*, which is the metre of the hymn. In these verses, he describes the various forms of the goddess Tara. In the last verse, he emphasizes that the goddess does not actually change forms, but much like a crystal, she appears different, depending on what is placed nearby.

बालार्कालोकताम्रप्रवरसुरशिरश्चारुचूडामणिश्री-
सम्पत्सम्पर्करागानतिचिररचितालक्तकव्यक्तभक्ती।
भक्त्या पादौ तवार्ये करपुटमुकुटाटोपभग्नोत्तमाङ्गस्-
तारिण्यापच्छरण्ये नवनुतिकुसुमस्रग्भिरभ्यर्चयामि ॥

Tarini, the one who carries across! Refuge in adversity! Arya! Out of devotion, with my head bent with delight at the crown that are my hands brought together in supplication, I worship – with garlands of flowers which are novel praises – your feet, in which there is an instant pattern of lac made by the colouring caused by contact with the glorious splendour of the crown jewels of the chief gods, which are red like the brilliance of the young Sun.

चूडारत्नावतंसासनगतसुगतव्योमलक्ष्मीवितानं
प्रोद्यद्बालार्ककोटीपटुतरकिरणापूर्यमाणत्रिलोकं।
प्रौढालीढैकपादक्रमभरविनमद्ब्रह्मरुद्रेन्द्रविष्णु
त्वद्रूपं भाव्यमानं भवति भवभयोच्छित्तये जन्मभाजाम्॥

When contemplated, your form – its shade the splendour in the sky caused by the Buddhas seated on top of the crest-jewels, filling up the three worlds with rays more brilliant than a crore young Suns rising, Brahma, Marut, Shiva, and Vishnu bowed by the weight of a single foot, stretched out in the proud *alidha* posture (left leg drawn back, right knee pushed forth) – brings about the removal of the fear of rebirth for those who are subject to birth.

पश्यन्त्येके सकोपं प्रहरणकिरणोद्दूर्णदोर्दण्डखण्ड-
व्याप्तव्योमान्तरालं वलयफणिफणादारुणाहार्यचर्यम् ।
द्विष्टव्युत्रासिहासोड्डुमरडमरुकोड्डुमरास्फालवेला-
वेतालोत्तालतालप्रमदमदमहाकेलिकोलाहलोग्रम् ॥

Some see your angered form, the space in the sky filled with your arms, raised along with the rays emanating from your weapons, with acts as terrible and unflinching as those of the hoods of coiled serpents, terrible in the tumult of the great intoxicated sport caused by the energy of the heady rhythms of the spirits at the moment the extraordinary drums are resounded by (your) laughter which terrifies the enemies.

केचित्वेकैकरोमोद्भ्रमगतगगनाभोगभूभूतलस्थ-
स्वस्थब्रह्मोन्द्ररुद्रप्रभृतिनरमरुत्सिद्धगन्धर्वनागं ।
दिक्चक्राक्रामिधामस्थितसुगतशतानन्तनिर्माणचित्रं
चित्रं त्रैलोक्यवन्द्यं स्थिरचररचिताशेषभावस्वभावम् ॥

Some (see your form), which is an object of worship for the three worlds, with humans, Maruts, Siddhas, Gandharvas, Nagas beginning with Brahma, Indra and Shiva safely on the sky-like expansive surfaces emerging from each hair on your body, beautiful with the limitless forms of the Buddhas in the rays which extend in the directions of the compass, responsible for bringing about the creation and inherent nature of all moving and unmoving things.

लाक्षासिन्दूररागारुणतरकिरणादित्यलौहित्यमेके
श्रीमत्सान्द्रेन्द्रनीलोपलदलितदलक्षोदनीलं तथान्ये ।
क्षीराब्धिक्षुब्धदुग्धाधिकतरधवलं काञ्चनाभं च केचित्
त्वद्रूपं विश्वरूपं स्फटिकवदुपधायुक्तिभेदाद्द्विभिन्नम् ॥

Some see your form with the redness of a Sun whose rays are redder than lac or vermilion, others, blue-like the powder from a crushed piece of a splendid, smooth sapphire, some see your form whiter than the milk of the agitated milk ocean, and some see it golden. Your form, which is the cosmic form, is varied because of variations in the placement of the conditioning factor, like a crystal.

Female Buddhas

The worship of the feminine has been a major characteristic in India for a millennia. It was just a matter of time, for Buddhism that emerged out of this cultural landscape, to participate in this celebration of the female. Tantric texts and Tantric temples provide ample evidence of an astounding range of imagery of female Buddhas.

Within the plethora of Buddhist goddesses there is the female Buddha. She is neither a spouse nor a consort or an attendant, but the female Buddha herself. On looking closer, a pantheon of female Buddhas known as the Dakinis, the Tantric form of a female practitioner or spirit, becomes apparent.

The Mahayana path

The matter of female Buddhahood was raised by Mahayana Buddhists. They asserted there is one path to universal Buddhahood and that is Ekayana, or one path or one vehicle. For these, both the sexes had the nature of the Buddha.

American scholar of Buddhism Diane Y Paul, in *Women in Buddhism*, questions, "But what did Buddha nature then suggest for women's physical and psychological nature… if women were truly capable of having a Buddha nature in this lifetime without undergoing any sexual transformation, this would implicitly indicate that women were not biologically determined as religiously psychologically and physically inferior to men."

The wise one

The Mahayana goddess Prajnaparamita (See pp 222–23) represents a fascinating development in the history of Female Buddhas. She appears, with no clear antecedents, on to the Buddhist firmament with spectacular rapidity.

While the question of whether there could be a female Buddha was taking shape in the theoretical arena, Prajnaparamita,

▽ **Wisdom womb**
The goddess Prajnaparamita, seen in this white sculpture, is known as the mother of all Buddhas. She is the personification of a Mahayana text of the same name.

though not a Female Buddha, was duly recognized at the pinnacle of the pantheon, as the "wisdom womb" who gives birth to all Buddhas.

She personified wisdom that was such an essential ingredient for liberation. A woman could attain liberation, but was denied Buddhahood. Yet it was Mahayana Buddhism that had made Buddhahood the collective goal of all the practitioners – monks and nuns – regardless of their gender.

New deities

The Buddhist pantheon expanded under Tantric inspiration introducing new deities. The most remarkable theological achievement was explicitly affirming the possibility of attaining Buddhahood in a female body. Female Buddhas added a wonderfully colourful and robust dimension to not just Buddhist iconography, but also nuancing the aspect of soteriology, or the doctrine of salvation.

The first female Buddha

Tara (See pp 232–33) became the first female deity to be crowned with the title of Buddha. Once the perception of female Buddhahood was decisively ensconced, Tantric Buddhism advanced a number of female Buddhas encapsulating enlightenment and teaching esoteric yoga. In Tantric Buddhism, enlightenment is characterized as the realization of emptiness and sublime bliss. Tara fulfilled the goal of the very coveted liberation, not in some distant future or in

> **IMPACT OF FEMALE BUDDHAS**
>
> The presence of female Buddhas in Tantric iconography was a positive revolution for women. Especially because Tantric doctrine states that Buddhahood can be achieved in the present lifetime in the present body. Therefore, the introduction of female Buddhas was appropriate. Since bodies are both male and female the absence of a female Buddha would effectively exclude women from the Tantric goal of Buddhahood in the present body. Instead, Miranda Shaw notes that an older doctrine of innate Buddhahood is elaborated into a Tantric identification of men as male Buddhas and women as female Buddhas. This helps resolve the issue of women being able to attain Buddhahood both rationally and gender-wise.

another lifetime but in tandem with Tantric beliefs, in the present lifetime. Typical of the female Buddhas, if they are not depicted alone, then they have only females in their retinue, mostly yoginis. Among attributes in iconography, some appear to be standard, such as the knife and the skull bowl. These are tantric ritual implements which inherently have esoteric symbolic meanings.

Miranda Shaw, American scholar of religious studies, explains in her book, *Buddhist Goddesses of India*, "In Tantric symbology the object held in the right hand signifies the male principle of skillful means or techniques of attaining liberation. The object in the left signifies the female quality of enlightened insight or realization of emptiness."

△ **This c. 1300–25 gilt** copper statue is of a Dakini from either Nepal or Tibet. The Dakinis are an energetic female form and are usually seen in action in their iconography.

"Envision the **Buddhas** of the ten directions
In the form of Tara…
They **purify all beings** with rays of wisdom light,
Establishing them as Buddhas.
From now until complete **enlightenment**, pray
Quickly to become **Buddha Tara**"

MIRANDA SHAW, *PASSIONATE ENLIGHTENMENT* (1994)

Iconography of Tantric and Mahayana goddesses

Iconography is important in deciphering the purpose and role of each Buddhist goddess, whether she is from the Mahayana or Tantric school of thought.

The distinction between Mahayana and the Tantric Buddhist goddesses is clear in their philosophies and even more explicitly apparent in their iconography. Each feature of the Mahayana figures reflects the power of the goddess. At the other end of the spectrum are the Tantric goddesses whose varied motifs provide a reference to the yogic and ritual practices attached to them.

The protectors

Within the Mahayana tradition, which evolved in c. 2nd century, are goddesses (See pp 228–29) replete with their influences. They are often called upon to help individuals. This is because they are seen as saviours in their own right, evolved and powerful. Crucially, they do not provide the penultimate enlightenment.

Their iconography too seems to convey this, for they are usually depicted in a rather stately, seated stance. They are extravagantly attired in silken garments. They are lavishly embellished with stone jewellery and their hair is intricately coiffed.

▷ **Mandala and the goddess**
This 19th-century image depicts a Tibetan mandala often used in Buddhist and Hindu worship. Mandala is the Sanskrit word for circle. At its centre is the goddess Vajrayogini, worshipped for the prevention of death.

Triumph over selfishness

A Tibetan Buddhist Thangka painting of Vajravarahi from Nepal

Vajravarahi literally means adamantine she-boar. She is the wrathful form of the goddess Vajrayogini (See pp 244–45). Scholars, at times, use the names interchangeably. She is often described as the queen of the Dakinis, or the sky dancer, and is therefore seen in a dancing form. This is a traditional Thangka painting, an art form from Tibet, which means something rolled up. These paintings or drawings are made on cotton or other woven material. They are held up by a cane rod, which can be easily rolled up.

1. She is red, the hue of the essence of female accumulated life force – blood. The colour also signifies her passion. It is also a visual allusion to the fiery energy she abounds in through yogic practice. Her face exhibits intense concentration and ferocity. She is unencumbered by clothing.

2. Vajravarahi wears a garland of skulls, or a *mundamala*, and other human bone ornaments. She holds a skull bowl, like a chalice, in the right hand. It is brimming with the blood of gods and demi-gods. It also represents emptiness. The human bone ornaments are indicative of freedom from conventional dualisms of purity and impurity, of life and death.

3. In the right hand is her vajra, a small curved blade knife, that she brandishes in a threatening way. With this, she is said to cut off dualistic thinking, destroy illusions and a negative mindset.

4. She is encircled with flames. The blazing fire signifies wisdom as per Buddhist thought.

5. She treads on the corpse of her former self, which she has left behind in the course of her journey to Buddhahood. This shows the triumph over negative and self-centred mind states. Metaphorically, this means that the spiritual growth of a being entails the death of their selfishness.

6. On the crook of the left arm, she supports the *khatvanga*, or a mystical staff. Firstly, it represents her male consort as she is not celibate. She embraces the staff pole just as she wraps her arm around his waist when she dances with him in sacred union. Secondly, the staff symbolizes the ultimacy of her attainments. It is elaborate in design, bedecked with a vase of nectar supporting two heads in varying degrees of decay and a dry skull.

Devis in Jainism

The worship of the female divinity may have been a later addition to the Jainism faith, but played a crucial role in its spread. These goddesses performed a specific function – to help the devotee with everyday problems.

It is generally believed that Jainism, ascetic and puritanical as it was, kept away from goddess worship. Quite contrary to this belief Jaina sects, especially those associated with Digambaras, were engrossed in Tantric practices where veneration of the Yakshi formed an integral aspect of devotion. In fact, Yakshas and Yakshis are considered part of the entourage of the *Jina* image.

The need for a goddess

The faith of Jainism developed when Mahavira, a 6th-century chieftain of a republican kingdom, gained enlightenment and became known as the *Jina*, or victor. His path that lay emphasis on austerity and penance gained popularity and is today mostly practised in western India. It is important to understand how goddesses came to be accepted within traditions that were quite antithetical to their existence in the formative phases.

It could have been because the abstract nature of core Jain teachings needed some embellishments, which came in the form of goddesses. Perhaps, it stemmed from the need to keep the social base intact. The absence of a god denied the lay person from identifying with the supernatural, who could be invoked in the hour of crisis. Yet another reason could have been because the *Jina* does not give any boons. He is depicted either in *dhyanamudra*, the sacred hand gesture or in the *kayotsarga*, a standing posture, which literally means "dismissing the body".

A matter of inclusion

Indian scholar Virendra Singh Bithoo notes that it was in this context that there was a "need to incorporate existing local gods and goddesses who could grant boons to worshippers." It was easier, he writes, to "expand any religion in specific local and regional contexts when local elements are appropriated and assimilated." At the same time, he alludes that by integrating them, Jainism could easily spread into regions where their worship was more popular.

It helped too that goddesses could intervene in human affairs, unlike *Jinas*, who are liberated, perfect souls, completely detached from everyday human experience. American scholar of comparative religion, John Cort

> "**Jaina goddess** traditions constitute a **distinct strand** within the **complex history** of goddess **worship** in **India**."
>
> JOHN CORT, "MEDIEVAL JAINA GODDESS TRADITIONS",
> *INTERNATIONAL REVIEW FOR THE HISTORY OF RELIGIONS* (1987)

writes that while these goddesses could not "grant the devotee salvation, for that is a condition greater than themselves", there were indications of them taking on the role of "savioressess". However, mostly, the goddesses were "worshipped as *jagadanandadayini*, the goddess who grants the pleasures of the world".

Advocates of Jainism had also included Shasana *devatas*, or deities of teaching who protect and spread the message of the Jina along with Yakshas and Yakshis, in their pantheon, myths, and ritual. By the 10th century, they had become independent goddesses at the centre of their own cults. Today, Padmavati, Ambika, and Chakreshvari are esteemed deities and worshipped along with the Tirthankaras.

INFLUENCE IN THE SOUTH

Several shrines to the goddess Padmavati came up during the reign of the Western Ganga dynasty that ruled Karnataka from 350 to 1000 CE. Indian historian K Rajan says that Jainism was influenced by Tantric ideas and practices in the early medieval period. In c. 10–11th century, important treatises on Jain Tantrism were written in Karnataka. The *Jvalinikalpa Harivapadmavatikalpa* was dedicated to these goddesses, which has a lot of Tantric references.

Maternal instincts
This sandstone sculpture, created in the 6–7th century in Shahabad, Bihar, depicts Ambika with a child in her lap. Her beatific expression is representative of her nurturing and protective characteristics.

Ambika

The one who protects and nurtures

"She has remained a **popular** household **deity of fertility** and abundance among the lay **community of Jains**."

PRATAPADITYA PAL, *INDIAN SCULPTURE*, VOLUME 2 (1988)

Considered one of the most important goddesses in the Jain tradition, Ambika is the Yakshi, or female attendant deity, of Neminatha, the 22nd Tirthankara, or Jain spiritual teacher.

Sometimes, she is described as his consort, but is also known as Shasana Devi, or the protector goddess. In Jainism, many of the goddesses are seen as attendants to the male deity. Ambika, on the other hand, is a goddess, who, over time, was deified and is seen as very much an independent goddess in her own right.

The name Ambika literally means mother. She goes by several names including Ambai, Amba, Kushmandini, and Amra Kushmandini. Incidentally, Ambika is also an appellation of the goddess Parvati (See pp 108–19) from the Hindu pantheon.

Legend

According to an account in the 14th-century text *Ambika Devi-kalpa*, Ambika plays an important role in rescuing her devotees.

Similar to the other Yakshis, she extends her help to commoners as well as monarchs. In one such case, it is believed that she helped King Kumarapala of the Solanki dynasty accede to the throne in the 12th century in the region of Gujarat.

Iconography

Sculptures and artwork depicting Ambika are distinct. She almost always has four hands with the right ones holding a mango and a branch from a mango tree. She holds a rein and her two sons in her left hands. She is also seen under a tree, most often a Shala or Sal tree, with a lion, her vahana, at her feet. These relate directly to the legend surrounding her origin (See pp 252–53) and emphasize her link to children and motherhood.

Her sculpture in the Durga Temple complex of Aihole, Karnataka, shows her surrounded by female attendants. Sometimes she is also seen as a part of a pair with her consort Gomedha, following the Shvetambara tradition, with a small Tirthankara image on the top.

Role of Ambika

Most temples dedicated to Ambika are located in Rajasthan and Gujarat. Today, she is worshipped as the mother goddess, and is seen as the deity for material prosperity, safe childbirth, and protection of women. She is also said to represent fertility and plays an important role in protecting her followers against evil.

IN TODAY'S TIMES

SHAKTI VESHALU

On the last day of the Bonalu festival that takes place every year in Hyderabad and Secunderabad in Telangana, a group of male performance artists, called Shakti Veshalu, can be spotted centre stage in elaborate costumes. They come from diverse backgrounds and religions to play goddesses such as Ambika and Lakshmi. They take over 14 hours to dress and wear makeup, before performing in the processions as nine goddesses in 30 avatars. Art in this region is for all and truly has no religion.

A goddess is born

The myth behind Ambika's transition to a goddess can be seen as an analogy for how even a mere mortal can strive for the divine.

There once lived a content family of four – the father, the mother, and their two sons – in the land of Gujarat. Some legends call the mother Ambika, while others call her Agnila. One day, the husband invited several Hindu Brahmans for an important ritual and a feast, and the family cooked food for the occasion. While Ambika was busy with the preparations, she heard a sound and looked up. She saw a Jain monk outside the house, asking for food.

Ambika did not think twice, and out of the goodness of her heart, gave him some food. Her husband returned later, and became angry when he heard that she had given the monk food meant for the Brahmans. He considered this a grave transgression.

Furious, the husband told Ambika to leave the house. She wept and pleaded, but he refused to listen. Ambika had no choice. With tears streaming down her face, she took her two sons and left the only home she knew, absolutely bereft. She did not know what to do, for she had no food, money, or means to travel.

She had no choice but to make her way to a nearby forest. She walked through the woodland until she saw a withered mango tree next to a dry lake. Ambika knew that she and her children would starve, so she sat under the tree and waited for death.

In just a matter of time, before disaster struck, the tree produced sweet mangoes for them. Meanwhile, the dried-up lake provided water. The three, by a sheer miracle, survived.

Time passed and Ambika's husband grew repentant. He realized that he had made a mistake and went looking for his wife and two children. He finally made his way into the forest. As he approached the tree where Ambika had sought shelter, his wife saw him and did not realize that he wanted to take her home. She searched for a place to hide, but could only see a well. So she jumped in along with her sons, and died.

Because Ambika was a good person and had done no one any harm, she was reborn as a Yakshi to Neminatha, the 22nd Tirthankara, or Jain spiritual teacher. Her husband was reborn too, but as a lion, forever meant to rest at her feet and serve her as her vahana.

The protector
Cave 32, on the first floor of the Ellora caves in Maharasthra, has a typical carving of Ambika. The stone sculpture shows her with her two sons under a tree, with her mount, the lion, at her feet.

A resplendent vision
This is a white marble statue of Padmavati from a Jain temple in Mumbai, Maharashtra. As is the common tradition, the small image on the top is possibly of Parshvanatha, the Tirthankara associated with her.

Padmavati

The serpent goddess

"… on whose head is the **lord of serpents**, whose seat is an abundant **red lotus**…"

BHAIRAVA PADMAVATI KALPA

Seated on a lotus flower under a canopy of snake heads, Padmavati presents a tranquil image of a goddess. Even though she is associated with a creature as deadly as a snake, she is hardly fierce. One frequently encounters her in alcoves at temple entrances where she is dressed in the finery of silken clothes, resembling a bride. Just like the Hindu goddess Lakshmi, she is bountiful and bestows wealth. Jain devotees invoke her to dispel distress and attain *siddhi*, or accomplishment.

Assimilation into the Jain fold

Although Padmavati's origins are unclear, she was probably originally a *kula devi*, or a clan deity, and people invoked her to cure snake bites. She was integrated into the Jain system after the 10th century as a replacement for another snake goddess Vairotya. At this point, she was elevated as the Yakshi, or the guardian deity, of Parshvanatha, the 23rd Tirthankara, or spiritual teacher, who, like her shares a close relationship with snakes. That Padmavati has, over the centuries, acquired an independent status is clear from her many individual depictions where Parshvanatha is a small image in her crown.

Representations

The most common representation of Padmavati is one with four arms. However, she could have as many as 24 arms. She wields scores of things, ranging from *padma*, or lotus, *pustaka*, or book, and *veena*, a stringed instrument, to *divya phala*, or divine fruit, *ankusha*, or elephant goad, and *pasa*, or noose. Her hands could be in the *varada mudra* to indicate that she dispenses boons, and at times, it could be replaced by a serpent. She mostly sits in the yogic posture of *lalitasana* on either a rooster or a serpent. The serpent indeed is the most distinctive feature in her iconography.

Her worship

Padmavati is worshipped by both Digambaras and Shvetambaras, and just like Jvalamalini (See pp 258–59), her most prominent stronghold is Karnataka, where she was widely worshipped in the medieval period. In fact, she also figures in the foundation myths of the Western Ganga dynasty, which ruled ancient Karnataka between the 4th and 10th centuries. Even today, the region is dotted with many temples dedicated to the goddess.

Tantric modes of worship are often applied to revere this goddess. Her Tantric leanings are obvious from the "Padmavati Stotra", a hymn in her praise, which addresses her as the celebrated Tantric goddess Mahabhairavi. There are many Tantric texts that relate her rituals. Of these, the 12th-century text *Bhairava Padmavati Kalpa* is the most well known. It discusses rituals such as *stambha*, or immobilization, *vasya*, or subjugation, and *akarshana*, or attraction.

IN TODAY'S TIMES

PADMAVATI BASADI

Humcha, or Hombuja, a village in Shivamogga, Karnataka, is home to the most famous temple in the world dedicated to Padmavati. Although the current structure came up in the 11th century, its origins can be traced to the 7th century when it was established by Jinadatta Raya, founder of the Santara dynasty of Karnataka. According to legend, Jinadatta Raya had a dream in which Padmavati told him to establish his kingdom in Humcha. He constructed the shrine in her honour, near the tree under which he had the dream. The temple has been a prominent Jain centre ever since.

In all her glory
This is a wall carving of Chakreshvari seated on the mythical eagle, Garuda outside the Panchasara Jain Temple in Patan, Gujarat. She can be seen holding her trademark *chakras* in all four of her hands.

Chakreshvari

One who wields the chakra

"... the four-armed **Chakreshvari** rides a *garuda* and **bears discs** in her two arms."

MARUTI NANDAN PRASAD TIWARI, *ELEMENTS OF JAINA ICONOGRAPHY* (1983)

The guardian goddess or the attendant deity (Yakshi) of Rishabhanatha, first of all *Jinas*, or Victors, Chakreshvari is one of the most popular goddesses in the Jain pantheon. She is a Shasana devata, deity of teaching, who helps protect and spread the message of her Jina. Over time, she developed a separate identity as a powerful goddess.

Attributes

As with all attendant deities, the texts attribute specific features, characteristics, and powers to her. Her symbol, the *chakra* or disc, is one of the main weapons in the mythology of the Indian subcontinent, and her vehicle is the mythical eagle Garuda. This makes her similar to two Hindu gods – the goddess Vaishnavi whose vehicle is the Garuda and Vishnu who also wields the *chakra*. Chakreshvari's male counterpart is the Yaksha Gomukha, but, unlike her, he does not have an independent status.

Difference in nomenclature

The two principal sects of Jainism – the Digambara and the Shvetambara traditions – refer to Chakreshvari differently. The Shvetambaras call her Chakreshvari and Digambaras know her as Apratichakra, but this distinction is not watertight. Each gives her different attributes, yet they retain the *chakra* as her symbol.

Rites and rituals

She is sometimes associated with magic or occult practices that are the Tantric modes of worship. Unlike more orthodox Jain rites, worshippers invoke the goddess under her different names and visualize her using mantras to assist meditation. They perform various rites with the help of yantras, intended to appease evil forces and win the favour of the goddess. These take the form of hymns of praise composed in Sanskrit. The *Chakreshvari Ashtaka*, a hymn, is one such example.

Imagery and iconography

In all her sculptures and paintings, Chakreshvari is shown holding the *chakra* in at least one of her hands. The number tends to vary. A lot of the iconography related to her comes from Deogarh, Uttar Pradesh, which has one of the richest centres of Jain religious art in India, spread over the 9–12th century. Depicted with two, four, six, eight, 10, and running up to 20 arms, Chakreshvari's visuals are replete with numerous elements related to sacrosanct Jina images. These include adorers, attendants bearing *chamara*, or fly-whisk, flying *muladharas*, or the root *chakra*, elephants, small *Jina* figures, and also well-known goddesses Sarasvati and Padmavati (See pp 254–55). All these diverse images indicate her importance in Jainism.

IN TODAY'S TIMES

ATTEWALI, PUNJAB

The village of Attewali in Sirhind, Punjab, is home to an extremely popular temple dedicated to Chakreshvari. Believed to have come up during the reign of Rajput warrior-king Prithviraj Chauhan, the goddess and her *Jina* Rishabhanatha are portrayed as beautiful, white, stone idols. A popular legend states that the goddess instructed a group of touring pilgrims, carrying her idol, to install it at this site.

Jvalamalini

The dreadful goddess with flames

"She is the **destroyer of evil**, but she '**destroys** in order **to liberate**'."

S SETTAR, "THE CULT OF JVALAMALINI AND THE EARLIEST IMAGES OF JVALA AND SYAMA" (1969)

Emanating flames from her head, Javalamalini is the *Vahni Devi*, or the fire goddess. The fire she symbolizes is the medium that bridges the gap between the human soul and the supreme soul by engulfing every obstacle that restricts the attainment of the highest level of consciousness.

Independent authority
Jvalamalini is the Yakshi, or the guardian spirit, of Chandraprabhanatha, the eighth Tirthankara, or spiritual teacher. Her characteristics are detailed in a 12th-century Kannada text called *Chandraprabha Purana* where she is described in connection with Chandraprabhanatha.

Even so, she is one of the few Jain goddesses who are worshipped independently. Digambaras worship her for protection against evils and diseases. Despite some hymns dedicated to her within the Shvetambara tradition, the Shvetambaras do not attach many religious connotations to her.

Puranic connections
Although Jvalamalini is primarily a Jain goddess, Indian historian S Settar has traced her antecedents to the Puranic form of Devi as Mahishasuramardini. He says that the concept of the fiery goddess Mahishasuramardini (See pp 86–89) was incorporated into the Jain fold and gave rise to Jvalamalini. The Jain goddess who appeared was, however, slightly muted in her conceptualization. She also appears in various Puranas, such as the *Brahmanda Purana* and the *Matsya Purana*, where she is associated with Shakti, and the *Vayu Purana*, which associates her with Shiva.

The hub of her worship
Settar has also argued that Jvalamalini's worship was more popular in South India, particularly Karnataka, than in North India. Perhaps, due to this, her earliest representations also come from the Virupaksha Temple in Karnataka. It has yielded an 8th-century image of the goddess wherein she is perched under a canopy and has eight arms, each wielding a weapon. That the worship of Jvalamalini flourished the most in Karnataka is also clear from her many temples that were built in the 12th and 13th centuries.

Tantric affiliations
Jvalamalini is also worshipped according to Tantric traditions. Indian scholar of Tantra NN Bhattacharyya notes that mantras, yantras, mudras, and *nyasa*, or touching specific body parts while reciting the mantras, form an important feature of her worship. The Tantric cult associated with her gets a reference in the well-known historical text *Jvalamalini Kalpa*, which was composed by Jain acharya Indranandi and other Digambara monks of Karnataka in the 10th century. Her cult was started by Helacharya, a Jain Tantric teacher and leader of the monastic order Dravida-gana, who invoked her to drive out an evil spirit from one of his students.

IN TODAY'S TIMES

JWALAMALINI BASADI

One of the most famous and chief centres dedicated to Jvalamalini is in Chikkmagaluru, Karnataka. The temple traces its origin to the Vijayanagara period. Unlike most idols of Jain goddesses that are often white, the idol here is black, perhaps to indicate her fierce form. It portrays the goddess in her most typical form, with eight arms, each holding a weapon.

> "Tantric manuals suggest that **the figures** are not icons of **beings**, be it god or human, but that they are **icons of ideas** in a stylized mode."

PRANSHU SAMDARSHI, "THE CONCEPT OF GODDESSES IN BUDDHIST TANTRA TRADITIONS", *THE DELHI UNIVERSITY JOURNAL OF THE HUMANITIES AND THE SOCIAL SCIENCES* (2014)

Unfettered and free

Tantric Buddhism grew steadily ever since its emergence in c. 7th century, popularized as it was, by Siddhacharyas, or mystic poets, with their Tantric yogic practices, notes scholar Pranshu Samdarshi. Though Tantric Buddhism had its footing in Mahayana philosophy, it was different for it lay emphasis on practice and technique rather than philosophy. Tantric Buddhism used the language of imagery to illustrate deeper thoughts. In fact, some profound notions were epitomized through the symbolic union of male and female figures.

This is where the goddess announced a new stage of Buddhism in theory and practice, notes American scholar of religious studies, Miranda Shaw. They had a "more dynamic, passionate persona", she notes, and her "sole interest" was liberation. So, for instance, they looked fierce and their hair open much like female sages. The goddess accomplished the highest spiritual position in Buddhism – Buddhahood, the absolute zenith of the pantheon.

Deciphering Vajrayogini

In compliance with this concept, the Tantric goddess Vajrayogini (See pp 244–45), has a more energetic, ardent identity. Her visage is one of intense concentration and may even appear to be a bit on the fierce side. Her body is unclothed. She is described as *digambari*, which means "garbed in space" or "sky clad". This may suggest different things, such as being in consonance with

a renunciant lifestyle. It also indicates simplicity and a state of oneness with nature and all of creation. In Tantra, she is visualized as the centre of the solar orb where she stands in a heroic posture with her left leg forward. She holds her decapitated head in her left hand and a sword in her right, while blissfully drinking from the stream of blood gushing from her headless body. Her unbound hair indicate unfettered freedom and a disdain for convention. She is heavily ornamented, not unlike other goddesses, but her jewellery is made of bones.

Scholars, such as Samdarshi, suggest that visualization is a major constituent to Tantric practice. This is because most of the Tantric goddesses are seen with multiple heads, arms and legs that represent the multiple functional nature of an enlightened being.

▽ **A 1651 painting** of Vasudhara, the goddess of abundance from Nepal

GOLDEN GODDESS

Mahayana figures are in direct contrast to their Tantric counterparts. So, for instance, the goddess Vasudhara is seen calm and serene in her iconography. She appears golden or bronze, colours that are associated with opulence, fertility, and generosity. She also wears jewellery and an elaborate headdress that identifies her as a Bodhisattva.

The dancing goddess
Vajrayogini is often described as a Dakini, which loosely means sky dancer. In this metal sculpture, the goddess as a Dakini is depicted in her Tibetan form. She wears a necklace and a crown made of skulls.

Vajrayogini

The surveyor of the world

"The **dancing goddess**, Vajrayogini,
Is crowned with a **topknot**
And has the **third eye** of omniscience.
She pervades the **universe**…"

A NEWAR TANTRIC SONG, TRANSLATED BY MIRANDA SHAW,
BUDDHIST GODDESSES OF INDIA (2006)

It may be said that the principal supreme female Buddha is Vajrayogini. She is not only beautiful but an embodiment of compassion as well. She features in some of the earliest Buddhist scriptures from c. 7–8th century CE and remained significant in India through the 12th century. Today, she is still important in the living traditions of Tibet and Nepal.

Liberation

American scholar of religious studies Miranda Shaw translates vajra to mean adamantine, which refers to the indestructible state of enlightenment. She also characterizes Vajrayogini as a Dakini, "a tantric form of female practitioners who moves freely in space and dances in the sky". Her depiction in fact is that of the goddess leaping in a blissful manner. Her actions are much like a dance, but with an upward-bound movement, and buoyant with a kind of inexplicable joy – the joy of being liberated. Her hair, flowing, sways with her, as do her ornaments. Her ever-present chalice of a human skull seems to brim with ambrosia.

Vajrayogini is a Tantric female Buddha. She and her type mark a radical departure from the female archetypes of the Mahayana movement. The maternal nurturing quality of the Mahayana goddess gives way to the dynamic fiery Dakini whose sole task is to bring about liberation to her worshippers. She severs their "bonds of attachment", writes Shaw, and "removes all duality and delusion". She flies away from the world's limitations and sets forward to a stratosphere of great potential.

Vajrayogini embodies the pinnacle of spiritual enlightenment. She offers a striking visual portrayal of this enlightenment in the female form.

The Yogini

It is significant that the word yogini is part of her name. This means a woman who attained perfection through the practice of yoga, and grants the fruits of her yogic practice to her followers.

Shaw writes, in *Buddhist Goddesses of India*, "Her youthfulness is not primarily a mark of conventional beauty but rather a sign of yogic perfection, for mastery of the inner yogas regenerates the body, reversing the results of aging and restoring vigour, flexibility, and a smooth and radiant complexion."

IN TODAY'S TIMES

CHARYA NRITYA

The Newars, the indigenous people of Nepal, are known for performing a spiritual dance called Charya Nritya, which means dance as a spiritual discipline. Still practised today, this Buddhist dance form goes back to more than 1,000 years. Previously unknown and practised in secret, this art form is now in the spotlight because of social media. The dancers represent deities such as Vajrayogini and Tara. It involves disciplined yogic meditation practices and rituals. Dancers make different mudras and poses to reflect each deity.

The temple of the protector
The Pathirakali Amman Temple, also known as Pathirakali Ambal Kovil, in Trincomalee, Sri Lanka is a c. 11th-century temple dedicated to the goddess Bhadrakali, a manifestation of Kali. The elaborate and intricate ceiling, as seen here, and the temple's exterior exemplifies typical Dravidian style of architecture.

The legend of Kannaki

A fascinating and complex model of womanhood, Kannaki presents an interesting example of deification and Buddhist and Hindu syncretism. Her story is told in a popular Tamil epic, the *Silappatikaram*.

The worship of Kannaki, an iconic character in a popular Tamil epic in India, is unique to Sri Lanka. There are two distinct strands connected to her. The first lies in her transformation into a unique Hindu deity and the second, in incorporation into the Buddhist pantheon.

Story from the epic

Even though she was first enshrined in Kerala, Kannaki's origins are deeply rooted in Tamil Nadu. One first encounters her as the protagonist of the classical Tamil epic, *Silappatikaram*, or the "Tale of an Anklet", composed between the 2nd and the 6th centuries.

In the poem, Kannaki, an ordinary Tamil woman, marries Kovalan, the son of a rich merchant. He gets involved with a dancer and spends all his wealth on her. Penniless, he realizes his mistake and returns to his wife, who had remained faithful to him throughout. Kovalan hopes to recoup his fortunes through trade in the city of Madurai, ruled by the Pandya king Nedunjcheliyan I. In order to do so, he decides to sell Kannaki's precious anklet. However, as he tries to strike the deal, the anklet is mistaken for the queen's stolen anklet. Kovalan is accused of theft and beheaded without trial.

Kannaki learns of her husband's death and becomes furious and sets out to prove her husband's innocence. In the royal court, she breaks open her anklet and shows the king that it contains rubies, not pearls as in the queen's anklet. Realizing that there has been a huge miscarriage of justice, the king kills himself. Even so, Kannaki remains firm in her resolve to avenge the cruelty inflicted upon her and her husband. She tears out her left breast and sets the city on fire. Madurai, the capital of the Pandyas is engulfed in flames. It is only at goddess Meenakshi's request that Kannaki calms down. Due to her devotion to her husband, she is bestowed with divine strength and elevated to the status of a goddess.

Prominence in Sri Lanka

Sri Lankan anthropologist Malathi de Alwis notes that though there are no longer any temples to Kannaki in Tamil Nadu, a few shrines exist in Kerala, where she is worshipped as Bhagavati, an avatar of goddess Kali (See pp 126–29).

It is quite the reverse in Sri Lanka, where she has a devout following in every province of the island. Hindus, particularly in the eastern and northern regions, believe that Kannaki came to Lanka after setting Madurai on fire, in order to cool her anger. She visited two places in the north and seven in the east. These sites now have important temples dedicated to her. Here, the goddess is shown holding an anklet in each hand and is revered as a symbol of chastity.

▽ **Sri Lankan dancers** performing a traditional ritual dance during Gammaduwa in Nawagamuwa Pattini Devalaya temple in Colombo.

"When we hear your **anklets tinkling** and we see your **miracles, tears flow** from our eyes… rain your blessings on us!"

A SRI LANKAN SONG, TRANSLATED BY MALATHI DE ALWIS IN "THE INCORPORATION AND TRANSFORMATION OF A 'HINDU' GODDESS: THE WORSHIP OF KANNAKI-PATTINI IN SRI LANKA" (2018)

Buddhist and Jain overtones

Kannaki is also the only female deity venerated within Theravada Buddhism, the dominant religion in Sri Lanka. Sri Lankan anthropologist Gananath Obeyesekere has found distinct Jain overtones in *Silappatikaram*. He argues that Kannaki is a Jain goddess, not a Hindu one, which is why she was so easily assimilated into the Sri Lankan Buddhist polity. He claims that the deity was Jain and Buddhist even in her Indian milieu. It is possible, he notes, that her cult was rooted in the cult of the Mother Goddess of West Asia. This most likely came to South India as a function of mercantile and maritime contacts between West Asian merchants and their Indian heterodox counterparts in coastal Kerala. He suggests that Buddhist migrants from Kerala, fleeing South India because of an increasing Hindu hegemony and persecution between the 8th and 13th centuries, first introduced Kannaki to Sri Lanka and adapted her cult to suit the new culture.

▽ **In Sri Lanka**, people venerate Kannaki during the festival of Gammaduwa seeking relief from adversities. Seen here is a man creating a piece of decoration for the festival.

PROVIDER OF STRENGTH

In Sri Lanka, those battling diseases, poverty, death, and unemployment, often consider Kannaki as a symbol of resilience and find in her worship a coping mechanism. Devotees fasten their hopes and wishes in the form of coins wrapped in coloured pieces of cloth onto a "wish tree" in the belief that the goddess would quell their miseries. Women beat their chests while weeping for sick and dead children. As they pray, they shut their eyes tight until wrinkles appear on their forehead.

TANTRA AND THE GODDESS 5

Capsizing the Vedic and Puranic forms of worship, the Tantric traditions present an alternative way to experience the Goddess. The Tantric Goddess is extraordinary in Her overt form and bold nature. The only way one can experience Her is by striking a union with Her, that is, embodying the Goddess in one's own body.

Hindu tantric texts

The esoteric practices of Hinduism, Buddhism, and Jainism are enumerated in a body of literature called Tantras. This corpus presents itself as an antithesis to the Vedas and covers several esoteric subjects.

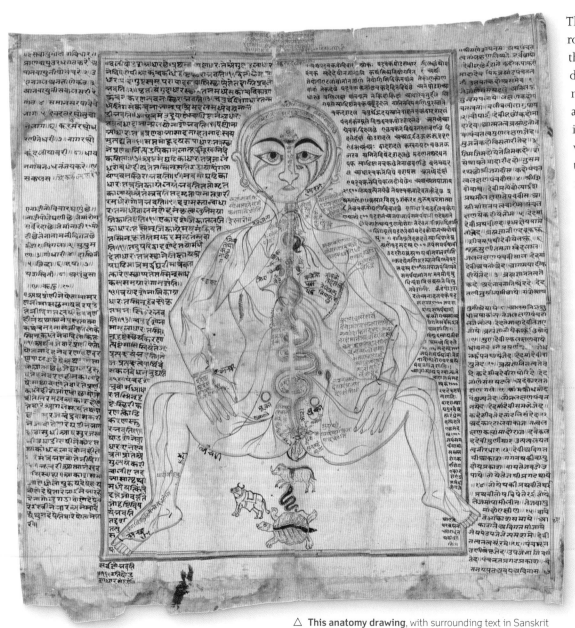

△ **This anatomy drawing**, with surrounding text in Sanskrit and old Gujarati, shows the flow of *prana*, or breath, through the body of a Tantric practitioner.

The history of Tantrism is rooted in a diffusion of ideas that occurs through two distinct but interdependent modes of transmission – oral and written. Tantric ideas are informed by scriptures as well as oral and unrecorded traditions, collectively referred to as Tantras. Although the number varies, they are believed to be 108, and dated around the 7–11th century, though the concepts expressed may be much older. By this time, Tantrism had imbued all major religions in the Indian subcontinent, including Buddhism and Jainism.

Unearthing the meaning

Just like the Vedas (See p 18), the Tantras also claim to have the status of revelation. They regard themselves a secret that can be revealed by a guru only with the appropriate initiation. This means that axiomatic to

"I make prostration to **Shiva and Parvati**… who **reveal themselves** in forms of ever-renewing novelty with the **progress of meditation**…"

ADI SHANKARACHARYA, *SHIVANADALAHARI*, TRANSLATED BY SWAMI TAPASYANANDA

the study of the Tantric texts is the necessity of oral interpretation by living initiates. This undoubtedly places limits on the interpretation of these texts. It is also one of the reasons why Tantras may sometimes appear to have obscure meanings for the uninitiated. Adding to this conundrum is their cryptic and difficult language. It is designed to exclude the uninitiated, partly because the texts prescribe transgressive practices and are heavily symbolic in order to uphold their secretive nature.

Sectarian division

The Hindu Tantras are divided along sectarian lines – the Shaiva Agamas, which focus on Shiva, the destroyer, the Vaishnava Samhitas, which revolve around Vishnu, the preserver, and the Shakta Tantras that gives prime importance to the feminine divine. Even so, regardless of the sect, as a general rule in the Tantras, the feminine divine, either in the form of Shakti or individual goddesses, acquires immense significance.

Structure of the narrative

The dissemination of knowledge in the Tantras is generally in the form of dialogue. In the Vaishnava Samhitas, there is dialogue between Vishnu and Lakshmi, and the Shaiva Agamas encapsulate exchanges between Shiva and Shakti. In both, the goddess, as the disciple, asks the questions and Shiva or Vishnu, as the master, answers. In the Shakta Tantras, it is Shiva who does the asking and the Goddess replies. This narrative structure reflects the importance and centrality of the guru in Tantrism as it is in the same method that disciples receive wisdom from their human masters.

Shakti and Shiva

The Shakta Tantras are among the most important texts crucial to understanding Shakti. They provide one of the earliest references where the concept is explored in detail. These Tantras, imbued with reverence for the divine feminine, represent the Goddess as the focus and the all cognizant one. They highlight Shakti as the creative aspect of the male gods and when unified with the male principle, She is the absolute truth. The Shakta Tantras treat the Goddess as equal and an essential part of the cosmic existence.

In a way, the Shakta Tantras are related to the Shaiva Agamas as the belief is that Shiva and Shakti are two aspects of the same truth and Shiva's dynamic power is Shakti.

The theosophy presents the masculine and feminine principle in a state of elemental, supreme, perfect harmony, expressive of the non-duality of Shiva and Shakti – the ultimate goal for the Tantric sadhaka.

KAULA

In the 10th century, Hinduism witnessed the emergence of a new Tantric tradition called Kaula. According to this school of thought, the manifest reality is perceived as *kaula*, a derivate of *kula*, or lineage, and the deity is termed *akaula*, or one who is beyond *kula*. In this system of worship, emphasis is given on group practices.

The practice and the practitioners

The esoteric practice of Tantra and the role of the Goddess within it can only be truly understood by unwrapping the elaborate rituals that form the core of its practice.

With secrecy lying at its very core, Tantrism evokes a mix of reverential fear and dark fascination. Demystifying its closely guarded ritualistic practices can only be speculative. The absence of credible anecdotal material further muddies any true understanding of Tantrism.

As early as the 5th century, Tantrism influenced a variety of sectarian traditions thriving at the time. It also started to pervade Hinduism, with its emphasis on the cult of divine feminine power. Indeed, the fluidity between the two in certain aspects can blur the boundaries between Hinduism and Tantrism.

The five essentials

Shrouded in secrecy, Tantrism's esoteric rituals set it apart from mainstream Hinduism. Central to these is the practice of *Panchmakara*, which focuses on the offerings of the *panchatattva*, or five substances. *Panchamakara* derives its name from these five essentials beginning with the letter "m" – *madya*, or alcohol, *mansa*, or meat, *matsya*, or fish, *mudra*, or hand gestures, and *maithuna*, or ritualized sexual intercourse. Performed by exclusive groups of worshippers, Panchamakara is also referred to as Shakti puja, yoni puja, *duti* puja, Yogini puja, and, finally, on account of its extreme secrecy, *gupta* sadhana.

These five essentials help the practitioner in overcoming the duality of clean and unclean, sacred and profane, while unshackling them from a world that is considered artificially

▷ **A modern interpretation** of the yoni, the symbol of Shakti or the primordial force of creative energy, and key to the practice of Tantra.

"… **facets** of Tantric… practice are **relevant** to all who… are **sincerely engaged** in the noble task of **spiritual self-transformation.**"

GEORG FEUERSTEIN, *TANTRA: THE PATH OF ECSTASY* (2000)

fragmented. The fifth and central Tantric *sadhana*, *maithuna*, can be performed with a woman previously initiated and transformed into the manifestation of the goddess.

The goal of Tantrism

The Tantric practice is an attempt to raise humanity to the level of divine perfection by the awakening kundalini shakti, or the force within.

The highest goal is the transformation of the body into divinity. Tantric practitioners view the body as a microcosm of the universe and focus on it as the only vehicle for attaining powers and liberation. By means of essentially personal rituals, the practitioner sacrifices his ego and thereby conjures the Shakti. This is called *sadhana*, or meditation.

Tantric texts explain how to compel lesser divinities and outcaste women, or Matangis, female flesh-eating demons, or Pishachas, and the ghouls or Dakinis. These state that the deities should be compelled, rather than persuaded, by uttering the right mantra in the correct manner. Mantras are believed to reveal the unity of the deity, the guru, the practitioner that is to be initiated, and the mantra. The *sadhaka*, or the follower of the *sadhana*, must know and repeatedly recite the goddess mantra, or *japa sadhana*, throughout the worship. It is imperative to correctly imagine and internalize the goddess. This can be achieved by drawing the correct magical mystical diagrams, or yantra.

The objective is to force the gods to bestow magical power on the worshipper, leading to bliss, the ultimate goal. For example, the *Shri Chakra* is one of the most famous yantras. It has a fascinating mathematical structure and is an indicator of the metaphysical sophistication of

the Shri Vidya tradition (See pp 280–81). The various parts of the chakra correspond to parts of the human body. The Goddess is regarded as the vital force pervading the chakras, the physiological and spiritual centres of energy in the body and rising as the kundalini energy through them. She is visualized geometrically in the complex triangles, circles, and other figures comprising the design of the *Shri Chakra* and is invoked by a secret mantra.

When invoking the Goddess through hymns and prayers, *sadhakas* should make their wishes known to the deity. They have to identify with the Goddess to have a vision of Her. This makes tantric worship strongly individualistic. Mantras are disguised and must be decoded by those with special knowledge. A guru plays an important part and transmits the mantra to the initiated individual. While the teacher is dedicated to awakening the student, the disciple must also be willing to engage in this process by cultivating loving regard towards the guru. The guru gives the information only after determining the capability of the disciple. There are many schools of Tantrism with variations in practices and norms – but what unites them is that they are highly ritualistic.

TANTRISM IN THE INDIA

Tantric practices were probably pan-Indian by the 10th or the 11th century. Scholars suggest that Tantrism was prevalent in Kashmir and Nepal, based on the manuscripts that have been found in the early medieval era. Bengal and Assam were also important centres for Tantrism before it spread to the far south. Many Tantras have been translated into Tamil and are used in South Indian temples.

The ten goddesses

The Dasamahavidya is a group of 10 Tantric goddesses or Mahavidyas. They are the manifestation of Shakti, the divine feminine – each with their unique characteristics and origin stories.

The character of the goddesses changed quite dramatically with the emergence of Tantrism. They became far more visible in texts as well as visual representations. The theology too became unequivocally centred around the devi. In fact, by the 15th century, Tantric goddesses had gone beyond growing firm roots and were coming into their own.

Among them is a striking cluster of 10 goddesses known as the Dasamahavidya, so diverse they have their own identity and attributes. Here, the adjective *maha*, meaning supreme and the expression vidya has been loosely translated as "knowledge" by modern scholars. But, it does not do justice to the fascinating characterization of these Tantric goddesses. Some are bloodthirsty and terrifying, while others are the epitome of grace. While one carries her own severed head, another enthrals and hypnotizes.

The name and order of the sequence of the Dasamahavidyas vary, but there is a general listing. This includes: Kali (See pp 126–29), Tara, Tripurasundari, Bhuvaneshvari, Chinnamasta, Bhairavi, Dhumavati, Bagalamukhi, Matangi, and Kamala. Of these, scholars note, Kali, Tara, and

> "The Mahavidyas are **not mere consorts** of male deities – here, Shakti takes centre stage to bring forth **time**, space, **evolution**, and **destruction**."
>
> KAVITHA M CHINNAIYAN, *SHAKTI RISING* (2017)

Chinnamasta are the most important and worshipped as individual goddesses as well. Here, Kali, notes American scholar of religious studies David Kinsley, emerges as "personified wrath" of Sati in this myth, and of Durga and Parvati elsewhere.

The fierce ones

The Mahavidyas are usually associated with Shiva's spouse, Sati (See pp 98–101) and their emergence ties into incidents leading up to Daksha's sacrifice (See pp 102–03).

The *Devi Bhagavata Purana* tells of an argument between Shiva and Sati about his not allowing her to attend Daksha's *yagna*, or sacrifice. Unable to bear this refusal, Sati decides to reveal her supernatural powers and appears before Shiva as Kali, naked, dark-skinned, and wearing a garland of skulls. Frightened, Shiva tries to run, but Sati's 10 forms manifest themselves, encircling the god. He then gives Sati permission to go to the sacrifice.

SHAKTAPRAMODA

The Shaktapramoda, a 17th-century text, is one of the best known Tantric ritual manuals of worship devoted to the 10 goddesses of the Mahavidya pantheon. It is a living text and passages from it have been quoted frequently in shorter, cheaply produced versions readily available in local marketplaces.

△ **The Mahavidyas**
This c. 1800 *rumal*, or handkerchief, from Basohli, Himachal Pradesh depicts the 10 Mahavidyas. The goddesses have been embroidered with silk on a cotton cloth.

Kinsley notes that these manifestations are not "mere feminine versions" of the Dasavatara (See pp 24–25). They are "not described as warriors" and their "fearsomeness" does not "seem to be related to upholding the cosmic order". Their sole aim, he notes, is to terrify Shiva and even establish her dominance over him. This "dramatically alters the traditional myth of Sati", writes Kinsley.

The origins

It is difficult to assign a definitive date of the formation of the group of Mahavidyas. When compared to the Ashtamatrikas (See pp 144–47) and the Chaunsatha yoginis (See pp 316–18), they seem to belong to a later period. Their earliest mention is in the *Mahakala Samhita* from the 12th century.

Despite their esoteric nature, their presence is expansive, seen north to the east, in temples, life-sized, painted icons, and popular calendar art. Some scholars draw a connection between Brahmanical Hinduism and local deities, calling the Mahavidyas, a result of a consistent, complementary interaction between the two.

Deciphering the goddesses

The principal aim of the Tantra is to overcome differences which would be stifling to individuals. The Dasamahavidyas facilitate the escape of such artificial shackles because they themselves are "social antimodels", notes Kinsley. These goddesses, who once thrived on the fringes, advocate different types of transgressive practices that flaunt or undermine the distinctions between the category of pure and impure. This is what created the composite worship of a hybrid group of goddesses.

The integration of Devis from diverse regions and with different doctrines gives prominence to marginalized goddesses such as Matangi, Dhumavati, and Bagalamukhi. Each goddess has her own point of origin, and have many versions. They retain their ethnic trait, making them fascinating and creating a fabric that is fundamentally inclusive.

The fierce one
This lithograph of Tara in watercolour is from Kolkata, West Bengal. Here, she is depicted as dark blue with a potbelly and clad in animal skin. Her hair is matted, just like Shiva, on whom she is standing.

Tara

The guide, the rescuer, and the saviour

"I have **studied the map** of the **invisible worlds**. I am the battle's head, the journey's **star**."

SRI AUROBINDO, *SAVITRI*

Tara belongs to the edge of the refined world. She is the power of the golden embryo, or Hiranyagarbha, from which the universe evolves, writes Indian author and monk Swami Harshananda. She is the "void or the boundless space". Second to Kali in the Dasamahavidya pantheon, on a soteriological level, her representation and real nature are closely related to her function as a saviour or liberator.

Tara's features

In Tantric texts, she is often referred to as Ugra Tara or the fierce Tara. She is similar to Kali in physical appearance. They both have dark complexions and their iconography often depicts them as standing over a corpse. Tara, however, differs from Kali as she is full-breasted and with a large, protruding belly. In the *Tantrasara*, a 16th-century text, her forbidding presence is described as being short and her location is often associated with cremation grounds.

In the hymn devoted to her in the *Mundamala Tantra*, she is called one who likes blood, is smeared with blood, and who enjoys blood sacrifice. The word *mundamala* means a garland of heads or skulls, often spotted on iconography dedicated to the Mahavidyas.

Origins and worship

It is likely that the Hindu Mahavidya Tara developed from the Bodhisattva Tara (See pp 232–35), who occupies a central position in Tibetan Buddhism.

The Hindu Tara is not as widely worshipped as Kali or Lakshmi, though there are temples dedicated to her in North India and Nepal. The most famous of these is the temple and cremation ground of Tarapith (See box) in West Bengal, a powerful centre of goddess worship.

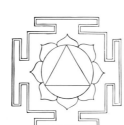

TARA'S YANTRA

According to the goddess Sati's myth (See pp 102–03), this is where Sati's third eye fell. A central stone image inside the temple depicts Tara nursing Shiva, the destroyer. This is a far cry from her more "fierce" displays and emphasizes her maternal and nourishing traits.

It appears that, just like Kali, Tara is associated with Shiva, but in diametrically opposite ways. She wears her hair knotted on top of her head in a *jatajuta*, or matted locks, in the style of an ascetic. This shows her propensity toward asceticism and yogis, which is essentially Shiva's ecosphere. In some depictions, the figure beneath her feet is Shiva.

Uninhibited and somewhat rough she is identified with the fires of cremation grounds. She, in essence, represents the final destruction.

IN TODAY'S TIMES

TARAPITH

Tarapith, a Shakti *pitha*, in Birbhum district, West Bengal, is the most well-known for the worship of Tara. There are many myths surrounding the establishment of this temple, the most popular of which traces its origins to the story of Sati (See pp 98–101). The idol of Tara inside the temple is made of rock and adorned with a silver crown and red vermilion. Followers usually gift a sari, which is then draped over the idol. An unusual aspect of this popular Tantric temple is that it is next to a cremation ground.

Tripartite rendition
This image, taken in 1990, shows a three-faced idol of goddess Tripurasundari from a Tantric temple in Tewar village in Jabalpur, Madhya Pradesh.

Tripurasundari

The queen of all the worlds

"The **dawn** is your robe. **Past, present, and future** are your **body**, and the **scriptures** are your **words**."

VANAMALI, *SHAKTI: REALM OF THE DIVINE MOTHER* (2008)

The conqueror of the three cities of the Asuras, she is the universal creative energy. Her manifestation may be gentle and benign, yet she encompasses all forms of Shakti, including the more fearsome aspects. She goes by several names, such as Lalita, Rajarajeshvari, Sodasi, Shrividya, and Shridevi, though she has no connection to Vishnu's spouse. Considered an aspect of Parvati (See 108–11), she is *sundari*, or the fair one, and her representation is that of a 16-year-old girl.

American scholar of religious studies David Kinsley describes Tripurasundari as "the cosmic queen from whom everything originates, in whom everything inheres, and by whom everything will be dissolved."

Beauty past compare

The 8th-century Indian philosopher Adi Shankaracharya has dedicated his composition *Saundaryalahari* (See pp 288–95) to her. In this, he describes her from the hair on her head to the toes, that is *Keshadi-padantam*. This is especially significant as the devotees finally find themselves at her feet.

The *Tantrasara* by Indian philosopher Abhinavagupta describes how, as Brahma, the creator, and Vishnu, the preserver, prostrated, the jewels from their crowns fell at her feet. These illuminate her as she sits on her throne.

TRIPURASUNDARI'S YANTRA

Her exercise of power is subtle, for she is not a warrior goddess. The hymn is a meditation in the present tense and not the recollection of a golden past. Unlike the earliest paean – the *Devi Mahatmya* – what is being worshipped is beauty and not fighting skill and manoeuvring.

Symbolism

Though married to Shiva, she is independent. She asserts this by sitting on different manifestations of the supreme gods, Shiva, Vishnu, Brahma, and the god of all Devas, Indra. Her iconography portrays her as holding various symbols of beauty and fertility. Her aura is one of domesticity and power, albeit of an understandable, and, so, acceptable kind.

Representations

American scholar of religious studies Kathleen M Erndl in her chapter on the Shakti tradition in *The Hindu World* quotes the Indian theologian Bhaskaraya, who noted three significant manifestations "which partakes equally in the illuminative and reflective aspects. These are physical (*sthula*), which is the iconic Lalita Tripurasundari; the subtle (*sukshma*), which is the Shrividya-*mantra*; and the supreme (*para*), which is the diagrammatic *shricakra* or *yantra* form."

Seated on Shiva
This painting is celebrated South Indian artist S Rajam's rendition of Lalita Devi. As is her typical depiction, she is shown seated on her husband Shiva's body, and is bedecked with jewellery to resemble a married woman.

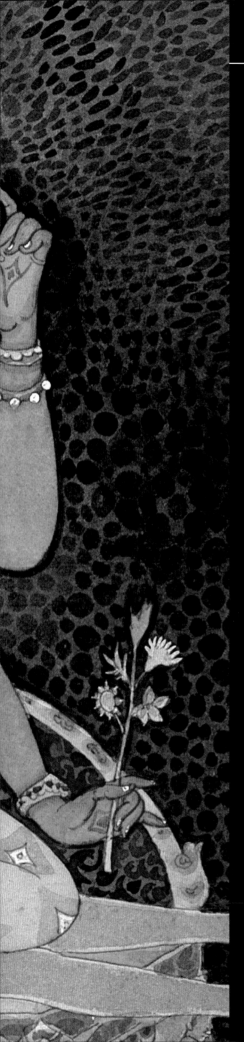

The emergence of Lalita Devi

The story of Lalita Devi and the war against Bhandasura in the Sanskrit text *Brahmanda Purana* is not only about good versus evil, but also establishes her supremacy as the goddess of all creation.

Shiva, the destroyer, was in deep meditation, when Manmatha or Kama, the god of love, interrupted him. Furious, he opened his third eye and turned his wrath on Manmatha, reducing him to ashes. One of Shiva's attendants, Chitrakarma, collected the ashes and shaped them into the idol of a man. When Shiva looked at the idol, it came to life. Happy, Chitrakarma told the man to recite the "Shatarudriya", a powerful hymn to Shiva from the Vedas.

The man performed severe austerities as he recited the hymn, until Shiva, pleased with him, granted him several boons. Among them were promises of a life that was 60,000 years long, invincibility, and power over the world.

Brahma, the creator, dismayed at Shiva's generous blessing, cried, "Bhand! Bhand!" So, the man came to be known as Bhandasura. He ruled over the Devas and the Danavas, and caused them great distress. Desperate to be rid of the Asura, Indra, the god of heavens turned to Narada, the heavenly sage, for advice.

The sage told the god to seek the great goddess Parashakti's help, but in order to do so, he would have to perform a great sacrifice. Indra followed Narada's instructions. As he performed the rituals, a great chakra arose from the sacrificial fire. In the midst of it was Lalita Devi, glowing brighter than the Sun.

Everyone came to see her and pay their obeisance. Brahma declared that no person who remained single was fit for sovereignty, and that she had to choose a partner. Of all the gods, only Shiva, as Kameshvara, was suited to marry the beautiful goddess. However, she had a condition. She told the gods that no matter whom she married, she would remain completely and totally independent. Shiva agreed.

After the wedding, Lalita left for her battle against Bhandasura. Three great chariots made up her army. She rode the first, the Chakraraja, or king of all chariots, which had Shaktis and warrior goddesses, each armed with every weapon conceivable. Her commanders rode two chariots – one that had goddesses who could bemuse the minds of the enemy and the Bhairavis, while the other carried the gatekeepers of all the directions. A fierce fight raged for four days, until Bhanda and all his kinsmen and followers were decimated and his capital razed to the ground.

Lalita Devi returned victorious and made Shrinagara her home, which was built on one of the peaks of Mount Meru. She brought Kama back to life as well. The overjoyed gods prayed to her, and called her Tripurasundari. They then praised her in a beautiful hymn called the *Lalitasahasranama* (See pp 278–79).

The Lalita corpus

The *Lalitopakhyana* and the *Lalitasahasranama* are important scriptures within Shaktism. Together, they present a systematic overview of the mythology and theology of the goddess Lalita.

▽ **This is a 20th-century painting** of Tripurasundari from Nepal, where she is also known as Purnachandi.

The worship of goddess Lalita is beyond the rigid compartmentalization of Tantric and Brahmanic ways of worship. She isn't tied down by any cultic or ideological affiliations, for anyone who wishes to gain favours from her can chant her mantras.

In addition to the *Saundaryalahari* (See pp 288–95), one encounters her most vividly in the third and last part of the *Brahmanda Purana*, known as Uttarbhaga, which includes the epilogue, referred to as Upasamharapada. In it, chapters 5 till 44 are delineated as the *Lalita Mahatmya*, also called the *Lalitopakhyana*. Composed of two words Lalita and *upakhyana*, or story, the *Lalitopakhyana* means the great narrative of Lalita. It is presented in the form of a dialogue between sage Agastya and Hayagriva, an avatar of Vishnu, the preserver.

Later addition

Even though the *Brahmanda Purana*, with its kernel dated to c. 200 CE, is widely believed to be one of the earliest Puranas, the *Lalitopakhyana* seems to have been composed later, probably in the 12th century. Sanskrit scholar GV Tagare in his translation of the *Brahmanda Purana* gives enough evidence

to show that the episode was composed as an independent text and appended to the Purana by Shakta devotees much later, perhaps to legitimize it and give it popularity. In turn, its insertion also gave the *Brahmanda Purana* a "Shakta colouring".

The Lalita tradition

The *Lalitopakhyana* recounts the complete mythology and theology of goddess Lalita. The text is preoccupied with presenting the goddess as the ultimate reality. This is clear as at several points, the narrative takes on the form of a eulogy. For instance, in chapter 13, the Devas sing in her praise. They address her as the one who is "greater than the greatest", "the embodiment of Brahman", and "the protectress of three worlds", amongst many such epithets.

Its overarching myth is her origin out of a sacrificial fire to slay Asura Bhanda (See pp 276–77). In this context, Indian monk and scholar Swami Tapasyananda compares it to the *Devi Mahatmya*. However, he perceives the battle and the Asura in the *Lalitopakhyana* as being far more "refined".

The *Lalitopakhyana* also contains the philosophy and rituals of Shri Vidya (See pp 280–81) and the ideas enunciated in it resonate with the philosophy of Advaita, or non-duality.

Lalitasahasranama

Towards the end of the *Lalitopakhyana*, there is a powerful devotional composition in the form of a mantra, consisting of 1,000 epithets for Lalita. Known as the *Shri Lalitasahasranama*, it

---

LALITA AND THE YOGINIS

Through the thousand names of Lalita, one gets a vision of her physicality, such as her slender waist, her wavy hair, her ornaments and armaments, and other characteristics. For instance, verse 237 describes her as one "who is attended on by a host of sixty-four crores of Yoginis". She is described as wearing a girdle of tinkling bells, often seen in the Yogini stone sculptures of Bhedaghat, Madhya Pradesh. This is an apposite example of the correspondence between the scripture and the sculpture and demonstrates her alliance with the Yoginis.

provides a beautiful description of the goddess and explains how to worship her. These 1,000 names are not mere titles. They encapsulate powerful descriptions of the goddess, for example, *Sarvastrakhandini*, or the splitter of all missiles, *Gandhakarshini*, or the one who attracts smells, and *Baudhadarshangani*, or the one who has Buddhist philosophy as one of her limbs.

The *Shri Lalitasahasranama* also exists as an independent text comprising three chapters – an introduction, the *namavali*, which lists the 1,000 names, and the *phala shruti*, which talks about the rewards as the result of observing the required practices.

Some scholars view the text as a sequel to the *Lalitopakhyana*, perhaps because of the same frame narrative. In the introduction, Agastya asks Hayagriva why he has not included the 1,000 names of the goddess in his narrative. Hayagriva replies that he thought it was a secret. He proceeds to enunciate the names and adds that they were composed by the goddesses of speech at the command of Lalita herself.

Popularity

Famous for its lucidity and clarity, the *Shri Lalitasahasranama* is a gem of the Tantric corpus as some of the names embody the

> ## "Salutations to Her who ever **promotes** the cause of **divine forces**… who is **radiant** as a **thousand suns rising together**."

VERSES 5–6, *SHRI LALITASAHASRANAMA*, TRANSLATED BY SWAMI TAPASYANANDA

major tenets of Tantrism. At the same time, any devotee of Lalita can chant it. It is indeed recited regularly in many parts of South India. French scholar of Tantra André Padoux in his essay "Mantra" says, "… the mantra of a deity is not the same thing as that deity's name. But since Vedic times lists of names of deities have existed, the recitation of which was prescribed and considered ritually efficacious or as salvific… Hinduism proposes a large number of namastotra, hymns of praise to the Name, or sahasranama, Thousand Names of deities, and there are cases where the name or names of a deity is/are to be uttered like, and with the same expected effects as, a mantra."

▽ **Women reading Sahasranamas** is a common sight in many Hindu temples in South India. This image is from a temple in Chennai, Tamil Nadu.

Shri Vidya

One of the most elaborate and popular spiritual practices in Tantrism is that of Shri Vidya, dedicated to Lalita Tripurasundari. Here, the devotee worships the goddess either in her geometrical or yantra form or by reciting the mantra in her name.

A significant Tantric tradition of the Shaktas, Shri Vidya is centred around the goddess Lalita Tripurasundari (See pp 274–75). She is invoked by a 15-syllable mantra called Shri Vidya – which lends this practice its name – and worshipped as a sacred diagram, the Shri Yantra, also known as the *Shri Chakra*.

Literary references
The cornerstone of knowledge and devotion leading the devotee to the goddess can be found in two medieval texts, both traditionally credited to Advaita Vedanta philosopher and theologian Adi Shankaracharya.

The first is the *Saundaryalahari*, or Wave of Beauty, which consists of Ananda Lahari, or Flood of Bliss. It constitutes hymns that promise the practitioner the attainment of the knowledge of *mantra shastra* and Kundalini yoga. It charts a course of appropriate ideas and practices for the ultimate union with the goddess. She is addressed in the Tantric form – the spiritual-material (*moksha-bhoga*), the auditory (from her ordinary appellation to her sacred mantra), and the visual (from her visible form to the yantra).

The other text, *Lalitasahasranama*, or The Thousand Names of Lalita, makes elaborate references to ritualistic worship such as Shri Chakra Puja, or the worship of the deity in a diagram form. Chanting the text is the concluding part of another prayer, the Shri Vidya Upasana. To recite this text is to expand the divine energy of the devotee's body before being initiated. Anyone can chant it. These are

shlokas, or poetic verses in Sanskrit, which speak of the benefits of reciting this hymn, which include harmony at home and protection from diseases. Each name of the goddess is deemed so potent that reciting even a few of her names is beneficial.

A living tradition
The ritualistic recitation of the *Lalitasahasranama* has been a regular feature in South India, particularly in the states of Tamil Nadu and Karnataka, where a large number of Hindu devotees follow the Shri Vidya Sadhana. Scholars argue that Shri Vidya, which developed and became popular in South India, may have had some connection to Kashmiri Tantric roots. The tradition, over time, became aligned with orthodox Vedanta and with the monastic tradition of the Dasanamis, or ascetics who belong to one of the 10 orders, at Sringeri, Karnataka and Kanchipuram, Tamil Nadu. It also became integrated with the Saiva Smarta community, traditionally believed to be founded by Adi Shankaracharya.

△ **Sometimes, the Shri Yantra** may also be depicted in a three-dimensional form. In this form, it is known as Mahameru.

SHRI VIDYA AND DUALITY

Shri Vidya integrates dualism and non-dualism. It says that the non-dualistic Shiva, the destroyer, and Shakti, the creator of the dualistic world, are inseparable. There is a distinction within the Shri Vidya between those who reject the use of the five makaras (See pp 268–69) of Tantrism and those who incorporate them. However, the Shri Vidya sect tends to distance itself from the extreme Tantric groups.

"… the Sakta… **Tantric tradition**… **originally transgressive**, became absorbed within the Brahminical tradition, so it became… **respectable**…"

GAVIN FLOOD, "TANTRA: THEORY AND PRACTICE" (2019)

Scholars hold Shri Vidya as more recent and "refined" in its form. Some of the extreme Tantric practices were considered unpalatable, especially those pertaining to animal sacrifice to appease the divine. Adi Shankaracharya is said to have pacified those deities by installing *Shri Chakra* in prominent Shakta temples across India, and prohibiting animal sacrifices in those places. British scholar of comparative religion Gavin Flood finds resonance of this in the Brahmanizing of later medieval traditions of Tantrism.

Concept and practice

Shri Vidya helps impart material prosperity and self-realization. Details of belief may vary across texts, but the general principles are similar to those within Trika Shaivism or Kashmir Shaivism, a non-dualistic tradition of Shaiva-Shakta Tantra. Three modes are prescribed for worshipping Lalita Tripurasundari: with the mind, with speech, and with the body. These translate into meditation or visualization of her form; repeating mantras; and performing external worship with flowers, incense, and vegetarian offerings. Initiation is a prerequisite for access to Shri Vidya, qualification for which must be determined by a guru.

▽ **The triangles in the** two-dimensional Shri Yantra represent creation and the intersection of the female Shakti and the male Shiva.

She who fulfills all desires
The Pathivara or Pathibhara temple is one of the most significant Shakti *pithas* in Nepal. Situated at around 3,794 m (12,448 ft), the temple is at the end of a four-hour hike, surrounded by snow-capped mountains. Devotees believe that a visit to the mountain goddess, who often requires ritualistic sacrifices, will fulfil all their dreams and wishes.

Shakta Upanishads

Encapsulating didactic knowledge, the Shakta Upanishads reflect some of the philosophical underpinnings of Shaktism. They draw upon the common leitmotif of Upanishads, but view Brahman and Atman as feminine.

"The Devi alone was, in the beginning. She created the egg-shaped world. She is known as Kamakala, which stands for the syllable IM. She is known as Shringarakala, which stands for the half-syllable (*ardhamatra*), after the a, u, and m, of the AUM." This quote from a Shakta Upanishad extols the Goddess. It is a part of eight minor Upanishads related to Shaktism theology of the Devi as the supreme being. They, along with other minor Upanishads, are classified as separate from the 13 major Principal Upanishads (See pp 18–19).

The Shakta Upanishads are believed to have been composed between the 9th and the 15th centuries. This makes them among the most recent minor Upanishads.

In the praise of the Goddess

The Shakta Upanishads contrast from other groups of minor Upanishads as they constitute an important source of information on Devi worship and Tantra-related theology. They are notable for declaring and revering the feminine as the supreme. They also deal with metaphysical concepts, such as Brahman, or ultimate reality, and Atman, or soul. The philosophical premises in many Shakta Upanishads is syncretism of two schools of Hindu philosophy – the Sankhya and Advaita Vedanta. The outcome is called Shaktadavaitavada, meaning, the path of monistic Shakti.

△ **19th-century gouache paintings** of Sarasvati (top), Lakshmi (middle), and Kali (bottom)

Goddess as the ultimate reality

Many of the Shakta Upanishads deal with the idea of monistic Shakti directly. The *Devi Upanishad* refers to Mahadevi (See pp 160–61) as representing all goddesses. It states that the Goddess is the Brahman and from her arises *prakriti*, or materiality, and *purusha*, or consciousness. She is bliss and non-bliss, the Vedas and what is different from it, the born and the unborn, and all of the universe.

Similarly, the *Bahvricha Upanishad* describes Devi as identical to all truth and reality, and whatever is not as unreal, non-truth, and non-self. She is the Brahman, the ultimate unchanging reality, the consciousness, and the bliss which shines by herself. She is everywhere, within and without, asserts the Upanishad. She is pure, she is love, and she is symbolized as the goddess Tripurasundari (See pp 274–75).

Individuality

The Shakta Upanishads are a great resource to understand specific goddesses. The *Kali Upanishad* describes Kali's mantra and yantra. The *Tara Upanishad* gives a grandiose description of the *vira svarupa*, or the omniform aspect, of goddess Tara (See pp 272–73).

Goddess Tripurasundari's Upanishad proclaims the identity between the body of the worshipper and *kundalini shakti*, the symbolism of the *Shri Chakra*, and the esoteric meaning of the *upacharas*, or treatments. The Upanishad attached to the goddess Kamala extols the greatness of goddesses Vaishnavi and Mahamaya (See pp 78–79). The *Lakshmi Upanishad* presents its ideas through the goddess Lakshmi.

SHVETASHVATARA UPANISHAD

Composed as early as the 5th century BCE, this verse Upanishad is found embedded in the *Yajurveda*. It is unusual because it places loving attention on a personal god. Right at the start, the supreme being is addressed with the Vedic names Rudra, Isha, and Ishvara, and then one is introduced to Shiva, who even today has millions of devotees. Importantly, this does not take away from the Upanishadic ethos of the universal spirit realized by sages in the depth of meditation.

> "But **nowhere else** have I seen such a pure, lofty, heady **distillation** of **spiritual wisdom** as in the **Upanishads**, which seem to come to us from the very **dawn of time**."

EKNATH EASWARAN, *THE UPANISHADS* (1987)

It discusses true wealth, and presents Yoga meditation for spiritual attainment, away from material cravings and towards inner wealth. It presents Tantric concepts, such as nine chakras, as a part of yogic practice.

Intertwined with metaphysics

According to Indian historian Madhu Khanna, each Tantra includes a sectarian proto-Upanishad. The inclusion of these short, but immortal, philosophical treatises was possibly motivated by a new impulse to give a philosophical foundation to the liturgical literature. These are essentially practical manuals concerned with providing practical techniques of worship with a sprinkling of meta concepts. The insertion of "mock" Upanishads in the compilation may have served to fill this gap.

A more plausible reason for providing a metaphysical underpinning was to relate the sectarian Upanishads to earlier Upanishads that enjoyed the popularity and prosperity of *Shruti*, that is "revealed literature". Sectarian cultures, such as Shaiva, Shakta, and Vaishnava, recreated their ancient affinities with a legitimizing reference to the authority of *Shruti*. This *Shruti*-based mock literature imitates and adopts the language of the earlier classical Upanishads. It proclaims the identity of the creator Brahma. Khanna points out that in reflecting the meta principles of their deity, the text may quote, paraphrase, and reframe ideas of the classical Upanishads by which they are influenced.

△ **Seven chakras** – the crown, third-eye, throat, heart, navel, pelvic, and root

ஸ்ரீ பாலாதிரிபுர சுந்தரி

லக்ஷ்மி

பிரம்மா

விஷ்ணு

ஈஸ்வரன்

ருத்ரன்

கணேஷர்

ஸ்ரீ

சக்கரம்

ஷண்முகர்

Unparalleled beauty

Tripurasundari's representation in a contemporary lithograph

The lithograph (facing page) resembles a celestial world, of deities – Shaiva and Vaishnava. In the centre of this world sits its queen, the resplendent Tripurasundari, commanding and controlling the functioning of the universe she has created. It is an extraordinary enunciation of the theological idea of feminine supremacy over the entire cosmos.

1. She is seated on a remarkable throne. The male gods make up its legs. These are Brahma, the creator, Vishnu, the preserver, and Shiva, the destroyer, represented as Rudra and Ishana (from left to right). This shows Tripurasundari's authority over masculine assertions of Brahman, or ultimate reality, and how without her Shakti the great gods are rendered lifeless and immobile.

2. The theme of servility is not restricted to male gods, for she has the ultimate supremacy. The goddesses Lakshmi and Sarasvati stand on either side and attend to her, holding fly whisks made of peacock feathers. This symbolizes their subservience to her.

3. She is attired as a typical *sumangali*, or happily married woman, with gold jewellery studded with gems and fragrant flowers in her hair. This form is to stress the idea that Tripurasundari is the most beautiful form of Shakti.

4. She is seated on the body of Shiva, her husband. That she is the wife of Shiva is clear as she wears his most distinct marker, the *chandra kala*, or crescent moon. Her intimate depiction with Shiva may imply completeness through the union of male and female.

5. Her maternal instincts and her role as the divine mother, the source of everything, including male energies, is clear through the depiction of her children, Ganesha and Kartikkeya (below, left to right).

6. Like most goddesses, she also wields different weapons in her many hands. The five-spiked weapon she holds indicates her control over five senses, representing her as the penultimate consciousness. Her most distinct weapon, however, is the bow in the form of a sugarcane. Sugarcane is the source of the sweetest nectar and bow is the weapon of choice of Kama, the god of desire. By holding such a thing, the goddess shows her benign and lovely form.

7. Her diagrammatic form has at its centre a *bindu*, or dot, which emanates a web of intersecting triangles, symbolic of a womb. The four triangles with tips pointing upwards stand for masculine, and the five triangles with tips pointing downwards represent the feminine. Their union leads to the formation of the universe, depicted through circular rows of lotus petals.

Saundaryalahari

The *Saundaryalahari* is a hymn to the allure of the goddess
Tripurasundari. Its primary sentiment relates to the realization of her
unparalleled loveliness. It draws upon the idea that her beauty is not
restricted by physicality, but has the power to move minds and souls.

The *Saundaryalahari*, meaning "the waves of beauty", is a 100-verse Sanskrit hymn in praise of the goddess Tripurasundari (See pp 274–75). Dated between the 8th and 9th centuries, its authorship, by tradition, is almost unanimously ascribed to the philosopher and theologian Adi Shankaracharya. The text is usually understood to come under the broad umbrella of the Shaiva tantric devotional tradition and is meant for the followers of Shri Vidya, an esoteric tradition.

It positions the goddess as the supreme principle of the universe. The first 41 verses, called "Ananda Lahari", deal with the goddess as Shakti. It talks about *ananda*, or bliss, a factor that

is experienced from within rather than from any outer vision. The mandalas, chakras, yantras, mantras, and tantras are written about as representing the psychic states or experiences of the yogi.

Verses 42–91, specifically called the "Saundarya Lahari", extol the beauty of the goddess from the head to toes. This section delineates, in graphic and vivid categorization, each physical feature.

The final 10 verses invoke the goddess to save the world. The secret mantra of the goddess, believed to bring about transcendental bliss, is encoded in the hymn.

Wave of beauty

The following are a selection of verses from the *Saundaryalahari*.
Highly descriptive as well as figurative, these verses contextualize
the aesthetic experience of the goddess. They highlight the idea
that her stature in the celestial world is profound, no doubt,
but her beauty comes from her devotion to Shiva.

शिवः शक्त्या युक्तो यदि भवति शक्तः प्रभवितुं

न चेदेवं देवो न खलु कुशलः स्पन्दितुमपि ।

अतस्त्वामाराध्यां हरिहरविरिञ्चादिभिरपि

प्रणन्तुं स्तोतुं वा कथमकृतपुण्यः प्रभवति ॥

Shiva is only capacitated to act when he is joined with Shakti – otherwise,
the god is not capable of even a twitch. So, without first having acquired
merit, who would have the capacity to worship or praise you, who are an
object of worship for even Vishnu, Shiva, and Brahma?

तनीयांसं पांसुं तव चरणपङ्केरुहभवं

विरिञ्चिस्सञ्चिन्वन् विरचयति लोकानविकलम् ।

वहत्येनं शौरिः कथमपि सहस्रेण शिरसां

हरस्संक्षुद्यैनं भजति भसितोद्धूलनविधिम् ॥

Brahma collects the tiniest bit of pollen from your
feet-lotuses, and tirelessly creates the worlds. Shesha
somehow bears it with his thousand heads. And Shiva,
crushing it up, partakes in the act of sprinkling ash.

त्वदन्यः पाणिभ्यामभयवरदो दैवतगणः
त्वमेका नैवासि प्रकटितवराभीत्यभिनया ।
भयात् त्रातुं दातुं फलमपि च वाञ्छासमधिकं
शरण्ये लोकानां तव हि चरणावेव निपुणौ ॥

> The multitude of gods other than you grants fearlessness and boons with
> their hands – you alone haven't manifestly acted out the granting of
> fearlessness and boons – for, Refuge of the worlds, your feet alone are enough
> for protecting from fear and granting fruit greater even than desire!

त्वदीयं सौन्दर्यं तुहिनगिरिकन्ये तुलयितुं
कवीन्द्राः कल्पन्ते कथमपि विरिञ्चिप्रभृतयः ।
यदालोकौत्सुक्यादमरललना यान्ति मनसा
तपोभिर्दुष्प्रापामपि गिरिशसायुज्यपदवीम् ॥

> Daughter of the snow-mountain! Poets, beginning with Brahma,
> attempt with great difficulty to compare your beauty, out of eagerness
> to see which the divine women mentally attain the state of identity
> with Shiva, difficult to attain even with austerities.

भवानि त्वं दासे मयि वितर दृष्टिं सकरुणा-
मिति स्तोतुं वाञ्छन् कथयति भवानि त्वमिति यः ।
तदैव त्वं तस्मै दिशसि निजसायुज्यपदवीं
मुकुन्दब्रह्मेन्द्रस्फुटमकुटनीराजितपदाम् ॥

> Bhavani! (You) Bestow a compassionate glance unto me, a servant – unto a
> person who, desiring to pray to you thus, says "Bhavani (may I be) you", You
> immediately grant the status of being united with you, the feet of which (state)
> are irradiated with the bright crowns of Vishnu, Brahma, and Indra.

जपो जल्पः शिल्पं सकलमपि मुद्राविरचना
गतिः प्रादक्षिण्यक्रमणमशनाद्याहुतिविधिः ।
प्रणामस्संवेशस्सुखमखिलमात्मार्पणदृशा
सपर्यापर्यायस्तव भवतु यन्मे विलसितम् ॥

> In the state of self-offering, let my prattle become *japa,* or repetition of mantras;
> all gesticulation, the composition of mudras; movement, circumambulation;
> all manner of consumption, the procedure for oblation; lying down, prostration;
> and all pleasures enjoyed, synonymous with service unto you.

किरीटं वैरिञ्चं परिहर पुरः कैटभभिदः
कठोरे कोटीरे स्खलसि जहि जम्भारिमुकुटम् ।
प्रणम्रेष्वेतेषु प्रसभमुपयातस्य भवनं
भवस्याभ्युत्थाने तव परिजनोक्तिर्विजयते ॥

> "Sidestep the crown of Brahma before you! Here you slip on the hard crown
> of Vishnu, the destroyer of Kaitabha! Avoid Indra's crown!" – Let these
> statements of your entourage when you rise to receive Shiva returned home,
> as all these (gods) are bowing before you, be victorious.

स्वदेहोद्भूताभिर्घृणिभिरणिमाद्याभिरभितो
निषेव्ये नित्ये त्वामहमिति सदा भावयति यः ।
किमाश्चर्यं तस्य त्रिनयनसमृद्धिं तृणयतो
महासंवर्ताग्निर्विरचयति निराजनविधिम् ॥

> One who is worthy of honour! The eternal one! What surprise is it if the fire of the Great
> Dissolution waves the lamp of worship before the one who, rendering a mere twig the
> prosperity of the three-eyed Shiva, contemplates you, surrounded by the rays beginning
> with Anima which have emerged from your own body, as his own Self?

ललाटं लावण्यद्युतिविमलमाभाति तव य-
    द्द्वितीयं तन्मन्ये मकुटघटितं चन्द्रशकलम् ।
विपर्यासन्यासादुभयमपि संभूय च मिथः
    सुधालेपस्यूतिः परिणमति राकाहिमकरः ॥

> Your forehead, immaculately effulgent with the splendour of
> its beauty, appears to me as a second crescent moon in your
> crest. If the two were to turn around and come together in a
> pair, it would turn into the full moon, emitting nectar.

अहः सूते सव्यं तव नयनमर्कात्मकतया
    त्रियामां वामं ते सृजति रजनीनायकतया ।
तृतीया ते दृष्टिर्दरदलितहेमाम्बुजरुचिः
    समाधत्ते संध्यां दिवसनिशयोरन्तरचरीम् ॥

> Your right eye, being the sun, creates the day, and your left, being
> the lord of night, creates the night with its three watches. Your
> third eye, whose splendour is that of a golden lotus in bloom,
> produces Twilight, the wanderer between day and night.

शिवे शृङ्गारार्द्रा तदितरजने कुत्सनपरा
    सरोषा गङ्गायां गिरिशचरिते विस्मयवती ।
हराहिभ्यो भीता सरसिरुहसौभाग्यजयिनी
    सखीषु स्मेरा ते मयि जननी दृष्टिः सकरुणा ॥

> Mother! Your glance is dense with love for Shiva, contempt for all
> others, angered towards Ganga, incredulous at the acts of Shiva,
> afeared of Shiva's serpents, triumphant over the beauty of the lotus,
> smiling at your companions, and compassionate towards me.

निमेषोन्मेषाभ्यां प्रलयमुदयं याति जगती
तवेत्याहुः सन्तो धरणिधरराजन्यतनये ।
त्वदुन्मेषाज्जातं जगदिदमशेषं प्रलयतः
परित्रातुं शङ्के परिहृतनिमेषास्तव दृशः ॥

> Daughter of the king of mountains! The wise ones say world attains
> dissolution and arising from the opening and shutting of your eyes.
> I suspect that your eyes have given up blinking to save this entire world,
> which has been produced by the opening of your eye.

मृणालीमृद्वीनां तव भुजलतानां चतसृणां
चतुर्भिः सौन्दर्यं सरसिजभवः स्तौति वदनैः ।
नखेभ्यः सन्त्रस्यन् प्रथममथनादन्धकरिपो-
श्चतुर्णां शीर्षाणां सममभयहस्तार्पणधिया ॥

> Terrified of the nails of Shiva, the enemy of Andhaka because of the earlier
> destruction (of the fifth head), the Lotus-born praises with his four faces the
> beauty of your four arm-vines, slim as the lotus fibre, in the hope that you
> would simultaneously place a fearlessness-granting hand upon each.

समं देवि स्कन्दद्विपवदनपीतं स्तनयुगं
तवेदं नः खेदं हरतु सततं प्रस्नुतमुखम् ।
यदालोक्याशङ्काकुलितहृदयो हासजनकः
स्वकुम्भौ हेरम्बः परिमृशति हस्तेन झडिति ॥

> Goddess! May this dyad of your milk-giving breasts, drunk by
> Kartikeya and the elephant-headed Ganesha, remove our
> distress, anxious upon seeing which, Ganesha quickly feels his
> frontal protuberances with his hands, causing amusement.

श्रुतीनां मूर्धानो दधति तव यौ शेखरतया
ममाप्येतौ मातः शिरसि दयया धेहि चरणौ ।
ययोः पाद्यं पाथः पशुपतिजटाजूटतटिनी
ययोर्लक्षालक्ष्मीररुणहरिचूडामणिरुचिः ॥

> Mother! Mercifully place upon my head too your feet, which the heads of the Vedas bear as their crest, the water from washing which is the river in the matted locks of Shiva, and the light of whose red dye is the splendour of Vishnu's red crest jewel.

हिमानीहन्तव्यं हिमगिरिनिवासैकचतुरौ
निशायां निद्राणं निशि चरमभागे च विशदौ ।
वरं लक्ष्मीपात्रं श्रियमतिसृजन्तौ समयिनां
सरोजं त्वत्पादौ जननि जयतश्चित्रमिह किम् ॥

> What is strange in it, Mother, that your feet – which are experts in living in the snow-mountains, brightest in the dead of night, and grant Lakshmi to your worshippers – are victorious over the lotus, which is destroyed by snow, slumbers at night, and merely bears Lakshmi?

गिरामाहुर्देवीं द्रुहिणगृहिणीमागमविदो
हरेः पत्नीं पद्मां हरसहचरीमद्रितनयाम् ।
तुरीया कापि त्वं दुरधिगमनिःसीममहिमा
महामाया विश्वं भ्रमयसि परब्रह्ममहिषि ॥

> Those who know the scriptures call you Speech, the wife of Brahma; Padma, the wife of Vishnu; and the daughter of the mountain, Shiva's consort. You are the fourth one, the consort of the supreme Brahman, whose greatness is limitless and incomprehensible, and who delude the world as the Great Maya.

Dance of devotion
On Maha Shivratri, a festival dedicated to Shiva, the destroyer, devotees throng the streets, celebrating the day. Some dress as the god himself, others as the goddesses Kali, Parvati, or Durga, who represent Shakti, much like this image from Chennai, Tamil Nadu. Here devotees, dressed as goddesses from the Hindu pantheon, dance to the beat of the drums, in honour of the god.

The golden goddess
This image of the goddess Bhuvaneshvari is a part of a chromolithograph printed by the Calcutta Art Studio, known for publishing images based on Indian mythology. Here the goddess has a rich golden complexion, is wearing gold jewellery, and a bright red sari.

Bhuvaneshvari

Queen of the cosmos

"Bhuvaneshvari is the **Space** that contains and sustains, the... Support of all **manifestations**."

S SHANKARA NARAYANAN, *THE TEN COSMIC POWERS* (1975)

She is the mistress of the world, linked to the cosmos. The 3rd Mahavidya, her connection to the universe is also reflected in her name – *bhuvana*, or the world.

There is an early reference to her in the *Prapanchasara Tantra*, a popular Tantric text that can be traced to the 10–14th century. In this, she is referred to as Prapancheshvari. *Prapancha* is a synonym for the world constituting the five elements – earth, water, fire, wind, and ether. This means that she is one with *prakriti*, or nature. She is also referred to as Pradhana, meaning the most important or prime.

Creation

A popular myth describes her as an emanation of the goddess Tripurasundari (See pp 274–75) who assumed the form of Bhuvaneshvari after she created the three worlds with Surya, the sun god. In a hymn in her praise, Bhuvaneshvari is described as a sovereign queen of the cosmos and the mother of Brahma, the creator, Vishnu, the preserver, and Mahesha, or Shiva, the destroyer. She upholds and protects the Earth and is called Jagaddhatri, or the one who carries the world.

Identity

The goddess Bhuvaneshvari does not manifest until the world is created. She is strongly identified with the physical world and its resources. Her worship is said to bring about auspiciousness, material success, and wellbeing. She is often also associated with the goddess Sarasvati (See pp 186–195), a patron of music, arts, speech, wisdom, and learning. This is why she is also called Vageshvari, or the mistress of speech.

In the same vein, Bhuvaneshvari is identified with *Shabda Brahman*, the ultimate reality in the form of sound, and *vac siddhi*, according to which anything one says comes true. Like the other Mahavidyas, her yantra is considered powerful. She also has her own *bija* mantra, a one-syllable sound used in meditation and *hrim*, a mantra that can calm the mind. These are key tools for practitioners and devotees.

Beauty unsurpassed

Texts often refer to Bhuvaneshvari's loveliness, such as in the 16th-century text *Tantrasara*, which describes her with a golden complexion and beautiful face framed by flowing hair. She is seen with the crescent moon on her forehead and adorned with many ornaments.

She is said to be so beautiful that Shiva produced a third eye to view her more thoroughly. Her connection to Shiva is a result of her being an aspect of Parvati. In her 100 *nama stotra* in the 17th-century text *Shaktapramoda*, she is described as a beautiful young girl.

BHUVANESHVARI'S
YANTRA

The headless goddess
This 19th-century coloured woodblock print from Kolkata, West Bengal, of Chinnamasta is a classic depiction of the goddess. Here, she is accompanied by her attendants, as she stands on Rati, the wife of Kama, the god of love, as the couple make love on a lotus.

Chinnamasta

Cycle of life, sustenance, and death

"Chinnamasta is the **thunder destroying** all the **anti-divine forces**; she is **the hidden radiance** in the **heart** of the cloud."

S SHANKARA NARAYANAN, *THE TEN GREAT COSMIC POWERS* (1975)

Perhaps one of the most electrifying images among all the Dasamahvidyas belongs to Chinnamasta or she whose head is severed. The self-decapitated nude goddess is usually seen standing or seated on a divine couple, copulating on a lotus. The couple depicted are the god of love Kama and his wife Rati.

Chinnamasta carries her severed head in one hand and a *khatri*, or a scimitar, in the other. Three jets of blood gush from her neck. Her head drinks from one stream of blood, while the attendants standing on either side, drink from the other two streams. This stark and gory imagery is enough to leave the viewer riveted.

There seems to be no real early prototype for the goddess Chinnamasta before her appearance in the Mahavidya group.

Symbolism of Chinnamasta

Scholars offer several interpretations of the symbolism behind this depiction. In the spiritual tradition, this is a sacrifice symbolized by the cutting off of the head. It indicates the separation of the mind from the body, implying the freedom of consciousness from the physical body. It is how one achieves spiritual awakening, self-realization, and the awakening of the *kundalini*, or spiritual energy.

Within the implication of the renunciation of attachment and ownership of the material lies the philosophy that one is nothing but the body. This suggests that the goddess helps the practitioner or devotee transcend the mind and its functions and face the reality that sooner or later death takes us all.

Attributes

Chinnamasta represents *atma-yajna*, or self-sacrifice. This manifests when a devotee offers one's own being to the Godhead, through an act of the sacrifice of the mind, in order to live fully, in unity with the divine consciousness.

Chinnamasta is a life-giver and a life-taker and an embodiment of sexual energy. By analyzing the copulating couple which is her pedestal, she also symbolizes the renewal of life. She is often described as destruction as well as life itself. The 17th-century text *Shaktapramoda*, describes Chinnamasta as one who represents death, temporality, and destruction as well as life, immortality, and recreation.

Chinnamasta is a significant Tantric deity, worshipped among esoteric Tantric practitioners. At times, she is also linked to Chinnamunda, a form of Vajrayogini (See pp.244–47), the Tibetan Buddhist goddess.

CHINNAMASTA'S YANTRA

Bhairavi

She who annihilates

"You **maintain the world** by your power **as the sun**, and you **dissolve the world** in **your form as fire**."

SARADA TILAKA, IN DAVID KINSLEY'S *THE TEN MAHAVIDYAS: TANTRIC VISIONS OF THE DIVINE FEMININE* (1997)

Ferocious and terror-inducing, Bhairavi's primary role in the cosmic process is annihilation. Considered the female form of, and consort to, Bhairava, a manifestation of Shiva, the destroyer, the goddess is the 5th in the Mahavidya pantheon.

German-American cultural anthropologist Wolf-Dieter Storl suggests that Bhairava would be helpless without this female power. It is believed that in his energetic female form he himself is the goddess.

Bhairavi has many forms and some texts indicate that she has as many as 12 different forms.

American scholar of religious studies David Kinsley describes some of them. As Tripura Bhairavi, she resembles a thousand rising suns. As Chaitanya Bhairavi, she is seen holding a noose, a goad, and a skull. She sits on a corpse and wears a garland of freshly severed heads that gush blood over her breasts. Sometimes, she is clothed in the skins of the Asuras she has killed. Her hands hold a rosary and a book, and make the mudras of *abhaya* and *varada* to indicate her fearless and boon-granting nature.

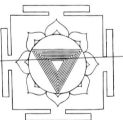

BHAIRAVI'S YANTRA

Etymology of Bhairavi

Indian scholar of Tantra NN Bhattacharyya suggests that, among the followers of Tantra, a female shamaness is called Bhairavi. She relieves her worshippers from all types of distress. Her name is formed by the letters "bha" symbolizing *bharana*, or maintenance, "ra" symbolizing *ramana*, or sport like creation, and "va" symbolizing *vaman* or release. Bhairavi also means terror.

Interpretations

In some traditions, Bhairavi is seen as one who oversees and empowers the three male deities associated with creation, preservation, and destruction – Brahma, Vishnu, and Shiva. She is independent of them and transcends them. She is said to control passion and arouse it.

Kinsley notes that some scholars identify her "with Mahapralaya, the great dissolution at the end of a cosmic cycle, during which all things, having been consumed by fire, are dissolved in the formless waters of precreation."

Dhumavati

The smoky one

> "Her **complexion** is like the **black clouds** that form at the time of **cosmic dissolution**."
>
> *BHAIRAVA EVAM DHUMAVATI TANTRA SHASTRA*

She who is made of smoke, or Dhumavati, personifies the dark side of life. The 7th goddess of the Mahavidyas, she is often described as an ugly widow clad in grey rags. American scholar of religious studies David Kinsley notes that the goddess has no known presence outside the Mahavidyas. He adds that she, interestingly, bears a likeness to the earlier Vedic goddesses (See pp 40–43), such as Nirrti, the goddess of disease and decay, Jyeshtha, the goddess of inauspicious things, and Alakshmi, the goddess of misfortune. She is nothing but smoke, and often dissipates and travels just as easily as smoke does.

Origins

There are a couple of key stories around Dhumavati's origin, which Kinsley notes in his book *Tantric Visions of the Divine Feminine.*

The first is connected to the myth of Sati and her death (See pp 102–03). It is said that as Sati's body burnt, the smoke led to Dhumavati's creation, embodying the mood of affronted outrage. The second myth tells of a time when Sati was so ravenous that she asked her husband Shiva, the destroyer, to get her something to eat. He refused, so Sati swallowed him instead. When Shiva asked her to release him, she refused. Furious, he cursed her to live as a widow and suffer like one. Smoke began to emit from Sati's body, her beauty almost vanished, and she appeared clad like a widow. Her name was now Dhuma, meaning smoke, or Dhumavati. She separated from Shiva and lived a solitary existence. Her new abode became the cremation ground, a smoky place.

Iconography

Dhumavati is usually depicted as carrying a winnowing basket in her hands, used to separate the grain from the chaff. It metaphorically denotes the Upanishad concept of *viveka*, or mental discrimination between the permanent and the fleeting. She is described as tall, usually in dirty clothes. Sometimes, she is dressed in white. She is toothless, her breasts are pendulous, and her nose is long and crooked.

A common feature in her iconography is her association with the crow. A carrion eater, the bird symbolizes death in some cultures. It is a fitting companion for a goddess of misfortune, decay, and loss. Occasionally, it is quite large and serves as her vahana, or mount. Sometimes, a number of crows accompany her.

In some temples, especially the one in Varanasi, Uttar Pradesh, her idol is made of black stone and she receives offerings, such as liquor, cigarettes, and meat. She holds a broom and a pot in her other two hands, while with the fourth she makes the *abhaya mudra*, which is the sign of fearlessness.

DHUMAVATI'S YANTRA

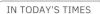

IN TODAY'S TIMES

DHUMAVATI TEMPLE

Today, believers worship Dhumavati seeking protection against their enemies. There are not many known temples to her name. One of them, however, is in the holy city of Varanasi in Uttar Pradesh. Here, devotees make peculiar offerings, such as meat, *bhang*, or a preparation made from cannabis leaves, cigarettes, and alcohol. Sometimes, devotees even make blood sacrifices.

Destroyer of enemies
This 19th-century drawing in opaque watercolour on paper from Nepal depicts the goddess holding the tongue of a man, probably the Asura Madan, who misused his power of speech.

Bagalamukhi

The one who paralyzes the enemies

"The wicked person turns good…
O Bagalamukhi, the **eternal auspicious mother**, daily our obeisance to thee?"

S SHANKARA NARAYANAN, *THE TEN GREAT COSMIC POWERS* (1975)

One of the most fascinating of the Mahavidyas, Bagalamukhi has some of the most divergent myths associated with her origin. In all of them, however, she is the goddess who, armed with a cudgel or a club, destroys her followers' adversaries and misunderstandings. She "stupefies the opponent", paralyses their *vac*, or speech, and has hypnotizing powers. Her name is derived from the Sanskrit words, *bagala*, or bride, and *mukhi*, or face.

Fondness for yellow

It seems that her preferred colour is yellow. One of her epithets is Pitambaradevi as she is supposed to have a yellow complexion. Temples devoted to her are painted yellow, sweets of the same colour are offered to her, and devotees wear yellow garments when they pay her obseisance.

Origins

According to one of the myths, she was discovered in Haridra, the lake of turmeric. Once, Vishnu, the preserver, was at the lake worshipping Tripurasundari (See pp 274–75), the supreme goddess, when a cosmic storm appeared.

It threatened to destroy the world. Scared he begged the goddess for help. Tripurasundari emerged as Bagalamukhi, calmed the storm, and restored balance.

In another myth, an Asura named Madan, received the boon of *vac siddhi*, or the power of speech, as a reward for his austerities. This meant that anything that he would say would come true. The power went to his head and he began abusing his gift and killing people.

Seeing the destruction, the gods prayed to Bagalamukhi. She appeared and grabbed Madan's tongue, taking his speech away from him. This is why, American scholar of religious studies David Kinsley notes, she is often depicted holding a tongue in one hand.

BAGALAMUKHI'S YANTRA

Connections in the name

Another myth connects Bagalamukhi to Parvati and Shiva, the destroyer. Once a famished Parvati implored Shiva to get her some food. He ignored her and continued his meditation. Enraged, she swallowed him, just like a crane. Kinsley feels that this may be why she is called Bagalamukhi. Other scholars, however, feel that her name comes from Valgamukhi, or the ability to control one's enemies. The latter seems to hold true in her defeat of the Asura, Madan.

Matangi

Goddess of the hunter tribe

"Reverence to… Matangi, **the outcast** and **residue**, who gives **control** over all creatures."

MATANGI MANTRA

The Moon adorns Matangi's head. She has three eyes and an emerald green complexion that signifies knowledge and life-energy. The 9th goddess in the Mahavidya pantheon, she wields magical powers, especially the power to exert control over the others. American religious studies scholar David Kinsley translates her name to mean "she whose limbs are intoxicated with passion".

It is said that Matangi lives in speech or in the forest. She is often depicted as holding the string instrument *veena* and a parrot, a representations of her powers over speech. She is also shown holding a sword, shield, noose, and goad in her four hands.

Association with tribes

In all her origin stories, she is described as someone belonging to a lower caste. Tantric texts associate her with tribes, such as in the *Matanga Parmeshvara Tantra*, which indicates that she originally belonged to the Matanga tribe.

The Matangas seem to have played an important role in different regions across India. One tale indicates that she was the daughter of the hunter-king Matanga. She is also connected to the Chandalas, Shavaris, and some hunter tribes. It is believed as the goddess of the hunter tribes, she has the power over creatures in the nature.

As a Mahavidya

The incorporation of a goddess such as Matangi, possibly of tribal origin, into the Mahavidyas fold, appears to be an effort to assimilate and give sanction to otherwise marginal deities. Indian art historian Vidya Dehejia points out that Matangi also appears in one of the Yoginis lists and her vahana, or mount, is a donkey.

Shaiva links

Matangi has deep connections to Shiva, the destroyer. One origin story calls her Shiva's sister who looked upon the god's lifestyle and habits with sheer disgust. Angry, Parvati (See pp. 108–11) cursed Matangi to be reborn in an untouchable community. Matangi was so unhappy that Shiva finally blessed her with a boon – people on pilgrimage to the holy city of Varanasi, Uttar Pradesh, would have to worship at her shrine before their journey to consider their pilgrimage complete.

Many stories also associate her with *ucchishtha*, or polluted leftovers. It is believed that one of her forms arose from the scraps of food that fell as Shiva and Parvati were eating. It is why devotees are expected to offer *ucchishtha* in a "state of pollution", which in itself is a reversal of the usual etiquettes for worship of Hindu deities – that is one must wash or bathe before praying.

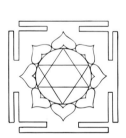

MATANGI'S YANTRA

Kamalatmika

The lotus goddess

"The **manifestation** of the **consciousness**, the **beauty revealed** in all its **glory**, the **exquisite charm** expressed is **Kamala**."

S SHANKARA NARAYANAN, *THE TEN GREAT COSMIC POWERS* (1975)

The Mahavidya goddess Kamalatmika, or Kamala, meaning she of the lotus and which is also an epithet for the goddess Lakshmi (See pp 168–71), has perhaps the oldest tradition of worship outside the Mahavidyas. There are references to her in the Vedas and she is seen in early sculptures. The Buddhists and Jains worship her as well. Adored widely, it would not be an exaggeration to say that she is one of the most ubiquitous of all goddesses.

Association with Lakshmi

She is recognized as one who bears metaphysical ideologies and transcendent cosmic functions but perhaps not with the same aura as her fellow Mahavidyas. Kamala's inclusion among the Mahavidyas does seem odd and it is an interesting appropriation of a "higher" goddess, such as Lakshmi.

There are some key differences. She is almost never depicted or described in her *dhyana*, or meditation mantras, with Vishnu, the preserver, or any of his avatars. She is not connected to the domestic or connubial sphere.

Iconography and features

Similar to the goddess Lakshmi, Kamala is usually depicted with four (not two) large elephants who grasp pitchers in their trunks and pour sacred water over her. Metaphorically, elephants relate to clouds and rain that signifies fertility, which is important in an agrarian economy. Elephants also suggest royalty and authority, as they were the preferred mount for kings during processions and military campaigns. She can be described as the goddess of wealth, fertility, and prosperity. She holds a lotus in one hand, while the other hands make the mudras, or gestures, indicating the granting of boons and giving assurance.

She is often depicted alone. But the importance of a Mahavidya lies in the goddess's independence. She is associated with the goddesses Varahi and Vaishnavi of the Saptamatrikas (See pp 144–47), the group of seven goddesses linked to the Mahavidyas. At times she is also linked with Shiva, the destroyer, as his consort.

Her qualities make her fierce as well as auspicious and desirable. The *Lakshmi Tantra*, a Tantric text dedicated to the goddess Kamala, retains her benign features, but integrates her fearful features within her eulogies.

Indian historian Madhu Khanna believes that Kamalatmika's role, "is to connect the Mahavidya pantheon with the mainstream Vaishnava worship thereby co-opting an all-inclusive model for the Mahavidya pantheon."

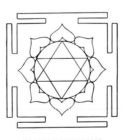

KAMALATMIKA'S YANTRA

Cradle of creation

A significant seat of Shakti worship, the Kamakhya temple in Assam holds deep meaning for the followers of the goddess.

Every year, after the first rains of the monsoon, in June, the temple of Kamakhya in Guwahati, Assam, comes alive for Ambubachi, one of the holiest festivals dedicated to the goddess. As the waters that run through the inner sanctuary turn red with iron oxide, devotees throng the temple to celebrate the goddess's menstruation.

Much like the other *Shakti pithas* (See pp 104–07), Kamakhya does not have a female icon or statue. Instead, followers worship a natural formation that symbolizes the yoni or vulva of the goddess.

Of the 10 temples dedicated to the goddess on the Kamarupa hill overlooking the massive River Brahmaputra, Kamakhya is the most important. The earliest mention of the site is about the 4th century, but the temple itself was built in the 16th century by the Koch dynasty. Today,

it has gained a reputation as a place of mystery, which sees the practice of esoteric Tantric rituals. It is, however, also a place of considerable significance within the Shakta culture. A place that, notes American scholar of religious studies David Kinsley, "reveres and enshrines a sacred place that is affirmed to be the creative orifice of a goddess whose larger body is the earth itself or at least the local mountain and region".

The temple at Kamarupa

Kamakhya traces its origins to the story of Sati (See pp 102–03) who steps into the holy fire after her father, the king Daksha, insults her husband, Shiva, the destroyer. As Shiva wanders the Earth with her corpse, Vishnu, the preserver, uses his *chakra*, or discus, to scatter her body across the land. Her yoni falls in Guwahati and

△ **Celebrating fertility**
Devotees throng the Kamakhya temple in June during the Ambubachi festival.

△ **Seeking blessings**
Bells and *chunnis*, or bright red scarves ,embroidered with golden thread are given as offerings.

△ **At their feet**
Devotees pay obseisance to carvings of gods along the sides of the temple.

becomes the site for Kamakhya. The temple itself has a long, low elevation comprising a sanctuary and three halls. The sanctuary and the innermost hall have octagonal and 16-sided domes. Stone carvings within the plain brick walls of the sanctuary depict musicians and guardian figures. The sanctuary is a cave. Here, one finds a cleft made of two sloping faces of stone. It remains moist because of water from a perennial natural spring. The hollow, some 10 inches deep, is a vulva-shaped depression that devotees worship.

Worshipping the goddess

Indian art historian Vidya Dehejia notes that unlike other rituals in goddess worship, those at Kamakhya are distinct. She notes that the festival of Ambubachi is similar to the one that takes place in southern India in Chengannur, Kerala, at the temple of goddess Bhagvati.

The festival of Ambubachi finds association with the menstruation of the goddess. For believers, the change in water colour, Indian scholar of Tantrism and art history Ajit Mookerjee notes, symbolizes *rajas* or *ritu*, or the goddess's menstrual blood. Devotees, especially practitioners of Tantric rites, gather at the temple on this occasion to touch the waters and seek the goddess's blessings.

"**Kamarupa** is the **sacred land** of the Goddess... **Elsewhere** the **Goddess** is **rare**; in **Kamarupa** she is in **every house**."

WORSHIP OF THE GODDESS ACCORDING TO THE KALIKAPURANA, TRANSLATED BY KR VAN KOOIJ (1972)

Religious studies scholar Patricia Dold writes that the "use of red water symbolizing menstrual blood as *prasad* and the closure of the temple during the goddess's annual menstruation provide one example of the interplay at Kamarupa between a transgressive Tantric orientation and orthodox standards of purity". She records the belief among devotees that this was "the best place to worship Shakti, the source of all creation, because this was the only place where the yoni... was worshipped. This understanding was also reflected in the words of the anonymous *bhakta* who said that the yoni at Kamarupa was the source of all: 'We are all born from the *joni* (sic) here'."

△ **An offering to the goddess**
A family sits before a priest at Kamakhya with offerings for the goddess in search of divine favour.

△ **Holy women**
Sadhvis, or women ascetics, prepare to participate in the annual Ambubachi festival

Bells of faith
A priest (left) performs a ritual at the Kamakhya temple, one of the *Shakti pithas*, located in Guwahati, Assam. Bells, as seen here, are a common sight in Hindu temples. Often, devotees ring them as a sign of respect, informing the deity that they have arrived. They are also considered auspicious and as a way to banish evil. Sometimes, bells are used as offerings for wish fulfilment.

The Yogini cult

A collection of obscure goddesses emerged across India sometime in the early medieval period. Though many temples to them are lost today, scholars are trying to unravel who they were and what they represented.

Among the category of cluster goddesses, the Yoginis have sustained their power to enthral. The air of enigma, part of their aura for over a century, is now being lifted with scholarly trails leading towards Tantric texts that are being translated and studied. There is not just a multitude of Yoginis, but a plurality in the descriptions, rituals, and traditions subsumed under the umbrella of the cult. There is a lot that needs to be understood, of who they were and what they entailed. And, there is a strong chance that much will not be understood or interpreted in an accurate manner.

Matter of identity

The word "Yogini" has a broad definition within Indian culture and there is often a blurring of boundaries between goddesses and women within this cult. It has been used to define attendants, sorceresses, or even demons. In Tantra, it is a term for women who perform the required rituals to become Yoginis. Indian scholar of Tantra, NN Bhattacharyya suggests that they could have been women or priestesses who were "possessed by goddesses and in the course of time they were elevated to the position of deities".

▽ **The unique circular structure of** the Chausath Yogini Temple in Hirapur, Odisha, can be seen quite clearly in this image. Elaborate rituals are sometimes still practised in these temples.

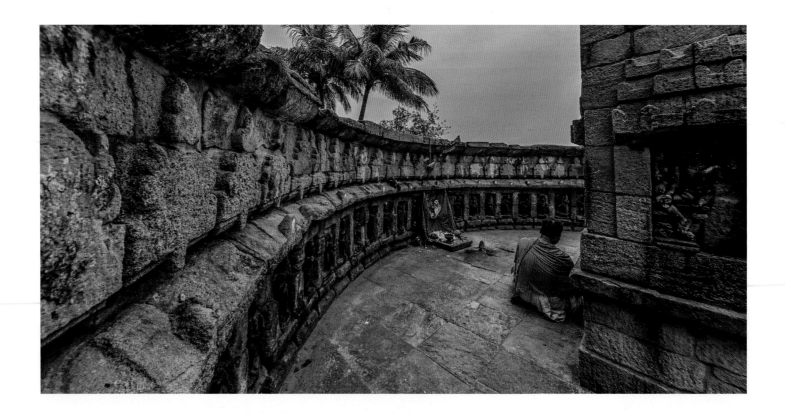

> "Some of them are **dancing and singing** with their **girdles and waistbands** tinkling sweetly. Some of them are **clapping their hands** in front of those **who dance**."

VERSE 28, *LALITA MAHATMYA*

Indian art historian Vidya Dehejia references ancient Indian texts that tell of Yoginis (or even Dakini and Sakini as references to female deities or spirits) as wielders of supernatural powers which also involved them turning people into animals. "The stories highlight the awe and dread with which they are regarded," she notes. However, drawing upon the 64 Yoginis mentioned in the Puranas, Dehejia states that in some traditions they could have been "varying aspects of the Great Goddess who, through these Yoginis, manifested the totality of her presence".

It is interesting to note that the Yoginis are rarely spoken of in singular, often seen as group divinities and worshipped collectively. Unlike other goddesses, they do not have any associations as spouses or consorts and seem independent of mainstream Hindu male deities. Dehejia suggests that the 64 Yoginis were perhaps "patron deities" for those who followed the unorthodox Kaula *marga*, a Tantric tradition.

The list and brief description of the 64 Yoginis find their earliest reference in the *Agni Purana*, dated around the 9th century. Dehejia notes that for such an unorthodox cult to find mention in the Puranas "must testify to the powerful hold it exerted over its increasing fold of followers". However, they are also treated as outsiders with no real mythology associated to them. There are references to the Yoginis and their worship within the *Lalitasahasranama* (See pp 278–79), which was appended to the *Brahmanda Purana* to give it a Shakta tone.

The iconography

In their material form, the Yoginis are large, life-size, seated or standing images. These alluring and magnificent sculptures in stone, mostly full-bodied and voluptuous with dissimilar expressions – calm or frightening – are found often in the several open-air temples dedicated to them across parts of central and northern India. Each temple has its set of Yoginis with varying characteristics (See pp 320–21).

Many temples are found near what were once capitals of ruling dynasties, indicating a belief that the Yoginis protected the land and consolidated the dynastic positions of the kings who may have built a temple to them.

There is no uniformity in the iconography and each group appears to have a separate identity. Occasionally, a group may have their names inscribed on pedestals. The images are usually accompanied by other figures or are simple sculptures of the Yogini in isolation.

VILLAGE DEITIES

The origins of the Yoginis can be seen in village cults or in the worship of the grama devatas or village goddesses where they are favoured deities. They are concerned with day-to-day matters, such as marriage, fertility, snake bites, or diseases as mentioned. Over time, it seems that these goddesses transformed and consolidated into groupings of 64, 81, 42 Yoginis. Each Yogini temple reflects a localized tradition of yoginis. The shrines of Hirapur and Ranipur Jharial present us with goddesses who were worshipped in two areas of Odisha during the 7th and the 8th centuries. Some, it seems, have reverted to their original village goddess status. For instance, Vaseli, who is mentioned in an Odia text as a Yogini, is today worshipped as a village goddess in the coastal villages of Odisha as a vermilion-stained stone

» Therianthropism is quite common among these sculptures as there is ample sculptural and textual representation of animal elements. So, Yoginis may have animal heads as seen in images from Lokhari, Madhya Pradesh, which can range from horses and lions to birds and snakes. There are a variety of body types. Some are old with drooping breasts, while others, like those in Bheraghat, Madhya Pradesh are heavily ornamented with multiple necklaces and garlands. Each Yogini has a halo and most have multiple arms.

Rites and rituals

It is important to interpret the cult within the context in which the Yoginis appear. The circular walls of their temples seem to have bounded a consecrated space where a series of rites and practices collectively known as Mahayaga were enacted. These important rituals aimed to please and placate the Yoginis in one's journey for occult powers. It was believed that the Yoginis could be cruel and wrathful when displeased, but would bestow the disciple with all manner of powers if the worship was done in an appropriate manner.

The Shri Kamada sculpture in the Bhedhaghat temple in Madhya Pradesh has an interesting Tantric rite carved into its pedestal. Kamada is one of the names of the Devi in the Kalika Purana where Kama, the god of love, is identified with sexual love while Kamada removes frigidity. The rite seems to be a depiction of what appears to be yoni puja.

There are enough literary and iconographic sources depicting independent linga worship removed from the yoni. However, yoni worship, though known to be prevalent in the Tantric texts, rarely has such an explicit rendering of the act, in stone or otherwise. Here, two sages, their hands folded, bow to the yoni, which is an anatomically accurate rendition of the female vulva. Its significance cannot be overlooked. The understanding is that the man, the worshipper, cultivates pure vision on seeing the woman as a deity and by extension her sexual organ as the seat of enlightenment.

> " … one of many **meanings** of *yogini* and closely related terms is "**tantric sorceress**"… a notion carried into the **modern world**… with tragic **consequences**…"

SHAMAN HATLEY, "YOGINI" (2020)

Indian cultural activist and writer Pupul Jayakar writes that rites were centred around the physical worship of woman and the sex organs in which the woman's body became the kshetra or the enclosed field of power, itself the instrument of magic and transformation. This may be a rendition of stripuja also known as secret worship or guhyapuja. The theoretical basis of this practice is the belief that women are embodiments of goddesses and that worship of women is a form of devotion that female deities explicitly require, notes American scholar of religious studies Miranda Shaw.

Names and nature of the Yoginis

Yoginis have telling names that hint at personality. Shri Takari means a particular part of a woman's pudenda while Shri Lampata translates to mean the lustful or licentious one. Some other names include Shri Vibhatsa, the dreadful one or Shri Bhisani the terrifying one. Shri Rauravi references the Yogini who makes loud sounds or has the voice of a jackal, while Rakhtapriya is someone who loves to drink blood. There is also Garbhabhakshi who is the eater of foetus.

Judging by their names it appears that they came from villages and were originally folk divinities (See box on p 317). Their names do not reveal Sanskrit origin, while others reveal a Sanskrit root, but several are grammatically incorrect.

◁ **One of the most famous** sculptures is that of the Yogini Vrishanana from 10–11th century. She wields a club in her right hand. A swan pecks at the fruit she holds in her left hand. This buffalo-headed Yogini was once stolen from a village temple and sold to an art collector in Paris. It was later returned to India.

The Yogini temples

These mysterious temples dedicated to the Yoginis once housed stunning sculptures of female deities. Today, many of them lie empty or abandoned, their real purpose still a matter of speculation among scholars.

Most Hindu temples have a few elements common to them, whether it is the grandeur of their size, the square shape, or pillared hallways. Ornate carvings grace the exterior of the structure that is topped by a spire. The Yogini temple, on the other hand, has an exceptional structure that gives short shrift to any normative canon of architecture. It has two features that render it instantly recognizable – defining circular shape and hypaethral or roofless and open to the sky.

Home of the yoginis
Dating to the 9–12th century, these unique sandstone temples have simple exteriors. Within its circular walls are niches,

which contain life-sized stone images of the Yoginis. Each sculpture has its own enclosure and faces an open courtyard in the centre. The temples, most commonly have 64 (or Chaunsath, as they are called in the vernacular) Yoginis. There have been instances where the centre has a Shiva temple, but scholars feel it may have been a later addition.

Most of the temples are in Madhya Pradesh, Uttar Pradesh, and Odisha, but many do not have the sculptures, having failed to survive time and invasions or fallen victim to pilfering. The three that still have sculptures are at Ranipur Jharial and Hirapur in Odisha and Bhedaghat in Madhya Pradesh. Scholars note that Yogini worship was prevalent until the beginning of the 16th century, but disappeared from the 17–18th century. Most of these temples were largely

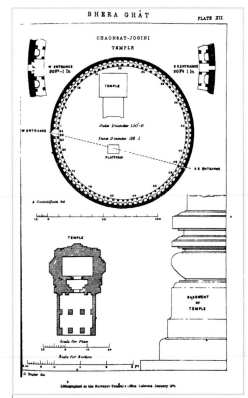

△ **Circular rendering**
A floor plan of the Yogini temple at Bhedaghat detailing the 81 niches.

△ **A former home**
The spectacular Yogini Temple at Mitauli, Madhya Pradesh, once, it is believed, had space for 64 Yogini sculptures and one for the Great Goddess. Today, the space holds Shiva icons.

abandoned but have, in recent times, attracted worshippers once again, who sometimes leave behind evidence of their worship.

The largest Yogini temple is in Bhedaghat, near the town of Jabalpur in Madhya Pradesh. It is 38 m (125 ft) in diameter and unlike others has 81 Yoginis. Indian art historian Vidya Dehejia notes that the worship of 81 Yoginis was specific to royalty and suggests that this could have been a "royal chapel".

The temple in Hirapur, Odisha, is the smallest with a diameter of 9 m (30 ft) and houses 64 carved, grey chlorite, standing Yoginis. Temples bereft of sculpted Yoginis, but still extant, can be found in places, such as Mitauli and Dudahi, in Uttar Pradesh, Khajuraho, Mausuhaniya, and Badoh in Madhya Pradesh.

Many temples were located in isolated areas on hilltops. Scholars believe it could have been because some of the rituals may have invited derision. Perhaps, it could have also been because of a need for a quiet space, away from the hustle and bustle of townships.

A question of shape

Scholars note that despite the elaborate sculptures, the temple's design itself is akin to simple village or tribal shrines. In terms of its shape, a rectangular temple, such as the one in

"To those **eternal Yoginis** by whose **glory** The **three worlds** have been established, to them I bow down, to them I pray."

KULARNAVA, IN *YOGINI CULT AND TEMPLES* BY VIDYA DEHEJIA (1986)

Khajuraho, is rare. Scholars feel its shape was chosen more for practical reasons – the ridge where it is built was too narrow. The preferred circular shape is in itself intriguing. In the Puranas, the Yoginis, who moved as a group of 64 in the sky, formed a circle on descent. It also lends itself quite perfectly to the Hindu view of a cosmos, viewed as a continuum. The shape may suggest a spatial translation of the Yogini chakra or it may replicate the shape of the female vulva.

German religious scholar Heinrich von Stietencron analyzes the Hirapur temple as a "cosmographically conceived edifice that reflects the heavenly bodies, the deities associated with them, and the cycle of all determining time."

△ **Ranipur Jharial, Balangir district, Odisha**
An image of the dancing Shiva is at the centre of this small temple that also houses dancing Yoginis.

Yoginis

Yoginis are diverse, yet nameless, each bearing their own unique characteristic. Some have the face of animals, or voluptuous figures and bear distinct weapons or objects. Others look fierce, exude sensuality, or dance with gleeful abandon.

Khatvanga, or a skull staff

Hand on breast as a gesture of self-reflection

Goose vahana

△ **KANCHIPURAM YOGINI**
Region Kanchipuram, Tamil Nadu
Period c. 10th century

Hair splayed in a halo arrangement from behind her head gives her a wild, fierce appearance. Her mount is a corpse, there is a skull in her headband, and she wears snake armlets and has a human hand as an earring.

▷ **WINNOW BEARING YOGINI**
Region Kanchipuram, Tamil Nadu
Period c. 10th century

She holds a winnow that could be used for cooking or creating or tending a fire. Another hand has a head of corn and a skull cup. She has an elaborate hairdo with tight curls. This Yogini as well as some of the others in this collection expunge binaries of gender distinctiveness displaying the sacred thread that upper-caste Hindu men wear across their chest.

▷ **KETTLEDRUM CARRYING YOGINI**
Region Hirapur, Odisha
Period 9th century

She balances on two wheels placed on the back of a mouse. She holds a kettle drum in one of her four hands. The expression on the face of this Yogini is one of restrained beauty.

▷ **UNKNOWN**
Region Hirapur, Odisha
Period 9th century

Carved from black chlorite, this Yogini could possibly be Yamuna, as she stands on a tortoise. Her one foot in on its head and the other on the tail. Her hair is splayed behind in tight curls and she appears to carry a winnow.

Tortoise vahana

▷ **ANKLET ADJUSTING YOGINI**
Region Hirapur, Odisha
Period 9th century

She stands on one foot and adjusts the anklet on the other foot. She is the epitome of sensuality with wide hips, rounded breasts, and graceful figure. Her eyes, eyebrows and lips have a delicate shape. She stands on what appears to be a dog.

Elaborate chignon with small tight curls

◁ **ANTAKARI**
Region Bhedaghat, Madhya Pradesh
Period c. 9th century

Antakari, or she who destroys, has a menacing face, with bulging eyes and a gaping mouth. A headpiece of snakes surrounds a crown of skulls that sits on her head.

▷ **SHRI ERUDI**
Region Bhedaghat, Madhya Pradesh
From c. 9th century

Shri Erudi is theriomorphic, as she has the face of a horse. The animal head only seems to enhance her sensuality, as does her curvaceous body, with a narrow waist and broad hips. A cow sits at the base of her seat.

Woman paying obeisance

△ **SHRI VAISHNAVI**
Region Eastern India
From c. 11–12th century

This Yogini has two index fingers placed on either corners of her slightly open mouth as if to make a sound. Her mount is Garuda, the king of birds. She appears to be Vaishnavi with her feet placed firmly on a bird mount as she wields a spear and a sword in both hands.

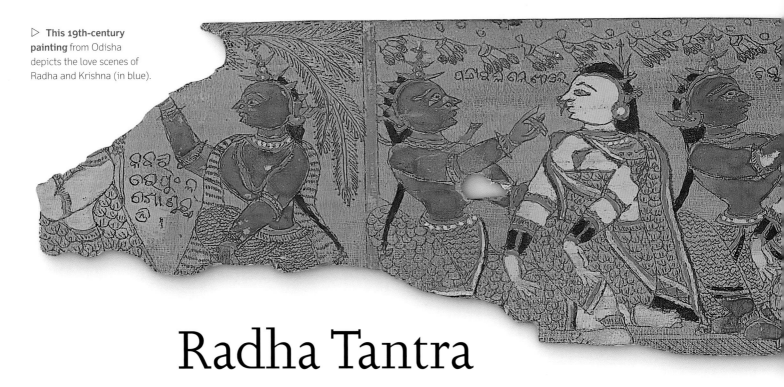

▷ **This 19th-century painting** from Odisha depicts the love scenes of Radha and Krishna (in blue).

Radha Tantra

An unusual text, the *Radha Tantra* falls at the crossroads of Vaishnavism and Shaktism. It is a prime example of a synthesis between two disparate religious streams wherein Shakta Tantrism reimagines a Vaishnava idea.

The celebrated Vaishnava story of Radha and Krishna is given a Tantric spin in the *Radha Tantra*. The has 1,745 Sanskrit verses spanning 37 *patalas*, or chapters. Since its title incorporates the name of the Vaishnava figure Radha, people commonly mistake the *Radha Tantra* to have Vaishnava affiliation. However, as scholar of religious studies Måns Broo in his translation of the text says, "it is a Shakta text giving a Shakta reinterpretation of a Vaishnava story". He further states that while its authorship remains unknown, it seems to have been written by someone with no complete knowledge of Sanskrit and who chose the language only for the purpose of legitimacy.

Origin in Bengal
Scholars argue that the text was likely composed in Bengal during the 17th century. Its emergence, deeply embedded in what Broo calls "Tantric revival" in Bengal that started in the 15th century. It was also in response to the Bengali Chaitanya Vaishnavism (See box). Its strong Bengal connection is evident because of the large number of manuscripts found in the region and its nearby areas.

CHAITANYA MOVEMENT

The 16th century in Bengal and Odisha witnessed the emergence of a new devotional movement inspired by the medieval saint Chaitanya. An ardent devotee of Radha and Krishna, he perceived their relationship as the highest expression of love between God and a human. A major characteristic of this movement was *kirtana*, the practice of collectively singing hymns and reciting Krishna's name repeatedly. Chaitanya's disciples, known as *gosvamins*, were instrumental in developing his ideas as a full-fledged theology.

Plot

The text, also called *Vasudevarahasya*, or the secret of Vasudeva, another name for Vishnu, the preserver, has a peculiar structure. Presented as a classic Agama text, it opens with a conversation between Shiva, the destroyer, and Parvati. The goddess requests her husband to retell the story of Radha and Krishna in the form of a Tantra.

The story goes that one day Vishnu, the preserver, requests Shiva for a mantra who, in turn, gives him the goddess Tripurasundari's mantra. Vishnu goes to the holy region of Varanasi and surrenders himself to its recitation. When the mantra does not bear any fruit, the perplexed god returns to Shiva's abode where he encounters the Goddess as Tripurasundari.

She tells Vishnu that mere recitation will not suffice as it stimulates only the mental faculty. It is essential to combine the rituals associated with both the body and the mind. She tells him that one needs to perform the Kaula practice, which incorporates secret rituals with one's partner. The goddess explains the process and gives him a yantra and a lotus garland imbued with magical powers. She also prophecies about his union with Radha on Earth. Content, he returs to his abode, Vaikuntha. The garland slips and falls in Vrindavan on Earth and Radha

> ## "This goddess and mistress awards the four goals of life, she **enchants** the world, she is **beautiful**, **most worshippable**, and **devoted** to protecting the world."

PATALA 1, *RADHA TANTRA*, TRANSLATED BY MÅNS BROO

emerges. After some years, she is united with Vishnu in his Krishna avatar and the two fall in love. Eventually, Radha becomes his guru and instructs him in the complex Kaula rituals.

Tantric theology

The Tantric leanings of the text are clear in its conceptualization of Radha and Krishna. They are presented as emanations of Tripurasundari and Vishnu, who are also forms of Shakti and Shiva. The text attempts to infuse Tantric elements in the worship of Krishna. Broo writes, "This Tantra is unusual in being first and foremost a polemical treatise, where ritual procedures are subsumed under a strong theological message."

DIVINE
LANDSCAPES ❋ 6

Local encounters with the Goddess have engendered numerous manifestations of Her, surrounded by distinct ways of worship. Through these interactions, the Goddess has permeated into the interiors of India, giving rise to an imagined sacred landscape. Here, She embodies geography and informs the geographical landscape in its conceptualization.

Sacred geography

In the eyes of a Hindu pilgrim, India is a consecrated geography.
Every element that it encompasses – be it geographical features, such
as mountains and rivers, or administrative units, such as towns and
cities – has a connection with the divine.

Although it is not unusual to find ancient
cultures in the world venerating the
landscape, the phenomenon in India is
unique, because of the immense number
of areas that are considered sacred and
its seamless continuity with the past. In
contemporary India, the idea of "sacred
geography" remains very much alive.
There is a deep veneration for rivers,
mountains, hills, caves, and groves, all of
which are accorded an aura of religiosity.
These sacred regions are therefore tirthas
or *pithas*, or seats of the divine.

Reciprocal relationship
People throng to these sacred spots to
experience the divine. The journey itself can be
formidable and can bring about a catharsis in
the pilgrims. Like the avowed practice of
circumambulation of a temple or a deity,
pilgrims attempt to circumambulate the entire

sacred site itself. The sacred regions therefore
represent the topographical manifestation
of the deity.

There appears to be a symbiotic relationship
between the sacred regions and the pilgrims
because the pilgrims are likewise involved in
a personal marking of the territory. In these
regions, they experience the numinous and by
their faith further contribute to the spiritual
aggrandizement of this symbolic geography.

Deifying natural structures
In India, if there is an unusual protuberance
or geological formation that resembles the
body, believers look upon it as an object
worthy of reverence. Its uniqueness
is suggestive that it may have a special
religious character and hence it is sanctified.
Such formations fill devotees with awe and
curiosity and ultimately, they become a part of
their religious belief. In the majority of the

> "This landscape not only **connects places to the lore of gods**… but it **connects places to one another** through local, regional, and transregional practices of **pilgrimage**."

DIANA L ECK, *INDIA: A SACRED GEOGRAPHY* (2012)

cases, the physiographic phenomena are perceived to be the body of the Goddess Herself. This is most explicit in the tradition and faith associated with Vaishno Devi (See pp 364–65).

Over time, myths are created to authenticate the belief and when wishes are granted then, in no time, the sites become popular pilgrimages with transformative qualities.

Goddess for cities

Another process at play is how cities and towns are created around the Goddess. For instance, the city of Mumbai in Maharashtra takes its name from the protective goddess Mumba Devi. She is the patron deity of salt collectors and fisherfolk, who are the original inhabitants of the area. She is Maha Amba, or the great mother, from where the word *mumba* may have been formed. The renaming of Bombay as Mumbai in 1995 was in honour of this goddess and acknowledges the preeminent position and reputation of this divinity and also the important role of

her shrine. Even though the Mumba Devi temple is tucked away in the teeming lanes of Mumbai's market area, it is still visited by hundreds of devotees every day.

The other instance where a city benefits from a major temple dedicated to a female divinity is in West Bengal. The Kali temple at Kalighat on the River Hooghly in Kolkata, dating from the end of the 17th century when the city was first founded, is responsible for lending the city its name.

CHAR DHAM

In India, besides the tirthas and the *pithas*, there are also the *char dhams*, or the four abodes, first popularized by Indian philosopher Adi Shankaracharya. They are strategically situated in the four cardinal directions. There is Badrinath in Uttarakhand in the North, Dwarka in Gujarat in the West, Puri in Odisha in the East, and Rameswaram in Tamil Nadu in the South. Hinduism prescribes that every Hindu should make a pilgrimage to these four in order to achieve moksha.

The victorious goddess
Bharat Mata has become an iconic symbol of India. She is seen here in the colours of India's flag – saffron, white, and green. A tiger or lion, her mount, traditionally associated with the goddess Durga, accompanies her.

Bharat Mata

India as a goddess

> "Limbs **glistening** under **brilliant sun**,
> Clothed **in the glory** of the **ascetic's garb**!
> Hail to you! **Beloved India**!"
>
> POEM BY SRIDHAR PATHAK

Hinduism has evolved over centuries in response to social, political, economic, and psychological forces. Many divinities have emerged from this cauldron, the manifestations sometimes serving a particular need. Bharat Mata – the personification of the Indian subcontinent – is one of them.

Origin

In the late 19th and early 20th century, as the nationalist movement picked up speed, it looked towards the theme of the Earth goddess, transforming her into Mother India or Bharat Mata.

Indian novelist and poet Bankim Chandra Chatterjee, in his book *Anandmatha* published in 1880, visualized her as the image of the land of India. Indian artist Abanindranath Tagore captured this vision in his painting *Bharat Mata* in 1905. Here, she was a four-armed goddess clad in saffron clothes with a halo around her head, a testament to her status as a goddess. Other early depictions included a map of India superimposed with a goddess – a form of Durga or Lakshmi.

Significance

Indian art historian Vidya Dehejia writes that Tagore's painting was not associated with any deity, but was an "artistic icon" for India during the freedom struggle. At that time, invoking the geographical entity of India as a goddess became important to foster a sense of nationalism and unity among Indians. Indian gender and culture scholar Rajeswari Sunder Rajan notes that the concept of Mother India was primarily used as a tool to mobilize women and elevate their status. Most of all, it was to "provide an inspirational symbolic focus – as in the evolution of the Bharat Mata figure – for national and communal identity".

Worshipping Mother India

In 1936, amid rising communal tension in the city of Varanasi, Uttar Pradesh, Mohandas Karamchand Gandhi inaugurated a temple to Bharat Mata. He saw it as a representation of unity. The temple has a marble relief map of India, with its rivers, mountains, and sacred places.

Later, other temples came up, including one in Haridwar, Uttarakhand. Built in 1983, this white, seven-storeyed marble temple has an entire floor dedicated to Bharat Mata. Here, much like the temple in Varanasi, the goddess stands at the head of a detailed map of India. American scholar of religious studies Diana L Eck, writes in her book *India: A Sacred Geography*: "This map-goddess emblem became a pictorial representation of the idea of India, popularized and deployed in nationalist, and later explicitly Hindu nationalist contexts."

IN TODAY'S TIMES

THE MOTHERLAND

It has been said that the people of India address their country not just as the "motherland" but as a "Mother". This notion views India as a mother in the spiritual and geographical sense. In fact, often in public arenas, or during sports and competitions, the most common cry or slogan used to invoke a feeling of patriotism is *Bharat Mata ki jai*, or Hail Mother India.

Local goddesses

Local divinities are often ancient autochthonous figures and form the root of the Puranic pantheon. They may have, over centuries, been assimilated into the Brahmanical fold through the process of osmosis, but have retained their regional local flavour.

There are many tiers of goddesses within the Hindu pantheon. The "high" level Devis have a somewhat national homogeneity in names and forms, such as Lakshmi and Sarasvati. At the opposite end of the spectrum, are countless "local" Devis, who are exclusive to specific regional pockets and clans. These local goddesses do not always find mention in the literate tradition and do not necessarily belong to the established order. Instead, they are personalized, demonstrating the ability of a village or a clan to choose their own goddess.

The village goddess

The most immediate presence in India's thousands of villages, no matter how small or isolated, is the exceedingly local Grama Devi or Devata, literally the village deity. A village may have its own unique deity or many villages may share a common one. Although they could be male or female, the majority of them are goddesses. Gangamma, Mariamma, and Kolaramma are some examples of female village deities from the southern peninsula of India.

▽ **This is an idol of a village goddess** from Puducherry in southern India depicted in a sleeping position.

"In the detailed maps of **districts and villages**, one sees that the worship of **Siddhas**… **Yogis**… coexists with the blood-thirsty rites to the **Grama Devatas, the village mothers**."

PUPUL JAYAKAR, *THE EARTH MOTHER* (1980)

Unlike the major Brahmanical deities who are in charge of the celestial world and cosmic cycles, a Grama Devi presides over the welfare of a village and acts as its guardian. She keeps the village boundaries protected and secure from enemies and safeguards villagers from the evil eye. People pray to her to seek protection from diseases and disasters and to ensure that the village is blessed with good health, that the women are fertile, and that fields produce good crops.

Grama Devis do not always have an anthropomorphic form. Their representations range from rough and uncarved stones to trees. Their shrines are simple and often built on the village boundaries where entire communities gather during important ceremonies.

The worship of Grama Devis does not require complex rituals as prescribed in texts for other great goddesses. They receive simple offerings of milk, honey, rice grains, and coconut. Now and then, animal sacrifices, usually of a goat, may be conducted to appease some of them.

Since Grama Devis live in small, restricted areas, the myths surrounding them remain within the local oral tradition. Women narrate these during significant occasions, such as weddings and births.

The clan goddesses

Another type of local goddesses are those specific to particular clans. Known as Kula Devis, they are traditionally worshipped over generations. While the male children of the family carry on the tradition and pass it on to their next generation, for female children the Kula Devis change after their marriage as they carry on their spouse's tradition.

The clan-based deities are usually local representations of the "higher" gods and goddesses. For instance, in Maharashtra, Khandoba and Bhavani, who are manifestations of Shiva and Shakti, enjoy immense popularity. Hindu families often make a pilgrimage to the Kula Devi temple to obtain her blessings after an auspicious occasion, such as a wedding. It is believed that rites done at the temple benefit all those genetically connected to the one performing the ritual. Scholar of religious studies Lindsey Harlan points out that in Rajasthan, Rajput men worship their Kula Devis for martial purposes and the women revere them to seek protection for their husbands and families.

◁ **This is a metal bust of Tujla Bhavani**, who is a popular deity in Maharashtra, but is also revered in Telangana, Karnataka, and Nepal.

KHOBARGHAR

In villages across India, women regularly adorn the external walls of their homes with tiny mirrors, seeds, clay reliefs, and paintings of Puranic deities. However, the *khobarghar*, or inner room, of the houses incorporates the Kula Devis. The *khobarghar* is made auspicious every day with fresh plaster and lotus mandalas, signifying fertility. This is where newly weds spend their initial marital period and where subsequently babies are born.

The desired goddess

The elasticity of Hinduism gives individuals the independence and agency to revere the deities they most believe in. This personal relationship with the divine is indeed one of its exceptional characteristics.

△ **Ishta Devis** can also be chosen from an assortment of mainstream goddesses in the Hindu pantheon, such as Lakshmi, Tripurasundari, and Sarasvati. This is an image of goddess idols from Rockfort Temple in Tiruchirappalli, Tamil Nadu.

Hinduism presents a unique phenomenon where individuals have the autonomy to choose their preferred deity. Referred to as Ishta Devis or Ishta Devatas, literally cherished divinities, they are considered personal deities.

One from many

There is no restriction for individuals when it comes to the selection of their special god or goddess. People can adopt their Ishta Devi or

SMARTA PHILOSOPHY

Indian philosopher Adi Shankaracharya conceptualized the Smarta tradition, an important sect within Hinduism. This school of thought emphasizes the worship of five deities, that is *Panchayatana*. These include Vishnu, the preserver; Shiva, the destroyer; the elephant-headed god Ganesha, Surya, the Sun god, and Durga, the Shakti. The Smarta tradition is inspired by Smriti literature, including the epics and the Puranas.

Devata from the group of mainstream divinities or from countless local deities that punctuate the religious fabric of Hinduism. So one could be attracted to any one of the avatars of Vishnu, the preserver, any manifestation of the Devi, any deity that is exclusively worshipped in some remote area of the country, or even a saint. This concept is mostly free from the clutches of any sectarian or cultic divisions and presents a somewhat personalized monotheism where the chosen deity represents everything to a devotee.

American scholar of religious studies Diana L Eck gives the example of Venkateshvara in Tirupati, Andhra Pradesh. She notes that there are differences of opinion whether this deity is a form of Vishnu, of Shiva, the destroyer, Shakti or Skanda. So, individual devotees see their preferred deity in his image. In this way, the darshana that a worshippers receives is according to their *bhavana*, or sentiment.

Sometimes, devotees who are initiated by a guru are often given an appropriate Ishta Devi or Devata along with their mantra. This is because a true guru is believed to be the best judge of which divinity would be the most compelling and of greatest value to the disciple.

Personal experience

Once individuals have selected their Ishta Devi or Devata, he or she becomes that one consecrated personage that individuals focus on for divine contemplation and bestow upon them special honour, love, devotion, and adoration.

The drive for a particular divinity depends on one's temperament and sometimes even circumstance. It seems logical that human diversity would demand that individuals have a chosen deity in sync with their needs, specifically addressing their individualities.

Even in a single family, members may have different personal deities, according to *bhavana* and inner disposition. The concept is neither universalized nor imposed on others. However, people are not bound to such divinities for their entire life. They are free to switch from one deity to another, depending on their situation in life. Reverence to an Ishta Devi or Devata does not mean the negation of others. It simply denotes special personal attachment to an extraordinary idiosyncratic belief in a single figure. Therefore, the concept of Ishta Devi or Devata is driven by the personal as opposed to the public.

Spiritual connection

Most Hindus believe in direct private communion with their chosen Ishta Devi or Devata, without any intermediary, such as a priest. In this way, this concept elaborates Hinduism's belief in spiritual focus because individuals choose such divine forms in order to satisfy their spiritual longing.

It is especially significant to the Smarta (See box) and Bhakti schools because one who enters the path of Bhakti yoga needs a concrete object to whom one can offer one's worship and emotion.

> "**Self-study** leads towards the realization of God or communion with **one's desired deity**."

VERSE 44, CHAPTER 2, PATANJALI'S *YOGA SUTRAS*, TRANSLATED BY BKS IYENGAR

◁ **Religious markings and oil lamps** on a wall in Harsiddhi Mata Temple in Ujjain, Madhya Pradesh

The face of a goddess
On the banks of the River Gomati in Chabimura, Tripura, surrounded by cascading lush green trees is a medieval architectural marvel. The steep hillside has a rock carving of the goddess Durga with her hair spread out and 10 distinct arms. This has been dated to either the 15th or the 16th century.

The saviour
Santoshi Mata is usually depicted seated in a meditation posture. She has four arms carrying the trident, sword, a rice bowl, and displaying the *abhaya* or fear-not mudra.

Santoshi Mata

She who grants wishes

> "… **No one** is happy… contentment can come, only when **the Mother divine**, Santoshi Mata is pleased and **blesses them**."
>
> LM SHARMA, *THE STORY OF SANTOSHI MATA* (2002)

In the 1960s, Santoshi Mata, as a goddess, was virtually unknown, her story and worship relegated to pamphlets written in the vernacular or transferred word-of-mouth among devotees. Then, in 1975, Indian director Vijay Sharma made the low-budget Hindi film *Jai Santoshi Maa*. The impetus was his wife's visit to a temple dedicated to the goddess in Jodhpur, Rajasthan. She prompted her husband to make a film on her return. The tale of the goddess and her ardent devotee on the Earth became a runaway hit in cities as well as rural areas and a cult favourite.

Soon, the goddess, American scholar of religious studies John Stratton Hawley notes in *Devi: Goddesses of India* "became one of the most important and widely worshipped goddesses in India, taking her place in poster-art form in the altar rooms of millions of Hindu homes."

Five temples dedicated to her in parts of northern India were identified and her shrines were added to several existing temples. She had been catapulted to a deity of pan-Indian significance.

Integration into the pantheon

Many scholars have drawn a comparison between Santoshi Mata and the lion-riding Sheranvali popular in northwestern India, and insist that there is nothing new about her. They see her as a manifestation of divine feminine power. They suggest that she could have been a part of a process where local deities and myths become identified with deities from the Brahmanical tradition.

The goddess bears many attributes reminiscent of older goddesses. She wields the sword and trident, much like Durga (See pp 80–83), and her iconography portrays her either seated or standing on a lotus like Lakshmi (See pp 168–71). This resonated with her "new devotees", writes Hawley, who recognized in her traits of "goddesses long since familiar to them". Her origin draws from the broader Hindu pantheon as well – she is the daughter of Ganesha, the elephant-headed god.

Worship

The goddess of fulfillment and contentment (her name comes from *santosha*, which means contentment), Santoshi Mata's worship is done through the *vrata-katha* method. This is performed at the home of a devotee without the intervention of a priest. The worshipper, usually a woman, takes a *vrata*, or vow, to partially fast on 16 consecutive Fridays. During this time, the devotee can eat one meal sans bitter or sour food. Offerings to the goddess include simple foods, such as unrefined sugar and gram, which is then fed to cows or distributed as offerings. Fasting women read the goddess's *katha*, or story, during their prayer on Friday. At the end, the devotee performs an *Udyapan* by feeding eight boys.

IN TODAY'S TIMES

TELEVISION

Deities are often immortalized on the small screen. *Santoshi Maa* was one such show. The Hindi mythological series that aired from 2015 to 2017 became so popular that it was dubbed in three regional languages: Telugu, Bhojpuri, and Bengali. The plot runs on two tracks – on the Earth about a girl named Santoshi and an ardent devotee of the goddess and in Devloka, the land of the gods, where Santoshi Mata lives.

The goddess within

Reverence to goddesses is so entrenched in Indian culture that women in Hindu households are often compared to them. So, they can be as eloquent as Sarasvati, as pious as Sita, or even as wild as Kali.

Hindu goddesses are powerful entities, superhuman even, for they do belong to a different biosphere. Yet there are moments when they experience a periodic human transference, either through their depictions in iconography or in mythology.

Another extraordinary, yet commonplace, occurrence is when human beings enter the Goddess's world. Lajja Gauri is a classic example of a goddess portraying a typical human function. Most of her iconography shows her in the midst of childbirth, which is also often seen as a symbol of fertility (See pp 54–55). Every month, Kamakhya Devi in Assam menstruates as does Bhagvati in Kerala. Often, temple festivals in these areas and agricultural cycles are interlinked and, it is believed, the goddesses experience a periodic reproductive cycle similar to women.

The goddess in a woman

There are also moments when the goddess presides over common situations and features in the day-to-day activity and life cycle of women. This is when women, as children, in their youth, or when old, experience comparisons to the goddess. Sometimes it is in their name, physical features, or in society's perception of their behaviour.

The most common goddess, often mentioned in this way is Lakshmi (See pp 168–71). If a baby girl is born, the congratulatory statement will be to say that her birth is akin

to Lakshmi entering their homes. This probably acts to soothe families in a country that often favours the birth of a male child. A new bride is also called Lakshmi. These linguistic parallels are common across India. It serves to remind people that the goddess is a harbinger of everything auspicious and that their lives have become beautiful with the latest addition to their midst.

Families often compare a woman who is a good cook to Annapurna (See p 111). Of course, she must be prudent enough to calculate the exact amount of food that needs preparation to avoid wastage.

There is a deep reverence for eloquence within Hinduism. The best praise paid to a good orator – male or female – is that

▽ **Classical Indian dance** forms interpret the goddess through a variety of poses and mudras. Here, a Bharatanatyam dancer plays the veena (left) in a possible depiction of Sarasvati. Another Bharatanatyam dancer depicts the devi (centre), while a Kuchipudi dancer uses the Pathaka mudra to represent Lakshmi (right).

Sarasvati is residing on their tongue. Studious girls could be Sarasvati as well. Sita (See pp 62–63), Rama's wife, is used as a metaphor as well. Her name is invoked to describe an accommodating girl, who could withstand adversities, much like Sita. It is also a compliment awarded for submissive or good behaviour. A sacrifice earns the moniker "Sati Savitri", a reference to the legend of a princess who saved her husband from Yama, the god of death.

Rituals during Navaratri, the nine-day festival, view pre-pubescent girls as embodied versions of the Goddess. Here, the perception of the Goddess is that of a *kanya*, or young girl, who is worshipped and offered feasts and gifts.

The fiery ones

Rarely are women asked to emulate the fierce Durga (See pp 80–83). Instead, many Indian cultures tend to reprimand feisty women or teenage girls with that particular name. The goddess,

> ## "Exalting women to a goddess is common in Hindi... A daughter is often... Lakshmi of the house."

CLARA SARMENTO, *EASTWARDS/WESTWARDS* (2007)

whose Sheranvali manifestation (See pp 94–95) is popular in northern India, may be a warrior, but possesses characteristics that cause discord.

Often followers perceive a powerful female religious or political leader as embodying the goddess. Many media houses called India's first female prime minister Indira Gandhi Durga, after the country's success in the Indo–Pakistan War of 1971 during her tenure.

In some regions of South India, if a woman does the opposite of what is asked of her, or if she is prone to fights and arguments, Chandi or Chamundi become favourable adjectives. This goddess is another manifestation of Durga.

It is also not uncommon for children to tease an elderly unkempt woman by calling her Kali (See pp 126–29). Children also sing a rather cruel ditty in the gullies of Uttar Pradesh and Uttarakhand: "Kali mata has come... run children as calamity has arrived" (Kali *mai dipak jalai bhago bacchon aafat ai*). This goddess is also an adjective for women who lose their temper.

THE LEGEND OF ALOPI DEVI

Prayagaraj, Uttar Pradesh, has a unique temple to Alopi Devi where she is worshipped as a *doli*, or a bride's carriage. Locals tell of a time when the region was a dense forest and a hotbed for dacoits. A marriage procession cutting through the forest found itself surrounded by them. After the dacoits killed everyone, they looked inside the *doli* and found it empty. The bride had disappeared. Sometime later, a temple emerged at the site, where the bride known as Alopi Devi, is worshipped. People seek her blessings during festivals and important occasions such as weddings.

Creation of a goddess

Almost every problem, no matter how big or small, has a goddess in the Hindu pantheon that the ardent devotee can turn to for help with a solution, to worship, or for solace.

△ **In India, the Banyan tree** has immense religious significance. Apart from being worshipped in its own right, it is also considered an auspicious site for installing idols. People often offer items such *kumkum*, or vermilion, and bangles, as a part of its worship.

Since there is no one central authority and no one sacred text within Hinduism for belting out norms for gods, the celestial world has flourished in the most imaginative manner.

A matter of need

As the Goddess exists within each of us as consciousness, there is a belief that one can "create" a new goddess, especially if she appears in a person's dream and directs the person to start worshipping her. Personal impulses, intense psychological yearnings have not been disparaged nor discarded, giving birth to an array of goddesses. The root of this lies in the fact that goddess worship is an ancient tradition. New goddesses encapsulate this very Hindu phenomenon.

The very names of these goddesses speak of their contemporaneousness as they deal with issues of a current nature, rather than cosmic concerns. This "Goddess production" is a dynamic process. It often takes place during a crisis or when believers seek some form of divine solace. These new goddesses fulfil this need for protection, nurturing, and care, and help their believers deal with adverse situations.

Though not a very new goddess, Nimishamba, perhaps an incarnation of Parvati (See pp 108–11), is said to remove her devotees's obstacles within a minute. *Nimisha* means minute and *amba* means mother in Kannada. Amba is also an epithet of Parvati, and her temples are dotted across South India.

In Rajasthan, villagers across the state often worship Kheda Devi, seeking her blessings for the protection, safety, and wellbeing of their cattle. During the nine-day festival of Navaratri, the Dangis, or cattle-herding communities, gather at Sapetiya village near Udaipur to worship Kheda Devi. They bring with them milk, which they use to make *kheer*, or rice pudding. This is done in the temple. After the *kheer* is offered to the goddess, it is distributed to all her devotees as *prasad*.

The unique ones

Goddesses can manifest themselves in different places. For instance, Rodi Mata, said to be the creator of manure, which helps sustain life and fertility in homes and the fields, is often worshipped in a garbage heap, across parts of Rajasthan. She has links to Mother Earth.

According to the tradition, Rajasthani women invite Rodi Mata to all family weddings by singing traditional songs of welcome. To invite her, women go to their area's garbage dump and sing as they drive a long iron nail into the ground. The iron nail symbolizes determination, fidelity, and acts as a ward to protect the newlyweds. The morning after the wedding, women formally escort the couple to the garbage heap, where they sing songs thanking the goddess, as they remove the nail. The couple make offerings of flowers, turmeric, *kumkum* or vermilion, and rice. They also seek her blessings so that the marriage results in the birth of many children.

> "Our **repeated**... obeisance to the Goddess who is **present** in all beings as **consciousness**."
>
> DEVI STUTI

Rivers have always been worshipped across India (See pp 348–49) as they sustain life. However, they are also an important part of the final Hindu ritual for the dead, that of the immersion of ashes. It is perhaps why the roads leading to them are also worshipped. It is believed that roads that provide safe passage to the living and the dead is a goddess. This road goddess is known as the Path Wari Mata or the deity of the road. She is praised in songs, as the one who offers food to the hungry and water to the thirsty.

India also has an extended tradition of worshipping gods for removal of diseases. Among them is Shiva, the destroyer, who in the *Rigveda*, is invoked for not bringing disease to humans or cattle, much like Kheda Devi. This same stream of thought is explored during disease outbreaks (See pp 374–77). Goddesses are invoked for specific health problems as well. Among them is the Chhink Mata, the goddess who cures sneezing fits.

ANGREZI DEVI

There is a unique temple in the tiny village of Banka, Uttar Pradesh dedicated to Angrezi Devi or the goddess of English language. This goddess is believed to help the Dalit community so that they have a better future and escape poverty. The bronze statue of the goddess wears a hat and carries a pen to empower the community as well as the Constitution of India, which gave Dalits equal rights. The belief behind the concept of this goddess is that one must know the English language in order to succeed and Angrezi Devi exists to encourage and bless them.

The golden goddess
This artist's digital impression of Meenakshi shows her in gold jewellery standing in front of the temple dedicated to her. As is typical of most portrayals, she is green with a parrot perched on her shoulder.

Meenakshi

The one with the beautiful fish-shaped eyes

"… the deity of Madurai… the goddess Minatci [Meenakshi] is fiery and independent."

PAUL YOUNGER, *THE HOME OF DANCING SIVAN* (1995)

The goddess Meenakshi, or Minakshi, is the pivot around which the ancient city of Madurai in Tamil Nadu revolves. She is the guardian of the city and of its rulers. Her name, which means the carp-eyed one, can have different etymologies. An interesting theory on the name is that she always keeps her eyes open, like fish, watching over her devotees.

While the state of Tamil Nadu has many shrines dedicated to Amman or the goddess, the most impressive is the temple of Meenakshi in Madurai. The founders of the city, the Pandya monarchs, commissioned it in the 11th century. One approaches the temple through high-walled, rectangular, towered enclosures called gopuras, which are the highest in the state. The complex also has elaborate mandapas, or pillared pavilions.

As a deity

Scholars believe that Meenakshi could have once been a local deity, who is now considered an avatar of Durga or Parvati and receives similar orthodox forms of worship. The rituals include bathing the image of the goddess every morning, elaborate adornment, offering of rice and lentils, and performing obeisance by way of incense and lamps. Indian art historian Vidya Dehejia notes that this is a process of an embodiment whereby the priests invoke the goddess and entreat her to enter and temporarily reside within her image.

The myth of Meenakshi

The 13th-century text *Tiruvilaiyatarpuranam* tells the story of the goddess Meenakshi. Once, the king Malayadhwaja Pandya and his wife Kanchanamalai performed a *yagna* or sacrificial offering, seeking a male child for succession. Instead, a daughter was born to them, as a three-year-old and with three breasts.

Worried, the parents prayed to Shiva, the destroyer, who told them to treat her like a son. She would lose the third breast once she met her husband, he told them. Raised as a boy, she grew up and ascended the throne after being crowned the successor. She soon went to battle seeking to expand her empire. Invincible, she destroyed her enemies until she went to Mount Kailash to fight Shiva.

As soon as she saw him, she transformed into a modest maiden. American scholar of religious studies, David Kinsley calls this transformation typical of many myths where powerful goddesses and deities "are subjugated or tamed by gods". In many ways this, he notes, "reinforces social norms". "In the human realm marriage is assumed not only to complete a woman but to tame her… the god or the male is seen as a civilizing, calming, ordering presence. Alone, goddesses and women are perceived as powerful and dangerous," he writes in *Hindu Goddesses*.

Meenakshi's wedding

A fascinating annual festival takes place every spring in the ancient city of Madurai. Here, amidst jostling crowds and elaborate rituals, the goddess marries her husband Sundareshvara.

Every year, for two weeks, the ancient city of Madurai resounds to the reverberations of traditional windpipes, cymbals, and drums. Devotees congregate in the streets to catch a glimpse of their beloved goddess Meenakshi, the fish-eyed one, to witness her coronation, and then wedding to Sundareshvara, a manifestation of Shiva, the destroyer.

Meenakshi is the patron deity of Madurai and the temple to her sits in the heart of the city, its magnificent spire dominating the skyline. While she shares space with Sundareshvara, who has his own shrine within the complex, devotees flock to the city mainly to seek the goddess's blessings.

The celestial couple

In the Tamil Talapuranas, which constitute the sacred history of a particular place, there are scattered references to Shiva being wild, unpredictable and at times even insulting. Yet, he is a model bridegroom for the king's daughter Meenakshi (See pp 344–45) and marries her as Sundareshvara. The priests in the temple, in fact, treat the couple much like a human one, with the routine performance of elaborate rituals that establish the relationship between the two.

The ceremonial visitation of Sundareshvara to Meenakshi's bedchamber is ritually enacted every evening, so that the celestial couple may spend the night together. In the morning, priests "awaken" the couple asleep in their

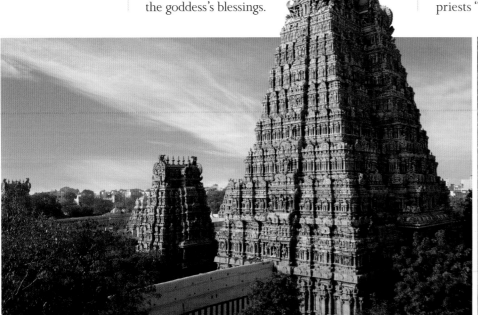

△ **The twin shrines**
The towering gopuras, or gateways, dominate the city skyline. Each panel has elaborate carvings that detail scenes from Hindu mythology and legends.

△ **Inside the temple**
This image of Shiva and Meenakshi, adorned with garlands, is in one of the pillar halls of the temple.

bed-chamber and an image of Sundareshvara is taken to his shrine. Scholar of anthropology CJ Fuller notes that the celestial couple "explicitly seen as lovers, are brought together, and only at night are they united, for during the day they are in separate shrines".

Holy wedding

Fuller draws attention to this ritual "theme of movement between separation and unity", which is also seen during the annual Chithirai Thiruvizha or Chithirai festival.

On the 1st day of the two-week festival, the two deities are taken through the different streets of the city in different vahanas. The coronation takes place on the 8th day of the festival, followed by the grand celestial wedding on the 10th day. On this day, the two deities are married with all the pomp and show of a Hindu wedding. Meenakshi, adorned in bridal clothes and jewellery, marries Sundareshvara, as devotees sing devotional songs and more than 50 priests perform special rituals.

Rites and rituals

A feature of the festival is the processions that make their way through the city every morning and evening. Icons of the two deities are placed on elaborately festooned, chariot-like vehicles that devotees drag through the streets. Priests, decorated elephants, musicians, and devotees carrying royal emblems walk alongside.

Fuller notes, "Each procession is always a circumambulation of the temple in the auspicious clockwise direction but it is also a circuit by Madurai's divine rulers of their temple and the city, and by symbolic equivalence their kingdom, the world, and the cosmos as well." The processions often halt at pavilions as the deity rests for a while, notes Indian art historian Vidya Dehejia. At this time, devotees who are not allowed or able to worship at the temple, can see their deities.

> "O Goddess **Minakshi**
> … with **long eyes** shaped **like a carp**
> … provides release from the fetters of life
> … who **conquered** Shiva
> … **Grant me bliss**."

A KIRTANAM BY MUTHUSWAMI DIKSHITAR, VIDYA DEHEJIA, *INDIAN ART* (1997)

△ **A matter of belief**
Devotees throng the two temples daily, seeking an audience with their deities.

△ **The holy couple**
Every evening, Sundareshvara is taken to Meenakshi's bedchamber as seen here.

Sacred rivers

It is true that wherever there is water, there is life. Hinduism celebrates its significance by according it divine status. Therefore, many rivers are perceived as physical manifestations of the divine, and are also likened to the greatest *tirthas*.

Most rivers in India are considered deities, specifically female divinities, as their life-giving waters are looked upon as possessing Shakti. Interestingly, Hinduism presents an allegory between rivers as a geographical feature and rivers as divinity personified. In a tropical and agrarian country, such as India, the waters are a big blessing for irrigation but in times of heavy deluge during the monsoon season, they could also result in life-menacing floods. These contrasting traits – *saumya*, or peaceful, and *ugra*, or fierce – resemble the dual nature of many goddesses in Hindusim, who could be benevolent and generous and yet have the potential to harm.

Inception

The concept of worshipping rivers as goddesses has been prevalent since the Vedic times. In the *Rigveda*, one encounters the sages paying obeisance to the River Sarasvati (See p 187) as a goddess to accept their sacrifices.

According to Indian art historian Vidya Dehejia, the inception of the phenomenon of sanctified rivers became popular by the start of the current era.

▽ **Hogenakkal Falls**
on the River Kaveri, between Dharmapuri district of Tamil Nadu and Chamrajnagar district of Karnataka

"The great **rivers of India** have been called "**mothers**" from the time of the **ancient Vedas**, hymns sung as long as 3,500 years ago."

DIANA L ECK, *ENCOUNTERING GOD: A SPIRITUAL JOURNEY FROM BOZEMAN TO BANARAS* (1993)

Ways of worshipping

In India, rivers are venerated as maternal figures and are referred to with the epithet of Nadima-Mata, or Mother River. Particularly seven rivers, collectively called *saptanadi*, are considered sacred. These include Ganga (See pp 352–55), Yamuna, Sindhu, Narmada (See pp 362–63), Kaveri, Godavari, and Krishna.

Devotees offer these rivers aarti, food, and flowers as a way of paying obeisance. In the evenings, they place lit diyas in the waters, which float along with the current, carrying with them the deep desires of the worshippers.

Sometimes, a sari is "draped" over the rivers by holding the cloth across banks. This perhaps symbolizes the strong notion of femininity associated with the rivers.

In Hinduism, the river waters are also significant because of their purifying powers. Devotees take a holy dip to absolve themselves of their past sins. The rivers are also an important site for *asthi visarjan*, or the practice whereby the ashes of the cremated dead are immersed in the waters. This ensures moksha to the departed.

Mythologizing rivers

Over centuries, these rivers were elevated to the status of goddesses by weaving a variety of legends and myths around them. For instance, Kaveri's origins can be traced to the myth of the churning of the ocean (See pp 174–75). In it, she emerged as Lopamudra to help Vishnu, the preserver, and eventually metamorphosed into a rock.

In another legend, Brahma, the creator, bestowed a boon on a childless king named Kavera. According to it, whatever he touched first would come to life as his child. The king inadvertently touched a rock, which instantly turned into a maiden. Kavera named her Kaveri and she went on to marry the sage Agastya on the condition that she would always be by his side in her riverine form in his *kamandalu*, or water pot. One day, in a region afflicted with drought, Ganesha, the elephant-headed god, in the form of a crow, tipped the sage's *kamandalu* and thus the river began to flow across the Earth.

The origin of Godavari is attributed to the sage Gautama who lived with his wife Ahalya in the mountainous region of Brahmagiri, now in Karnataka. One day, a cow ate all the rice that the couple had stocked. The sage attempted to drive away the cow with Durbha grass, but it died suddenly. Inordinately, the sage had committed the grim sin of *gau hatya*, or killing of a cow, a holy animal.

In order to absolve himself of this sin, he prayed to Shiva, the destroyer, requesting him to allow a part of Ganga to flow close to his residence so that he could purify himself with its waters. Shiva granted this wish and Godvari took birth as a river. This is one reason why the river is also called Dakshina Ganga, or Ganga of the South.

BRAHMAPUTRA

River Brahmaputra, literally the son of Brahma, one of the longest rivers to flow through the eastern part of India, is revered as a male deity. The story goes that the river was born as a part of sage Shantanu's divine plan. The son, who bore a striking resemblance to Brahma, was named Brahmakunda. The sage installed his son as a lake between four great mountains. Then, one day, Vishnu's avatar, Parashurama split one of the mountains and Brahmaputra began to flow across the lands.

Rituals at dusk
Every evening, the ghats of River Ganga witness a beautiful spectacle where devotees gather in large numbers to offer prayers to the goddess Ganga. Popularly known as the Ganga Aarti, it includes the ritual of offering lit lamps while singing hymns in praise of the goddess. Within no time, the riverside is illuminated with countless diyas, resembling a sparkling night sky. Seen here is a group of priests performing the Ganga Aarti in Rishikesh, Uttarakhand.

Ganga

On the path to salvation

"For Hindus it is the **River of Heaven**, **flowing** from the **foot of Vishnu**, falling to the **head of Shiva**, touching the earth on top of its **highest mountain**... with **streams of blessing**."

DIANA L ECK, *ENCOUNTERING GOD:*
A SPIRITUAL JOURNEY FROM BOZEMAN TO BANARES (1993)

It is said that physical contact with the Ganga has almost a magical, transformative effect on the devotee. It's why pilgrims revere it – for a dip or even a mere sip of its waters washes away one's sins, purifies the soul, or sets one on the path to salvation. The river does not forsake anyone.

The river, within the collective psyche of Hindus all over the world, is a personification of water so sacred that there is no other. As scholar Diana L Eck writes, "The Ganga as a goddess is more than a single river. She functions in India as the archetype of sacred waters."

Traversing India

The river emerges from the Gangotri glacier in the western Himalayas, in the northern state of Uttarakhand, where it is popularly known as Bhagirathi, a reference to its mythological origins. As it makes its way down the mountains, it meets the River Alakananda at the holy town of Devprayag, and it is here, at this confluence, that the river becomes known as Ganga. From here, she flows into the plains past the ancient cities of Prayag and Varanasi, turning east through the Gangetic plain of north India into Bangladesh before emptying into the Bay of Bengal.

Over centuries, several key *tirthas* or places of pilgrimage have emerged along the banks of the 2,510-km (1,560-miles) river, a testament to its sacrality.

The descent to earth

The earliest mention of the Ganga is in the *Rigveda*, when Indra set the river free to bless the earth. The mythologies get richer in detail in subsequent centuries through the Puranas and epics. Some texts refer to Ganga as Mandakini, flowing from Vishnu's toe in the celestial world.

The origin story is well-known. The king Bhagiratha prayed that Ganga be released from the heavens so that she may purify the ashes of his ancestors – the 60,000 sons of King Sagara. The sage Kapila had burnt them with an angry glance when they had disturbed his penance. The divinities did not overlook his sincere and arduous penance and

Personifying the river
Ganga rides a giant carp as monsoon clouds tear across the sky in this painting from Mandi, Himachal Pradesh, dated c. 1650–1675. Two long-nosed gharials from the crocodile family and an elephant accompany the goddess who carries a vessal of sacred water and a lotus.

Ganga had no choice but to comply. It is from Bhagirath that the Ganga also gets one of her epithets, Bhagirathi.

Ganga began her descent, reluctant and furious. Shiva, the destroyer, expecting her wrath to devastate the earth, caught the river in the labyrinth of his *jata* or tangled locks, in order to cushion her cascade.

For years, Ganga remained locked in the god's hair, meandering and dividing into streams and rivulets, breaking her force. When she became calm, Shiva set her free, allowing her to reach the earth. This is why Shiva is known as Gangadhara or the "carrier of Ganga", and the river is lauded as Harashekhara or Shiva's crown.

Relationship with the gods

Shiva and Ganga are seen as an example of perennial love renewed every instant by a stream that knows no end. It is why she is also called the "liquid consort", writes Eck and notes that there are times when she is referred to as Shiva's second love or Parvati's co-wife.

◁ **The Ganga–Jamuna** lota or water container, named after the contrasting colours of the two rivers is from Thanjavur, Tamil Nadu.

ANIMALS ASSOCIATED WITH GANGA

The River Ganga is home to countless creatures, some of which are associated with the Goddess herself. It is home to gharials, mugger crocodiles, and saltwater crocodiles. Ganga is often related with the *makara* (See p 196), a mythical sea creature, which resembles a crocodile. She is also often seen in her iconography seated on a fish. Incidentally, the river is home to over 350 fish species, many of which are endemic to the river and crucial to the ecosystem.

> **"River of the Divine Beings**! Which one among the rivers that **flow from mountains** has mounted the **matted locks of Siva**, the slayer of the (three) cities? By which river have the **lotus-like feet of Vishnu** been washed? **Could poets compare** any such river with even a **small part of you**?"

VERSE 22, *GANGALAHARI*

This has led to many colourful myths and some folktales say it's one of the reasons behind Parvati's desire to merge with Shiva as Ardhanarishvara.

As a goddess, Ganga is perhaps the only deity who has been a consort to all three supreme gods. She travels as the creator, Brahma's companion in his brass water pot. She flows from the preserver, Vishnu's toe and, along with Sarasvati and Lakshmi, is one of his three wives. Scholars note that it is with Shiva, however, that she shares the most intimate relationship. After all, he is the one who caught her in the tangles of his hair.

In fact, her descent from the heavens and then on to Shiva's hair is reenacted symbolically, countless times, every day, in temples as devotees follow the ritual of pouring water upon the Shivalinga.

Iconography

The myth behind Ganga's descent became a source of inspiration for artists and has been rendered in stone many times. One of the most outstanding representations is the tableau relief on two boulders in the beach town of Mamallapuram, Tamil Nadu from the Pallava dynasty, dated to around the 7th century. When Ganga is depicted with Shiva, she is shown as a tiny figure caught in the god's locks, but her

◁ **Bhagirathi (left) and the Alakananda** meet at Devprayag in Uttarakhand to become the Ganga.

independent images are very different. In them, she is a young woman standing sometimes on a river alligator with long thin jaws or on the *makara*, a mythical sea monster, which serves as her vehicle. She often holds a lotus and a waterpot, which reifies water as distinct from the river.

Significance within Hinduism

Eck notes that Ganga's descent from the heavens led to her name Trilokapathagamini, or she who flows in the three worlds – the heavens, earth, and the netherworld. It is why she has "become a place of crossing for human beings, both the living and the dead". This perhaps links to the belief that even a drop of Ganga jal (Ganga's water) in a dying person's mouth will assure them a place in heaven.

Practitioners of Hinduism usually ensure that they keep phials or small pots of the water in their home shrines, and use it for a variety of religious rituals. It is why devotees can often be seen collecting the river's waters from along its banks in certain sacred places, such as Gangotri, Haridwar, or Varanasi.

There are several shrines along the banks of the river containing anthropomorphic images of the Ganga that are worshipped. However, as evening comes around and the ritual of paying obeisance by lighting the lamp or aarti begins, priests and worshippers turn their attention from her representation as shakti in a temple to the "liquid shakti", as Eck calls it, in the river. For, no matter how long and convoluted the river's history and mythology may be, the Ganga will always be, writes Eck, "a river that flows with the waters of life".

Gangalahari

⟐

A beautiful, evocative Sanskrit poem, the *Gangalahari* eulogizes
the River Ganga. Composed by the 17th-century poet, musician,
and scholar Jagannatha Pandita, the poem is made up of 52
verses and translates to "Wave of Ganga".

⟐

Praying to the Ganga
Worship along the banks of the river is a common sight, as in this image from Varanasi, Uttar Pradesh. The goddess Ganga, seated on the top of crocodile, her vahana, is seen in the background. Many practitioners of the Hindu religion believe that the river has the power to purify the mind, body, and soul.

The *Gangalahari* addresses the river as a mother, who forgives and embraces everyone, especially those who have been abandoned.

Composed by Jagannatha Pandita, a Telugu Brahman, the poem is not just a homage to the river but a lament as well. The story goes that Pandita moved to Delhi under the patronage of the Mughal emperor Shah Jahan and his son, the poet-prince Dara Shikoh. Here, he fell in love with a Muslim woman and was exiled, not just by the court, but also by his community.

He went to the holy city Varanasi, Uttar Pradesh, to re-establish his standing within the community, but failed. He and his beloved then made their way to the Panchaganga Ghat, where, it is said, the five rivers – Ganga, Sarasvati, Dhupapapa, Yamuna, and Kirna – converge. It is here, while sitting at the top of the 52 steps that he composed the *Gangalahari*. As he composed each verse, the river rose, almost in tandem, until the waters lapped at their feet, purifying them, before sweeping them away. Scholar of religious studies Diana L Eck writes that Jagannatha, in his ode, says, "There are plenty of gods who will care for the good… but who will care for the sinner, except Ganga?"

Today, in Gangotri, a temple town near the source of the Ganga in Uttarakhand, the prayer to the river concludes with the singing of this long and wonderful hymn.

Wave of Ganga

The following verses reflect Jagannatha Pandita's devotion to the River Ganga. Within a single *stotra*, or hymn, one encounters different approaches to addressing and pleasing the deity. This is either by describing her greatness, focusing on one's wretchedness, or even by engaging in complex poetic descriptions.

दरिद्राणां दैन्यं दुरितमथ दुर्वासनहृदां
द्रुतं दूरीकुर्वन् सकृदपि गतो दृष्टिसरणिम् ।
अपि द्रागाविद्याद्रुमदलनदीक्षागुरुरिह
प्रवाहस्ते वारां श्रियमयमपारां दिशतु नः ॥

May that flow of your waters, swiftly removing the misery of the wretched and the sin of ones with evil intent when it has come in the line of sight but once, which is the initiatory preceptor in this world in the quick destruction of the tree of ignorance, bestow upon us limitless prosperity.

तवालम्बादम्ब स्फुरदलघुगर्वेण सहसा
मया सर्वेऽवज्ञासरणिमथ नीताः सुरगणाः ।
इदानीमौदास्यं भजसि यदि भागीरथि तदा
निराधारो हा रोदिमि कथय केषामिह पुरः ॥

Because of your support, mother, all gods have suddenly been delivered to the path of disregard by my heavy pride. Daughter of Bhagiratha! If you now assume neglect, alas! Tell me, before whom shall I cry in this world, bereft of support?

स्मृतिं याता पुंसामकृतसुकृतानामपि च या
हरत्यन्तस्तन्द्रां तिमिरमिव चन्द्रांशुसरणिः ।
इयं सा ते मूर्तिः सकलसुरसंसेव्यसलिला
ममान्तःसन्तापं त्रिविधमपि पापं च हरताम् ॥

It removes the inner sluggishness even of those men who have not performed good deeds when it is remembered, like a stream of moon-rays removes darkness – may that form of yours, whose waters are worshipped by all the gods, remove my threefold inner heat and sin.

———— ⚭ ————

अपि प्राज्यं राज्यं तृणमिव परित्यज्य सहसा
विलोलद्वानीरं तव जननि तीरं श्रितवताम् ।
सुधातः स्वादीयस्सलिलभरमातृप्ति पिबतां
जनानामानन्दः परिहसति निर्वाणपदवीम् ॥

Mother, their bliss mocks the state of liberation who, having suddenly given up a prosperous kingdom as a twig have taken refuge on your banks where reeds sway, and who drink to their fill an abundance of your waters, more delicious than nectar.

———— ⚭ ————

महादानैर्ध्यानिैर्बहुविधवितानैरपि च यन्
न लभ्यं घोराभिः सुविमलतपोराशिभिरपि ।
अचिन्त्यं तद्विष्णोः पदमखिलसाधारणतया
ददाना केनासि त्वमिह तुलनीया कथय नः ॥

Granting indiscriminately to everybody the inconceivable state of Vishnu, which is unattainable even by great acts of charity, meditations of various kinds, and immaculate masses of fierce penance – tell us, to whom can you be compared?

निधानं धर्माणां किमपि च विधानं नवमुदां
प्रधानं तीर्थानाममलपरिधानं त्रिजगतः ।
समाधानं बुद्धेरथ खलु तिरोधानमधियां
श्रियामाधानं नः परिहरतु तापं तव वपुः ॥

An abode of merits, the creator of fresh bliss, the foremost of forts,
the immaculate garb of the three worlds, the resolution of intellect,
and the termination of ignorance, the producer of prosperity – may
your body remove our burning pain.

मरुल्लीलालोलल्लहरिलुलिताम्भोजपटली-
स्खलत्पांसुव्रातच्छुरणविसरत्कौङ्कुमरुचि ।
सुरस्त्रीवक्षोजक्षरदगरुजम्बालजटिलं
जलं ते जम्बालं मम जननजालं जरयतु ॥

Spreading the colour of saffron from the sprinklings of pollen falling off the
multitudes of the lotuses swayed by the waves moved by the play of wind,
thickened with the clay that is the fragrant powder flowing off the breasts of the
divine women, may your flower-strewn water destroy the web of rebirth for me.

विधत्तां निःशङ्कं निरवधि समाधिं विधिरहो
सुखं शेषे शेतां हरिरविरतं नृत्यतु हरः ।
कृतं प्रायश्चित्तैरलमथ तपोदानयजनैः
सवित्री कामानां यदि जगति जागर्ति जननी ॥

Ah, may Brahma fearlessly establish unending meditative absorption, let Vishnu
happily sleep on the Shesha serpent, let Shiva ceaselessly dance; enough of
expiatory rites, and enough of austerity, charity, and sacrifice – if the Mother,
who is the progenitrix of desirable results, is awake in the world.

अनाथः स्नेहार्द्रां विगलितगतिः पुण्यगतिदां

पतन् विश्वोद्धर्त्रीं गदविगलितः सिद्धभिषजम् ।

सुधासिन्धुं तृष्णाकुलितहृदयो मातरमयं

शिशुः सम्प्राप्तस्त्वामहमिह विदध्याः समुचितम् ॥

As one orphaned to the one drenched in affection, as one slipped from status to the one who grants auspicious states, as one falling unto the one who uplifts the world, as one vanishing from sickness to the well-known doctor, as one with a heart desperate of thirst to the nectarine waters – this child, I, have come to you, the Mother. Do as is fit.

ललाटे या लोकैरिह खलु सलीलं तिलकिता

तमो हन्तुं धत्ते तरुणतरमार्तण्डतुलनाम् ।

विलुम्पन्ती सद्यो विधिलिखितदुर्वर्णसरणिं

त्वदीया सा मृत्स्ना मम हरतु कृत्स्नामपि शुचम् ॥

It attains comparison with the younger Sun in the destruction of darkness when (even) playfully placed as a mark on the forehead by people in this world, and quickly wipes off the series of bad letters written by fate – may that mud of yours destroy all my sorrow/lustre.

यजन्त्येके देवान् कठिनतरसेवांस्तदपरे

वितानव्यासक्ता यमनियमरक्ताः कतिपये ।

अहं तु त्वन्नामस्मरणकृतकामस्त्रिपथगे

जगज्जालं जाने जननि तृणजालेन सदृशम् ॥

Some offer sacrifices to the gods, others, exceedingly difficult services. Yet others, detached from this expanse, are intent upon restraints and regulations. I, on the other hand, whose desires are all fulfilled by the remembrance of your name, three-streamed one, regard the web of the world as a web of twigs.

A force of nature
Located on the River Narmada in the town of Bhedaghat, Madhya Pradesh, are the Dhuandhar Falls, which translates to a smoky stream. Unlike the classical description of Narmada, these waters are harsh and loud.

Narmada

The river goddess

"…The waters of the Sarasvati **purify one in**… five days… **Yamuna in seven days**… Ganga **instantaneously**, and of the Narmada at the **mere sight** of it."

VERSE 8–12, CHAPTER 186, *MATSYA PURANA*

Rising from the Maikala mountain range in eastern Madhya Pradesh, the River Narmada makes its way across the state passing into Gujarat, before emptying into the Gulf of Khambat. Like Ganga, Narmada too has elaborate mythology and spiritual significance and is among the country's most sacred rivers.

The birth of a river

The *Skanda Purana* tells an interesting version of Narmada's emergence. Once, Shiva, the destroyer, in the midst of severe penance, starts perspiring. His sweat collects to become the Narmada river. This perhaps accounts for the popular Hindi phrase *Shankar ka pasina* that tells of Narmada's birth from the sweat of Shiva.

Perspiration is also a plot device in another legend. In this, Shiva and his wife Parvati are busy love sporting and a beautiful daughter is born from their sweat. The girl roams the three worlds and soon the gods, Asuras, and the men find themselves attracted to her. Shiva declares that only the most valorous would win her hand. The suitors begin arguing, each claiming a right. Almost immediately, the girl vanishes and appears a yojana (about 12.6 km or 9 miles) away. She continues doing this for 1,000 years. Seeing this, Shiva bursts into

laughter. He names his daughter Narmada, which means she who has been given, or *da*, hearts, or *narma*, by the gods. Narmada remains unmarried and is known as a Brahmacharini, or a celibate woman.

American scholar of religious studies Diana L Eck notes that a hymn in the *Skanda Purana*, devoted to Narmada's praises, has several other names, including Maheshvari Ganga.

A place of pilgrimage

Eck notes that there are several references to the Narmada in the Puranas, far more than even Ganga. The texts detail all the holy places along the river's banks that number about 100 million *tirthas*, or places of pilgrimage. The *Padma Purana* is full of praise for the Narmada as a place of *tirtha*. Some scholars suggest that Narmada is considered holier than any other river in the country. The riverbed also has the *bana linga*, a cylindrical stone, which can be worshipped as Shiva without consecration.

A popular way of paying obeisance to the river is by conducting a *parikrama*, or circumambulation. Approximately 2,800-km (1800-miles) long, it runs from the source in Amarkantak, a town in Madhya Pradesh, to Bharuch. The pilgrimage can, however, start at any point along the banks.

IN TODAY'S TIMES

AMARKANTAK

The pilgrimage town of Amarkantak in Madhya Pradesh is located at the meeting point of the Vindhya and the Satpura ranges. The Narmada begins from one of its hills, and its source, people and devotees believe has a shape like the mouth of a cow. The town is known as *Teerthraj*, or the king of pilgrimages. Locals also believe that the forests around the town are filled with plants with medicinal properties, adding to the town's holy charm.

To the Goddess

The Indian landscape is dotted with many sacred places and people visit these religious sites in large numbers regularly. The journey itself is significant and the travails of travel are themselves an act of devotion.

Every year, thousands of Hindu pilgrims trek up many kilometres on the three-peaked mountain Trikuta in Jammu & Kashmir to seek the darshana of Vaishno Devi in her cave shrine. There, the devotees encounter the goddess in the form of three *pindis*, or stone protuberances, believed to represent the three goddesses, Mahasarasvati, Mahalakshmi, and Mahakali, symbolizing the three aspects of creation, preservation, and destruction.

Mythology

There are different legends relating to the origin of the goddess and her cave shrine. Some believe that this is where Sati's skull or right arm fell. This is why the shrine is also called a *Shakti pitha*. A popular myth relates the story of a woman named Vaishnavi and her transformation into the goddess, Vaishno Devi. According to this story, the Earth was once ravaged by Asuras and the gods were helpless. So the goddesses combined their *tejas*, or heat energy, to create a beautiful young woman. They named her Vaishnavi and instructed her to dwell on the Earth for its protection. Her ultimate goal, they told her, is to merge with Vishnu, the preserver, once she has achieved the highest level of consciousness.

Vaishnavi took birth as the daughter of King Ratnakar Sagar. Sometime later, she left her house to engage in penance by the seashore. There, she met Rama, Vishnu's avatar, who was on his way to Lanka to rescue Sita. She requested him to take her as his wife. Rama, being already married, could not accept her offer, but told her that

△ **From the sky**
This is an aerial view of Vaishno Devi shrine. The right side of the image shows the track leading to the shrine.

△ **In the name of the goddess**
A devotee on her way to the shrine, along with her child. Both of them are wearing a headband with the slogan "Victory to the Mother".

"One by one they **crawl**… into the **chamber** of the goddess. The ritual crawl has all the **symbolism of gestation and birth**, even though Vaishno Devi is a **virgin goddess**."

DIANA L ECK, *INDIA: A SACRED GEOGRAPHY* (2012)

he would visit her again and if she is able to recognize him, he would accept her as his wife.

Rama, disguised as an old man, returned, but Vaishnavi could not discern his true form. She was disappointed. Rama, however, promised her that they would be united in the future when he returned to the Earth in his Kalki form. He also asked her to meditate on the foot of the Trikuta Hills.

There, a Hindu Tantric, Bhairav Nath, saw her and fell in love with her. In an attempt to escape his advances and continue her meditation, Vaishnavi went into the mountains, to a cave. Bhairav Nath, however, followed her. Angry, she beheaded him and decided to live in the cave permanently, immersed in her prayers. She gave up her human form and became a rock with three heads.

The call of the goddess

Over the years, the abode of Vaishno Devi has become a popular pilgrimage centre. Many people undertake this hours-long arduous journey in the hope that she will fulfil all their wishes. While on their journey uphill, devotees sing the slogan of *Jai Mata Di*, or Victory to the Mother. Once they reach the cave, in order to encounter the goddess, they have to first crawl through a narrow and small opening.

An interesting concept associated with Vaishno Devi is that of a *bulawa*, or the call of the goddess. It is widely believed that the goddess herself calls her children for a *darshana*. If she is keen to bestow her blessings upon someone, they will invariably end up at her shrine, but without her will, no one, regardless of effort, money, and power, can reach her.

▽ **During festivals, such as Navaratri,** people take out elaborate processions in the honour of the goddess. This image shows a tableau with a miniature of the shrine and a girl dressed as the goddess.

△ **An efficient way**
These days, newer and easier ways, such as cable cars, are used to reach the shrine.

△ **Prayer ties**
Devotees often tie *chunnis*, or short scarves, at the shrine to make a wish.

To the source
The River Ganga, or Bhagirathi as she is
known in this region, emerges from Gaumukh,
at 4,023 m (13,200 ft). The name, meaning
the mouth of a cow, is given to the point from
which the waters surface from the Gangotri
glacier. The 17-km (10.5-mile) arduous trek
to Gaumukh is popular among pilgrims, who
make the journey under the shadow of the
Bhagirathi massif that looms over them at
6,856 m (22,493 ft).

Imagery of Mookambika
The goddess Mookambika is often portrayed seated with her legs crossed on an altar or a lotus, as seen in this traditional Indian mural. She holds Vishnu's Sudarshana chakra in one hand (left) and a conch in the other.

Mookambika

The goddess of good fortune and education

> "When Goddess Saraswati, Goddess Lakshmi and Goddess Kali **merged** with Lord Brahma, Lord Vishnu and Lord Mahesh, **the ultimate manifestation** was Maa Mookambika Devi"
>
> KAREN RAJESH AND VISHAL DESAI, *DEVI'S GRACE: MAA MOOKAMBIKA DEVI* (2011)

The small, but legendary, temple of Mookambika Devi along the foothills of the lush Western Ghats in Kollur, a temple town in Udupi district of Karnataka, is a prominent place of Shakti worship in southern India.

Here, the goddess is an embodiment of Mahalakshmi, Parvati, and Sarasvati. American scholar of religious studies Diana L Eck calls this a part of the "triune goddess" theology. This is not an uncommon representation of the Great Goddess, the Mahadevi or Parashakti (See pp 160–61). Here, when the Goddess manifests as "*sattva* (purity), she is Mahalakshmi; as *rajas* (power or passion), she is Mahasarasvati; and as *tamas* (darkness), she is Mahakali." Mookambika, too, Eck notes, is a part of this concept.

Representation in Kollur

The main icon of worship in the Kollur temple is in the form of an *udbhava linga*, or a self-manifested phallus. A gold line runs through it, almost dividing it, and the two sides represent *purusha*, or the male, and Shakti, the female. Indian philosopher Adi Shankaracharya is said to have installed the idol of the goddess Mookambika at this temple.

The legend of Mookambika

The goddess's origin story has many versions, echoing in many ways the story of Durga and Mahishasura, and also reflecting local legends.

In it, the Asura Kamasura desires nothing more than to become the ruler of the three worlds. After great penance, Brahma, the creator, grants him the boon he asked for – that only a woman may kill him. Pleased, Kamasura returns but grows worried on hearing the story of Durga and Mahishasura. The Asura prays to Shiva, the destroyer, as only he can truly grant the power of immortality. The penance is long and hard, but the Asura manages to please Shiva.

Indra, the god of the heavens, realizes that the boon of immortality would make Kamasura unstoppable, so he prays to Sarasvati. The goddess takes away the Asura's power of speech and Shiva, unable to hear his wish, disappears. Enraged, Kamasura, now known as Mookasura, or the mute Asura, attacks all the other gods and soon defeats Indra, becoming the king of the three worlds.

Aghast, the gods pray to the Trimurti – Brahma, Vishnu, and Shiva – who invoke the Goddess. From Her emerges a new goddess with an arsenal of weapons from Sarasvati, Lakshmi, and Parvati. She defeats Mookasura and comes to be called Mookambika.

IN TODAY'S TIMES

THE MYSTERIOUS PILLAR

Close to the Mookambika Temple in Kollur is an iron pillar, considered about 2,000 years old. Local legends indicate that this was a part of the trident Mookambika used to slay Mookasura. Metallurgists suggest that the 8.7-m (28.5-ft) tall pillar was made with iron produced by an indigenous process similar to those used by India's tribal communities.

The mountain goddess
Nanda Devi, the western summit of
the two-peaked massif, is seen from
the Garhwal region of Uttarakhand.
Its access is through the Nanda Devi
National Park, today a UNESCO World
Heritage site. The much-lower eastern
summit (not pictured) is often called
Sunanda Devi or Nanda Devi East.

Nanda Devi

The bliss-giving goddess

"... Nanda Devi, **queen of them all**, held aloft her proud **shapely head**, her **slender shoulders** draped with **snow-white braid**."

ERIC SHIPTON, *NANDA DEVI* (1985)

The giant massif of ice and granite has a distinct shape and form, as it rises up from between a fortress of snow-clad mountains. Sometimes, a plume of smoky clouds caress the tip, a veil, devotees believe, protecting the goddess from curious eyes.

For geographers and mountaineers, this is Nanda Devi, the second-highest mountain in India standing at 25,646 feet (7,817 metres). For believers, she is the patron mountain goddess of the Garhwal and Kumaon regions of the state of Uttarakhand.

Links

There is a direct link between Nanda Devi and Shiva, the destroyer, in that she is, locals believe, married to the god. Some scholars believe that she is a manifestation of the goddess Parvati (See pp 108–11). There are many folk songs that tell of her relationship with Shiva and of the battles she undertakes to protect her followers, including one with the buffalo-demon, much like Durga and Mahisha.

A folk song, translated by anthropologist William S Sax, draws a connection between Nanda Devi and the Great Goddess who created the universe and the gods. In it, upon her death, the Goddess's head becomes Shiva, while her torso is reborn as Gaura, another name for Nanda Devi.

A matter of geography

Nanda Devi's remote, almost impregnable, location only serves to magnify the lore around her. Here, 12 peaks over 21,000 ft (6,400 m) surround Nanda Devi, along India's border, forming a "vast crater-like ring" as British mountaineer Hugh Ruttledge noted in the 1930s. A key point of access is in Garhwal, by way of precipitous cliffs, narrow paths with steep drops, and the Rishiganga gorge. Ruttledge wrote, "In no circumstances will access to the Goddess be easy."

Lending to the legend

It's no wonder that the goddess Nanda Devi and the mountain are inseparable in their mythology and divinity. Even the mountains surrounding Nanda Devi, locals believe, serve the goddess. In his conversations with them, American mountaineer H. Adams Carter noted that the peak Nanda Khat was considered her bed, Nanda Kot, her fortress, and Nanda Ghunti, the headdress. The mountain Trisul was her trident and Changabang provided light to the goddess. The Rishiganga gorge too was named after the seven sages who sought her protection.

"So tremendous is the aspect of the Rishiganga gorge that Hindu mythology described it as the last earthly home of the Seven Rishis. Here, if anywhere, their meditations might be undisturbed," Ruttledge wrote.

IN TODAY'S TIMES

NANDA DEVI UNSOELD

When American mountaineer Willi Unsoeld saw Nanda Devi, he decided to name his daughter after the mountain. Many years later, in 1976, he and his daughter, now a mountaineer, returned to scale the peak. The 22-year-old, however, died of acute high altitude sickness while climbing. Unsoeld, unable to bring her back, buried her on the mountain. A memorial to Devi in the Nanda Devi Sanctuary carries the following words from her diary: "I stand upon a wind-swept ridge at night with the stars bright above and I am no longer alone but I waver and merge with all the shadows that surround me. I am part of the whole and I am content."

The royal pilgrimage

The Nanda Devi Raj Jat Yatra is in honour of Nanda Devi, the mountain, the goddess, and the married daughter of Uttarakhand.

For three weeks, every 12 years in August–September, an elaborate procession winds its way through the Garhwal Himalayas in the state of Uttarakhand. Pilgrims cross villages, navigate turbulent rivers, and trek through high-altitude meadows, lakes, and snow-bound passes, as a part of the 280-km (174-mile) royal pilgrimage called the Nanda Devi Raj Jat Yatra.

It represents the goddess Nanda Devi's journey from her maternal home to that of her husband, Shiva, the destroyer, high up on Mount Kailash in the Himalayas. This journey, also known as a *jat* or pilgrimage, is in many ways, emblematic of the lives that women in Uttarakhand live – the journey they too must make once they are married, leaving their home and friends behind, as they transition to their husband's home. It mirrors the pangs of loneliness a woman may feel being away from her birth home and all that is familiar, the joy of returning to her place of childhood on a visit, and the despair of leaving it yet again.

Leaving home

In Uttarakhand, Nanda Devi is as much a goddess as she is a *dhiyani* or daughter married into another village, notes anthropologist William S Sax. Desperately lonely in her icy abode on Mount Kailash, she goes home to Nauti. When it is time for her to return, priests and devotees place an image of her in a decorated bridal palanquin, infused with the spirit of the goddess. A four-horned ram, adorned with colourful clothes and carrying gifts for Nanda Devi, leads the procession. People bid her goodbye to the tune of folk songs, cymbals, and drum beats, with all the poignancy of a human bride leaving her home for the first time.

△ **Twin peaks**
Nanda Devi (left) and the much-smaller Sunanda Devi are considered sisters in Kumaon mythology.

△ **Escorting her home**
Devotees and priests carry the decorated *doli* or bridal palanquin with an icon of the goddess.

Many villages including those from the Kumaon region join the procession carrying their own idols of the goddess. At some points during the journey, the priest possessed with the spirit of the goddess turns back, as if to return, but is coaxed to continue. Every halt is significant, connected to the many local legends around the goddess, of her interactions with her devotees, her fiery curses, and even battles with local demons.

The procession finally makes its way up to Bedni Bugyal, a high-altitude meadow at 3,354 m (11,000 ft). It then goes to the mysterious ice lake of Roopkund at 5,029 m (16,500 ft), before reaching its final destination, Hom Kund. This lake, at 3,756 m (12, 323 ft) is near the base of Trishul, the mountain that the locals call Kailash. Here, the ram is set free and the procession turns back. It is believed that the ram makes its way to Kailash and Nanda Devi's home.

The goddess travels

The Nanda Devi Raj Jat Yatra is in some ways a reversal of the pilgrimage that devotees make. For, here, it is the goddess who travels to her marital abode. Yet, participants of this journey – the devotees and the priests carrying the goddess's palanquin – must follow rituals and rules as a way of exhibiting their devotion. So,

"**I must go**, my son, to Swami's **Kailash**, I must go. **I must go**, my son, I am the ***dhiyani of the Sages***."

A FOLK SONG, TRANSLATED BY WILLIAM S SAX, *MOUNTAIN GODDESS: GENDER AND POLITICS IN A HIMALAYAN PILGRIMAGE* (1991)

during the smaller, annual *jat yatra*, devotees and priests may only sleep in a certain place, or eat a certain type of food else they would invoke the ire of the goddess. Or, in the case of the Raj Jat or Royal Pilgrimage, devotees must remain barefoot throughout the journey.

Sax in his seminal work *Mountain Goddess* notes that the procession is called the "*jat* not of the pilgrims but of the goddess". He compares this journey to the processions of deities and village gods across South Asia where "pilgrims travel with, rather than to, the deity who is the object of their devotions, where the deity moves among people who, primarily because of caste restrictions, might not otherwise get so close to him or her."

△ **Bidding her goodbye**
As the palanquin makes its way through villages, devotees gather and sing songs and dance in her honour.

△ **Into the mountains**
The priests participating in the Nanda Devi Raj Jat Yatra have to hike through high-altitude meadows.

Goddesses of epidemics and diseases

From the beginning of time, whenever there has been an epidemic, believers have turned to goddesses seeking their protection. Mostly they shield the devotee from the disease, but sometimes, they cause it as well.

▽ **This c. 10–11th century bronze trident** depicts Mariamman (centre), one of the main goddesses in South India.

Most villages in India have a resident mother goddess who is closely linked to the wellbeing of the place of her origin. She has a symbiotic relationship with her people. Her job is to protect and provide, and in return she expects propitiation in an appropriate manner. At the same time, she metes out punishment and has an undeniable association with disease.

Scholar Richard L Brubaker calls this the goddess's "ambivalent" nature. She protects her devotees, no doubt, but is responsible for inflicting them with disease as well. "She is both the scourge and the mistress of disease demons," he writes. "...she delights in the disease, is aroused by it, goes mad with it; she kills with it and uses it to give new life."

The diseases could also be considered a manifestation of the Earth Mother's anger, suggests Indian cultural activist and author Pupul Jayakar, who describes the goddess as a "skeleton bodied lady with terrible features, a complexion black as the darkest night and bloodshot eyes".

The myth of Shitala

The connection between goddesses and epidemics becomes apparent in the legends surrounding the virulent and contagious smallpox virus. The affliction was often

"To **worship Sitala**, to pay attention to what she represents, is to **provide oneself** with a more realistic, less **fragile view of life**, which in turn makes the inevitable outburst of disease or tragic **occurrences less devastating.** "

DAVID KINSLEY, *HINDU GODDESSES: VISION OF THE DIVINE FEMININE IN THE HINDU RELIGIOUS TRADITION* (1998)

regarded as a visitation or "possession" by the smallpox goddess and this association continued even after its eradication in the 1970s in India. Instead, it expanded to include other viruses such as chicken pox and measles that continue to wreak havoc.

While there are several goddesses connected to this disease, Shitala or Sitala seems to enjoy a special position. Considered an incarnation of Durga (See pp 80–83), she was worshipped in the 19th century in Bengal and North India, as one who can cure smallpox. Her name translates to mean "the cool one" and the virus was considered a manifestation of her personality. The burning fever and pustules that marked her entry into the body demanded ritual rather than therapeutic responses. For believers, recourse to any form of treatment was impious, likely to provoke the goddess and further imperil the child in whose body she resided.

American scholar of religious studies David Kinsley refers to Shitala's presence in the virus as her "grace". He adds that, according to linguist and scholar Edward Dimock, this may be interpreted as her "ability to permit people a wider vision of reality". He adds, "Sickness, death, disease, and suffering generally seem to come and go, according to this way of viewing things."

"A synchronic view of reality… in which past, present, and future are collapsed, in which sequential time is seen to be a mere construct, superimposes the whole range of human events – blessings, tragedies, good times, and bad times."

Shitala continues to hold a place of reverence in parts of the country. She is depicted as haggard, emaciated, and ugly, wearing red and seated on a lotus or a donkey. Her victims are seen as possessed and "cooled" with water and milk, as a way of appeasing wrath.

The legend of Mariamman

There are several goddesses, much like Shitala, who have a regional connection, and are not identified with pan-Hindu deities. While Shitala's appeal is restricted mostly to the eastern or the northern parts of India, Mariamman (See pp 378–79) and Yellammma have a unique place in South India. The two goddesses find references as early as the Sangam age, c. 200 BCE to 300 CE.

▷ **The goddess Yellamma, worshipped** across much of southern India, shares her origin story with Mariamman, though she has definite tribal roots.

There are several interesting origin stories around the Dravidian goddess of pustular disease. In one, she is the virtuous wife of a sage who turns three gods into children when they approach her. They curse her and her face becomes pockmarked, much like smallpox. In another, she is the wife of the Tamil poet Tiruvalluvar, notes Indian scholar of Tantra NN Bhattacharyya, who fans herself with Margosa leaves and cures herself of the disease.

However, the one legend that seems significant is linked to the Puranas, but has no connection with the disease. In this, Parashurama, the sixth incarnation of Vishnu,

△ **Priests in a temple** in Coimbatore can be seen here praying to Corona Devi, who is also known as Corona Mata. At the bottom, is a visual depiction of the COVID-19 virus, which are seen as demons.

cuts off his mother's head at the request of his father, as she has an unchaste thought. In most myths, Parashurama receives a boon from his father and wishes that his mother be restored to life. Parashuram mistakenly places the head of Renuka on the body of an untouchable woman. The body with the Brahman head was worshipped as Mariamman while the one with the untouchable woman's head came to be called Yellamma.

Henry Whitehead in his 1921 book, *The Village Gods of South India*, notes that this "probably describes the fusion of the Aryan and Dravidian cults in the days when the Aryans first found their way into South India." Mariamman's body, he writes, describes the Shaiva cult, while Yellamma's body could "describe some of the cults of the ancient Dravidian deities, modified by Brahman ideas and influences". Kinsley, while quoting scholar Richard L Brubaker underlines Mariamman's "ambivalent nature and her role as a village goddess exemplifying the social status quo in which Brahmans are at the head of the social system".

Local goddesses

There are many other such goddesses, their names varying from region to region. Many of them retain their role of protecting the devotee from the pox. For instance, Bijasenamata or Chechak Mata protects against smallpox in Bastar, Chattisgarh. The names give a clue to their role: *bija* means a spot like the mark of measles or chicken pox and *chechak* translates to eruption on the skin. The goddess is

CORONA MATA

During the COVID-19 pandemic, a new goddess, called Corona Mata, emerged. It is believed that, in Durga-like fashion, she will slay the Coronavirus demon. Artists depict Corona Mata wearing a mask as she slays the virus. She is armed with gloves and carries sanitizers, masks, and other medical equipment. Her worship is most prominent in Bihar, Jharkhand, Assam, and Bengal. A temple to her has also been established on the outskirts of Coimbatore, Tamil Nadu.

> "The **protectress**… has to protect them from **disease and other troubles**. That is why… Village Mothers have… been … **associated** with disease. "

NN BHATTACHARYYA, *INDIAN MOTHER GODDESS* (1999)

enshrined as a stone, painted yellow with auspicious, yellow–orange powder called sindoor and draped in a red sari. Her silver eyes are the only human feature. The goddess is honoured after the birth of a child and asked to protect the new-born against the pox. Priests carry portable shrines of this goddess to the areas of Bastar, so that she can be propitiated by one and all. Bija is said to have an army of 25 *virs*, or heroes and 64 Yoginis or female attendant goddesses.

In Andhra Pradesh, the Buddhist goddess Hariti who went from stealing children to protecting them (See pp 224–25) is known as Erukamma, goddess of smallpox and other contagious diseases. She even finds mention in Chinese monk and traveller Hiuen Tsang's 7th-century account of his visit to India.

Other well-known village goddesses of southern India include Gangamma, Bhadrakali, and Pidari who are worshipped outside villages walls with turmeric or kumkum, or vermilion.

Bhattacharyya also lists goddesses, such as Bombai Mai who is worshipped as the plague mother in Gaya, Bihar, and Olai Chandi or Oladevi, the goddess of cholera in Bengal. The latter is also known as Didi Thakrun and is worshipped by Hindus and Muslims alike. He notes how, in Bundi, Rajasthan, at the onset of cholera, believers would take the goddess Mari across the Chambal in a cart painted black and request her to never return.

People protector

Idol of Mariamman in Sri Veeramakaliamman Temple, Singapore

Mariamman was first worshipped as a fertility goddess in the rural areas of southern India, with references to her from as early as the Sangam period, spanning roughly between the 2nd century BCE and the 3rd century CE.

Her association with fertility explains why she eventually came to be known as a goddess who bestows rain. Over the centuries, her worship became popular and transitioned to the cities. Soon, she came to symbolize much more than fertility as people turned to her for protection against diseases such as smallpox.

Mariamman is often depicted in a regal image. Red-hued and beautiful, yet sombre, the image on the right is her gratifying and peaceful form. This is in stark contrast to her terrifying form, where she has fangs. She sits in the *lalitasana*, or the royal position, with one foot on the decapitated head of what appears to be a Rakshasa.

Her most common depictions represent her with two to four arms. This image shows her with eight arms. In the left hands, she holds a lotus, a trisul, a *sarpam damaru*, or serpent-pellet drum, and a knife. The lotus signifies the Sahasrara chakra, or the thousand-petalled lotus, which is one of the primary yogic chakras. The trisul can symbolize either the three primal *gunas*, or qualities, or the Trimurti, composed of Brahma, the creator, Vishnu, the preserver, and Shiva, the destroyer.

The *khadga*, or sword, reflects the sharpness of intellect and knowledge. The *sarpam damaru*, along with the trisul, show her connection with Shiva as it is his preferred musical instrument. The serpent hood is indicative of her association with chthonic elements.

In the right hands, she holds a *pinaka*, or bow, a *pasha*, or lasso, and a *kapala*, or skull cup. The *pinaka* represents her tribal origins and also emphasizes her association with the yogic practice of *ekagrata*, or one-pointed attention. The *pasha*, held by Yama, the god of death, is symbolic of how the human mind ought to be detached from worldly pleasures. She holds the blood-filled *kapala* to quench her thirst from the blood of evil forces.

Mariamman's worship includes an assortment of offerings. Apart from bangles and saris, she is often offered a lemon garland, believed to absorb negative energy and to cool her fierceness. Devotees also carry pots of water mixed with turmeric and neem leaves to her shrine to ask for protection against diseases.

Serpent hood

Sarpam damaru, or serpent-pellet drum

Decapitated Rakshasa head

Red and green saris as offerings

Pasha, or noose

Lemon garland

Sari with lotus motif

Glossary

amrita
The elixir of life, produced during the churning of the ocean by the Devas and the Asuras.

Ardhanarishvara
The composite form of Shiva, the destroyer, and his consort Parvati. It symbolizes the fusion of the intrinsic duality present in all nature. The half-male and half-female figure represents the two energies of the universe – masculine, that is *purusha*, representing consciousness, and feminine, that is *prakriti*, representing nature. The two elements are discrete but inseparable – complete and creative when united.

Aryans
A term used to describe people who are known to speak an archaic Indo-European language. Among other regions, they inhabited the northern region of the Indian subcontinent.

Asuras
These are supernatural beings with immense powers who were constantly in conflict with the Devas, or the gods. According to one myth that explains the etymology, Varuni, the goddess of liquor, emerged during the churning of the ocean, and liquor was claimed by the gods. Thereby, gods came to be called Suras (with liquor) and their opponents Asuras (those without liquor).

atman
The soul or the principle of life which is believed to be imperishable and present in all creation. It is different from the physical body, mind, and consciousness. According to Advaita Vedanta, it is the same as the Brahman, the essential energy of the cosmos.

avatar
In Hindu mythology, an incarnation of a god or a goddess on the Earth. Some of them may have many different avatars. In Sanskrit, the word literally means "a descent".

Brahman
The focal metaphysical concept of Hindu philosophical thought, which has been defined in several ways. It is the essence of the universe, the cosmic principle within and behind all existence, the ultimate unchanging reality, and the absolute consciousness.

Brahmans
The highest-ranking class according to the Hindu caste system, or varnas. A privileged and priestly group, its members hold the hegemonic position by virtue of their birth. They are said to be the repositories of knowledge and they are the only ones who can perform *yagnas* and rituals to propitiate the gods.

Bodhisattvas
Highly enlightened Mahayana Buddhist beings who delay nirvana so that they can devote themselves to the service of others. Bodhisattvas can be both female and male.

chakras
In yoga, they are the mystical energy centres in the body, usually believed to be seven in number. It is also used to refer to a discus or a wheel, which is a very powerful and deadly weapon wielded by Vishnu, the preserver, and all his avatars.

Daityas
Daityas are descendants of Diti, the granddaughter of Brahma, the creator, from whom their name is derived. A type of Asuras, Daityas were known to fight with the Devas because of jealousy.

Danavas
A race that descended from Danu, who was the daughter of Daksha, one of the agents of creation. Danavas are also a type of Asuras.

Devas/Devis
Heavenly divine beings worshipped by Hindus, Jains, and Buddhists. The male form is known as Deva, while the female is called a Devi. The Devas and the Devis have to be regularly propitiated with prayers and offerings by human beings. The root of the word Deva comes from the word *div*, which means to shine.

darshana
A glimpse or view of the divine. It is a process through which the divine also sees the worshipper, who believes to have been blessed.

dharma
Hindu scriptures describe dharma as a way of life that follows the path of righteousness. The objective of dharma is the attainment of moksha or ultimate liberation.

Digambaras
One of the two major schools of Jainism. A Sanskrit term, it translates to sky-clad, which is a euphemism for nudity. Male monks of this sect do not wear any clothes.

Dravidian
A group of people residing in South Asia, specifically in the southern part of the Indian subcontinent. They are believed to be the indigenous population of the country. They speak Dravidian languages, such as Tamil, Kannada, Telugu, and Tulu.

Gandharvas
A group or class of minor Hindu deities who are divine musicians and are known for their beauty. Their name comes from the word *gandha*, which means smell. The Gandharvas ate sweet-smelling herbs and their vestments emanated heavenly fragrances.

guru

A learned teacher or expert in a particular field of knowledge. It also refers to a spiritual guide, who reveals the meanings and potential of life, and shows the path to self-realization.

Hindu calendar

A Hindu calendar is based on lunar months, that is, the cycles of the phases of the Moon. Each year is made up of 12 months (354 days). The discrepancy between a 365-days solar year and lunar year is bridged by the inclusion of one extra month in the lunar year every 30 months. The 12 months are: Chaitra, Vaishakha, Jyeshtha, Ashadha, Shravana, Bhadrapada, Ashvina, Kartika, Margashirsha, Pausha, Magha, and Phalguna.

Indic religions

Religions that originated in the Indian subcontinent, such as Hinduism, Jainism, Buddhism, and Sikhism.

jagarana

Also known as *jagarata*, it is a ritual prevalent among Hindus in North India. It involves an all-night vigil with songs and dance in honour of a female deity.

mantra

A sacred sound, word, or verse. In Sanskrit, the word literally translates to instrument of thought. A mantra is used in many ways, such as to invoke deities or to build concentration during meditation.

maya

An illusion, maya is anything that seems to be that which it is not. In everyday use, maya is trickery and magic while spiritually, it is any existence other than the ultimate reality. It also refers to the capacity of the divine whereby the phenomenal world comes into being.

moksha

Refers to liberation of the atman from the cycle of birth, death, and rebirth. In most Hindu traditions, moksha is the ultimate goal of life.

Mahayana

The Greater Vehicle school of Buddhism that emphasizes the importance of Bodhisattvas.

mandala

A circular diagram that symbolizes the universe and is used in meditation by Hindus and Buddhists.

mudras

Symbolic hand gestures made by deities. It is derived from the Sanskrit word, *mud* that means joy and *ra* that means produce. As a result, mudras mean gestures that produce joy and happiness. Many of the goddesses in their iconography are seen showing these. The most popular ones are the boon-giving and the fear-not mudras.

Nagas

Semi-divine, serpent-like beings who can assume any form at will. They are the protectors of nature, particularly of waterbodies, where they dwell.

Navaratri

A nine-day Hindu festival that is celebrated in September or October. Navaratri is observed in honour of the divine feminine, the Devi.

parikrama

Clockwise circumambulation of a deity or a holy site.

Rakshasas

Supernatural beings who have the power to change their appearance at will. They were created by Brahma from his breath while he was asleep. Once they were created, they were so hungry that they started consuming Brahma himself. In protest, he shouted, *rakshama*, which means protect me, and Vishnu, the preserver, banished them to the Earth. This is how they get the name Rakshasa.

Rishis

Thinkers who devoted themselves to understanding the ultimate truth, metaphysical, spiritual, and religious ideas.

shloka

A form of verse that lends itself to the oral tradition of transmission of learning. Most Sanskrit verses are composed as couplets of 16 syllables.

Shri Vaishnavism

A Hindu sect that originated in South India and pays allegiance to Vishnu. The sect follows the teachings of the 11th-century philosopher Ramanuja.

Shvetambaras

One of the two major schools in Jainism. A Sanskrit term, it means clad in white. It refers to the practice of Shvetambara monks wearing white clothes, setting them apart from the Digambaras.

sutras

Ancient and medieval texts from Hinduism and Buddhism. The sutras preserve important teachings of their respective faiths and guide a follower who is adherent on the path devoid of ignorance and entrapment in the endless cycle of rebirth and death towards spiritual liberation.

Tirthankara

The 24 religious teachers who are worshipped by Jains.

Upanishads

Written between 800 BCE and 100 CE, these are collections of texts that elaborate on the philosophy contained in the Vedas. They discuss metaphysical ideas, such as the nature of the atman and the Brahman.

Vahanas

These are vehicles or animal mounts of Hindu deities. The term is derived from the Sanskrit *vahanam* which means that which carries or pulls. Goddesses and gods are often seen either seated on their vahana, or next to it. Some of the most popular ones are Sheranvali's lion, Parvati's tiger-lion, and Sarasvati's swan.

Vedas

The oldest scriptures of Hinduism, they are four in number. The *Rigveda* and the *Samaveda* are a collection of hymns, the *Yajurveda* contains instructions for rituals and the *Atharvaveda* is replete with spells.

Yakshas/Yakshis

Power and benevolent forest-spirits, who are believed to be the guardians of treasures and are very fond of riddles. They are often seen paired together in a lot of Jain iconography in temples.

yoga

A spiritual, mental, and physical discipline that leads to a union of the soul and the spirit. Such a balance requires discipline, promotes self-awareness, and leads to enlightenment.

yantra

A mystical diagram used in Tantric forms of worship. These are often used in the rituals associated with Dasamahavidya goddesses.

Yoginis

Female master practitioners of Tantra and yoga. They are also described as a sacred feminine force made incarnate as an avatar of the goddess Parvati. They are also worshipped in Yogini temples across the Indian subcontinent. As per historians, Yoginis were once thought to be local village goddesses, who were gradually grouped together during the rise of the practice of Tantra.

yuga

Ancient Hindu belief holds that time is cyclical. Each cycle of time comprises four ages or yugas. The first is Satya Yuga, the golden age, the best of all the yugas. This is followed by Treta and Dwapara, which see a gradual deterioration of humanity, the environment, and quality of life. The final age is Kali Yuga, which is a time of darkness and ignorance, when the spiritual is forgotten and the relentless exploitation of both humans and nature results in the destruction of the universe.

Index

Selected Bibliography

All the English translations of the *Devi Mahatmya* are taken from *Devi Mahatyam (Glory of the Divine Mother): 700 Mantras on Sri Durga* by Swami Jagadiswarananda, published by Sri Ramakrishna Math, 1953.

CHAPTER 1   INTRODUCTION TO THE GODDESS

Brockington, JL. *The Sacred Thread*. Edinburgh University Press, 1996.

Campbell, Joseph. *The Power of Myth*. New York: Doubleday, 1988.

Chattopadhyaya, Debiprasad. *Indian philosophy: A popular introduction*. People's Pub. House, 1964.

Clooney, SJ Francis X. *Divine Mother, Blessed Mother: Hindu Goddesses and the Virgin Mary*. Oxford University Press, 2005.

Lall, Manohar. Among the *Hindus: A study of Hindu Festivals*. New Delhi, Chennai: Asian Educational Services.

Majumdar, RC. *The History and Culture of the Indian People Vol 1: The Vedic Age*. Bombay: Bharatiya Vidya Bhavan, 1965.

Williams, George M. *Handbook of Hindu Mythology*. Santa Barbara: ABC-CLIO Inc, 2003.

CHAPTER 2   RISE OF THE GODDESS

Chitgopekar, Nilima, ed. *Invoking Goddesses: Gender Politics in Indian Religion*. Har Anand Publications, 2007.

Clooney, SJ Francis X. *Divine Mother, Blessed Mother: Hindu Goddesses and the Virgin Mary*. Oxford University Press, 2005.

Dalal, Roshen. *The Vedas: An Introduction to Hinduism's Sacred Texts*. Penguin Books, India, 2014.

Dehejia, Vidya. *Devi, The Great Goddess: Female Divinity in South Asian Art*. Washington DC, Ahmedabad, Cologne: Arthur M. Sackler Gallery, Mapin Publishing, Prestel Verlag, 1999.

Dowson, John, *A Classical Dictionary of Hindu Mythology and Religion, Geography, History and Literature*. London: Trubner & Co, Ludgate Hill, 1888.

Easwaran, Eknath. *The Upanishads*. Nilgiri Press, 2007.

Kenoyer, Jonathan Mark. *Ancient Cities of the Indus Valley Civilization*. Oxford University Press, 1998.

Kinsley, David. *Hindu Goddesses: Visions of the Divine Feminine in the Hindu Religious Traditions*. Berkeley, Los Angeles, London: University of California Press, 1988.

Khanna, Madhu, ed. *Saktapramodah of Deva Nandan Singh*. DK Print World Ltd, 2013.

Kosambi, DD. *The Culture and Civilization of Ancient India in Historical Outline*. Vikas Publishing House Pvt Ltd, 1997.

Ratnagar, Shereen. *Understanding Harappa: Civilization in the Greater Indus Valley*, Tulika Books, 2017.

Singh, Upinder. *A History of Ancient and Early Medieval India: From the Stone Age to the 12th Century*. New Delhi: Pearson Longman, 2008.

Upadhyaya, KD. "Indian Botanical Folklore". *Asian Folklore Studies*, Volume 23, Number 2, 1964.

CHAPTER 3   EVOLUTION OF GODDESS WORSHIP

Basham, AL. *The Wonder That Was India: A Survey of the Culture of the Indian Sub-Continent Before the Coming of the Muslims*. Sidgwick & Jackson, 1954.

Bhattacharji, Sukumari. *The Indian Theogony: A Comparative Study of Indian Mythology from the Vedas to the Puranas*. Cambridge University Press, 2007.

Bhattacharyya, NN. *History of the Tantric Religion*. New Delhi: Manohar Books, 1992.

Brown, C Mackenzie. *The Song of the Goddess: The Devi Gita Spiritual Counsel of the Great Goddess*. State University of New York Press, 2002.

Brown, C Mackenzie. *The Triumph of the Goddess: The Canonical Models and Theological Visions of the Devi-Bhagavata Purana*. State University of New York Press, 1990.

Chakrabarti, Kunal. *Religious Process: The Puranas and the Making of a Regional Tradition*. Delhi: Oxford University Press, 2001.

Chattopadhyaya, Debiprasad. *Indian Philosophy*: A Popular Outline. PPH, 1964.

Chaturvedi, BK. *Durga: Gods and Goddesses of India*. Delhi: Books For All, 1996.

Chaturvedi, BK. *Lakshmi: Gods and Goddesses of India*. Delhi: Books For All, 1999.

Chaturvedi, BK. *Saraswati: Gods and Goddesses of India*. Delhi: Books For All, 1998.

Chitgopekar, Nilima. *Encountering Sivaism: The Deity, the Milieu, the Entourage*. Delhi: Munshiram Manoharlal Publishers Pvt Ltd, 1998.

Chitgopekar, Nilima, ed. *Invoking Goddesses: Gender Politics in Indian Religion*. Shakti Books, 2002.

Chitgopekar, Nilima. *Rudra: The Idea of Shiva*, Penguin, 2007.

Choudhuri, Usha; Choudhari, Indra Nath. *Hinduism: A Way Of Life And A Mode Of Thought: A Way of Life and Mode of Thought*. Niyogi Books, 2013

Chopra, Capt Praveen. *Vishnu's Mount: Birds in Indian Mythology and Folklore*. Chennai: Notion Press, 2017.

Clooney, SJ Francis X. *Hindu Wisdom for All God's Children*. New York: Orbis Books, 1998.

Coburn, Thomas. *Encountering the Goddess: A Translation of the Devi-Mahatmya and a Study of Its Interpretation*. New York: State University of New York Press, 1991.

Cowell, Edward B; Thomas, Frederick William, tr. *The Harsa-carita of Bāna*. London: Royal Asiatic Society, 1897.

Darian, Steven G. *The Ganges in Myth and History*. Delhi: Motilal Banarsidass Publishers Private Limited, 2001.

Dehejia, Vidya. *Devi, The Great Goddess: Female Divinity in South Asian Art*. Washington DC, Ahmedabad, Cologne: Arthur M Sackler Gallery, Mapin Publishing, Prestel Verlag, 1999.

Dowson, John, *A Classical Dictionary of Hindu Mythology and Religion, Geography, History and Literature*. London: Trubner & Co, Ludgate Hill, 1888.

Eck, Diana L. *India: A Sacred Geography*. New York: Harmony Books, 2012.

Diana L. *Encountering God: A Spiritual Journey from Bozeman to Banaras*. Beacon Press, 2003.

Flood, Gavin. *An Introduction to Hinduism*. Cambridge University Press, 1996.

Flynn, Sean. *Why Peacocks? An Unlikely Search for Meaning in the World's Most Magnificent Bird*. Simon & Schuster, 2021.

Goldberg, Ellen. *The Lord Who Is Half Woman: Ardhanarisvara in Indian and Feminist Perspective.* State University of New York Press, 2002.

Goswami, Meghali et al. "Sapta Matrikas in Indian Art and their Significance in Indian Sculpture and Ethos: A Critical Study." *Anistoriton,* Volume 9, 2005.

Griffith, Ralph TH, tr. *The Hymns of the Rig Veda.* 1896.

Harshananda, Swami. *Hindu Gods and Goddesses.* Madras: Sri Ramakrishna Math, 2002.

Hawley, John Stratton and Narayanan, Vasudha, ed. *The Life of Hinduism.* New Delhi: Aleph Book Company, 2017

Hawley, John Stratton and Wulff, Donna Marie. *Devi: Goddesses of India.* Berkeley: University of California Press, 1996.

Hazra, RC. *Studies in the Puranic Records on Hindu Rites and Customs.* Delhi: Motilal Banarsidass Publishers Private Limited, 1988.

Hiltebeitel, Alf; Erndl, Kathleen. *Is the Goddess a Feminist: The Politics of South Asian Goddesses.* New York: New York University Press, 2001.

Jayakar, Pupul. *The Earthen Drum: An Introduction to the Arts of Rural India.* Delhi: National Museum, 1980.

Kinsley, David. *Hindu Goddesses: Visions of the Divine Feminine in the Hindu Religious Traditions.* Berkeley, Los Angeles, London: University of California Press, 1988.

Kinsley, David. *Tantric Visions Of The Divine Feminine: The Ten Mahavidyas.* Delhi: Motilal Banarsidass Publishers Private Limited, 1988.

Kinsley, David. "The Portrait of the Goddess in the Devī-māhātmya". Journal of the American Academy of Religion, Volume 46, Number 4, 1978

Krishna, Nanditha. *Sacred Animals Of India.* Penguin Books, 2008.

Ludvik, Catherine. *Sarasvati: Riverine Goddess of Knowledge from the Manuscript-carrying Vina-player to the Weapon-wielding Defender of the Dharma.* Brill Leiden, 2007.

Mahadevan, TMP. *The Hymns of Sankara.* Delhi: Motilal Banarsidass Publishers Private Limited, 1980.

Mahalakshmi, R. *Art and History: Texts, Contexts and Visual Representations in Ancient and Early Medieval India.* Bloomsbury Publishing, 2020.

McDermott, Rachel Fell; Kripal, ed. *Encountering Kali: In the Margins,* at the Center, in the West, 2003.

Meister, Michael W, ed. *Discourses on Çiva, Proceedings of a Symposium on the Nature of Religious Imagery.* Philadelphia, University of Pennsylvania Press, 1984.

Menzies, Jackie. *Goddess: Divine Energy.* Thames & Hudson, 2007.

Miller, Barbara Stoller, tr. *Bhartihari and Bilhana: The Hermit and the Love Thief.* Penguin Books, 1990.

Mohanty, Seema. *The Book of Kali.* New Delhi: Penguin Books, 2009.

Mookerjee, Ajit. *Kali: The Feminine Force.* London: Thames & Hudson, 2008

Nivedita, Sister. *Kali: The Mother.* Kolkata: Advaita Ashrama, 2005.

Otto, Rudolf. *The Idea of the Holy: An Inquiry into the Non-Rational Factor in the Idea of the Divine and its Relation to the Rational.* Oxford University Press, 1923.

Pattanaik, Devdutt. *7 Secrets of the Goddess.* Westland, 2014.

Pattanaik, Devdutt. *Lakshmi: The Goddess of Wealth and Fortune, An Introduction,* Mumbai: Vakils Feffer & Simons Pvt Ltd, 2002.

Pintchman, Tracy. *The Rise of the Goddess in the Hindu Tradition.* State University of New York Press, 1994.

Rhodes, Constantina Eleni. *Invoking Lakshmi: The Goddess of Wealth in Song and Ceremony.* State University of New York Press, 2010.

Satyananda Sarasvati, Swami. *Devi Gita.* Delhi: Motilal Banarsidass Pvt Ltd Publishers, 1991

Singh, OP. *Iconography of Gaja-Lakshmi.* Varanasi: Bharati Prakashan, 1983.

Sharma, Bulbul. *The Book of Devi,* New Delhi: Viking, 2001.

Sivananda, Swami. *The Devi Mahatmya.* Shivanandanagar: The Divine Life Society, 1957.

Storl, Wolf-Dieter. *Shiva: The Wild God of Power and Ecstasy.* Simon & Schuster, 2004.

Stietencron, Heinrich von. *Hindu Myth, Hindu History: Religion, Art, and Politics.* Ranikhet: Permanent Black, 2005.

Shreenivas, Jhaver P. *Spiritual Heritage and Cultural Symbols of India.* Jaico Publishing House, 1999.

Tagare, GV, tr; Bhatt, GP, ed. *The Skanda-Purana,* Part I. Delhi: Motilal Banarsidass Publishers Private Limited, 1995.

Tapasyananda, Swami, ed. *Sri Lalita Sahasranama.* Madras: Sri Ramakrishna Math, 1990.

Thapar, Romila. *A Penguin History of Early India: From Origins to AD 1300.* Penguin Books, 2003.

The Siva-Purana, Vol. I & II. Delhi: Motilal Banarsidass Publishers Private Limited, 1969.

Zimmer, Heinrick. *Myths and Symbols in Indian Art and Civilization.* Bollingen Foundation. Princeton University Press, 1946.

CHAPTER 4   BUDDHIST AND JAIN GODDESSES

Bhattacharyya, NN. *History of the Tantric Religion.* New Delhi: Manohar Books, 1992.

Cort, John, et al. Brill's *Encyclopedia of Jainism.* Brill Academic Pub, 2020.

Cort, John. "Medieval Jaina Goddess Traditions," *Numen,* Volume 34, 1987.

de Alwis, Malathi. "The incorporation and transformation of a 'Hindu' goddess". *The South Asianist Journal,* Volume 6 (1), 2018.

Greenberg, Yudit Komberd, ed. *Love in World Religions.* Denver, Oxford: ABC Clio, 2008.

Gupte, RS. *Iconography of the Hindus, Buddhists, and Jains.* Bombay: DB Taraporevala Sons & Co. Private Limited, 1972.

Kramrisch, Stella. *Exploring India's Sacred Art: Selected Writings.* University of Pennsylvania Press, 1983.

Mahalakshmi, R. *Art and History: Texts,* Contexts and Visual Representations in Ancient and Early Medieval India. Bloomsbury Publishing, 2020.

Paul, Diana Y. *Women in Buddhism: Images of the Feminine in the Mahayana.* University of California Press, 1979.

Pal, Pratapadiya. *Indian Sculpture.* Los Angeles County Museum of Art; University of California Press, 1988.

Pranshu Samdarshi The Concept of Goddesses in Buddhist Tantric Traditions, The Delhi University Journal of the humanities and the Social Sciences Vol 1 2014.

Obeyesekere, Gananath. *The Cult of the Goddess Pattini.* Chicago: University of Chicago Press, 1984.

Rajan, K. "Jwalamalini Cult and Jainism in Kerala", *Heritage Journal of Multidisciplinary Studies in Archaeology,* Volume 5, 2017.

Shaw, Miranda, *Buddhist Goddesses of India.* Princeton, Oxford: Princeton University Press, 2006.

Shaw, Miranda. *Passionate Enlightenment: Women in Tantric Buddhism.* Princeton, Oxford: Princeton University Press, 1995.

www.jainpedia.org

CHAPTER 5   TANTRA AND THE GODDESS

Brahmanda Purana. Delhi: Motilal Banarsidass Publishers Private Limited, 1984.

Broo, Mans. *The Rādhā Tantra: A critical edition and annotated translation.* Routledge, 2017.

Chattopadhyaya, Debiprasad. *Lokayata: A Study in Ancient Indian Materialism.*1959.

Chitgopekar, Nilima, ed. *Invoking Goddesses: Gender Politics in Indian Religion.* Har Anand Publications, 2007.

Clooney, SJ Francis X. *Divine Mother, Blessed Mother: Hindu Goddesses and the Virgin Mary.* Oxford University Press, 2005.

Dehejia, Vidya. *Devi, The Great Goddess: Female Divinity in South Asian Art.* Washington DC, Ahmedabad, Cologne: Arthur M Sackler Gallery, Mapin Publishing, Prestel Verlag, 1999.

Dehejia, Vidya. *Yogini Cult and Temples: A Tantric Tradition.* New Delhi: National Museum, 1986.

Feuerstein, Georg. *Tantra: Path of Ecstasy.* Shambhala, 2000.

Flood, Gavin. *The Blackwell Companion to Hinduism.* Oxford: Blackwell Publishing, 2003.

Harshananda, Swami. *Hindu Gods and Goddesses.* Madras: Sri Ramakrishna Math, 2002.

Hazra, RC. *Studies in the Puranic Records on Hindu Rites and Customs.* Delhi: Motilal Banarsidass Publishers Private Limited, 1988.

Keul, István, ed. *'Yogini' in South Asia: Interdisciplinary Approaches.* Routledge, 2017.

Khanna, Madhu, ed. *Saktapramodah of Deva Nandan Singh.* DK Print World Ltd, 2013.

Kinsley, David. *Hindu Goddesses: Visions of the Divine Feminine in the Hindu Religious Traditions.* Berkeley, Los Angeles, London: University of California Press, 1988.

Kinsley, David. *Tantric Visions Of The Divine Feminine: The Ten Mahavidyas.* Delhi: Motilal Banarsidass Publishers Private Limited, 1988.

McDaniel, June. "The Tantric Radha: Some Controversies About the Nature of Radha in Bengali Vaishnavism and the Radha Tantra," The Journal of Vaisnava Studies, Volume. 8.2, 2000.

Mittal, Sushil and Thursby, Gene, ed. *The Hindu World.* Routledge, 2007.

Monier-Williams, Monier. *A Sanskrit-English Dictionary.* New Delhi: Oxford University Press, 2000.

Mookerjee, Ajit. *Kali: The Feminine Force.* London: Thames & Hudson, 2008

Ratnagar, Shereen. *Understanding Harappa: Civilization in the Greater Indus Valley*, Tulika Books, 2017.

Tigunait, Rajmani; Halbfass, Wilhelm. "The Concept of Sakti in Lajsmidhara's Commentary on The Saundaryalahiri in Relation to Abhinavagupta's Tantraloka", A Dissertation in Asian and Middle Eastern Studies, 1997

Saraswati, Chandrasekharendra. Saundaryalahari. Bharatiya Vidya Bhavan, 2001.

Shankaranarayanan, S. *The Ten Great Cosmic Powers.* Samata Books, 2013.

Sharma, RS, ed. Indian society: Historical Probings. New Delhi: People's Pub House, 1974.

Shaw, Miranda. *Passionate Enlightenment: Women in Tantric Buddhism.* Princeton, Oxford: Princeton University Press, 1995.

Storl, Wolf-Dieter. *Shiva: The Wild God of Power and Ecstasy.* Simon & Schuster, 2004.

Tapasyananda, Swami, tr. *Sivananda Lahari of Sri Sankaracarya.* Madras: Sri Ramakrishna Math, 1985.

CHAPTER 6 DIVINE LANDSCAPES

An 'English goddess' for India's down-trodden,
Accessed at https://www.bbc.com/news/world-south-asia-12355740

Aitken, Bill. *The Nanda Devi Affair.* New Delhi: Penguin Books, 2000.

A temple for a language. Accessed at https://www.thehindu.com/books/a-temple-for-a-language/article17752224.ece

Bhattacharya, NN. *The Indian Mother Goddess.* New Delhi: Manohar Books, 1999.

Calasso, Roberto. *Ka: Stories of the Mind and Gods of India.* London: Vintage Books: 1999.

Carter, Adams H. "The Goddess Nanda and Place Names of the Nanda Devi Region". The American Alpine Club, 1977.

Chitgopekar, Nilima. *Encountering Sivaism: The Deity, the Milieu, the Entourage.* Delhi: Munshiram Manoharlal Publishers Pvt Ltd, 1998.

Dalal, Roshen. *The Vedas: An Introduction to Hinduism's Sacred Texts.* Penguin Books, India, 2014.

Dehejia, Vidya. *Devi, The Great Goddess: Female Divinity in South Asian Art.* Washington DC, Ahmedabad, Cologne: Arthur M Sackler Gallery, Mapin Publishing, Prestel Verlag, 1999.

Dehejia, Vidya. *Indian Art.* London: Phaidon Press, 1997.

Dehejia, Vidya. *Yogini Cult and Temples: A Tantric Tradition.* New Delhi: National Museum, 1986.

Eck, Diana L. *Banaras: City of Light.* Columbia University Press, 1999.

Eck, Diana L. *Darsan: Seeing the Divine Image in India.* Columbia University Press, 1998.

Eck, Diana L. *Encountering God: A Spiritual Journey from Bozeman to Banaras.* Beacon Press, 2003.

Eck, Diana L. *India: A Sacred Geography.* New York: Harmony Books, 2012.

Flood, Gavin. *An Introduction to Hinduism.* Cambridge University Press, 1996.

Fontein, Jan. *The Pilgrimage of Sudhana: A Study of Gandavyuha illustrations in China, Japan, Java.* The Hague, Paris: Mouton & Co, 1967.

Fuller, CJ. *The Renewal of Priesthood: Modernity and Traditionalism in a South Indian Temple.* Princeton University Press, 2003.

Hawley, John Stratton and Wulff, Donna Marie. *Devi: Goddesses of India.* Berkeley: University of California Press, 1996.

Hiltebeitel, Alf; Erndl, Kathleen. *Is the Goddess a Feminist: The Politics of South Asian Goddesses.* New York: New York University Press, 2001.

Iyengar, BKS. *Light of the Yoga Sutras of Patanjali.* Harper Collins, 1993.

Jayakar, Pupul. *The Earth Mother: Legends, Goddesses, and Ritual Arts of India*, Harper & Row, 1990.

Kinsley, David. *Hindu Goddesses: Visions of the Divine Feminine in the Hindu Religious Traditions.* Berkeley, Los Angeles, London: University of California Press, 1988.

Mason, Kenneth, ed. "Nanda Devi", *The Himalayan Journal*, 1933.

Rajan, Rajeshwari Sunder. "Is the Hindu Goddess a Feminist," *Economic and Political Weekly*, Volume 33, Number 44, 1998.

Sax, William. *Mountain Goddess: Gender and Politics in a Himalayan Pilgrimage.* Oxford University Press, 1993.

Sax, William. "Village Daughter, Village Goddess: Residence, Gender, and Politics in a Himalayan Pilgrimage," *American Ethnologist*, Volume 17, Number 3, 1990.

Sharma, LM. *The Story of Santoshi Mata.* Diamond Pocket Books Pvt Ltd, 2002.

Shipton, Eric. *The Six Mountain Travel Books.* Mountaineers Books, 1990.

US Climber Dies on Peak Whose Name She Bore. Accessed at https://www.nytimes.com/1976/09/18/archives/us-climber-dies-on-peak-whose-name-she-bore.html

Whitehead, Right Reverend Henry. *The Village Gods of South India.* 2020.

Acknowledgments

The publisher would like to thank:
Member of Parliament and author **Shashi Tharoor** for writing the Foreword.

Economist and author **Bibek Debroy** for his insights on the subject and helping with the initial planning of the book.

Nilima Chitgopekar for writing this book.
An associate professor in the department of history at Jesus & Mary College, University of Delhi, Nilima Chitgopekar has authored six books and edited one, along with several articles and essays. She has been the recipient of prestigious fellowships from the Oxford Centre for Hindu Studies (OCHS) and the Charles Wallace India Trust (CWIT). Her endeavour in her lectures, writings, and films is to convey the intricacies and complexities within Hinduism, simply, yet without compromising on the wonderful ambivalences that exist within it.

Tarinee Awasthi for translating extracts from *Adbhuta Ramayana* (pp 28–31), "Devi Sukta" (pp 46–47), *Devi Mahatmya* (pp 72–75), *Devi Gita* (pp 164–67), *Gita Govinda* (pp 210–13), *Sragdhara Stotra* (pp 238–39), *Saundaryalahari* (pp 290–95), and *Gangalahari* (pp 358–61).
A Sanskritist whose areas of interest span Mimamsa, Vedanta, and devotional traditions, Tarinee Awasthi is currently a doctoral candidate at Cornell University, and holds a Master's degree in history from Jawaharlal Nehru University.

Chitra Subramanyam for writing the text on Nanda Devi (pp 370–71) and the Nanda Devi Raj Jat Yatra (pp 372–73).

Chitra Subramanyam and **Vatsal Verma** for content planning, **Bipasha Roy** for editorial assistance, and **Sumedha Chopra** for help in picture research.

Every effort has been made to acknowledge those individuals, organizations, and corporations that have helped with this book and to trace copyright holders. DK apologizes in advance if any omission has occurred. If an omission does come to light, DK will be pleased to insert the appropriate acknowledgment in the subsequent editions of the book.

The publisher would like to thank the following for their kind permission to reproduce their photographs:

(Key: a-above; b-below/bottom; c-centre; f-far; l-left; r-right; t-top)

1 Dreamstime.com: Juliengrondin. **2 Brooklyn Museum:** Gift of Dr. Bertram H. Schaffner, 1993.106.2. **5 © The Metropolitan Museum of Art:** Rogers Fund, 1927 (cra). **Wellcome Collection:** Copper yantra meditation plaque, India, 1801-1900 / Attribution 4.0 International (CC BY 4.0) (ca). **6 Philadelphia Museum of Art:** Stella Kramrisch Collection, 1994, 1994-148-115. **7 © The Metropolitan Museum of Art:** Edward C. Moore Collection, Bequest of Edward C. Moore, 1891

(cra); Purchase, Friends of Asian Art Gifts, 2007 (cla). **Wellcome Collection:** Mystical body of tantric meditation, flow of the life force / Attribution 4.0 International (CC BY 4.0) (ca). **9 Los Angeles County Museum of Art:** Gift of Diandra and Michael Douglas (M.81.271.9). **12 Getty Images:** Heritage Images / Hulton Fine Art Collection. **14 Dreamstime.com:** Rusel1981. **15 Getty Images / iStock:** vbel71. **16 Dreamstime.com:** Marek Lipka Kadaj. **17 Dreamstime.com:** Oleg Doroshenko. **19 Dreamstime.com:** Mcmorabad. **20-21 Shutterstock.com:** Lal Nallath. **22 Wellcome Collection:** Tantrika painting / Attribution 4.0 International (CC BY 4.0). **22-23 Wellcome Collection:** Copper yantra meditation plaque, India, 1801-1900 / Attribution 4.0 International (CC BY 4.0). **24 Alamy Stock Photo:** Dinodia Photos. **26-27 Getty Images:** Jack Vartoogian. **28-31 Dreamstime.com:** Andrey Yanushkov. **33 Dreamstime.com:** Manjunatha S. **36 Getty Images:** DEA / G. Nimatallah / De Agostini. **37 Alamy Stock Photo:** Suzuki Kaku (b). **40-41 The Cleveland Museum Of Art:** Gift of Doris and Ed Wiener. **41 Los Angeles County Museum of Art:** From the Nasli and Alice Heeramaneck Collection, Museum Associates Purchase (M.69.13.4). **42 Shutterstock.com:** AstroVed.com. **43 Getty Images:** Angelo Hornak / Corbis. **44-45 Dreamstime.com:** Andreuma3. **44-47 Dreamstime.com:** Andrey Yanushkov. **48 The Cleveland Museum Of Art:** Gift of Maxeen and John Flower in honor of Dr. Stanislaw Czuma. **49 Shutterstock.com:** JoshiGraphy. **50 Oriental Memoirs, Vol. III:** James Forbes. **51 Los Angeles County Museum of Art:** Nasli and Alice Heeramaneck Collection, Museum Associates Purchase (M.78.9.16). **52-53 Getty Images:** gulfu photography. **54-55 © The Metropolitan Museum of Art:** Samuel Eilenberg Collection, Bequest of Samuel Eilenberg, 1998. **56 © The Metropolitan Museum of Art:** Rogers Fund, 1927. **57 Alamy Stock Photo:** Soumyajit Nandy. **60 Philadelphia Museum of Art:** Gift of Stella Kramrisch, 1975, 1975-148-1. **62 Los Angeles County Museum of Art:** Gift of The Walter Foundation (M.91.348.2). **63 Wellcome Collection:** Tulasidasa, Rama-carita-manasa. Miniature, Sita presenting the garland to Rama / Attribution 4.0 International (CC BY 4.0). **64-65 Dreamstime.com:** Ghanshyam P Ramchandani. **66 Dreamstime.com:** Soumen Tarafder. **67 Dreamstime.com:** Arijeet Bannerjee (crb). **Los Angeles County Museum of Art:** Gift of Marilyn Walter Grounds (M.82.225.2) (tr). **68-69 Getty Images:** STR / NurPhoto. **70-75 Dreamstime.com:** Andrey Yanushkov. **70-71 National Museum in Warsaw. 76-77 Dreamstime.com:** Nuttawut Uttamaharad. **78-79 Los Angeles County Museum of Art:** Gift of Paul F. Walter (M.84.229.5). **80 Getty Images:** Debajyoti Chakraborty / NurPhoto. **81 Shutterstock.com:** Shivram. **82 © The Metropolitan Museum of Art:** Gift of Mr. and Mrs. Peter Findlay, 1978. **83 Getty Images:** Deshakalyan Chowdhury / FP (tr). **© The Metropolitan Museum of Art:** Gift of Mr. and Mrs. Uzi Zucker, 1982 (bl). **84-85 Shutterstock.com:** Bappa Pabitra. **86-87 The Detroit Institute Of Arts:** Gift of Dr. and Mrs. Leo S. Figiel and Dr. and Mrs. Steven J. Figiel. **87 Alamy Stock Photo:** Artokoloro. **88 © The Metropolitan Museum of Art:** Purchase, Diana L. and Arthur G. Altschul Gift, 1993. **89 Dreamstime.com:** Saiko3p. **90 Wellcome Collection:** Durga kills the buffalo demon. Gouache painting by an Indian artist, 1800s.. **91 Brooklyn Museum:** Gift of Dr. Bertram H. Schaffner. **92 123RF.com:**

dinodia (tr, clb, c, crb). **93 123RF.com:** dinodia (t, cra, crb, bc). **Alamy Stock Photo:** Dinodia Photos (cl). **94 Shutterstock.com:** Sonia Dhankhar (bl); Rinku Dua (br). **95 Getty Images / iStock:** Gaurav Gupta (br). **Getty Images:** Saqib Majeed / SOPA Images / LightRocket (bl). **96-97 Getty Images:** Ashok Nath Dey / Hindustan Times. **98 National Gallery of Modern Art, New Delhi. 99 The Cleveland Museum Of Art:** Leonard C. Hanna, Jr. Fund (br). **100 akg-images:** Roland and Sabrina Michaud. **101 Dreamstime.com:** Siraanamwong. **102-103 Los Angeles County Museum of Art:** Purchased with funds provided by Dorothy and Richard Sherwood, Mr. Carl Holmes, William Randolph Hearst Collection, and Mr. Rexford Stead (79.1). **104 Shutterstock.com:** Mr. Mahato (bc). **Wellcome Collection:** Shiva carrying his wife in her Sakti form (bl). **105 Alamy Stock Photo:** Abhishek Singh (bl). **Shutterstock.com:** Imagine Rural (br). **106 Getty Images / iStock:** architecture and monuments photography (bl). **Shutterstock.com:** ImagesofIndia (br). **107 Getty Images:** Dinodia Photo (br). **Shutterstock.com:** Srikant Panda (bc). **108 Wellcome Collection:** Parvati, the wife of Lord Shiva, holding a lotus in each hand. Gouache painting by an Indian artist. **109 Brooklyn Museum:** Gift of Emily Manheim Goldman (tr). **110 Los Angeles County Museum of Art:** From the Nasli and Alice Heeramaneck Collection, Museum Associates Purchase (M.72.1.14). **111 Los Angeles County Museum of Art:** Gift of Marilyn Walter Grounds (AC1992.209.1) (tl). **Wellcome Collection:** Shiva begging from Annapurna. Chromolithograph. (br). **112 Getty Images:** Heritage Images. **114 ©The Metropolitan Museum of Art:** Purchase, Anonymous Gift, 2013. **115 Getty Images / iStock:** yands. **116-117 Getty Images:** Praful Gangurde / Hindustan Times. **118 Alamy Stock Photo:** ephotocorp / Shreekant Jadhav. **119 ©The Metropolitan Museum of Art:** Gift of Dr. J. C. Burnett, 1957. **120-121 Los Angeles County Museum of Art:** Harry and Yvonne Lenart Fund and Museum Acquisition Fund (M.88.51). **122-123 Alamy Stock Photo:** Dinodia Photos. **124 Alamy Stock Photo:** ephotocorp / Shreekant Jadhav. **126 Alamy Stock Photo:** Dinodia Photos. **128 Los Angeles County Museum of Art:** Museum Associates Acquisition Fund (M.80.3). **129 Los Angeles County Museum of Art:** Purchased with funds provided by Dorothy and Richard Sherwood and Indian Art Special Purpose Fund (M.80.101). **130 Los Angeles County Museum of Art:** Gift of Dr. S. Sanford and Mrs. Charlene S. Kornblum (M.2011.5). **131 Getty Images:** Debajyoti Chakraborty / NurPhoto. **132-133 Los Angeles County Museum of Art:** Gift of Paul F. Walter (M.70.70). **134 Dreamstime.com:** Danilo Mongiello. **135 Getty Images:** NurPhoto. **136-137 Getty Images:** Indranil Bhoumik / Mint. **138 Alamy Stock Photo:** North Wind Picture Archives (bl). **Getty Images:** Manakin (br). **139 Alamy Stock Photo:** Chris Hellier (bc). **The Missionary Repository for Youth, and Sunday School Missionary Magazine, 1850:** (br). **Wellcome Collection:** A goat being slaughtered at Kali Puja (bl). **140 Getty Images / iStock:** Easy_Asa (b). **©The Metropolitan Museum of Art:** Bequest of George C. Stone, 1935 (l). **140-141 Los Angeles County Museum of Art:** Purchased with funds provided by Mr. and Mrs. Paul E. Manheim and Paul F. Walter (M.83.25) (c). **141 Dreamstime.com:** Believeinme (br). **©The Metropolitan Museum of Art:** Bequest of George C. Stone, 1935 (t, cb); The

Collection of Giovanni P. Morosini, presented by his daughter Giulia, 1932 (ca). **Philadelphia Museum of Art:** Stella Kramrisch Collection, 1994 (bc). **142-143 Wellcome Collection:** Kali trampling Shiva. Chromolithograph by R. Varma. **145 Philadelphia Museum of Art:** Stella Kramrisch Collection, 1994. **146 Los Angeles County Museum of Art:** Gift of Doris Wiener (M.88.228). **146-147 Los Angeles County Museum of Art:** Gift of Paul F. Walter (M.80.157). **148 Los Angeles County Museum of Art:** Gift of Mr. and Mrs. Werner G. Scharff (M.91.232.11a-b) (tr). **Philadelphia Museum of Art:** Gift of Mr. and Mrs. Lessing J. Rosenwald, 1959 (cl). **148-149 Philadelphia Museum of Art:** Stella Kramrisch Collection, 1994, 1994-148-115. **149 The Cleveland Museum Of Art:** Andrew R. and Martha Holden Jennings Fund (c). **Dreamstime.com:** Shariqkhan (tr). **©The Metropolitan Museum of Art:** Purchase, Anonymous Gift and Rogers Fund, 1989 (tl). **Philadelphia Museum of Art:** Gift of Mr. and Mrs. Lessing J. Rosenwald, 1959 (br). **150-151 Getty Images:** Heritage Images / Hulton Archive. **152-153 Alamy Stock Photo:** WBC ART. **154-155 Getty Images:** K M Asad / LightRocket. **156-157 Dreamstime.com:** Amit Banerjee. **158-159 Dreamstime.com:** Elena Ray Microstock Library © Elena Ray. **161 ©The Metropolitan Museum of Art:** Fletcher Fund, 1996. **162-167 Dreamstime.com:** Andrey Yanushkov. **162-163 Dreamstime.com:** Anil Dave. **168 Alamy Stock Photo:** imageBROKER / Olaf Krüger. **169 The Cleveland Museum Of Art:** Gift of Dr. Norman Zaworski. **170 Dreamstime.com:** Manjunatha S. **171 Getty Images:** Veena Nair. **172 The Cleveland Museum Of Art:** Gift of John D. Proctor. **173 ©The Metropolitan Museum of Art:** Gift of Evelyn Kossak, The Kronos Collections, 1986. **174-175 Alamy Stock Photo:** Art Collection 4. **176 Alamy Stock Photo:** Manoj Attingal. **178-179 Getty Images / iStock:** ePhotocorp. **180 Shutterstock.com:** Akshath Photography. **182 Depositphotos Inc:** reddees (bc). **Dreamstime.com:** EPhotocorp (bl). **Getty Images:** Narinder Nanu / AFP (br). **183 Getty Images:** Narinder Nanu / AFP (br); Praful Gangurde / Hindustan Times (bl). **184-185 Alamy Stock Photo:** Andrew Mason. **186 Getty Images:** Heritage Images / Hulton Fine Art Collection. **188 ©The Metropolitan Museum of Art:** The Crosby Brown Collection of Musical Instruments, 1889. **189 Getty Images / iStock:** NSA Digital Archive. **190 Wellcome Collection:** Hindu goddesses Lakshami and Saraswati playing castanets and a tambura. Watercolour drawing.. **191 The Cleveland Museum Of Art:** Gift of William E. Ward in memory of his wife, Evelyn Svec Ward. **192 Dreamstime.com:** Olga Moreira (br); Murali Nath (bl). **193 Dreamstime.com:** Shaikh Mohammed Meraj (bl); Rudra Narayan Mitra (br). **194-195 Wellcome Collection:** Sarasvati with her sitar and peacock. Chromolithograph by R. Varma. **196 123RF.com:** snehit (bl). **Dreamstime.com:** Anil Dave (br); EPhotocorp (cl); Karthikeyan Gnanaprakasam (cr). **197 Dreamstime.com:** Panithi33 (cl); Gemini Prostudio (cra). **Getty Images / iStock:** Rangeecha (bl). Los Angeles County **Museum of Art:** Purchased with funds provided by Harry and Yvonne Lenart (M.85.159.1) (br). **198-199 Getty Images:** Burhaan Kinu / Hindustan Times. **200-201 The Cleveland Museum Of Art:** Edward L. Whittemore Fund. **202 ©The Metropolitan Museum of Art:** Cynthia Hazen Polsky and Leon B. Polsky Fund, 2003. **203 The Cleveland Museum Of Art:** Mr. and Mrs. William H. Marlatt Fund (br).

Los Angeles County Museum of Art: Gift of Mr. and Mrs. Hal B. Wallis (M.70.69.2) (tr). **204 Dreamstime.com:** Ajijchan (bl). **204-205 Getty Images / iStock:** Avishek Das. **205 Dreamstime.com:** Ajijchan (bc); Abhishek Mittal (br). **206 Dorling Kindersley:** Mamta Panwar. **208-213 Dreamstime.com:** Andrey Yanushkov. **208-209 The Cleveland Museum Of Art:** Bequest of Mrs. Severance A. Millikin. **216 Dreamstime.com:** Jjspring (tr). **216-217 Getty Images:** Jeremy Woodhouse. **218 © The Metropolitan Museum of Art:** John Stewart Kennedy Fund, 1915. **219 © The Metropolitan Museum of Art:** Rogers Fund, 1931. **220-221 © The Metropolitan Museum of Art:** Gift of John and Evelyn Kossak, The Kronos Collections and Mr. and Mrs. Peter Findlay, 1979. **222 Los Angeles County Museum of Art:** From the Nasli and Alice Heeramaneck Collection, purchased with funds provided by the Jane and Justin Dart Foundation (M.81.90.6). **224 © The Metropolitan Museum of Art:** Gift of Steven Kossak, The Kronos Collections, 1981. **226-227 Dreamstime.com:** Sergeychernov. **228 © The Metropolitan Museum of Art:** Zimmerman Family Collection, Purchase, Lila Acheson Wallace Gift, 2012. **229 © The Metropolitan Museum of Art:** Purchase, Friends of Asian Art Gifts, 2007. **230 Dreamstime.com:** Bhuwan Chalise. **231 Dreamstime.com:** OneWalker. **233 © The Metropolitan Museum of Art:** Zimmerman Family Collection, Purchase, Oscar L. Tang Gift, in honor of Agnes Hsu, 2012. **234 Alamy Stock Photo:** robertharding / Godong (bc). **Los Angeles County Museum of Art:** Gift of Mr. and Mrs. Werner G. Scharff (M.91.232.7) (r). **© The Metropolitan Museum of Art:** Gift of Florence and Herbert Irving, 2015 (cl). **235 Alamy Stock Photo:** Nick Bobroff (bl); Ivan Vdovin (c). **Depositphotos Inc:** Waikeat (tr). **© The Metropolitan Museum of Art:** Purchase, Lila Acheson Wallace Gift, 2001 (br). **236-237 Getty Images:** Godong / Universal Images Group. **236-239 Dreamstime.com:** Andrey Yanushkov. **240 Dreamstime.com:** Jill Shepherd. **241 Los Angeles County Museum of Art:** Purchased with funds provided by Harry and Yvonne Lenart (M.85.221). **242 Alamy Stock Photo:** CPA Media Pte Ltd / Pictures From History. **243 © The Metropolitan Museum of Art:** Purchase, Friends of Asian Art Gifts, 2004. **244 Alamy Stock Photo:** CPA Media Pte Ltd / Pictures From History. **246-247 Alamy Stock Photo:** Art Directors & TRIP. **248-249 Alamy Stock Photo:** Dinodia Photos. **250 Los Angeles County Museum of Art:** Purchased with funds provided by Robert H. Ellsworth in honor of Dr. Pratapaditya Pal (M.90.165). **252-253 Dreamstime.com:** Shailen Photography. **254 Shutterstock.com:** Hitman H. **256 123RF.com:** dinodia. **258 Alamy Stock Photo:** Abbus Archive Images. **260-261 Getty Images / iStock:** OscarEspinosa. **262-263 Alamy Stock Photo:** Pacific Press Media Production Corp.. **263 Dreamstime.com:** Maithreebhanu. **266 Wellcome Collection:** Mystical body of tantric meditation, flow of the life force / Attribution 4.0 International (CC BY 4.0). **268 123RF.com:** daemonbarzai. **271 Los Angeles County Museum of Art:** Gift of Anna Bing Arnold (M.80.4). **272 Wellcome Collection:** Taraka standing on a dead body. Coloured lithograph.. **274 akg-images:** Roland and Sabrina Michaud. **275 Dreamstime.com:** Al4k14. **276-277 Alamy Stock Photo:** Dinodia Photos. **278 © The Metropolitan Museum of Art:** Purchase, Nancy Fessenden Gift, 2018. **279 Alamy Stock Photo:** Sondeep Shankar. **280 Dreamstime.com:** Fortton. **281 123RF.com:** Dirk Czarnota. **282-283 Dreamstime.com:** Michal Knitl. **284 Wellcome Collection:** Saraswati, the Hindu goddess of learning and knowledge and the wife of Brahma. Gouache painting by an Indian artist. (cra, c, br); Lakshmi, the goddess of wealth and prosperity and the wife of Lord Vishnu. Gouache painting by an Indian artist. (cra, c, br); Goddess Kali dancing on Shiva. Gouache painting by an Indian artist. (cra, c, br). **285 Dreamstime.com:** Zanna Bojarsinova (br). **286-287 Wikimedia Commons. 288-289 Alamy Stock Photo:** Dinodia Photos. **288-295 Dreamstime.com:** Andrey Yanushkov. **296-297 Getty Images:** Arun Sankar / AFP. **298 Wellcome Collection:** The ten Madavidyas. Chromolithograph.. **300 Alamy Stock Photo:** The Picture Art Collection. **302-303 © The Metropolitan Museum of Art:** Purchase, Lila Acheson Wallace Gift, 2011. **305 © The Metropolitan Museum of Art:** Purchase, Marie-Hélène Weill Gift, 2015. **306 Los Angeles County Museum of Art:** Gift of Ann Rohrer (M.84.58.2). **308 Alamy Stock Photo:** History and Art Collection. **311 © The Metropolitan Museum of Art:** Purchase, Marie-Hélène Weill Gift, 2015. **312 Dreamstime.com:** Saurav Purkayastha (bl, br). **Shutterstock.com:** Saurav022 (bc). **313 Dreamstime.com:** Oscar Espinosa Villegas (bl). **Getty Images:** Biju Boro / AFP (br). **314-315 Dreamstime.com:** Samrat35. **316 Shutterstock.com:** AnilD. **319 Getty Images:** Godong / Universal Images Group. **320 Alexander Cunningham:** Report of a Tour in the Central Provinces in 1873-74 and 1874-75. **320-321 Shutterstock.com:** Kevin Standage. **321 Dreamstime.com:** Jyoti Prakash Dash. **322 Alamy Stock Photo:** PA Images / Yui Mok (cl). **Shutterstock.com:** Bishwambers Photography (br); Kali Justine (bc). **Wikimedia Commons:** Daderot / Arthur M. Sackler Gallery, Washington, DC, USA (tr). **323 Alamy Stock Photo:** ephotocorp / Shreekant Jadhav (tc). **Getty Images:** B P S Walia / IndiaPictures / Universal Images Group (cl, bc). **Wikimedia Commons:** Daderot / Matsuoka Museum of Art (r). **324-325 Getty Images:** Sepia Times / Universal Images Group. **328-329 Dreamstime.com:** Biplab Roy Chowdhury. **330 Shutterstock.com:** Iamtejasvisingh. **332 Alamy Stock Photo:** Dinodia Photos. **333 Dreamstime.com:** Laxman Navghane. **334 Dreamstime.com:** Dmitry Rukhlenko. **335 Dreamstime.com:** Poornima Singh. **336-337 Shutterstock.com:** balajisrinivasan. **338 Getty Images:** Dinodia Photo. **340 Getty Images:** IndiaPix / IndiaPicture (bc, br). **341 Getty Images:** IndiaPix / IndiaPicture. **342 Getty Images:** Anand Purohit. **344 Getty Images:** Godong / Universal Images Group. **346 Dreamstime.com:** Saiko3p (br); Vladimir Zhuravlev (bl). **347 Dreamstime.com:** Lakhesis (bc); Vladimir Zhuravlev (br). **348 Alamy Stock Photo:** ephotocorp / Sunil Kulkarni. **350-351 Getty Images / iStock:** Vivek_Renukaprasad. **353 Philadelphia Museum of Art:** Gift of Stella Kramrisch, 1987. **354 © The Metropolitan Museum of Art:** Edward C. Moore Collection, Bequest of Edward C. Moore, 1891. **355 Chitra Subramanyam. 356-357 Dreamstime.com:** Bidouze Stephane. **356-359 Dreamstime.com:** Andrey Yanushkov. **362 Shutterstock.com:** ImagesofIndia. **364 Dreamstime.com:** Mdsindia (bl). **Getty Images:** Arijit Sen / The India Today Group (br). **365 Dreamstime.com:** Mdsindia (bl). **Getty Images:** Channi Anand / IndiaPictures / Universal Images Group (br). **Shutterstock.com:** Shahid Iqbal Shaikh (bc). **366-367 Getty Images:** Frank Bienewald / LightRocket. **368 Shutterstock.com:** AjayTvm. **370 Dreamstime.com:** Daniel Prudek. **372 Dreamstime.com:** S4sanchita (bl). **Getty Images / iStock:** Winterline Production (br). **373 Shutterstock.com:** Stocksvids (bl, br). **374 Getty Images:** DEA / G. Dagli Orti / DeAgostini. **375 Getty Images / iStock:** yogesh_more. **376 Getty Images:** AFP. **379 Getty Images:** Godong / Universal Images Group. **380 Dreamstime.com:** Juliengrondin. **382-383 Philadelphia Museum of Art:** Stella Kramrisch Collection, 1994

All other images © Dorling Kindersley